The Bab Ballads

THE BAB BALLADS

BY W. S. GILBERT

Edited by James Ellis

The Belknap Press of
Harvard University Press
Cambridge, Massachusetts
1970

Acknowledgments

I wish to acknowledge the contributions of a number of persons and institutions in the preparation of this book.

Mr. William H. Bond, Librarian of the Houghton Library, Harvard University, offered initial and much appreciated encouragement. Mr. Reginald Allen, now Acting Director of the American Academy in Rome, gave generously of his time, his wisdom, and the resources of his unrivaled Gilbert collection at the Pierpont Morgan Library, New York City. In London, Messrs. Raymond Mander and Joe Mitchenson graciously placed their remarkable theater collection and enviable fund of information at my service. Miss Jane W. Stedman of Roosevelt University, Chicago, and Dr. Terence Rees of London have been of the utmost help and courtesy in providing both sound criticism and factual information on troublesome allusions.

In my research I received full cooperation from the staffs of the following libraries in England and the United States: the Bodleian Library, the Bristol Public Library, the British Museum, the Gabrielle Enthoven Collection of the Victoria and Albert Museum; the Robert Frost Library of Amherst College, the Boston Public Library, the Forbes Library (Northampton, Massachusetts), the Houghton and Widener Libraries of Harvard University, the Henry E. Huntington Library (San Marino, California), the Library of Congress, the New York Public Library, the Pierpont Morgan Library, the William Allan Neilson Library of Smith College, and the Yale University Library. Above all, I wish to thank Miss Nancy Devine and other members of the staff of the Williston Memorial Library, Mount Holyoke College, for handling my numerous requests with ingenuity, expedition, and patience.

My colleagues Mr. Joseph McG. Bottkol, Miss Dargan A. Jones, and Mr. Ben L. Reid aided me in matters critical, classical, and technical; Mr. John Bush Jones of the University of Kansas in matters Gilbertian. In England I was helped variously by Mr. and Mrs. John Cavanagh and specifically by Mr. Dennis Arundell, Mr. A. O. J. Cockshut, Mr. Archie Harradine, Mr. David Mayer, Mr. Colin Prestige, Mr. E. E. F. Smith (Clapham Antiquarian Society), and Mr. A. A. Whife ("The Tailor and Cutter"). Miss Elaine Griffiths of Oxford, England, and Dr. and Mrs. Carmer Hadley of Altadina, California, provided warm hospitality to a wandering scholar.

I am grateful to Mrs. Katharine Scott Ridley for diligent researching in my behalf and to three former students for assistance in exacting tasks: Mlle. Marie Hélène Jacquet for investigations in the newspaper archives of the Bibliothèque Nationale, Miss Andrea Sununu for alert proofreading of my manuscript, and Miss Penny Laurans for help in the collation of texts.

Permission to quote from published and unpublished sources has been granted by the following persons, publishers, and institutions: the Royal General Theatrical Fund, owner of the subsisting copyright in the writings of W. S. Gilbert; Miss Emily Driscoll; the *Gilbert and Sullivan Journal* (Colin Prestige, Editor); the Hamlyn Publishing Group Ltd. for material from *The Gilbert & Sullivan Book* by Leslie Baily; Harcourt, Brace & World, Inc., and the author for material from *The Archaeology of the Cinema* by C. W. Ceram; the Houghton Library of Harvard University; the Hutchinson Publishing Group Ltd. for material from *Old Days in Bohemian London* by Mrs. Clement Scott and *Victorian Days and Ways* by Mark Edward Perugini; London International Ltd. for material from *Gilbert: His Life and Strife* by Hesketh Pearson; the Pierpont Morgan Library; Yale University Press for material from *The Swinburne Letters*. I have been unable to locate the personal representatives of the publishers John Camden Hotten and Edward Wylam but hope they will pardon any breach of copyright in my brief quotations from their correspondence.

A summer stipend from the National Endowment for the Humanities in 1967 and awards from the Faculty Grants Committee of Mount Holyoke College have helped finance my research at home and abroad. I am pleased to be able to record my thanks for this support.

My debt to my wife, Virginia Ridley Ellis, for constant assistance, keen criticism, steadfast encouragement, and sheer endurance, is incalculable.

James Ellis

Granby, Massachusetts
October 1969

Contents

Introduction

Introduction

When the seventy-year-old W. S. Gilbert was knighted in 1907 by Edward VII, it was in belated recognition of his contributions in the previous century as a "playwright," as he was designated in the investiture list. Characteristically, Gilbert jibbed at the mechanical implications of the term—"There is an excellent word 'dramatist' which seems to fit the situation, but it is not applied until we are dead, and then we become dramatists as oxen, sheep, and pigs are transfigured into beef, mutton, and pork after their demise"[1] —but he would not have disputed the point that his plays were his greatest achievement. He wrote over seventy stage pieces, ranging from a Faust tragedy in blank verse to pun-laden burlesques of Italian opera, and was regarded as one of the outstanding dramatists of his day, though a retrospective glance at the drama from Tom Robertson to Shaw would show that this is at best a dubious honor. In our own day his fame rests slenderly but securely on the series of comic operas he wrote in collaboration with Arthur Sullivan, a collaboration so successful that many people who can "whistle all the airs from that infernal nonsense 'Pinafore'" cannot say which man was the librettist and which the composer.

The Three Bohemian Ones: Gilbert without Sullivan

There is another Gilbert besides the dramatist and author of the Savoy Operas, however, and he too seems destined to find a small and quaintly carved niche in the halls of immortality. This is the Gilbert who was popular journalist and comic artist, the author of the Bab Ballads. In one of these ballads, "The Three Bohemian Ones," his own triple career is adumbrated in the story of the prosperous but vile fate of the three wayward sons of the worthy merchant Jasper Porklebay (of Porklebay and Brown). Dan, the eldest, sinned first by going upon the stage and becoming a stock tragedian. The second son, Donald, tried journalism,

> And wrote amusing tales and scenes
> In all the monthly magazines.

Singleton, the youngest Porklebay, turned comic artist

> And made an income fairly good
> By drawing funny heads on wood.

Gilbert was all three of these misguided youths, and, like his own Pooh-Bah, all at once. From 1861 to 1871, while placating the Jasper Porklebays by preparing for the bar and practicing unsuccessfully before it, he found his

[1] Sidney Dark and Rowland Grey, *W. S. Gilbert: His Life and Letters* (London: Methuen, 1923), 196.

true—albeit sinful and remunerative—vocation by writing some score of plays and contributing hundreds of articles, stories, criticisms, poems, and "funny heads" to various weeklies, monthlies, and annuals, most especially to *Fun,* the best of the many rivals to *Punch.* Much of what he wrote was hackwork and deserves only to be forgotten; but his poems, which he came to call the "Bab" ballads (the name with which he signed his drawings), are possibly the best—and surely the best illustrated—comic verse in the English language.

Gilbert saw fit to rescue some of these whimsical ballads, together with the grotesque little figures which accompany them, from the certain oblivion of penny journalism by publishing collections of them in 1869 and 1873. Since then the "Babs" have sold by the tens of thousands in various editions published both in England and the United States. No edition published during the author's lifetime contained more than eighty of his poems and no later edition more than eighty-six, although one hundred thirty-seven can be located. Furthermore, in 1898 Gilbert committed an unforgivable act of vandalism upon his own work by replacing a majority of the insect-like creatures infesting the poems with sweet, amiable, inoffensive, and wholly inappropriate drawings. Since then it has been these latter-day saints who have greeted readers of the "Babs," but their good manners and refined lines are quite out of place in that bold, bad world. The present edition offers all of Gilbert's poems with all the original illustrations and proves beyond question that the two younger Porklebays in Gilbert were as talented as their theatrical brother.

The Undecided Man: Gilbert's Poetic Career

While still a boy, Gilbert was taken to France to recover from typhoid fever, which had left him thin and temporarily bald. One day he saw Napoleon III and the Empress Eugénie go by in the imperial coach and, so the family story went, memorialized the scene with these lines:

> When the horses, white with foam,
>   Drew the Empress to her home
> From the place whence she did roam,
>   The Empress she did see
>   The Gilbert Familee.
> To the Emperor she said:
>   "How beautiful the head
> Of that youth of gallant mien,
> Cropped so neat and close and clean—
>   Though I own he's rather lean."
> Said the Emperor: "It is!
> And I never saw a phiz
> More wonderful than 'is."[2]

[2] Gilbert's niece, Mrs. Francis Carter, recollected this poem many years later. Leslie Baily, *The Gilbert & Sullivan Book* (London: Cassell, 1952), 12–13.

Perhaps it is just as well that no more of his schoolboy verse survives, and that the anonymity of contributions to the comic papers makes it difficult to identify his earliest professional efforts. We have just enough to feel confident that we do not want any more.

The first poem Gilbert tried to publish was a quasi-humorous piece entitled "Satisfied Isaiah Jones," which did not quite satisfy the editor of *Once a Week* because of its length, but which he found "clever and amusing."[3] Thus encouraged, Gilbert wrote more poems and articles and sent them to more papers, of which there was an astounding number. It was the heyday of comic journalism: ever since *Punch* had shown the way in 1841, every young man about London (and some still at Oxford and Cambridge) thought he could improve upon the original with his own unlimited wit and limited capital. Most of these magazines lasted for only a few years and have long since been forgotten—*Judy, Toby, Banter, The Bat, The Porcupine, The Tomahawk.* When the indefatigable H. J. Byron decided to found his third comic journal in 1877 and asked J. R. Planché to provide the introduction, that grand old man of hundreds of extravaganzas, burlesques, and pantomimes was probably not jesting when he began:

> "Mirth. A new humourous Magazine!" Preserve us!
>   Another can the Public really need?
> It is enough to make Minerva nervous,
>   They seem so fast each other to succeed;
> "Follow," perhaps, would be the better reading,
> For some, 'tis said, succeed without succeeding.

Mirth achieved that sort of success, lasting for only a dozen issues. This had not been the case with Byron's first attempt, *Fun*—"a close copy of *Punch* in all its particulars," an early contributor admitted[4]—which survived under various editors and owners until early in the present century, when it merged into another magazine. Gilbert made his debut as comic writer and artist in *Fun;* years later he could still recall the occasion vividly:

> In 1861 *Fun* was started, under the editorship of Mr. H. J. Byron. With much labour I turned out an article three-quarters of a column long, and sent it to the editor, together with a half-page drawing on wood. A day or two later the printer of the paper called upon me, with Mr. Byron's compliments, and staggered me with a request to contribute a column of "copy" and a half-page drawing every week for the term of my natural life. I hardly knew how to treat that offer, for it seemed to me that into that short article I had poured all I knew. I was empty. I had exhausted myself: I didn't know any more. However, the printer encouraged me (with Mr. Byron's compliments), and I said I would try. I did try, and I found to my surprise that there *was* a little left, and enough indeed to

[3] Edith A. Browne, *W. S. Gilbert* (London: John Lane, The Bodley Head, 1907), 18.
[4] E. L. Blanchard, the writer, critic, and theater historian. See Clement Scott and Cecil Howard, *The Life and Reminiscences of E. L. Blanchard* (London: Hutchinson, 1891), I, 260.

enable me to contribute some hundreds of columns to the periodical throughout his editorship, and that of his successor, poor Tom Hood![5]

The owner of the magazine, Charles Maclean (his name in conjunction with his constant smile was too much for the ever-punning Byron, who referred to him as "Maclean teeth"[6]) had been the one who first saw promise in Gilbert and urged the editor to publish him. Maclean may possibly have feared the outcome if the young poet were rejected: his own son had threatened to shoot Queen Victoria for not reading his verses and had been sent to Broadmoor in consequence.

The staff of *Fun*, under the editorship of Byron and Hood, included a number of writers who were to dominate the popular literary and journalistic worlds of the later Victorian period; mostly young and carefree, they were frequenters of the Arundel Club until it became too tame, whereupon they migrated to that Bohemian haven the Savage Club. The regulars were Gilbert and his fellow dramatist Tom Robertson, the two subsequently influential theater critics E. L. Blanchard and Clement Scott, and three men extremely popular as characters and writers in their own time but almost forgotten now, Henry Leigh, Arthur Sketchley, and Jeff Prowse. The list of less frequent contributors contains a few names still remembered today: F. C. Burnand, who later became editor of *Punch;* the two Americans Artemus Ward and Ambrose Bierce;[7] the journalists Thomas Catling and T. H. S. Escott; the poets C. S. Calverley and Austin Dobson; and those two jacks-of-all-liter-ary-trades G. R. Sims and George Augustus Sala. An impressive array of talent, especially for so unsubstantial a magazine, whose budget was as light as its contents. All contributors were paid the same—one pound per column, prose or verse, with fractions of columns paid at proportionate shillings and pence. Illustrations were paid for according to size; a series of four or five figures for one of the later ballads brought Gilbert £1 5s. Altogether, with the text of a poem running about a column and a half, Gilbert earned

[5] "William Schwenck Gilbert: An Autobiography," *Theatre,* n.s., I (2 April 1883), 218. In an "Illustrated Interview" with Harry How, *Strand Magazine,* II (October 1891), 339, he describes the event somewhat differently, giving the impression that Byron had solicited his contributions from the start. "Poor Tom Hood" was the son of the more illustrious Thomas Hood, and was always careful to maintain this distinction in their given names.

[6] F. C. Burnand, also with *Fun* in its early days, found Maclean's fixed smile "inexpressibly irritating. . . . It never expanded to a grin, although he made a point of showing his teeth, whose whiteness and brightness quite illuminated his imperturbable visage." See his *Records and Reminiscences* (London: Methuen, 1904), I, 411.

[7] Ward, whose real name was Charles Farrar Browne, was in some ways the American counterpart to Arthur Sketchley, who created the popular character of "Mrs. Brown" (no relation to Charles) in *Fun*. Sketchley's real name was George Rose (not Brown). Bierce really was Bierce, but in *Fun* and elsewhere he wrote under the name "Dod Grile." When his book *The Fiend's Delight* was published by Hotten in 1873, it bore on the title page a drawing of a most wicked gentleman calmly holding a baby in a pair of tongs over a blazing fire. The drawing was by Gilbert and had appeared previously in *Fun,* on 5 November 1864, in a series called "The Comic Mythologist."

something under three pounds for a typical "Bab." Not a great sum perhaps, but of course he was writing other material, and for other journals.

From the first issue of *Fun* on 21 September 1861 until the new series began under Edward Wylam's ownership and Tom Hood's editorship on 20 May 1865 there is no record of the authorship of its columns, but because the illustrations are mostly initialed some of Gilbert's early drawings can be spotted.[8] In the eighth issue a full-page cartoon is signed with the familiar "Bab," a name he did not use again in *Fun* for almost four years; usually he identified himself as "W. G." or "W. S. G." It is tempting but not necessarily valid to label any writing connected with these illustrations as his work. Several poems have been wrongly attributed to him in this way, most notably "The Lie of a Lifetime," an inordinately tedious polemic in heroic and longer couplets aimed at Napoleon III that ran for sixteen installments in 1864 and totalled almost a thousand lines. Gilbert provided illustrations for the first six rounds of this dreary tract, but "the absurd verses," he assured a correspondent later, "were not written by me."[9] In five instances, however, the text of a poem is so closely related to the accompanying Gilbert drawings as to be almost certainly his work. The same is true of a number of prose series, the best of which was "The Comic Physiognomist," which ran for twenty-five numbers in 1863–1864. These quaint drawings and devastating verbal descriptions of facial types prepared both Gilbert and his readers for the "Babs" which followed. He had fashioned his weirdly constructed toys; he had only to provide the animation of metrical narrative.[10]

During Hood's first months as editor of *Fun*, Gilbert was writing simultaneously for *Fun* and *Punch*. By December 1865 he had published two articles, the illustrations for another, and a poem that technically ranks as the first "Bab" ballad (it is the earliest with an illustration so signed) in the older, more prestigious, and better paying journal. The Bab Ballads might have become a regular feature of *Punch* but for two decisions by its editor, Mark

[8] The identification of these drawings is only tentative, as Gilbert may not have been the only "W. G." contributing to the old series of *Fun*. The proprietors' files of the new series, identifying each contributor and the sum he was paid each week, have been preserved and are now in the Henry E. Huntington Library, San Marino, California. For many years this set belonged to the descendants of the Dalziel Brothers, engravers for *Fun* and, from 1870 to 1893, owners of the magazine, who had purchased it for £6,000 from Edward Wylam, who wished "to devote his entire attention to the development of 'Spratt's Dog Biscuits,' the patent for which he had recently purchased." See George and Edward Dalziel, *The Brothers Dalziel*. . . (London: Methuen, 1901), 272. Dark and Grey refer to a set of *Fun* possessed by Gilbert, with his penciled indications of his contributions, but it seems to have disappeared. A good summary of Gilbert's early cartoon work for *Fun* is given by Jessie Cattermole, "Gilbert's Bow in 'Fun,'" *Gilbert and Sullivan Journal*, VIII (January 1962), 93.

[9] Letter to E. Bruce Hindle, dated 29 January 1885, in the Reginald Allen Collection, Pierpont Morgan Library, New York City.

[10] Another column, "Gossip of the Week," would also seem to have been Gilbert's: it includes a reference to that democratic railway company the Diddlesex Junction that later appeared in *Thespis* and introduces the joke about sitting down on the spur of the moment, which Gilbert, always economical with his humor, repeated in *Ages Ago* and *The Yeomen of the Guard*.

Introduction   Lemon. The first was refusal to publish Gilbert's "The Yarn of the 'Nancy Bell'" on grounds that it was "too cannibalistic for his readers' tastes."[11] Then, when Gilbert offered him another batch of articles and drawings, he attempted to steal Gilbert from *Fun* without assuring him of a place at the *Punch* table. "I was told by Mark Lemon, or rather a message reached me from him, that he would insert nothing more of mine unless I left 'Fun.' ... This I declined to do unless he would take me on the regular staff of *Punch*. This *he* declined to do, and so the matter ended."[12] So, too, did Gilbert's literary associations with *Punch*. One week after his last piece in that magazine appeared, he played host in his chambers in Clement's Inn to a new club of his founding called "The Serious Family."[13] All the members were *Fun* regulars, and Hood was appointed "head of the family." Gilbert, most appropriately and prophetically designated "l'enfant terrible," agreed, in lieu of dues, to provide the group each week with "a rump-steak, cold boiled beef, a stilton cheese, whiskey and soda and bottled ale," an arrangement he later admitted was the worst bargain and best decision he had ever made. He had declared himself on the side of a paper with a demonstrably hearty appetite and robust constitution, and the following March the ancient mariner from the "Nancy Bell" told his story in *Fun*, where he was very well received.

The antagonism between Gilbert and *Punch* did not cease, however. His plays, from first (the comedietta *Uncle Baby* had been mercilessly and justifiably attacked on 28 November 1863) almost to last, came in for frequent abuse from the magazine. Mr. Punch was quick to accuse Gilbert, who rightly applied the stock theatrical phrase "new and original" to his plays, of borrowings and thefts. Shirley Brooks added insult to injury by inadvertently publishing in *Punch* what proved to be an altered version of one of Gilbert's very early poems from *Fun* (see my note to "The Advent of Spring"). Burnand, who succeeded Brooks as editor, exceeded him in antagonizing Gilbert by

[11] Gilbert recounts this in the "Preface" to *Fifty "Bab" Ballads* (1877), but by calling the poem "the first of the series" he implied that he had written no verse for *Fun* previously. This was not the case, nor could it be termed the earliest poem in this or any other collection of "Babs."

[12] M. H. Spielmann, *The History of "Punch"* (New York: Cassell, 1895), 528. See also Kate Field, "W. S. Gilbert," *Scribner's Magazine,* XVIII (September 1879), 753. R. G. G. Price, *A History of Punch* (London: Collins, 1957), 86, describes the loss of Gilbert as Mark Lemon's "biggest failure" in spotting talent for the magazine. Ironically, he thinks what "finally emerged as the *Punch* tradition" of light verse owed as much to Gilbert as to the university wits actually on the staff (pp. 137–138). Upon Lemon's death it was rumored that Gilbert might be in line for the editorship. Shirley Brooks, writing to Percival Leigh, was "unconvinced" by such talk, and with good reason—a few days later *he* was named to the post. See George Somes Layard, *A Great "Punch" Editor* (London: Sir Isaac Pitman & Sons, 1907), 401. Other useful discussions of Gilbert's associations with *Punch* are Charles L. Graves, *Mr. Punch's History of Modern England* (London: Cassell, 1921), II, 280–281; and "Gilbert and 'Punch,'" *Gilbert and Sullivan Journal,* VII (May 1958), 232.

[13] See Hesketh Pearson, *Gilbert: His Life and Strife* (London: Methuen, 1957), 25–26. The name was taken from the title of a popular farce by Morris Barnett. Gilbert describes the club in fictionalized form in his story "Tom Poulton's Joke," *The Dark Blue,* I (March 1871), 107–113.

referring to his tragedy *Broken Hearts,* always a favorite with its author, as "Broken Parts" in a letter to Clement Scott. Scott, by this time drama critic for the *Daily Telegraph,* thought the remark amusing enough to publish, which brought this response from Gilbert:

> My dear Scott,
>
> I consider the article you have written in yesterday's news most offensive, and likely to cause a great deal of injury to my play. Burnand's attempt at wit is silly and coarse, and your desire to bring it into prominence in the worst possible taste. I am not by any means a thin-skinned man, but in this case I feel bound to take exception to your treatment of me and my serious work.[14]

Gilbert got his own back at Burnand at a dinner party. The story is variously told, but in essence he asked Burnand if *Punch* ever received any good unsolicited poems; on being told that it did, he snapped back, "Then why don't you ever publish them?" Burnand, a more genial and forgiving sort than Gilbert, even had the audacity to inquire some years later whether he would like to submit an article to *Punch.* Gilbert was understandably amazed, but not in the least mollified:

> Dear Burnand,
>
> I am just off yachting for four months or so—off & on—so I couldn't possibly do the article you suggest.
> I am simply lost in astonishment that you who have for so many years, systematically decried my work, should think it deserving of insertion in the columns of your paper.
>
> Yours very truly,
> W. S. Gilbert[15]

By Christmas 1866, all three of the Bohemian Ones in Gilbert were beginning to meet with success. As a dramatist he was represented by a pantomime at Astley's (*Hush-a-Bye Baby,* coauthored by Charles Millward) and an extravaganza based on Donizetti's *L'elisir d'amore* at St. James's (*Dulcamara*), as well as by an unperformed burlesque published in Warne's Christmas Annual. As a journalist he had contributed over sixty pieces to *Fun* during the year, a quarter of them poems. One of these, "The Story of Gentle Archibald," a fanciful tale with three ludicrous illustrations, could be termed the first true and complete Bab Ballad. As an artist, he placed others of his figures besides those in *Fun* in Warne's annual and in *The Magic Mirror,* a volume of children's stories by his father, William Gilbert. The next year brought more—much more—of the same. Five of his dramatic pieces

---

[14] Mrs. Clement Scott, *Old Days in Bohemian London* (London: Hutchinson [1919]), 70–71.
[15] Letter, dated 27 May 1884, in the Pierpont Morgan Library.

were performed, including a burlesque (*Robinson Crusoe*) written by five members of the *Fun* staff. His output for the journals was even more impressive: articles in *Belgravia, The Graphic, London Society, Once a Week,* and three annuals. In *Fun,* the Comic Physiognomist had returned with a series of fourteen columns on "Men We Meet," together with almost a hundred "Bab" drawings of them. These were followed by another genuine Bab Ballad, "General John," and then, from August through December, twenty more, each seemingly better than the last. During these months Gilbert wooed and wed Lucy Agnes Turner, then took her to France for a honeymoon; he is said to have written one of the "Babs" while on the train to Folkestone with his bride.

During the next year and a half, through May 1869, most of his effort was applied to ballad writing. He had two extravaganzas produced and began his association with the German Reeds at their Gallery of Illustration with a musical sketch called *No Cards;* wrote a few articles for *Fun, Tom Hood's Comic Annual,* and *London Society;* and did some more illustrations for his father's stories. For the most part, though, he wrote poems—forty-nine of them for *Fun,* three for Hood's annual, and one for *Belgravia Annual.* Then, quite abruptly, the balance swung the other way and Gilbert the dramatist reasserted himself for good. The next twelve months witnessed six new plays, but only a dozen poems and about as many prose pieces in *Fun.* Only a handful of poems appeared in 1870, but there were four plays, including *The Palace of Truth,* his first dramatic triumph. The next January brought two more plays, *Randall's Thumb* and *A Sensation Novel,* and the last Bab Ballad to appear in *Fun,* "Old Paul and Old Tim." By the end of the same year his most successful drama of all, *Pygmalion and Galatea,* was playing at the Haymarket, while at the Gaiety J. L. Toole and Nellie Farren appeared in an operetta by Gilbert and a certain young composer of growing reputation. Gilbert had made his final bow in *Fun* as a Bab balladeer at the opening of 1871; by the end of the year he had taken his first as librettist of the Savoy Operas—Gilbert and Arthur S. Sullivan had written *Thespis,* and the remarkable partnership had begun.[16]

Gilbert was finding the stage more rewarding esthetically and financially than comic journalism, with its constant rush and frequent deadlines. When the Dalziels had become the proprietors of *Fun* in 1870, he had turned down their request for more contributions to the magazine with a crisp, "I am sorry to say that my numerous engagements place it out of my power, for the present at all events, to undertake any new work."[17] A few years later he

[16] Strictly speaking, "Savoy Opera" should be applied only to the nine Gilbert and Sullivan pieces produced by Richard D'Oyly Carte at his elegant and electrified Savoy Theatre, which opened on 10 October 1881 with the transference of *Patience* from the Opera Comique. It is usual to apply the term to all fourteen of their works, however, though least appropriately to *Thespis,* given at the Gaiety under John Hollingshead's management and forever excluded from the repertory of the D'Oyly Carte Opera Company because most of the music has been lost.

[17] Letter, dated 9 February 1870, in the Houghton Library; by permission of the Harvard College Library. It is tipped in at the front of a copy of the first three volumes of *Tom Hood's Comic Annual* that once belonged to Gilbert Dalziel, a nephew of the engravers.

seems to have dickered with them for a salary, rather than the usual payment by the column inch. In the proprietor's copy the figure of two and a half pounds is entered as the amount due Gilbert for his last ballad; to this has been added the notation "3.—.—salary . . . Which is it to be?" Two weeks later the entry of payment for his review of his own comedy *Randall's Thumb* (which he describes as "a very loosely constructed and improbable play") is followed by "I have not seen him yet—this is the *measure* parg[?]."[18] For financial or other reasons, after 27 May 1871 Gilbert wrote nothing more for *Fun* until December 1874, when his excellent parody of *Hamlet* (or rather of Victorian productions of it), "Rosencrantz and Guildenstern," appeared in three installments. This piece must have been promised to Tom Hood, who had died on November 20. When Gilbert discovered that the new editor, Henry Sampson, was connected with "that blackguard publication the 'Hornet,'" he informed the Dalziels that he could not consent "to be associated in any way with him. I don't blame him, for it often happens that a young man can't choose his work—but at the same time, I could not, consistently with my self-respect, work under a man who is associated with the most disgraceful paper since the Age and the Satirist. . . . I have provided two columns for the next three numbers—these, of course, I will send."[19]

The young man stayed on as editor, and Gilbert wrote no more for *Fun*. He continued to be watchful of its policies, however, and within a few months was writing to the owners to complain about Sampson's treatment of the actor John Hare:

Dear Mr. Dalziel

I am stepping rather out of my province in calling your attention to the disgraceful attacks made on Mr. Hare in the last and next ensuing number of "Fun." I am quite certain that you would never allow your paper, hitherto so excellently conducted, to be made a medium for personal spite—& I am equally sure that you will see at once that the five separate attacks on Mr. Hare, in two numbers, cannot be reasonably assigned to a spirit of fair criticism. It is the "Hornet" over again.[20]

[18] The last word is difficult to decipher; one would like to read it as "pay[ment]."

[19] Letter, dated 30 November 1874, in the Pierpont Morgan Library. The Dalziels had always liked Sampson, but even if they had not they were almost honor-bound to make him editor. Hood's widow conveyed to them his last letter:

Sampson has long co-operated with me, and now so well understands the working of the paper that it has been of the greatest comfort and use to me to have, for the first time in my life, some one on whom I could entirely rely when I was disabled.

A more disinterested and faithful friend man never had, and I am sure if you transfer the bauble from my hands to his you will have secured fidelity and ability of no unusual [sic] order, loyalty and discretion, zeal and determination. It is my dying wish that he might be my successor on *Fun*. Of course I only express this as simply a wish of

Yours always,
Tom Hood

(*The Brothers Dalziel*, 282). In 1877 Sampson left *Fun* to found *The Referee*, where he made a great reputation as "Pendragon," and was replaced by Charles Dalziel.

[20] Letter, dated 27 March [1875], in the Pierpont Morgan Library.

Introduction Besides being merely annoyed with his interference, the Dalziels were disturbed to discover that the paper had reached Gilbert before its scheduled Wednesday appearance. This was all Gilbert could take:

> Dear Sirs,
>
> I am sorry that my note and my motive for writing it should have been misconstrued by you. I am a very old and intimate friend of Mr. Hare and I am also pardonably interested in the success of a paper with which I had the pleasure of being intimately associated for more than ten years. . . .
>
> With the mistake by which I was favoured with a copy of "Fun" three days earlier than you wished me to receive it, I have, of course, nothing whatever to do. With the view however of placing the recurrence of such a catastrophe out of the question, perhaps you will be so good as to instruct your publisher to discontinue sending me the complimentary copy with which, of late, I have been honoured.
>
> I am, Dear Sirs,
> Faithfully yours,
> W. S. Gilbert[21]

So ended his association with a periodical to which he had contributed hundreds of articles and woodcuts and over one hundred and twenty-five poems. As so often happened in his public and private affairs, he managed to bring things to a disagreeable close. Like his Fairy Queen, Gilbert never did things by halves. He was constitutionally unable to leave an ugly situation alone, and so his exacting sense of fair play in conjunction with an irascible temperament marred the major triumphs and associations of his career.

After *Fun*, Gilbert published only four more poems. In April 1872 his serious and sentimental "Eheu! Fugaces" appeared in *The Dark Blue*, to which he had contributed other work previously. In 1879, when his old friend Edmund Yates founded *Time: A Monthly Miscellany of Interesting and Amusing Literature*, Gilbert agreed to begin a "new series" of Bab Ballads there.[22] He kept his word for two issues and that was all. It was just as well, for in one of these poems, "Jester James," he had become too plausible for the reader to feel comfortable about abandoning poor James at the bottom of a well; in the other, "The Policeman's Story," Gilbert had become too indignant with courtroom injustices to have fun. He was now the famous author of *H.M.S. Pinafore*, the colleague of Arthur Sullivan, and the business associate of Richard D'Oyly Carte. Despite his profession, he was behaving less and less like any of the three Bohemian Ones and more and more like their sober father, Jasper Porklebay, with all his "righteous ways." In his final poem, "The Thief's Apology," published in the 1884 Christmas number of the *Illustrated Sporting and Dramatic News*, he bitterly condemns "a wicked world where dog eats dog."

---

[21] Letter, dated 4 April [1875], in the Pierpont Morgan Library.

[22] Yates had published Gilbert previously in *Tinsley's Magazine*. Years before there had been some talk that Gilbert would be Yates's successor as drama critic of the *Daily News*, but Hollingshead was awarded the job, which he held from 1863 to 1868.

Introduction

The Precocious Baby: Gilbert as "Bab"

Victorian cartoonists and illustrators frequently signed themselves with some sort of short and catchy nickname—one thinks immediately of "Phiz" (Hablot Knight Browne), "Spy" (Leslie Ward), and "Ape" (Carlo Pellegrini) —and so too did Gilbert. He hit upon the name he had been called as a child, "Bab," short for "babby" or "baby," much as Dickens chose "Boz," a name derived from the nickname of his youngest brother, Augustus, whom the family called "Moses" (from *The Vicar of Wakefield*) and then, nasally, "Boses" and finally "Boz."[23] It is just possible that Gilbert was consciously imitating his favorite author in this matter. Although he regularly signed his pictures "Bab" from 1866 on, it was not until his first collection of poems that he began to call them the "Bab Ballads." Soon after publication of this first edition, his new poems appearing in *Fun*, beginning with "The Two Ogres" (23 January 1869), were also titled "The Bab Ballads." The following "Bab," "Mister William," was designated as "No. 60"; from then on every one of Gilbert's poems in *Fun* except for "The Ghost to His Ladye Love" received a number, up to eighty-five, which was applied by mistake to the last two ballads. If we count backward from "Mister William" and include only ballads (not the two descriptive pieces about the holiday towns of Margate and Boulogne) and only those with illustrations, we find ourselves right back with "The Story of Gentle Archibald" as number one. The purist might be tempted to eliminate all other poems from an edition that calls itself "The Bab Ballads," but as Gilbert himself included unillustrated poems and verse that is neither light nor narrative under this title, my decision was to include all his poems in this volume.[24] The great majority qualify both as illustrated "Babs" and as ballads, with such ballad features as narrative form, commonplace figures and incidents, violent action, abrupt transitions and conclusions, and frequent use of dialogue—all twisted to serve comic rather than serious ends. The typical "Bab" stanza also approaches ballad form, but usually holds tight to tetrameter and to rhyme in all lines: Gilbert

---

[23] "Babby" was a common variant of "baby" in Gilbert's day. The poem "Babbage! A Burlesque," published in *The Comic News* and possibly the work of Gilbert, demonstrates this use of the word applied to a most precocious infant: "In Algebra when quite a child I dabbled, / Of Euclid when a babby Babbage babbled."

[24] Excluded are Gilbert's verse dramas, his opera lyrics, a few burlesque sketches in verse, some brief macaronics which he describes as French translations of poems by Thomas Moore, and a few bits of unworthy doggerel. For the record: the verse burlesques, with lyrics written to popular airs, are "The Derby Day Operatized" (3 June 1865), "Piccadilly" (1 July 1865), and "Electra; or, The Lost Pleiad" (27 July 1867); the translations, presented as letters to the editor, are "Ne t'en va pas" (27 May 1865), "Garryowen" (17 June 1865), and "Good-bye, Sweet-heart, Good-bye" (29 July 1865); the bits of filler are "In Re Dawkins" (10 June 1865), "To Mademoiselle Lucca" (21 October 1865), and "I Do Adore Thee!" (16 December 1865). All, of course, were printed in *Fun*, where the "Editor's" comment to one sums up the whole very well: "Oh! bosh!"

was almost wholly unable to resist a rhyme and had the comic versifier's special infatuation with the feminine sort.[25]

If inappropriate in the exceptional case, the name "Bab" fits most of the poems in one way or another. Several, such as "The Baby's Vengeance" and "The Precocious Baby," tell the remarkable histories of unusual infants and children. In other ballads adults who should know better suddenly break into baby talk; even that beer-drinking navvy Bob Polter, whose "hands were coarse, and dirty too," calls his feet his "tiddle toddle tootsicums." Still other ballads—"The Two Ogres" is a good example—are cast as though addressed to children and are complete with a "moral" in the last stanza. These are but surface indications of a more profound Babbishness, though, for the truth is that the "Babs" are addressed to the child in each of us—to that ineradicable part of us that delights in being selfishly asocial, in having its own way at all costs, in being spiteful and vengeful, in letting chaos come again—the child we try to outgrow or at least disguise. Hovering as it does between the naive and the diabolic, it is a quality which causes some to laugh and others to wince. The bizarre little creatures in the Bab Ballads, their illustrious positions in the army, the navy, the church, or business notwithstanding, have never really grown up. They are mentally and temperamentally children, masquerading as knights, bishops, generals, and sea dogs. We find the same quality in less exaggerated form in the characters of the Savoy Operas; it is perhaps partly for this reason that they can be so successfully performed by children. Gilbert must have sensed this when he presented *H.M.S. Pinafore* and *The Pirates of Penzance* with children's companies.

The enfant terrible of "The Serious Family" created dozens of variations on his own role, the willful child ready to use any means to gain his ends. This can be better understood from a look at the two baby pictures that Gilbert placed, one on each title page of the first two collections of "Babs"; the one he used first, and in most later editions, appears on the title page of this volume. We know what to expect when this baby, fists already clenched, is placed before the piano by an unseen and unheeded adult: in fact, we had already been warned in the subtitle to the poems, "Much Sound and Little Sense." Baby will gratify himself by banging at the keys and making noise; Baby has no intention of bringing beauty, delight, or consolation to others. And we don't blame Baby, we laugh at him and encourage him to go on. Bab must be treated in very much the same way.

An even more perfect, more revealing rendering of Bab is the first illustration to "The Precocious Baby" (see p. 129), which Gilbert promoted to the

---

[25] Gilbert was always fascinated by rhyme and intrigued by the challenge of supposedly unrhymable words. When a guest said to him one evening that "Decima" was not easy to rhyme, he instantaneously made up this limerick:

> There was a young lady, Miss Decima,
> Whose conduct was voted quite pessima;
> But she mended at last,
> On the eve of the fast
> Of the Sunday called Septuagesima.

See Rowland Grey, "The Author of Pinafore," *Century Magazine,* LXXXIV (October 1912), 852.

title page of his second book, *More "Bab" Ballads.* This "exceedingly fast little cad" standing pigeon-toed and in baby dress, but with hands held purposefully and manfully behind his back and a monocle screwed up tight in his insolent little face, is obviously in full command of the theater in whose dress circle he poses. His look is not so much that of the cat that has swallowed the canary as of the canary planning the details of an ingenious and lingering death for the cat.

Children can get away with murder, so to speak—the sort of social murder Gilbert often wanted to commit. In a few of his early and unguarded poems —"Tempora Mutantur," "The Pantomime 'Super' to his Mask," and especially, "Haunted"—he tells us directly what he thinks "of that charnel-house, Society." In propria persona he dared not attack the occupants of that house, but through the child-figures of his poems and operas he could. It is not within the scope of this introduction to offer a psychological analysis of Gilbert, tempting as that is, but it seems an inescapable conclusion that he found in his comic poems and plays an acceptable means of accommodating his aversions and hostilities.[26] His homunculi could do battle for him and be as sanguinary, as mercenary, or as hedonistic as they pleased, without fear of reprisal; Gilbert went about with them, disguised as the author. When secure in his role as comedian, he could even admit what he was doing, as he does through King Gama in *Princess Ida:*

> If you give me your attention, I will tell you what I am:
> I'm a genuine philanthropist—all other kinds are sham.
> Each little fault of temper and each social defect
> In my erring fellow-creatures I endeavour to correct.
> To all their little weaknesses I open people's eyes;
> And little plans to snub the self-sufficient I devise;
>
> .   .   .
>
> To compliments inflated I've a withering reply;
> And vanity I always do my best to mortify;
> A charitable action I can skilfully dissect;
> And interested motives I'm delighted to detect.

The explanation given by W. H. Auden for nonsense verse, "an attempt to find a world where the division of class, sex, occupation did not operate,"[27] might well be applied to Gilbert, who is not fundamentally a nonsense writer even though he has frequently been labeled one. Except for his earliest identifiable poem for *Fun* ("The Advent of Spring"), his sequence called "Something Like Nonsense Verses," and portions of "The Story of Prince Agib" and "Brave Alum Bey," he never wrote nonsense of the Edward Lear or Lewis Carroll variety. There are no little birds bathing crocodiles in cream, no Dong with a luminous nose, no Jabberwocky. The brave Alum Bey,

[26] In "The Fantasies of W. S. Gilbert," *Psychoanalytic Quarterly,* XXI (April 1952), 373–401, Arthur B. Brenner attempts a Freudian analysis of Gilbert's writings which is based on limited information and not altogether reliable evidence.

[27] "Preface," *The Oxford Book of Light Verse* (Oxford: Clarendon Press, 1938), xviii.

however perverse the application of Turkish words in his ballad, would not dream of going to sea in a sieve; he carefully dresses himself in cork jacket and trousers, so that when the boat goes down with all hands he bobs safely and smugly on the surface. When Lord B. addresses the Zommerzet farmers in "The Force of Argument," he speaks nonsense for the very sensible purpose of being rid of them and their pesky daughters. Gilbert's world, if not literally ours, is ours with a peculiar vengeance. The motives and methods of his characters are all too human, but by caricaturing them, by making strange stick figures of them and placing them in a hermetically sealed chamber like some display in a Victorian glass bell jar, the dissection can take place with almost no outcry from the victim within or without.

Only occasionally has a critic found Gilbert's operations more painful than pleasurable. The *Athenaeum* reviewer of the "Babs" thought them without humor because without heart.

> These "Bab Ballads" are the dreariest and dullest fun we ever met with; they have no real humour nor geniality, nor have they the broad farce of burlesque; they are wooden, both in the verses and in the illustrations; the jokes are entirely destitute of flavour. To have real fun you must have a real human heart, for fun requires sympathy quite as much as sentiment. Humour quaint and whimsical, like Charles Lamb's or Hood's, requires an insight into the most contradictory moods and tenses of human nature, and a power of love for all human things inspiring and underlying the sense of whimsicality. The "Bab Ballads" do not contain a single thread of interest, nor a spark of feeling. The illustrations are painful, not because they are ugly, but because they are inhuman.[28]

Quiller-Couch, lecturing on Gilbert at Cambridge, took much the same view: "The man, to summarize, was essentially cruel, and delighted in cruelty."[29] Such responses, unassailable if unappreciative, are those of a reader unable or unwilling to make the purely intellectual transformation of the scene that is demanded by Gilbert. The sentiment must give way in "a momentary anesthesia of the heart," to use Bergson's phrase. Anyone who objects to having his feelings "put under" will never find himself at ease among the Bab Ballads. Anyone who likes to give all feeling an occasional holiday will relish the "inhumanity" they momentarily afford.

[28] *The Athenaeum*, 10 April 1869, 502. But compare the response of James Payn, writing anonymously in *Chamber's Journal:* "Their excessive simplicity—their utter absurdity—take the reader by storm, and forbid him, unless he is one of those unfortunates who are nothing if they are not critical, to speculate upon the why and wherefore of his mirth. . . . The echoes of other metrical jokers besides Hood linger about this little book; you are reminded here of Thomas Ingoldsby, and there of the joint authors of *Bon Gaultier;* but in almost all the ballads there is something quite original too: the author holds the patent for a certain monopoly in absurdity which we have never seen infringed" ("Nonsense-Verses," XLVI [21 August 1869], 539, 541).

[29] "W. S. Gilbert," *Studies in Literature,* 3rd ser. (Cambridge: Cambridge University Press, 1929), 228.

Introduction   The "Babs" have always been admired by men of good humor and good sense. They were recited gratuitously by dignified M.P.'s and for pay by comic actors (Arthur Cecil, Brandon Thomas, and Beerbohm Tree, for example). They were the delight of the esthetical Swinburne in his age and of the scholarly Gilbert Murray in his.[30] G. K. Chesterton adored them and Max Beerbohm almost worshipped them:

> He has given me so many hours of pleasure, and is so illustriously enshrined among my minor gods. I think the lilt of his lyrics is always running somewhere in my sub-conscious mind. And the "Bab Ballads" —how shall I ever express my love of them? A decade ago Clement's Inn was not the huddle of gaudy skyscrapers that it is now; and in the centre of it was a sombre little quadrangle, one of whose windows was pointed out to me as the window of the room in which Gilbert had written those poems, and had cut the wood-blocks that immortally illustrate them. And thereafter I never passed that window without a desire to make some sort of obeisance, or to erect some sort of tablet. Surely the Muse still hovers sometimes, affectionately, there where "Bab's" room once was.[31]

In contrast to such ecstatic praise we have Gilbert's own estimation of his poems in later years: "The 'Bab Ballads' appear to me to be but indifferent trifling. . . ."[32] This would seem to be an instance not of modesty but of Gilbert's often poor judgment of his own best work. His easy dismissal of his poems, and to some extent even of his operas, fits the pattern which emerges from almost everything we know about his life and personality—he was not one man, but two. He was a bully and a tyrant who adored children and animals. He was a respected officer in the Aberdeenshire Militia for fourteen years who admitted to being unable to kill any creature whatsoever. He was an unconscionable flirt who was a devoted and honorable husband ("I'm too true to be good," he would say). Known for strong language and unprintable jokes at his clubs, he spent much of his professional life trying to rid the London stage of French indecencies. Litigious enough to go to court if cheated of a penny, he was generous enough to subscribe anonymously to numerous charities. He made his reputation from comic verse and his fortune from comic opera, yet thought of himself primarily as a serious writer. He who contrived some of the most whimsical lords of misrule in all literature lived scrupulously by the rule himself and demanded that others

[30] Swinburne was himself an excellent comic poet, as his parodies reveal. Murray was related to Gilbert and had been named after his father. It is not surprising that a man whose lively translation of an Aristophanic *pnigos* reads like a Gilbert and Sullivan patter song should admire the "Babs."

[31] "Mr. Gilbert's Rentrée (and Mine)," *Saturday Review,* XCVII (14 May 1904), 619. According to Clement Scott, *The Wheel of Life* (London: Lawrence Greening, 1897), 104–105, Gilbert lived first in ground-floor corner chambers in Clement's Inn, then "migrated" to South Square, Gray's Inn, "where he wrote and illustrated the best of the Bab Ballads." Beerbohm is probably wrong about Gilbert actually cutting his wood blocks.

[32] Letter, dated 29 January 1885, in the Pierpont Morgan Library.

do so, too. He who placed so many insubstantial fairy realms upon the stage lived himself in a world of strict business and high finance in which he amassed a fortune and prided himself upon his houses, his yachts, his art collection, his telephones, and his automobiles. He was a trenchant public caricaturist who, from some remote part of his being, saw only through the blur of sympathetic tears. He was a remarkable humorist with little or no sense of humor.

In the Bab Ballads, one Gilbert suppresses the other but does not drive him off the premises. The one becomes extravagant, irresponsible, and outlandish, while all the time realizing that the other is looking on cynically, angrily, acquisitively, or just wistfully. Gilbert developed a formula guaranteed to stress the fantastic features in a way that would allow the unpleasant truths to pass all but unnoticed. He would take one false premise or improbable situation ("Once a fairy / Light and airy / Married with a mortal") and treat it as though it were natural and ordinary. He would (in one play he actually did) turn things upside down and walk about on the ceiling as though nothing had happened. In "My Dream," one of the last of the "Babs," he generously gives the secret away, like Jack Point offering "The Merrie Jestes of Hugh Ambrose" to Wilfred Shadbolt: "I dreamt that somehow I had come / To dwell in Topsy-Turveydom!" In that country the two Gilberts could live harmoniously, the one indulging in harmless violence while the other fumed in silent wrath. After all, to be thoroughly consistent such a place must be one where the pathetic is greeted with laughter and the jester tells the saddest tales.

The Gilbert who despised cowards can occasionally be seen, as in the openly sardonic "Old Paul and Old Tim" with its attack on Frenchmen who had fled to London during the Franco-Prussian War; but usually the caricaturist dominated, creating unsoldierly soldiers and unsailorly sailors in situations too absurd to be taken seriously. The Gilbert who wore his heart on his sleeve and even put it in his titles to serious plays (*Broken Hearts* and *Sweethearts*) presents himself in a few ballads, such as "Only a Dancing Girl," but usually it is the caricaturist who portrays sweethearts as just so many Edwins and Angelinas who, while a chorus of jurors sings trial-la-law, reduce love either to a matter of appetite or to a business transaction. A very Shavian and very cynical point of view—or it would be if that ridiculous chorus would stop singing and dancing. We see this same antiromantic reduction of motive in many of the ballads. Captain Cleggs, for all his denials, visits the mermen's lair only because of their attractive mates; no wonder Gilbert replaces this hypocrite's legs with a tail and puts him on half-pay. Both little Ellen, who marries the Reverend Bernard Powles (in "First Love"), and Miss Biggs, who accepts "Lost Mr. Blake," claim they are doing so out of a sense of moral duty, but we are made to see that it is otherwise. "Oh, my friends," explains the respectable Mis Biggs, "it's because I hope to bring this poor benighted soul back to virtue and propriety"; but Gilbert adds parenthetically, "And besides, the poor benighted soul, with all his faults, was uncommonly well off." Not all the earnest wooing of the good curate Aaron Wood, with his honest income of fifty pounds a year, can prevent Ellen from sacrificing herself to the Reverend Powles:

Introduction

She wished him happiness and health,
        And flew on lightning wings
    To BERNARD with his dangerous wealth
        And all the woes it brings.[33]

The prominence of the church in mid-Victorian times made "scenes of clerical life" obvious targets for comic and satiric shafts, as Gilbert frequently demonstrates. It seems clear that long and unenlightened sermons displeased him, as attested by "Sir Macklin," "The Reverend Micah Sowls," "Lost Mr. Blake," "'Eheu! Fugaces,'" and most vehemently "Blabworth-cum-Talking-ton." Beyond this, however, it is not so much the institution or its representatives that is under attack as it is the inevitable hypocrisy that, it seemed to Gilbert, must result when the nature of a calling is at variance with human nature. He delights in portraying clergymen as vain, worldly, and ignorant, not to register displeasure with the Church of England or its ministers, but to demonstrate that *all* men, whatever their position, are so and are laughable to the extent that they deny it. It may not be a flattering judgment of humanity, perhaps not even a fair one, and it may even account for his failure as a serious writer; but the fact remains that he was fundamentally contemptuous of people. His indictment is of human nature, not of human institutions, which can do no more than heighten or stress man's weaknesses.

What may appear to the modern reader as intolerance in several of the "Babs"—of Protestants, Catholics, Jews, and Muslims, of Frenchmen and Turks, of blacks—is usually no more, and sometimes less, than the seizing of a stereotype in order to shake some pervasive and universal truth out of it. Gilbert may have been guilty of that Victorian smugness which judged anything foreign as ipso facto inferior—Papists inferior to Anglicans, Frogs inferior to Saxons, "niggers" (the word commonly used in mid-Victorian times, quite often with no pejorative sense) inferior to "massas"—but his violent Turks are amusing for their violence, his treacherous Frenchmen for their treachery, and his "man-eating African swells" for their appetites. In fact, what often provides the sustaining humor in his poems and plays is that his "foreigners" are not foreign at all. Just as the town of Titipu is peopled with English schoolgirls and English bureaucrats, so the brave Alum Bey and Pasha Bailey Ben are Englishmen right down to their names, in disguises that deceive no one.

The cannibalism practiced by the crew of the "Nancy Bell" proved difficult for some of Gilbert's readers to swallow, as it were, because he left it so starkly unadorned; so he blackfaced his cannibals like Christy Minstrels and let them play at being savages. With English costume on top of the burnt cork, the humor is compounded and yet still remains miraculously harmless and acceptable. The cast-off suits in which the Bishop of Rum-ti-Foo dresses his flock of twenty-three souls cannot change the fact that they

---

[33] Gilbert was often criticized for this sort of treatment of love and romance, but it is a commonplace of light humorists. A much more proper Victorian than he, C. S. Calverley, does the same thing in "Love": "Love me, bashful fairy! / I've an empty purse," pleads the young man to one "on the shady / Side of sixty" who is worth her weight in gold.

played the eloquent tum-tum,
And lived on scalps served up in rum—
The only sauce they knew.

More civilized folk have more refined tastes and higher-strung instruments, but their appetites are just as keen. Even the good bishop's sober garb was no proof against primitive responses. Provided with suitable rationalizations, he learns to dance the Cutch-chi-boo and even falls in love:

And to conciliate his see
He married Piccadillillee,
The youngest of his twenty-three,
    Tall—neither fat nor thin.
(And though the dress he made her don
Looks awkwardly a girl upon,
It was a great improvement on
    The one he found her in.)

No one is safe when Harlequin Gilbert—he once played the part in a benefit performance with studied perfection—takes his bat in hand. But just as with the bat or slapstick, it doesn't hurt as much as you'd think it would. There is a quality in the "Babs" that is very much akin to the pantomime, complete with the practical and often brutal jokes of the harlequinade and the startling surprises of the transformation scene. It is not by coincidence that the decade in which the ballads appeared was also the one in which Christmas pantomime enjoyed its greatest popularity.[34] Gilbert gave the readers of *Fun* a unique variant of that holiday treat about once every fortnight for two years—a special occasion in which to turn child once again and watch the merry antics of clowns, policemen, and nursemaids. But it was, after all, a performance, with peculiar little characters far less real than any seen at Drury Lane. It should have been Gilbert, not Thackeray, to say, "Come, children, let us shut up the box and the puppets, for our play is played out."

[34] See A. E. Wilson, *Pantomime Pageant* (London: Stanley Paul [1946]), 30. Gilbert's performance as Harlequin was in *The Forty Thieves,* written jointly (one act apiece) by him, Robert Reece, F. C. Burnand, and H. J. Byron. This memorable event is recorded in the poem "The Amateur Pantomime at the Gaiety" (*Mirth: A Miscellany of Wit and Humour* [London, 1878], 169), which includes these lines on Gilbert:
There was laughing and cheering, and shouts of surprise,
As Gilbert in glittering garb met our eyes;
And when the "positions" he showed well he knew,
A thrill of astonishment ran the house through . . .
And Gilbert through all danced and postured with grace,
With a very determined expression of face.
Townley Searle (and on his authority, presumably, the *British Museum Catalogue*) wrongly attributes this poem to Gilbert; see *A Bibliography of Sir William Schwenck Gilbert* (London: privately printed [1931]), 89. Initialled "B," the poem is possibly by Byron, *Mirth*'s editor.

Introduction

The Troubadour: Gilbert Set to Music

As every Savoyard knows, the Bab Ballads were the preparation and inspiration for the later operas, not just the prelude to them. They were Gilbert's Hugh Ambrose—the source of his original songs, his self-constructed riddles, his ingenious paradoxes—both in general conception and in specific instances of plot, character, and dialogue. *Trial by Jury* was lifted whole from a page of *Fun* and, with a few additions, placed upon the stage. *H.M.S. Pinafore* was carpentered from several ballads including "General John," "Joe Golightly," "Captain Reece," "Lieutenant-Colonel Flare," "Little Oliver," "The Baby's Vengeance," and "The Bumboat Woman's Story." "The Rival Curates" become the rival poets of *Patience,* and "The Fairy Curate" changes profession and becomes Strephon in *Iolanthe.* Of the early librettos for Sullivan, only *Thespis* and *The Pirates of Penzance* do not draw significantly upon one or more of the "Babs."[35] When the operas were being revived early in this century, Gilbert confessed to his self-plagiarism when addressing the O. P. Club at a dinner held in his honor: "And while I am dealing with 'Savoy opera,' I am anxious to avow my indebtedness to the author of the Bab Ballads —who, I am told, is present this evening, and from whom I have so unblushingly cribbed. I can only hope that, like Shakespeare, I may be held to have so far improved upon the original stories as to have justified the thefts that I committed."[36] Many critics have disagreed with Gilbert on this last point, among them George Moore, Max Beerbohm (who found "the wild magic never quite recaptured" in the operas), and Chesterton ("every single Savoy Opera is a splendid achievement as compared with every other attempt at such an opera in modern times. But every single Savoy Opera is a spoilt Bab Ballad. . . ."), but no one can deny the indebtedness, which took many forms.

In his poems Gilbert, who admitted to being tone-deaf and unable to carry a tune, perfected the metrical and aural talents that made him the ideal librettist for the most tuneful composer England has ever produced. It is one of the peculiarities of Gilbert's verse that, while it is ingenious in its rhymes and rhythms and apparently effortless in the neat, polished expression of eccentric ideas, it is almost entirely without the coloring, resonance, or sympathetic harmonics of the best serious poetry. The "Babs" are eminently recitable, with their carefully selected words all neatly clipped and set in rows, their spirited dactyls and anapests hurrying one along, their tempting but

[35] *Pirates* draws on one of Gilbert's musical pieces for the German Reeds: *Our Island Home. Princess Ida* was also a reworking by Gilbert of something he had done earlier, in this case *The Princess,* his "respectful perversion" of Tennyson's poem. Many critics treat the ballad sources of the operas; see especially A. H. Godwin's chapter "The Genealogical Tree," in his *Gilbert and Sullivan* (London and Toronto: J. M. Dent & Sons, 1926), and the anonymous article in the *Observer,* 20 January 1907, p. 6, "The Pedigree of the Savoy Operas."

[36] The speech was published as "Savoy Memories" in the *Daily Telegraph* on 31 December 1906, p. 12, and is reprinted in Baily, *Gilbert & Sullivan Book,* 388.

tongue-twisting alliterations and consonances, and their pompously reverberating syllabics; but they are not singable.[37] The lines are too well marshaled, the sounds and numbers too rigidly controlled, for the verses ever to lift off the page. Nor should they do so. They are asked to play their part in the working mechanism of toy figures magically constructed by a unique origami of word and picture. When Gilbert soars, or even bounds, in his comic verse, it is to mock that very action. There is a disparity between Sir Barnaby Bampton Boo's name and his age, between his bouncing gait and dignified state:

> This is Sir Barnaby Bampton Boo,
>   Last of a noble race,
> Barnaby Bampton, coming to woo,
>   All at a deuce of a pace.
>   Barnaby Bampton Boo,
>   Here is a health to you:
> Here is wishing you luck, you elderly buck—
>   Barnaby Bampton Boo!

Even the balladeer—and it is one of Gilbert's happiest inventions to thrust the narrator's private feelings into several of the poems—grows queasy and querulous after jogging along with Sir Barnaby for nine stanzas, toasting him and various residents of Tuptonvee, and is forced to conclude:

> O excellent Milly de Plow,
>   I really can't drink to you now;
> My head isn't strong, and the song has been long,
>   Excellent Milly de Plow!

In "The Story of Prince Agib," perhaps the most musical of the "Babs," the narrator, supported by "the concertina's melancholy string" and other appropriate instruments, addresses us like some half-witted Virgil:

>   . . . I sing!
> Of Agib, who, amid Tartaric scenes,
> Wrote a lot of ballet-music in his teens:
>   His gentle spirit rolls
>   In the melody of souls—
> Which is pretty, but I don't know what it means.

There's the rub; the couplet *is* pretty, and melodic—but the ballads are not. As a comic poet Gilbert needed to be a versifier rather than a singer, more a woodpecker than a warbler, and this he was to perfection. He was able, as Swinburne recognized, to provide "the simple and perfect modulation

---

[37] This is not to say that the ballads have not been set to music. The most ambitious attempt was by Adrian Wells Beecham in 1931.

which gives a last light consummate touch to the grotesque excellence of verses which might wake the dead with 'helpless laughter.'"[38]

Besides preparing him as a lyricist, the "Babs" also provided Gilbert with the challenge to compound, light, and explode ingenious little crackers of topsy-turvey adventures. The improbable conditions, unimpeachable logic, and unexpected denouements of the operas had already proven irresistibly successful in the ballads. So too had the mock-heroic tone in which the tales are told, a quality which both Gilbert and Sullivan were to find essential for the effectiveness of their work. Gilbert once commented that he thought "all humour, properly so called, is based upon a grave and quasi-respectful treatment of the ridiculous and absurd,"[39] and to prove his point he created hundreds of different characters who have one trait in common—they all take themselves with the utmost seriousness. They are so filled with self-importance that they lose all perspective, becoming preoccupied with some trivial situation: a sugar broker worries about his weight, an Englishman who holidays in Scotland cannot stand the sound of bagpipes. But these small matters are treated as large ones, thereby coming to calamitous and catastrophic resolution: the sugar broker swells to a perfect sphere and rolls helplessly on the carpet; the Sassenach brute seizes a claymore and divides the offending piper close to the waist.

What's more (and more crucial), the narrative voice is if anything even more solemn, more passionate, more determined than the characters, which leaves the joke exclusively to us. Anyone familiar with the Savoy Operas knows how important it is that the actors play their parts straight. When he turned from balladry to drama Gilbert lost his narrative voice, and so was forced to become director (or "producer") at the Savoy in order to tell his actors, "I don't want you to *tell* the audience you're the funny man. They'll find it out, if you are, quickly enough."[40]

The Baby's Vengeance: Gilbert versus "Bab"

In the preface to *A Bunch of Keys* (1865), Tom Hood explained that this Christmas book was the result of "the growth of friendly communion, of pleasant chats of an evening, of fellowship of taste and feeling" among six young men (Hood, Tom Robertson, Tom Archer, Clement Scott, Jeff Prowse, and Gilbert), and promised that if the public "like the notion as well as we do, next year will see a successor." There was a successor, *Rates and Taxes,*[41]

---

[38] *The Swinburne Letters,* ed. Cecil Lang (New Haven: Yale University Press, 1959–1962), III, 92.

[39] Percy Fitzgerald, *The Savoy Opera and the Savoyards* (London: Chatto & Windus, 1894), 14 n. 1.

[40] George Grossmith, *A Society Clown* (Bristol: J. W. Arrowsmith, 1888), 103.

[41] Gilbert's contribution to *Rates and Taxes* was a decidedly autobiographical story of two struggling young writers, "Maxwell and I": "For we were dramatic authors, Maxwell and I. Of course we were a great many other things besides, for dramatic authorship in England is but an unremunerative calling at the best of times; and Maxwell and I were mere beginners. We wrote for magazines, we were dramatic

followed in 1867 and 1868 by two volumes of *Savage Club Papers,* with numerous contributions by the *Fun* staff, and, also in 1868, by the first of *Tom Hood's Comic Annuals* (in imitation of the ones his father had edited thirty years before). The young men sought to capitalize on their light literary facility and heavy journalistic productivity through publication in a form more substantial and rewarding than the comic papers. They did so not only collectively, but individually: in 1866 Arthur Sketchley offered a delighted public the first of a series of collections of his columns on "Mrs. Brown";[42] even Gilbert's fellow poet on *Fun,* Henry S. Leigh, was arranging to have his verse, *Carols of Cockayne,* published before Christmas in 1868. Why shouldn't Gilbert do the same? In the "Preface" to *The "Bab" Ballads,* dated 26 October 1868, he makes a modest claim: "I have some reason to believe that the Ballads, which now appear for the first time in collected form, have achieved a certain whimsical popularity among a special class of readers. I hope to gather, from their publication in a separate volume, whether that popularity (such as it is) is a thing to be gratified with. With respect to the Ballads themselves, I do not know that I have anything very definite to say about them, except that they are not, as a rule, founded upon fact." He selected forty-four poems, the earliest of which was "Tempora Mutantur" (15 July 1865) and the most recent, "Gentle Alice Brown," which had appeared in *Fun* on 23 May 1868. Thirty-four of them were illustrated, and Gilbert needlessly apologized for his figures:

I have ventured to publish the illustrations with them because, while they are certainly quite as bad as the Ballads, I suppose they are not much worse. If, therefore, the Ballads are worthy of publication in a collected form, the little pictures would have a right to complain if they were omitted. I do not know that they would avail themselves of that right, but I should, nevertheless, have it on my conscience that I had been guilty of partiality. If, on the other hand, the Ballads should unfortunately be

---

critics, we were the life and soul (such as they were) of London and provincial comic papers, we supplied "London Letters," crammed with exclusive political secrets, and high-class aristocratic gossip, for credulous country journals; we wrote ballads for music publishers, and we did leaders and reviews for the weeklies. I had almost forgotten to add that we were barristers-at-Law...."

[42] The first collection, *The Brown Papers,* was published by the *Fun* office as "No. 1" of the "Fun" Library. A letter dated 28 July 1868 from *Fun*'s owner Edward Wylam indicates that Gilbert must have negotiated first with him for publication of the "Babs": "The terms on which I publish will be as you mentioned viz. the same as I had with Mr. Sketchley for the Brown Papers Vol. I—" (This letter is in the British Museum, Add. MS. 49330, *The Gilbert Papers,* XLII, 2.) The next year Sketchley offered *Mrs. Brown's Visit to the Paris Exhibition,* and in 1868 *Mrs. Brown at the Sea-side.* In autumn 1870 he started a paper called *Mrs. Brown's Budget,* to which Gilbert contributed. Burnand informs us that "it did not succeed," which may have been an understatement, as only four odd numbers of it are preserved at the British Museum and apparently none elsewhere. Mrs. Brown must not have budgeted very well, for Sketchley was unable to pay his staff; Gilbert, true to form, brought a suit against him which he later withdrew on being paid thirty pounds "in full satisfaction of all claims in the matter of 'Mrs. Brown's Budget'" (*Gilbert Papers,* XLII, 33).

condemned as wholly unworthy of the dignity with which Mr. Hotten has invested them, they will have the satisfaction of feeling that they have companions in misfortune in the rather clumsy sketches that accompany them.

Nevertheless, it is clear that his apology is not just modesty, for he became increasingly dissatisfied with the drawings.

As the publisher of such American humorists as Bret Harte and Artemus Ward, of Swinburne (when rejected by Moxon), and of Henry Leigh of *Fun*, John Camden Hotten was not, perhaps, in the best position to invest the "Babs" with much dignity, and he soon came to regret having invested in them at all. Negotiating through Edward Wylam, *Fun*'s proprietor, Gilbert demanded £90 for a first edition of 2,000 copies of the book, plus £50 for each additional printing of 1,000 copies. Hotten declared himself willing to pay £50 for 1,500 copies or £75 for 2,000, informing Wylam that "gentlemen always will persist in believing that publishers make larger profits than they actually do."[43] He came around to Gilbert's terms, however, and even, with a certain prophetic reluctance, to the request that the printing be done by Judd & Glass, printers of *Fun*.[44] Gilbert was to receive an additional £2 2s. for a frontispiece illustration and title-page vignette. The day of publication was to be no later than November 15 and the price of the book no less than 3s. 6d.

It would seem that Hotten had another method of assuring himself of profit from the "Babs." When Judd & Glass reported to him that they were over-stocked with paper for the book, he sent them a memorandum asking that they print 2,300 copies: "The oddment will do for press copies, author's copies, etc. . . . My order is for <u>2000</u>, but it is a pity to have this paper left over."[45] What proved to be more of a pity was that Gilbert found out through Judd that 263 extra copies had been printed and demanded to be paid the additional £50 specified in his contract. Hotten held back the prepublication press copies he was about to distribute and wrote Gilbert to say that "Mr. Judd has been instructed to destroy any odd sheets remaining after 2000 copies," and that he (Hotten) would prefer to give the book to another publisher.[46] Gilbert countered by agreeing to accept ad valorem payment for the extras (which came to £13 3s.), but he insisted that Hotten publish the book, and within two days: "By your delay I lose all the Xmas sale & notices."[47] Hotten complied but immediately thereafter severed connections with Gilbert, who transferred his business to Routledge, the firm which continued to publish the ballads until 1904, when Macmillan took over the sixth edition (since reprinted twenty times).

[43] *Gilbert Papers, XLII*, 8.

[44] Judd & Glass had been the publishers of William Gilbert's first two books, a short tract "On the Present System of Rating for the Relief of the Poor of the Metropolis" (1857) and *Dives and Lazarus* (1858), "the adventures of an obscure medical man in a low neighbourhood."

[45] *Gilbert Papers*, XLII, 12, letter dated 3 October 1868.

[46] *Ibid.*, 22v and 21, letter dated 14 December 1868.

[47] *Ibid.*, 24v, letter dated 17 December 1868.

Even before the Routledge issue of the first collection of poems came out, under financial arrangements far less generous than Hotten's,[48] Gilbert was writing to William Tinsley about a second collection: "I have a second batch of "Bab Ballads" (published in Fun)—it occurred to me that possibly you might feel disposed to publish them in a collected form. I have the copyright both of the ballads and the illustrations, and I can let you have them on the terms that I received from Mr. Hotten last year, for the first series. . . ."[49] Tinsley declined the offer, and it was a full three years before *More "Bab" Ballads* was published, by Routledge.[50] Bound in the same bright green cloth that had covered the first collection were thirty-five ballads, all illustrated, which had appeared in *Fun* between 6 June 1868 ("Pasha Bailey Ben") and 28 January 1871 ("Old Paul and Old Tim").

From this point on, Gilbert seemed perversely determined to spoil what he had achieved. On 19 September 1875 he is once again writing to Tinsley Brothers: "I propose to publish a new edition of the 'Bab Ballads'—selecting the most popular pieces from the First and Second Series, and illustrating them with new and carefully executed drawings by myself. It occurred to me that you might possibly feel disposed to undertake the work. If so, I shall be happy to attend to any appointment you may think proper to make."[51] The Tinsleys were still not so disposed, so Gilbert fell back upon Routledge once more, who agreed to the publication of *Fifty "Bab" Ballads,* but not to the "new and carefully executed drawings." In the "Preface" to this edition, dated August 1876, Gilbert tells something of the poems' history, which he hopes will justify what he has done:

> The "Bab Ballads" appeared originally in the columns of "Fun," when that periodical was under the editorship of the late Tom Hood. They were subsequently republished in two volumes, one called "The Bab Ballads," the other "More Bab Ballads." The period during which they were written extended over some three or four years; many, however, were composed hastily, and under the discomforting necessity of having to turn out a quantity of lively verse by a certain day in every week. As it seemed to me (and to others) that the volumes were disfigured by the presence of these hastily written imposters, I thought it better to withdraw from both volumes such Ballads as seemed to show evidence of carelessness or undue haste, and to publish the remainder in the compact form under which they are now presented to the reader.

His public howled with rage at what he had done ("I soon discovered that in making the selection for this volume I had discarded certain Ballads that

---

[48] Routledge's terms were £50 for an edition of 10,000 copies, selling at 1s. each, with the publisher entitled to print an extra "13th copy in every dozen" (*ibid.,* 26, letter dated 18 July 1870).

[49] Letter, dated 12 September 1869, in the Pierpont Morgan Library.

[50] Routledge agreed to this volume in a letter dated 19 March 1872, in which another printing of The "Bab" Ballads was also approved but Gilbert's play *The Palace of Truth* refused (*Gilbert Papers,* XLII, 55).

[51] Pearson, *Gilbert,* 23.

were greater favourites with my readers than with me"), and in 1882 he was forced to restore these disfiguring imposters.[52]

His final dispensation of the poems came in 1898, when he published in a single volume all eighty of the previously collected ballads together with eighty-seven lyrics from the Savoy Operas, under the inclusive title *The Bab Ballads with which are included Songs of a Savoyard.*[53] The order of the poems was the same random one of earlier editions, but between each "Bab" came a song. The edition, in bright red pictorial cloth and with a frontispiece photograph of the now dignified author, was out by Christmas, 1897. But numerous errors necessitated a second edition, "with alterations," in March. This one, in buff cloth, added an "Index to First Lines." Before the year was out a third edition appeared.

The worst feature of this volume was not the mixture of ballads and lyrics but the decision by the author, now twice as old, fifty times wealthier, and a hundred times more respectable than when he wrote for *Fun,* to replace the original wood-block illustrations with a set of finer line drawings. As early as 1882 he had suggested this: "Perhaps it would be as well to draw the blocks again and return the originals to the Dalziels? I could improve considerably on the original sketches."[54] When at long last he had his way, he offered

[52] Gilbert admits his mistake in the "Author's Note" to the 1898 edition of ballads and songs. *Fifty "Bab" Ballads* included the only poem Gilbert saw fit to collect from a source other than *Fun*—"Etiquette," which had appeared in the Christmas number of *The Graphic* in 1869. It was not included in any earlier edition or in that of 1882 but was restored in the 1898 volume. The "imposters," as Gilbert saw them, included seventeen of *The "Bab" Ballads* ("Tempora Mutantur," "General John," "Sir Guy the Crusader," "Disillusioned," "John and Freddy," "Lorenzo de Lardy," "The Bishop and the Busman," "Babette's Love," "Ben Allah Achmet," "The Folly of Brown," "Joe Golightly," "The Force of Argument," "The Three Kings of Chick-eraboo," "The Periwinkle Girl," "Thomson Green and Harriet Hale," "The Sensation Captain," and "The Reverend Micah Sowls") and thirteen poems from *More "Bab" Ballads* ("Pasha Bailey Ben," "The Cunning Woman," "The Modest Couple," "Sir Barnaby Bampton Boo," "Brave Alum Bey," "Gregory Parable, LL.D.," "Lieu-tenant-Colonel Flare," "Little Oliver," "The Two Ogres," "First Love," "A Worm Will Turn," "Damon *v.* Pythias," and "Old Paul and Old Tim"). As if to stress his new severity in *Fifty "Bab" Ballads* Gilbert placed the two most somber ones, "At a Pantomime" and "Haunted," last, ending on a gloomy note which he perhaps thought would convince his readers that "I can do something more than wear the cap and bells," as he had said to his first biographer, Edith Browne, when she chanced to praise the former poem.

[53] Sixty-nine of the lyrics had been published in 1890 as *Songs of a Savoyard,* with illustrations by the author. Of course the lyrics to the two operas produced after that date—*Utopia Limited* and *The Grand Duke*—were not included, but were added in 1898. Gilbert had originally thought of calling the book *The Savoy Ballads,* which would have stressed their kinship with the "Babs" (*Gilbert Papers,* XLII, 34–36). In the "Author's Note" to the 1898 edition he credits his publishers with the idea of "welding" the poems and lyrics together, but it was clearly a union he had desired.

[54] Philip James, "A Note on Gilbert as Illustrator," *Selected Bab Ballads* (Oxford: privately printed, 1955), 120. James argues, quite wrongly I think, that the extrava-gance of the original figures was due to the engraving of the Dalziels, not to Gilbert's drawing. He offers as further proof the similarity of Gilbert's work to Tenniel's illustrations for *Alice in Wonderland,* also engraved by the Dalziels and at about the same time, but inspection reveals a great difference between the "Alice" pictures

this extraordinary explanation: "I have always felt that many of the original illustrations to "The Bab Ballads" erred gravely in the direction of unnecessary extravagance. This defect I have endeavoured to correct through the medium of the two hundred new drawings which I have designed for this volume. I am afraid I cannot claim for them any other recommendation."[55] Of course, the illustrations erred in the direction of unnecessary extravagance. But, as Beerbohm said, "so did the 'Bab Ballads.'"[56] Gilbert had been blessed with two ideal collaborators in his career, Arthur Sullivan and W. S. Gilbert, and had managed to quarrel with both. Just as the operas survive not because of Gilbert's words alone but because of the perfect mating of his talents with Sullivan's, so the "Babs" are dependent upon their inimitable "funny heads on wood."[57] The little creatures form a race all their own, with their bulging faces and torsos and tiny limbs. "Bodies like eggs and mouths like frogs' and little legs like dancing insects'," was Chesterton's description. What makes for the real fun, though, and is another aspect of the masquerade, is that these odd bodies have been crammed into carefully drawn costumes of convincing and authentic design: they are dressed exactly like sailors, curates, and attorneys, yet no one is fooled for a moment—they have come from another planet to play at our life and reveal its ridiculous side. The new drawings have none of this effect; they are delicate, charming, a trifle simpering—but, fortunately, the ballads are not.

---

and the "Babs." Since the Dalziels did all the engraving for *Fun,* one would expect to find all the pictorial work very much in the same style, if the engraver were the dominant influence; but the illustrations are not all alike, and Gilbert's figures can be spotted instantly.

[55] This was a part of the "Author's Note," dated 4 December 1897. The original drawings, from which the plates for the new figures were made, were given to the British Museum by Gilbert's adopted daughter, Nancy McIntosh, shortly after Lady Gilbert's death in 1936. Not all of the ballads received new illustrations: 21 were left unchanged, 22 received partial replacements, and 10 previously unillustrated were provided with "Bab" drawings for the first time. Of the 258 drawings accompanying the poems, 148 are totally new, 11 have been modified, and 99 remain as they were in *Fun.* The copy of the ballads marked by Gilbert to indicate to Routledge which cuts should stay and which be replaced is in the Reginald Allen Collection at the Morgan Library, a gift to him from Nancy McIntosh.

[56] "A Classic in Humour," *Saturday Review,* XCIX (27 May 1905), 697.

[57] Apparently self-taught as an artist and draughtsman, Gilbert was not unique in illustrating his own work; many Victorian comic writers, including Thackeray, Du Maurier, Lear, and Lewis Carroll, did so. It is clear from Gilbert's letters that he did much or all of the drawing on the wood blocks himself. One letter to the Dalziels reads: "Thank you, very much, for your unexpected kindness in cutting my block without charge. I had no idea of this when I sent it to you" (letter, dated 21 October 1868, courtesy of Emily Driscoll, New York City). At another time he wrote them, "I send 10 blocks—There are three more still unfinished. You shall have these tomorrow" (letter, dated 2 August 1869, in the Morgan Library). See also Gilbert Dalziel, "'Bab' and his Ballads," *Gilbert and Sullivan Journal,* I (January 1927), 10. The woodcuts were necessarily simple and bold in design, just what the poems demanded. When he was preparing the new illustrations, however, Gilbert declared, "wood engraving is out of the question." Even the "process" of line engraving which he settled for did not satisfy him: "all the brightness and precision of the sketches is quite lost—but there's no help for it" (letter, dated 18 April 1897, in the Morgan Library).

Introduction   While almost nothing has been done since Gilbert's day in behalf of Bab's original drawings, there have been attempts to locate and publish the uncollected poems. Sidney Dark and Rowland Grey appended six "Lost Bab Ballads" to their biography of Gilbert and quoted two others in an early chapter of the book.[58] In 1928, in his excellent work *The Story of Gilbert and Sullivan*, Isaac Goldberg added thirteen more.[59] Three years later, in his eccentric and unreliable bibliographical study of Gilbert, Townley Searle, without mentioning Dark and Grey or Goldberg, listed exactly their appended poems as "The Lost Bab Ballads," and in 1932 published these poems and sixteen others under that title. Four of them were not by Gilbert, however, and three others were lyrics written for *The Mountebanks* but never scored, owing to the sudden death of the composer, Alfred Cellier.[60] The most ambitious attempt to list all the poems was that of J. M. Bulloch, who published two articles in *Notes and Queries* giving the "Babs" in chronological and alphabetical order.[61] Possibly because of his reliance on statements by Searle, Bulloch also made some errors, as well as some guesses which cannot be substantiated. Of the one hundred and forty-six poems he attributes to Gilbert, eleven are demonstrably by others, ten are unassignable poems from *The Comic News*, seven are stubbornly anonymous pieces from the old series of *Fun*, three are the opera lyrics mentioned above, and one is a prose item by Gilbert.

The Present Text and the Notes

Whereas Gilbert made radical and unacceptable changes in the illustrations of the 1898 edition of the Bab Ballads, his textual revisions were almost all minor ones which served to standardize spelling and punctuation, eliminate repeated words, clarify ambiguities, or improve a rhyme or rhythm. I have therefore generally adopted this edition, in its revised form, for the present text. In a few instances where a change would seem to have been prompted by the older Gilbert's desire to curtail exuberance, I have substituted an earlier reading. Stanzas that were eliminated after the original publication of the poems in *Fun* have been restored. All such changes, as well as all significant variations among the original texts and subsequent editions, have been indi-

---

[58] The two quoted in the text are "Down to the Derby" (one stanza only) and "Musings in a Music Hall." The appendix contains "The Story of Gentle Archibald," "Fanny and Jenny," "Sir Conrad and the Rusty One," "The 'Bandoline' Player," "The Three Bohemian Ones," and "Prince il Baleine." These six were later included by Deems Taylor in his omnibus volume of operas and ballads published by Random House (New York, 1932).

[59] Goldberg published "The Dream," "To My Absent Husband," "A. and B.," "Trial by Jury" (in facsimile, in the text), "Blabworth-cum-Talkington," "The Hermit," "The Phantom Head," "Woman's Gratitude," "The Policeman's Beard," "The Ghost to His Ladye Love," "The Scornful Colonel," "The Variable Baby," and "The Ladies of the Lea."

[60] See my article "Townley Searle and the Lost Bab Ballads," *Gilbert and Sullivan Journal*, IX (May 1969), 224–225.

[61] "The Anatomy of the 'Bab Ballads,'" CLXXI (14 November 1936), 344–348, and "The Bab Ballads by Titles," CLXXII (22 May 1937), 362–367.

cated in the notes at the end of this book. Unless otherwise noted, the text of *Fifty "Bab" Ballads* (1877) is the same as that of the 1869 and 1873 collections. Minor variations in spelling, punctuation, and typography have been ignored in the notes though considered in preparing the text.

All the poems have their "original" illustrations, including the ten early poems which first received theirs in 1898: this will enable the reader to see for himself the difference between the earlier and later Bab as artist. The format of the ballads with their figures varies, and the placement of the illustrations differs occasionally from that in *Fun* or the collected editions in order that they may appear at the most appropriate point in the narrative. The effect of some pages approximates that of the poem as it originally appeared on one two-column page of *Fun*.

The notes to the poems provide (1) the date and place of original publication, (2) significant textual variants and changes, (3) recognition of prototypes of Savoy Opera plots, characters, and phrases, and (4) assistance with topical references and other allusions which might not be understood by the modern reader. Should this book fall into the hands of an Englishman, his indulgence is begged for explanations intended solely for Americans.

The Bab Ballads

THE ADVENT OF SPRING

Under the beechful eye,
  When causeless brandlings bring,
Let the froddering crooner cry,
  And the braddled sapster sing.
For never and never again
  Will the tottering bauble bray,
For bratticed wrackers are singing aloud,
  And the throngers croon in May!

The wracking globe unstrung,
  Unstrung in the frittering light
Of a moon that knows no day!
  Of a day that knows no night!
Diving away in the crowd
  Of sparkling frets of spray,
The bratticed wrackers are singing aloud,
  And the throngers croon in May!

Hasten, O hapful blue,
  Blue of the thimmering brow,
Hasten to meet your crew,
  They'll clamour to pelt thee now!
For never again shall a cloud
  Out-thribble the babbling day,
When bratticed wrackers are singing aloud,
  And the throngers croon in May!

THE CATTLE SHOW

THE HALF-CROWN DAY

(By a very Heavy Swell)

No! I'm not in the least democratic,
  I object to a mob and a crush,
My tastes are too aristocratic
  My way through a crowd to push.
So when to the cattle I take my way,
It's on either a crown or a half-crown day!

I *in toto* object to the "people,"
  They are always so shockingly rude,
E'en on men on society's steeple
  Their sad vulgar remarks they'll intrude.
So you cannot wonder I'd rather pay
To see the show on a half-crown day.

On the high-priced days *c'est une autre*
  Chose tout à fait, if you please,
Then the place is quite filled with *les notres,*
  With the people one everywhere sees,
Who, like myself, much prefer to pay
To see the show on a half-crown day.

Need I say that *we* don't care a button
  For the beasts in which farmers delight;
As long as the sheep turn to mutton,
  And the oxen to beef, why it's right!
To see and be seen is for what we pay
At Islington on the half-crown day.

What to *us* are the tools used for farming?
  For our tenants they're all very well;
But there really cannot be a charm in
  Such things to the genuine swell.
And that being the case I prefer to pay
To see the show on a half-crown day.

THE SHILLING DAY

(By a very Low Fellow)

Pushing, crushing, panting, squeezing,
  Fat-faced farmers left and right;
Round the beasts scarce room for sneezing,
  Each one struggling for a sight.
That's the style, we like a mob,
And we've only paid a bob!

Into pigs umbrellas poking,
  Likewise sticks and parasols,
They're too fat to mind such joking,
  Thoughts of oil-cake fill their souls.
They are heedless of the mob
Who have only paid a bob!

Passing on, we next a visit
  To the fatted oxen make;
Prime indeed each sleek side is, it
  Makes us long to cut a steak.
Such things are not for the mob,
Who have only paid a bob!

Then the sheep claim our attention,
  Southdowns, Devons, Herefords;
This a medal's gained, that, mention,
  Gladness bringing to their lords.
What care we? the vulgar mob,
Who have only paid a bob!

To the implements for farming
  Next we turn, and drawing near,
Comes the thought there'd be no harm in
  Half a pie and bottled beer.
We eat and feel we're of the mob
Who have only paid a bob!

THE CATTLE SHOW

Five shilling day,
Rich people pay
Cattle-y fat they view, view.
Those whom you see
Little of the
Showery knowery do, do.

See them go by,
Eye-glass in eye,
Quizzery phizzery well, well:
Scions of the
Nobilitee,
Hobbery-nobbery, swell, swell.

Formal salute,
Dumb as a mute,
Elitery meet-ery bow, bow;
Little gent winks
Rudely, and thinks
He's-ery cheese-ry now, now.

The knowing and deep
Go on the cheap
Day-ery payery bob, bob;
Little they mind
Though they should find
Gent-ery scent-ery mob, mob.

See how they throng,
Pushing along,
Rushery crushery, shove, shove;
Countryfied swains,
'TILDAS and JANES,
Takery makery love, love.

People to show
How much they know
Sidery widery dig, dig;
Pulling the ears
Of heifers and steers,
Strokery pokery pig, pig.

SIXTY-THREE AND SIXTY-FOUR

Oh, you who complain that the drawing's insane, or too much
    for your noddles have found it,
But listen a minute, I'll tell you what's in it—completely explain
    and expound it.
With intellect weasely, artist has easily earned all his bacon and
    greens by it,
And now that it's done and all ready for *Fun*, it's my duty to say
    what he means by it.
First Beef-eaters, twain, who are hideously plain, with a very great
    deal too much flesh on,
Are placed, I dare say, to keep clear all the way, like the "pleece"
    in a civic procession.
Two pantomime actors—disgraceful char*a*cters, for each is a thief
    and a chartist
(The clown little charms, for he's weak in the arms, but of course
    that's the fault of the artist),
Stealing and shouting, and bad doggerel spouting, completely
    regardless of rhyme or ear—
Melody metrical, authors theatrical little regard at this time o'
    year;
Each of the pair you distinguish down there, a barbarous Pan or
    a Sat'r I call
(But stop, surely "rhyme or ear" scarce rhymes with "time o'
    year"—"metrical" don't with "theatrical").
Two gentlemen, then, stout, hale-looking men, and they carry the
    season's necessities—
What's that in the bowl? How it flames! on my soul, I've not the
    least notion, unless it is

Something to drink—it must be that I think; there is pudding
 and beef and a turkey,
Savoury sausages—offspring of coarse ages, round the fat gobbler
 lurk ye!
Ha! Ha! Christmas-boxes!—purveyors of oxes, greengrocer, and
 baker, whom HODGE I call.
(Fox plural is "foxes," so why not ox "oxes"? The language is
 strangely illogical!)
A well-bred young man, meeting JULIA and ANNE, puts a smile
 that he fancies will please on,
And offers on meeting, the usual greeting—the compliments, viz.,
 of the season
(Whatever they are, it's a phrase popular in the various elegant
 "sets" I know,
I pay them away, and I wish I could say, that with them I could
 pay all my debts, I know!).
The waits, wet and chilly, so long have missed WILLIE, the tie is
 quite broken asunder;
Now, utterly crazy, they envy the daisy, and long to be one, and
 no wonder!
"One more unfortunate," mutely importunate, huddled, a mass,
 in a corner,
Miseries harden her—pardon her, pardon her—think of the cold
 when you scorn her!
Just to the left of her, utterly deaf to ver-acity, idle men two are,
Begging a farden, as frozen-out gardeners—just as much gard'ners
 as you are!
Letters from editors, dunning from creditors, vile red and white
 intimations,
That rates not a few (made October) are due, and that these are
 the LAST APPLICATIONS.
The cursed collector he bullies like HECTOR, and duns in a
 manner which funny ain't;
How on earth I'm to pay, I'm unable to say, for the rates *may* be
 made, but the money ain't.
The thinking these things on insanity brings on, my brain
 thoughts of suicide enter,
I almost think I'll run myself on a file, like the man up above in
 the centre!
The poor wretched prisoner (right corner) is in a sad state—his
 thoughts melancholy ones;
His wicked mind wends to his open-air friends—they are thieves,
 but uncommonly jolly ones!
Time, the physician (sure no one could wish an adviser with
 aspect more knowing),

Is earning a fee of old year Sixty-three, who's beginning to think
about going!
The noisy church-bell is a-ringing his knell—it's a delicate favour
to do one;
Its JANUS-like tone kills two birds with one stone, for it heralds
the birth of the new one!

* * * * * *

He sleeps the long trance—not a ghost of a chance of renewal of
lease by his lessor;
Il est mort, ce pauvre roi! Shall we sorrow? *Pourquoi?* let us rather cry
"*Vive* his successor!"
Anxious, uncommon I, great Anno Domini, am to know what
you've in store for me,
What you will pour for me none can explore for me, which
you'll admit is a bore for me.
The kid (if you pliz, I don't know who he is) takes "steps"
Sixty-three for to score out,
And I hope that all we who've seen old Sixty-three will be here
to bow young Sixty-four out!

THE DREAM

I dreamt (I was deep in
The middle of sleepin')
That as it was leap-year, the ladies—the ladies,
Young bachelors stopping,
Forthwith began popping
The question—which bold JIM afraid is—afraid is.

My slavey she swore,
As she knelt on the floor
(I was cautioned by many a leer of it—leer of it),
She lived but for me,
If I'd only love she!
But I told her that I wouldn't hear of it—hear of it.

An elderly dame,
She confessed to a flame
(Though she's older by far than my mother—my mother)
Which, dreading my jeers,
For a number of years
She had struggled, but vainly, to smother—to smother.

So many a mile,
To the source of the Nile,
She had made up her mind she would carry me—carry me;
And having got there,
For a wedding prepare,
For she fully intended to marry me—marry me!

Attractive young girls,
And old maidens in curls
(I ascribe it to faulty digestion—digestion),
And ladies of rank,
Young and plump, old and lank,
All set to work popping the question—the question!

And I thought one and all,
Thin and fat, short and tall,
The alternative gave of a match or law—match or law!
Which opened my eyes
With excessive surprise,
For I am not a popular bachelor—bachelor.

THE BARON KLOPFZETTERHEIM;

OR,

THE BEAUTIFUL BERTHA AND THE
BIG BAD BROTHERS OF BONN

FYTTE THE FIRST

Near the town of St. Goar,
  On the bleak Rhenish shore,
Dwelt a terrible Baron—a certain KLOPFZETTERHEIM.
  I've not got it pat,
  But it sounded like that,
Though whether it's properly spelt to the letter, I'm
  Not at all sure; I
  Confess for this story
To memory (second-rate) only a debtor I'm.
  Indulgence I claim,
  It's a high-sounding name,
And a name, too, to which one can easily set a rhyme.

    A growling and gruff 'un,
    A ruthless and rough 'un,
A tyrant, a Tartar, a toothless and tough 'un;
His skull was as bald as the palm of my hand,
And surrounding its base was a silvery band
Of curly grey hair, and he brushed it well up
    From ear round to ear,
    So it looked, from the rear,
  Like a very smooth egg in a very white cup.
    He'd bricks, and he'd mortar;
    He'd wood, and he'd water;
Sheep, oxen, and poultry, calves, pigs, and—a daughter;
Whom, though generally such points rather lax on, he
Swore was the loveliest woman in Saxony.

    The Baron was wealthy, but horribly stealthy;
    He'd jewels from Ingy, but still he was stingy;
    Though rich from a babby, unbearably shabby;
    Though steeped to his eyes, sir, in wealth, yet a miser;
    From boyhood a dunce, always trying to shirk "*hic, hoc,
Haec,*" he was stupid and proud as a turkey-cock.
    Stealthy and stingy and shabby and miserly,
    Every morning his wont was to rise early;
    Search out each inch of his rocky dominions,
    Count all the eggs and the apples and inions,

Listen at keyholes for candid opinions
Propounded by uncomplimentary minions,
    In syllables bated,
    For so was he hated
By all his dependents, for reasons just stated.

    Superior far,
    To her horrid papa,
Was BERTHA. The daughters of barons oft are.
    Her hair was fair,
    And a flaxen rare;
In the fine land called Rhineland, the best, I declare;
Its charms, in a single comparison summing,
It looked like a "nimbus," but far more becoming;
Besides, you could brush it, and alter the sit of it,
Play with its folds (did decorum permit of it),
Tickle your cheek with a stray ray or so;
Now you can't do all that with a "nimbus," you know.
Flaxen, I said—I recant—not a bit of it;
    A glorified hue
    (You find it on few),
Gold mingled with brown—now I'm sadly put to
    For an elegant noun
    (It must be gold and brown)
To which I can liken this natural crown;
But commonplace thoughts prove effectual stoppers,
And I can't think of any but sovereigns and coppers.
    In length it was ample, as you may suppose,
    For when BERTHA so fair
    Let down her back hair,
It rippled away till it reached to her toes.
She'd have made (had necessity ventured to drive her)
    A *really* respectable LADY GODIVA.
It was long, it was silky, and wavy, and mellow,
And about as much "flaxen" as sunbeams are yellow.

    Then her eyes!
    Their size!
    Their glorious blue!
    I am sure it's a hue
That was solely invented our trials to leaven—
You'll find it alone in girls' eyes and in heaven!
    When nobody hailed them,
    She quietly veiled them,
    Humanely declining
To send you, by needlessly flashing their light at you,
    Hopelessly pining;

But when you addressed her she always looked right at you—
          Right in your face,
          With a maidenly grace,
    That spoke to the truth and sincerity there,
And misconstrue that innocent gaze if you dare!

          Now the Baron's old seneschal,
          Finding the Rhenish all
          Swallowed, he hied
For some more to the *marchand de vin,* who replied,
"Friend, never of Rhenish the worth of a penny shall
E'er again aid in his lordship's digestion,
Unless he first pays down the penny in question.
The Baron must think me as green as an olive! Hence he
Ne'er will get more without cash down. At all events he
Couldn't suppose I would act with such folly, ven, see"
          (Opening his books
          With disheartening looks),
"I am tottering just on the brink of insolyvency."
          So the seneschal thought
          It was time to report
To his master the crisis to which he was brought.

FYTTE THE SECOND

is time now, I grieve, to my story to
    weave two who love to deceive and to
    plunder and thieve;
And this, by your leave, I'll attempt to
    achieve in a style, I believe, known as
    recitative.

A neighbouring Pfalzgraf had three sons, and he in armour glistened 'em;
RUPERT, CARL, and OTTO, as their noble father christened 'em.
In Christendom than OTTO you would hardly find a finer knight;
He set the women's hearts a-fire, which blazed away like pine a-light.
To gain him, all the German mothers tried the worst rascalities,
For he possessed the greatest of the German principalities;
    In fact, it brought him clear
    THREE HUNDRED POUNDS A YEAR—
Enough, we know, to sanction matrimonial formalities.

Now as RUPERT was eldest, and CARL was the second,
And OTTO the youngest, I'll swear you'll have reckoned
That RUPERT and CARL were, to say the least, quite on
          A par, as to evil,

With Robert the Devil,
And Otto a second edition of Crichton.
In legends we know
That it always is so:
The eldest sons, villains unheard of are thought to be;
The youngest, however, is just what he ought to be.
Otto was graceful, and slender, and tall,
While Rupert and Carl were as round as a ball.
Otto was handsome and neat as a pin,
While Rupert and Carl were as ugly as sin.

Now Rupert and Otto and Carl one day,
As home from hunting they made their way,
They entered the wine-merchant's *cabaret;*
Two brandies and water were brought on a tray
(For excellent Otto
Knew he ought not to
Drink anything stronger than curds and whey);
Then listened awhile to the gossiping host,
Who merrily told
Of the miserly old
Baron Klopfzetterheim, rolling in gold—
Of his recent endeavour
To get wine, and never
Pay nobody not even nothing whatever;
Telling them further,
How nowhere on earth a
More opposite creature existed than Bertha
(His amiable daughter),
How lovely all thought her,
And how he drove off all the nobles who sought her.

Now Rupert and Carl were cunning and bold,
And resolved to get hold
Of the jewels and gold,
In which it was said that Klopfzetterheim rolled.
But Otto was cast in a different mould,
And couldn't help thinking of what he was told
Of the beautiful Bertha, shut up by her old
Unpopular father
(Proprietor, rather);
So high-minded Otto
Remarked (*voce sotto*),
"These matters a pretty condition have got to;
Quite free from this fetter I'm
Resolved for to set her—I'm
Dashed if I'll suffer the Lord of Klopfzetterheim

44

Thus to imprison
So lovely a miss, on
The highly illogical plea that she's his'n."

Now the two elder brothers resolved to confide
In the landlord, and promised with him to divide
   The results, if he'd let them bide inside
   Two barrels, and so to the castle ride,
        To the Baron's old Rhenish hall,
   As though 'twere the liquor so rudely denied
        To the Baron's old seneschal.
So each of these worthies was packed in a barrel,
But what with their size and their flowing apparel,
        'Twas such a tight fit,
        That they couldn't e'en sit,
   Turn, stoop down, or change their position a bit;
        Only waiting to ask
        For a lantern and mask,
They ordered the landlord to "head in the cask."

Fytte the Third

Good Otto, not knowing
   What matters were doing,
Or thinking in which way the wind it was blowing,
   Paid what was owing
   For what they'd been stowing
Away in their waistcoats—then thought about going,
   When he saw at the door
   A wine cart with four
Strong horses attached, and of Rhenish a store;
   And on asking the host
   How now lay the coast,
   Was astonished to find
   That he'd quite changed his mind,
And was going to send both the wine and the car on
To his lordship and eminent highness the Baron.

Now being a brave and intelligent unit, he
Thought he could see a first-rate opportunity
Of seeing Miss Bertha with perfect impunity.
      It was not to be lost;
      So he said to the host,
"If you'll dress me like one of your active young draymen
(I'm sure I shall look like a chick of the same hen),
I'll pay you right nobly, as I always pay men."
The host, though the most irreligious of laymen,

Responded to this with a clerical "Amen";
    And quickly equipped him,
    Be-frocked and be-whipped him,
And OTTO, on his part, unsparingly tipped him,
    Then started away,
    With the wine in the dray,
Completely disguised in the drayman's array.

    But pondering arter
    The Baron's fair darter,
He failed to remember his *role* as a carter,
And nearly created the dickens's own "to do,"
    For he knocked with a bang,
    And he noisily rang
As gentlemen visitors only are wont to do;
    Although I may tell
    You, he knew very well
That a modest appeal at the area bell
Would, in his new line of life, better have fitted him,
As the flunkeys, with justice, remarked, who admitted him—
Adding some curses which nearly concerned his eyes;
But OTTO, the mild, from these wicked men turned his eyes,
Contented with gently consigning to Bath them as
Hurled at his head those unholy anathemas.

    The Baron KLOPFZETTERHEIM—
    Deeply in debt, or I'm
Greatly deceived (how these German names fetter rhyme!)—
    Opened his eyes
    With excessive surprise,
As he saw the two casks of respectable size
With Rhenish replete; and he opened them wider

When OTTO suggested, by way of a rider,
His master's (the wine-merchant's) deepest regret
(Expressed in a note for his lordship's perusal)
    That his foreman had let
    A ridiculous debt
Occasion the Baron so coarse a refusal;
But as it was done without even his knowledge, he
Trusted the Baron would take his apology
    In the way it was meant,
    For the wine he'd have sent
In a second (the shortest space known in horology).

The Baron, delighted, was easily pacified,
    For when Rhenish fails
    He falls back upon ales,
And gets—p'raps not tipsy, but just rather BASS-ified

(The stages of drink are not easily classified—
I'm speaking or writing about it, just *as* if I'd
Studied a failing, which horrid and fell I call);
In short, he was just in a humour angelical.
So he ordered SIR OTTO to take down each cask
To the cellar, and told off MISS B. to the task
　　　　Of watching its storing
　　　　In wine cellar, roaring
And shaking his stick at poor OTTO (a penny thing);
He told her to watch lest he pocketed anything.

　　　　OTTO goes to the cellar
　　　　With BERTHA *la bella*
(Who, like a good girl, always does what you tell her),
Assisted by many a half-starved retainer;
　　　　But lost to his duty
　　　　In BERTHA's great beauty
(Many men have been dazzled by many a plainer),
He made a mistake that he didn't observe—he
Placed each of the casks on the ground topsy-turvey,
And the horrible consequence was, that instead
Of his feet, his two brothers stood each on his head!

FYTTE THE FOURTH

ow *figurez vous*
　　The terrible stew
Of two young noblemen (stout ones, too),
Each in a cask, which a clumsy crew
Had topsy-turvey placed, in lieu
Of setting it down as they ought to do!
Of course these people none of them knew
Of the couple of nice young gentlemen, who
Were turning a most unusual hue,

　　From scarlet and purple to indigo blue,
　　As the blood to their head in a cataract flew;
　　Who'd have raised a roaring hullaballoo,
　　But that they feared to furnish a clue
　　To their hiding-place, for they thought on a few
　　Of the terrible things that would then fall due.
　　So they cursed away at each clumsy boor,
　　And as their chances of life grew fewer,
　　They swore that gold should never allure
　　Their innocent minds to thoughts impure;
　　But in spite of these good resolves, these poor
　　Young men grew bluer, and bluer, and bluer.

It's always an awkward thing, popping the question—
Refusals agree with few people's digestion;
So nine out of ten men are dreadfully slow about it—
Their minds are unsettled and change to and fro about it,
Because they don't know how young people should go about it;
　　　They hesitate so about it,
　　　So frightened, I trow, about it;
They *deserve* to get married, and that's all I know about it.

　　　OTTO well knew
　　　That the right thing to do
Was to say what he meant, and in syllables few.
　　　So he ventured to say,
　　　In his tenderest way,
　　　"The man now before you
　　　Lives but to adore you."
(With all that he said I'm not going to bore you;
Not that I'm anxious to make any myth of it,
But I think you'll be satisfied, quite, with the pith of it:
He talked as talk WILKINSON, JOHNSON, or SMITH of it.)
　　　Then his right hand he placed
　　　Round her delicate waist,
As well as he was in the cellar pitch-dark able. He
Wound up by adding, "I love you re-mark-able-y";
And when BERTHA indignantly answered him, "What, man,
An offer—ha! ha!—from the family potman!
My father your hide with his cudgel shall flay, man,
And teach you respect, you impertinent drayman;
In a moment your insolent manners he'll cure!"

"I'm no more a drayman," says OTTO, "than you're—
A proof I'll afford you of this satisfactory."
And though an extremely indifferent actor, he
Took from his waistcoat a big parchment roll, and
Proceeded to go through "The fair land of Poland,"
And handed the deed at the ballad's conclusion
To BERTHA, who stood overwhelmed with confusion.

　　　She read the recitals
　　　Of honours and titles,
From the opening words of the deed—"𝕿𝖍𝖎𝖘 𝕴𝖓𝖉𝖊𝖓𝖙𝖚𝖗𝖊,"
To "In witness whereof," with the air of a bencher
(That she understood nothing, my fortune I'll stake on it).
Then remarking she'd no requisitions to make on it,
With appropriate action to OTTO returned it,
And let him shake hands; and I think he had earned it.

Oh, careful papa!
Oh, prudent mamma!
Oh, uncle! oh, brother! which ever you are,
Whose well-lighted halls
See parties and balls,
Whose daughters go out and pay stiff morning calls,
And who think this proceeding,
Of which you've been reading,
Not quite in accordance with ladylike breeding,—
Remember her father, detestably mean,
Whose servant for fifteen long years she had been—
Cooking poor dinners and scrubbing floors clean,
And that OTTO was always considered, I ween,
The handsomest noble that ever was seen.

FYTTE THE FIFTH

TTO told her the reason he wore a disguise
Was to bask unrestrained in the light of her eyes.
Then he made a neat speech about God of Love's dart,
And offered his house, and his hands, and his heart
(And whenever he mentioned that organ, he thumped at it);
She didn't reject it—I may say she jumped at it;
And OTTO had such a peculiar way with him,
She agreed to elope from the castle that day with him,
If he could but discover (she'd many a doubt of it)
Some way by which she might get unobserved out of it.
But OTTO's good luck set him in the right track again;
There were two empty casks, he remarked, to go back again,
And he thought that MISS BERTHA could nicely arrange
(With judicious curtailing of under apparel),
To cram herself comfortably in a barrel.
So she ran up-stairs once just to pack up a change;
This done to her own satisfaction, she bade an
Undoubtedly faithful (though saucy) handmaiden
Instanter prepare,
By smoothing her hair
And "cleaning" herself (which a washing with soap meant—
It's not a nice phrase), for a sudden elopement.

Then BERTHA and GRETCHEN descended to OTTO
(Who was wondering where in the world they had got to);
And at first he demurred, when he heard she preferred
To take with her a third, and he thought it absurd
That she'd not go alone in her OTTO's society,
And all for the purpose of playing propriety.

With squeezing and crushing,
And crowding and pushing,
And crying and flushing, and chuckling and blushing,
They entered the casks (each of which held a cushing).
Miss B. began brushing
The tears that were gushing,
And OTTO, outside, enjoined silence by "hush"-ing,
Reproving her tears with "pooh-pooh"-ing and "tush"-ing.
Then the serfs took away,
And placed safe on the dray,
The casks which had held the material for lushing.

Little more to be told,
Of the miserly old
Baron KLOPFZETTERHEIM, rolling in gold.
Of his beautiful BERTHA
He heard nothing further,
The clumsy old Baron could never unearth her;
He ne'er could make out where his daughter had got to,
For of course he knew nothing at all about OTTO.
From the date of the wedding he didn't live long;
Everything, after she left him, went wrong.

He broke a blood vessel, endeavouring to bless (or
To curse—I don't know which) MISS BERTHA's successor
(Appointed a few hours after she quitted),
Because accidentally she had omitted
His slippers to warm—he was much to be pitied!
He broke a big blood vessel up in his head,
And fell on the floor of his palace, as dead
As OTTO's big brothers deep down in the cellar,
And his fortune descended to BERTHA *la bella*.

* * * * * *

Few hours they tarried
Before they got married
In private—no bridesmaids, or breakfasts, or fitnesses;
The clerk and the pew-opener were the witnesses;
The bride (though in stuff) looked a beauty bewilderin';
They lived many years and had hundreds of childerin.

DOWN TO THE DERBY

WITH RHYMES ON THE ROAD

Waggon and cart, ready to start,
  Early in morning at six, six;
Gallons of beer, stowed away here,
  Twiggery, swiggery, quick sticks.
Empty before, fill 'em once more;
  Women look trim in their caps, caps;
Screaming in fun, never say done,
  Joking and poking the chaps, chaps.
Sweeps in a truck, swells out of luck,
  Laughery, chaffery, grin, grin;
Travelling show, dwarf hid below,
  Eye on his giantess' gin, gin.

Twiggery, swiggery, shinery, finery, laughery,
  chaffery, pokery, jokery;
Down to the Derby as all of us go,
These are the sights that we each of us know;
Yet off to the Downs as we often have been,
Still every year is some novelty seen.

Ten of the clock, carriages flock
  Round to the doors at the West-end;
People who seem, skimming the cream,
  To have laid hold of life at the best end.
Phaeton and pair, baronet there,
  Lovely young girl with a smile, smile;
Look all about, splendid turn out,

Everything done in good style, style.
Hampers retain lots of champagne,
  Hungerly, vulgarly, prog, prog,
Nothing more seek, nice little shriek,
  Missing him, kissing him, dog, dog.

Flunkeydom, monkeydom, finery, whinery, livery,
  shivery, fowlery, growlery—
      Down to the Derby, etc.

Clapham we pass, schools in a mass,
  Up at the windows we go by,
Playful as mice, governess nice,
  Thinkery, winkery, oh, fie!
Balham the dull, vote it a mull,
  Marchery, starchery, slow, slow;
Tooting the next, sticks to its text,
  Travelly, gravelly, oh! oh!
Sutton a whet, thirsty we get,
  Palery alery, take, take;
Smart four-in-hand comes to a stand,
  Legs of the longest ones ache, ache.

Drinkery, winkery, palery alery, laughery,
  chaffery, crash along, dash along—
      Down to the Derby, etc.

Trudging along, two dozen strong,
    Wearily, drearily, riff-raff,
Swells at them stare, singing the air
    Of Saturday's opera, "Piff paff."
Handful of coin all of them join,
    Rambling, scrambling, pick up;
Rowing for more, won't have "encore,"
    Frightening, tightening, stick up.
Posturers two come into view,
    Rummer set, summerset throwing;
Over they turn (don't try and learn),
    All that they get for it owing.

Palery alery, smokery, jokery, rambling,
        scrambling, crash along, dash along—
            Down to the Derby, etc.

Under the trees, beautiful breeze,
    Lilacs in blossom we smell, smell;
May at last out (long while about),
    Country looks charming we tell, tell.
Everything seen, looking so green,
    Picture of verdure and so on;
Wonder if we green, too, shall be,
    As to the horse we should go on.
Pike and "no trust," up comes the dust—
    Pay away, dray away, got, got;
Dustman before, oaths by the score,
    Fit for the drawing-room not, not.

Flurrying, worrying, holloing, following;
    lay away, pay away, crash along,
        dash along—
            Down to the Derby, etc.

Epsom at last, nearing it fast,
    Smackery, crackery, whip, whip;
There's the Grand Stand, now close at hand,
    Think it a nice little trip, trip.
Get a good view, this one will do,
    Squeezing it, seizing it, rush, rush;
Downs looking smooth, CARELESS's Booth,
    Go in and get a good brush, brush.
Every one here, seems to appear,
    "How d'ye do?" "How are you?" nod, nod;
Some friends about, can't find 'em out,
    Look for them, hook for them, odd, odd.

Smackery, snackery, scenery, greenery,
    Leger bit, hedge a bit, look about,
        shook about—
            Down to the Derby, etc.

Now take your place, this is the race,
    Universe, tune a verse, fame, fame;
Cards to be sold, everything told,
    Colours of riders and name, name.
Buzz! off they go, galloping so,
    Bothery, dothery, eye, eye;
Look as they pass, out with the glass,
    Can't find the focus to spy, spy.
Yonder they run, some horse has won,
    Up with the number and see, see;
Whichever is in, hundreds may win,
    But thousands will diddled like *me* be.

Cantering, bantering, cheering 'em, nearing 'em,
    spy away, fly away, dothery, bothery—
        Down to the Derby, etc.

Derby complete, something to eat;
    Out with the provender, crush, crush;
Somebody walks off with the forks,
    Bring out the bottles and lush, lush.
Plenty of pie, salad is nigh,
    Lettuces, let us seize, cool, cool;
POPKINS an ass, broken a glass,
    Grittling, victualling, fool, fool;
Take to the wine, your health and mine,
    Drinkery, thinkery, nice, nice;
Off with the cup, finish it up,
    Sopping it, mopping it, trice, trice.

Readily, saidily, rather unsteadily, trickling,
    prickling, toiletty, spoiletty—
        Down to the Derby, etc.

Stroll on the course—one of the force,
    Piping and wiping his brow, now;
Handkerchief missed, called to assist,
    Robbery, bobbery, row, row.
Off with a watch, guard but a botch,
    Tickery, quickery, fled, fled;
Fortune to tell, know it too well,
    Gipsying, tipsying, head, head.

Ground seems to turn, throat seems to burn,
　　Whirl about, twirl about, steer clear;
Find out the drag, quizzed by a wag,
　　Jokery, smokery, queer, queer.

Robbery, bobbery, watchery, botchery, dangling,
　　wrangling, mumbling, grumbling—
　　　　Down to the Derby, etc.

Eaten a snack, time to be back,
　　Hurrying, scurrying, start, start;
Road as before, crammed but the more,
　　With carriage and phaeton and cart, cart.
Out come the stars, light up cigars,
　　Brandy and soda you must, must;
Road dry again, where was the rain?
　　Smokery, chokery, dust, dust.
Come to a block, just at "The Cock,"
　　Famous inn, same as in past time;
Pale ale to boot, take a cheroot,
　　"Dal be, it shall be the last time."

Hurrying, scurrying, hampering, scampering,
　　smokery, jokery, crash along, dash along—
　　　　Up from the Derby, etc.

Come to a pike, just what you like,
　　Ticketing, stick it in, stop, stop;
Plenty of fun, never say done,
　　Hattery, flattery, drop, drop.
Driving along, "let's have a song,"
　　Mystery, history, none, none;

Dozens of keys, take which you please,
　　Blowing horns, showing horns—*Lon-don.*
Lamps down the road, near your abode,
　　Flare away, glare away, far, far;
Kennington-gate, longer to wait,
　　Loud din and crowding at bar, bar.

Ticketing, stick it in, hattery, battery,
　　flare away, stare away, splashery, dashery—
　　　　Up from the Derby, etc.

Home get at last, going it fast,
　　Lifery, wifery, look, look;
Had no excess, buy a new dress,
　　Made it all right with your "book, book."
Wake the next day, think of the way,
　　How will the debts you incur be;
Or more to your mind, glad that you find,
　　You did pretty well on the Derby.
Anyhow you think it will do,
　　Not going now to be vexed here;
Hoping to spend with a "party" or friend,
　　A holiday, jolly day, next year.

Theatre, be at a, upper rooms, supper rooms,
　　choppery, moppery, steakery, rakery,
　　　singing too, bringing too, holiday, jolly day;
Fun thus we see as of old on the road,
This is the channel through which it has flowed;
Often to Epsom as people have been,
These are the fancies that freshen the scene.

SOMETHING LIKE NONSENSE VERSES

1.—THE HIGHLAND JEW

I saw a red-haired Jew from Aberdeen,
    In a gaberdine,
    At the Tabard Inn,
He wore a sword which was its scabbard in,
    On a Wednesday!

2.—THE PIOUS Q.C.

I saw MR. BIG BEN DENISON,
    Ask a benison
    On some venison,
Which he bought of ALFRED TENNYSON,
    On a Wednesday.

3.—THE GREEK MAIDEN

I beg to state I love a yaller miss,
    Born at Salamis,
    And this gal, or miss,
Bound to meet me down at Balham is,
    Every Wednesday!

4.—THE WORTHY INDEPENDENT MINISTER

A worthy Independent minister,
    Born at Finisterre,
    Turning sinister,
Smothered his wife with fumes of *kinaster*
    On a Wednesday!

5.—THE UNHAPPY MARRIAGE

Once I married a cook from charity,
    But disparity,
    And hair carrotty,
Made me treat her with barbarity
    Every Wednesday!

6.—THE SENSATION OPERA TROUPE

I know a man who's going to offer GYE
    Anthropophagi
    (Or androphagi),
Who will sing with French hippophagi
    Every Wednesday!

7.—THE UNFORTUNATE REVELLERS

Tipsy gents, the type of snobbery,
    Drunk and slobbery,
    Make a bobbery,
And the victims are of robbery
    Every Wednesday.

8.—THE JEALOUS DANCER

As I waltzed with JANE deliciously,
    JONES officiously,
    Injudiciously,
Bumped against us both most viciously,
    On a Wednesday.

9.—THE POLITE STUDENT

A civil student at my college (he
    Learns horology
    And conchology)
Offers me a full apology
    Every Wednesday.

10.—THE UNDIGNIFIED NOBLEMAN

I know a nobleman whose publicity
    And complicity
    In mendicity
Is a fact of authenticity
    Every Wednesday.

11.—THE ABSURD CHANCELLOR

Once a chancellor of acidity
    And timidity,
    With rapidity
Used to sing out "Rum ti iddy ti!"
    Every Wednesday.

ODE TO MY CLOTHES

(OWED TO MY TAILOR)

Oh! isn't it hot!
Oh! isn't it hot!
And all is soft and clammy and damp,
No need to moisten your postage stamp!
The very stones
Have lost their tones
And don't re-echo the p'liceman's tramp!
And, oh! isn't it hot!

I puff and blow and tetter and trickle,
I feel like nothing so much as a pickle—
A strong, hot India-pickle!
It's a hot acetic vinegar pickles me,
Everything that touches me tickles me;
And, oh! if you knew how I hate my clothes,
Fathers and mothers of half my oaths!
But in broiling June
I'm out of tune,
And I swear too readily then, I fear,
If you gave me a thousand pounds a year,
I'd glare at you,
Stare at you,
Heartily swear at you,
For making a wealthy man of me,
With the thermometer ninety-three!

And, oh! how I hate my hat!
That box of roasted air!
With the hard hot brim that presses its rim
With all its main right into my brain,

And it leaves its red trail there!
And how I hate my blessed boots,
Of pedal agonies the roots!
Sources of throes and pangs and shoots!
And socks with aggravating holes—
Socks that ruck all under the soles!

And then my collar!
Peruvian ROLLA!
(Convenient rhyme)
In thy blest time
You wore no trousers, choker, collar, brace, or sleeve,
But went about,
In-doors and out,
In what young ladies call "square bodies," I believe.

Trousers, waistcoat, and coat,
You cost me a ten-pound note;
But back—back to your pegs.
Head, body, and legs,
Through you I have grown as thin as a lath.
Now learn that I
Intend
To spend
June and July
Prone in a six-foot icy bath—
It is so hot,
May I be shot
If I can find a rhyme to "bath"!

THE STUDENT

I have chambers up in Gray's-inn,
   Turning out from Holborn-bars,
Though there are as many ways in
   As in Dublin there are cars.

You from Gray's-inn-lane can enter,
   Or from * * among the trees,
Then there's * * in the centre,
   Or from * * , if you please.

(Here follows, in thirteen verses, a list of the various approaches to Gray's-inn.)

I am on the second story,
   Where my name, in sable tint,
You may find in all the glory
   Of the largest Roman print.

If you'd like to know what others
   Live within the same domain,
Why there's, first, COLLUMPTON BROTHERS,
   Then there's POGSON, COGS, and CRANE.

Then you come to——

(Here follow, in seven verses, the names of our contributor's fellow-lodgers.)

One fine morning I was sitting
   On my pleasant window-sill,
Little o'er my mind was flitting,
   As I nibbled at my quill;

Not of Mexico revolving,
   Nor of Portugal and Spain,
Nor of Parliament dissolving,
   Nor of smashed excursion train.

(Here, in twenty-seven verses, follows a list of subjects of which our contributor was not thinking.)

For of Mexico I'm weary,
   Parliament's a thing of nought,
Trains to me are always dreary—
   Trains of passengers or thought.

(Here, in nineteen verses, he explains his reasons for not thinking of the subjects enumerated in the preceding twenty-seven.)

Well, as I was sitting idly
   On my pleasant window-sill,
Speculating vaguely, widely,
   On my aunt's unopened will,

I perceived a silent student
   At a window, quite at home,
Stooping more than I thought prudent
   Over a Tremendous Tome.

As I watched the youth pursuing
   His * * * I exclaimed,
"Well I wonder what you're doing,
   And I wonder how you're named!"

P'raps to orders you're proceeding,
   P'raps I've found a lawyer keen—
Caught an Oxford man at Reading—
   Possibly your name is GREEN.

(Here, in thirty-five verses, he speculates on the youth's possible prospects, and suggests a variety of names, all or any of which may be his. He then, rather artistically, changes his metre, and bursts into the following impassioned appeal):—

"I ask an ap-
  Is it zo-
  Is it conch-
  Is it ge-
  'Lectro bi-
  Meteor-
  Is it nos- } ology?"
  Or etym-
  P'raps it's myth-
  Is it the-
  Palaeont-
  Or archae-

(And so on, through all the ologies—eighty-four
more lines.)

This in accents loud I shouted
  At the youth across the square,
* * * I never doubted
  * * * he was aware.

If he heard me, nothing wot I,
  For he studied still his lore,
And no sort of answer got I,
  So I shouted out once more,

"I ask an ap-
  Is it zo-
  Is it conch- } ology?"
  Is it ge-

(And so on, as before, through the ninety-six
ologies.)

Still no answer, sign, or motion
  Came from him across to me,
And to this day I've no notion
  What that student's lore might be,

    Whether zo-
    Whether conch- ology,
    Whether ge-

(And so on, as above.)

TEMPORA MUTANTUR

Letters, letters, letters, letters!
   Some that please and some that bore,
Some that threaten prison fetters
(Metaphorically, fetters
Such as bind insolvent debtors)—
   Invitations by the score.

One from Cogson, Wiles, and Railer,
   My attorneys, off the Strand;
One from Copperblock, my tailor—
My unreasonable tailor—
   One in Flagg's disgusting hand.

One from Ephraim and Moses,
   Wanting coin without a doubt,
I should like to pull their noses—
Their uncompromising noses;
One from Alice with the roses—
   Ah, I know what that's about!

Time was when I waited, waited
   For the missives that she wrote,
Humble postmen execrated—
Loudly, deeply execrated—
When I heard I wasn't fated
   To be gladdened with a note!

Time was when I'd not have bartered
   Of her little pen a dip
For a peerage duly gartered—
For a peerage starred and gartered—
With a palace-office chartered,
   Or a Secretaryship.

But the time for that is over,
   And I wish we'd never met.
I'm afraid I've proved a rover—
I'm afraid a heartless rover—
Quarters in a place like Dover
   Tend to make a man forget.

Now I can accord precedence
   To my tailor, for I do
Want to know if he gives credence—
An unwarrantable credence—
   To my proffered I O U!

Bills for carriages and horses,
   Bills for wine and light cigar,
Matters that concern the Forces—
News that may affect the Forces—
News affecting my resources,
   Much more interesting are!

And the tiny little paper,
   With the words that seem to run
From her little fingers taper
(They are very small and taper),
By the tailor and the draper
   Are in interest outdone.

And unopened it's remaining!
   I can read her gentle hope—
Her entreaties, uncomplaining
(She was always uncomplaining),
Her devotion never waning—
   Through the little envelope!

THE BACHELORS' STRIKE

(TO BE WRITTEN IN THE YEAR 1905)

'Twas early in July,
  In eighteen sixty-five,
When a tribe of males from old Marseilles
  Declared they never would wive.

For they thought on the costly style
  Of shawls and bonnets and veils,
And they saw with amaze the expensive ways
  Of the damsels of old Marseilles.

They vowed they'd marry no maid
  Unless she'd dress her more
In the cheap and chaste and simple taste
  Of two hundred years before.

But centuries twain before,
  As painted pictures show,
All dress was dear, and the bodies, I hear,
  Were worn extremely low.

But none of the men of Marseilles
  Had histories on their shelves;
But, strong in the heat of their blind conceit,
  They chuckled within themselves.

And there rose from old Marseilles
  A cry from the maiden crew,
"Six thousand head of girls to wed,
  And nobody comes to woo!

"Oh, come, ye knights of France,
  And knights of England true,
And teach these loons to dance to the tunes
  They'd have us dancing to!"

And three thousand British knights,
  And as many knights of France,
Came down on rails to old Marseilles
  To teach these cravens dance.

They smote them hip and thigh,
  And then each warrior true
Embraced his prize before the eyes
  Of the mercenary crew.

And having fairly done
  The task to them assigned,
Each rode away, as the stories say,
  With a maiden packed behind.

And the dreary, dreary tribe
  Of cravens are still alive,
Though years have gone by since that July,
  In eighteen sixty-five.

And none will make their beds,
  And none will scour and wipe,
And no little trippers will bring out their slippers,
  And fill their evening pipe.

And an awful story goes,
  That there's a stern decree,
That swear as they may, to their dying day,
  No button they e'er shall see!

MORAL

So fools reject a prize,
  And, offered wealth, disdain it,
Because that they object to pay
  For the caskets that contain it.

So fools—such fools are they,
  They're scarcely worthy blaming—
Decline the care of a picture rare
  Because it involves a framing.

So many a fool we find
  So blindly wed to Mammon,
That the foolish flat begrudges the sprat
  That he knows will hook a salmon.

A BAD NIGHT OF IT

"What, about to leave town?" Yes, we've got to go down to the THOMPSONS' at
    Weybridge, in Surrey,

For a week at the least, and the wind's in the east, and I'm ill and I'm wheezy,
    and Weybridge is breezy, and awfully slow, and I don't want to go, but my
    wife did it all in a hurry;

But THOMPSON is rich, and a bachelor, which is important to me, for his brother,
    you see, married POLLY's mamma (he may swear at his star, for her ma is a
    dame whom I podgy call),

So JACK THOMPSON's her aunt—no, her uncle. I can't in such weather as this,
    when you steam and you hiss like an engine, be genealogical.

And I'm thinking with dread of that awful spare bed; for you can't sleep a wink,
    but you lie and you think, when you're stopping in rooms that are new to
    you,

And to ask you to go to a place you don't know, and lay down your poor head
    in an unexplored bed, when the weather is hot and unpleasant, is *not* what a
    good sort of fellow would do to you.

You kick and you plunge, and you roll and you lunge, and you shake off the
    bed-clothes that cover you,

With a terrible tickling, torturing, trickling, tingling feeling all over you;

You curse and you swear at the garment you wear, and you do all you can to get
    colder;

And then sick of despairing, and cursing and swearing, the sleeves you are
    wearing you roll away up to the shoulder;

Then the moon, which you know half-an-hour ago seemed the veriest ghost of a
    crescent,

Is blazing away, turning night into day, and quite round, and extremely
    unpleasant;

So you make up your mind just to draw down the blind, as a step that may lead
    to your snoring,

And you jump out of bed, and you damage your head, and you hollo with dread
    as you find that you tread on a terrible tack in the flooring;

And you look at the clock, and you see with a shock that the night has all gone,
    and you're far on to dawn, and you're ready to weep, for you've not had a
    sleep all the while, and it now will be soon light;

Then you rattle the shins of your tottering pins (they're as feeble as lath) on the
    edge of the bath, which, you then are aware, is the only thing there which is
    not lighted up by the moonlight.

Once again into bed, but this time with your head where your feet ought to rest,
    and your quick-throbbing chest all exposed to such air as there may be;

But that move no sleep charms, and you fling out your arms till a faint little
    shriek (shrill enough, though it's weak), from a fat little dot in a
    neighbouring cot, proclaims you've assaulted the baby,

Which awakens your spouse, and you then count five thousand to send you to
    sleep, but a vigil you keep for a half-hour's rout, for she ups and lets out in
    a way that would frighten a Gorgon;

But still you go through "eighty-one, eighty-two, eighty-three, eighty-four," and so through many more, while she's talking away till it's far into day, for her mouth's an unwearying organ.

So now you will know why I don't want to go to the THOMPSONS' at Weybridge, in Surrey;

For old THOMPSON's a beast, and the wind's in the east, and I'm ill and I'm wheezy, and Weybridge is breezy and awfully slow, and I don't want to go, but my wife did it all in a hurry.

TO PHOEBE

"Gentle, modest, little flower,
　Sweet epitome of May,
Love me but for half-an-hour,
　Love me, love me, little fay."
Sentences so fiercely flaming
　In your tiny shell-like ear,
I should always be exclaiming
　If I loved you, PHOEBE, dear.

"Smiles that thrill from any distance
　Shed upon me while I sing!
Please ecstaticise existence,
　Love me, oh, thou fairy thing!"
Words like these, outpouring sadly,
　You'd perpetually hear,
If I loved you, fondly, madly;—
　But I do not, PHOEBE, dear.

OZONE

Did you hear of the use of ozone, ohone?
It's the best disinfectant that's known, they've shown.
     Though it doesn't appear
     To my mind very clear,
Yet we'll sing of the praise of ozone, ohone!
Oh! we'll sing of the praise of ozone!

I don't quite see how it can act—in fact
In a room where a hundred are packed it's lacked:
     In a tenanted place
     Not a ghost of a trace
Of the gas that is known as ozone is shown,
Not a trace of this useful ozone!

But if on Ben Nevis's top you stop,
You will find of this gas there's a crop—but drop
     To the regions below,
     And experiments show
Not a trace of this useful ozone is known,
Not a trace of this useful ozone!

In a desert 'twill cover the ground, all round,
And up in the clouds I'll be bound it's found;
     But oh, it's a pity
     That here in the city
The divvle a drop of ozone is blown,
Not a drop of this useful ozone!

It's because I'm an ignorant chap, mayhap,
And I daresay I merit a slap or rap,
     But it's never, you see,
     Where it's wanted to be,
So I call it Policeman Ozone—it's known
By my friends as Policeman Ozone!

TO THE TERRESTRIAL GLOBE

BY A MISERABLE WRETCH

Roll on, thou ball, roll on!
Through pathless realms of Space
    Roll on!
What though I'm in a sorry case?
What though I cannot meet my bills?
What though I suffer toothache's ills?
What though I swallow countless pills?
    Never *you* mind!
    Roll on!

Roll on, thou ball, roll on!
Through seas of inky air
    Roll on!
It's true I have no shirts to wear;
It's true my butcher's bill is due;
It's true my prospects all look blue—
But don't let that unsettle you:
    Never *you* mind!
    Roll on!

        [*It rolls on.*

THE MONKEY IN TROUBLE

Waiting, waiting for the halter,
   Hoping for release in vain—
Oh! the Rock of Gibberaltar!
   Would I saw you once again!

Active, nimble, able-bodied,
   Up the tallest trees I ran;
Now I'm taken up and quodded,
   Just as if I was a man!

Beating at my prison wildly!
   Yelling with a maddened yell!
For, to put it very mildly,
   This is a condemnëd sell!

They have locked me in the station,
   Just because, when driven wild,
In a fit of irritation
   I attacked a teasing child!

Well, of course, the fact before you
   With malignity seems rife,
But, indeed, I do assure you
   Mine's a very trying life.

When you're treated *idem semper,*
   Thrashed, and clothed in dresses tight,
Why, it tells upon your temper,
   And you feel inclined to bite.

Just suppose a great gorilla
   Came and took the learned beak,
Made him fire a gun for siller,
   Beat a tambourine, and speak.

Wear a brigand hat and feather,
   Sweep the floor and dance and fight,
Play in every kind of weather,
   Don't you think he'd want to bite?

P'raps they're now indictments framing
   To be signed and stuck on shelves,
Me as human fellow claiming—
   Am I then so like themselves?

Let me go—you're sure to mess it—
   'Tis indeed your wisest plan,
As Mr. Russell would express it,
   "No, by heavens, I am not Man!"

Condemned Cell, Marylebone Police-court

BACK AGAIN!

Back to the dust of the town,
   Back to the work at the mill,
Back to the wig and the gown,
   Back to the dun and the bill,
Back to Smith, Robinson, Brown,
   Back to the paper and quill!

No more of Biedecher's Guide,
   No more of French *table d'hôte,*
No more of bridegroom and bride,
   No more adventures afloat,
No more of *diligence* ride,
   No more of circular note!

Back to my drama at day,
   Back to my leader at night,
Back to the Westminster fray,
   Back to the novel I write,
Back to my stall at the play,
   Back to Pam, Gladstone, and Bright.

No more rouletting afar,
   No more of Baden or Ems,
No more disgusting cigar,
   No more of Belgians and Flems,
No more of channel and bar,
   No more upsailing of Thames!

Back to policeman and guard,
　　Back to the Ovals and Squares,
Back to the ill-treated Bard,
　　Back to the bulls and the bears,
Back to investments ill-starred,
　　Back to the slap-bangy airs!

No more of black *demi-tasse,*
　　No more *six-sous petit verre,*
No more liqueur as a *chasse,*
　　No Burgomeister or Maire,
No play worth seeing, alas!
　　No dining out in the air!

Back to the chimney-pot hat,
　　Back to the chop at the club,
Back to my dog and my cat,
　　Back to my evening rub,
Back—(I'm not sorry for that)
　　Back to my sponge and my tub!

No more ablution in bowl,
　　No more *absinthe* to be had,
No more fantastical roll,
　　No more excursioning cad,
And, to tell you the truth, on the whole
　　I swear I'm uncommonly glad!

TO MY ABSENT HUSBAND

ell me, EDWARD, dost remember
　　How at breakfast often we,
Put our bacon in the tea-pot
　　While we took and fried our tea?

How we went to evening parties
　　On gigantic brewer's drays?
How you wore your coats as trousers,
　　In those happy, happy days?

How we used to pocket ices
　　When a modest lunch we bought?
Quaff the foaming Abernethy,
　　Masticate the crusty port?

How we fished in deep sea water
　　For the barbel, tench, and carp?
Wore our rings upon our pencils
　　While we cut our fingers sharp?

How we cleaned our boots with sherry
　　While we drank the blacking dry?
How we quite forgot to pay for
　　Articles we used to buy?

How, a ruffian prosecuting,
　　Who'd been swindled, so he said,
We appeared at the Old Bailey,
　　And were done ourselves instead?

MUSINGS IN A MUSIC HALL

BY A YOUNG MAN FROM THE COUNTRY

When a man sticks his hat at the back of his head,
    Tell me, Oh, Editor, why do they roar?
And then, when he pushes it forward instead,
    Why do they scream twice as loud as before?
When an elderly gentleman rumples his hair,
    Why do they all go delirious as well?
When he uses a handkerchief out of repair,
    Why do they, why do they, why do they yell?

When a vulgar virago is singing her song,
    Why must she offer herself as a wife?
Why give applause about ten minutes long
    When a baby of seven imperils its life?
What does a singer intend to imply
    By "Whack fol the larity, larity, lay"?
What can he hope to convey to me by
    Singing "Rum tiddity, iddity!" eh?

PANTOMIMIC PRESENTIMENTS

Looking lately in at LACY's, at the photographic faces
Of the many Thespian races who are living or have gone;
I began aloud to wonder on the next dramatic blunder
Which my criticism's thunder would be exercised upon.

(Passing MENKEN as Mazeppa, on her omnibus high-stepp*ah*,)
There was glorious PAREPA—there were BILLINGTON and TOOLE;
There was BUCKSTONE slying winking—there was pretty Eily sinking,
There was Rip Van Winkle drinking like a poor besotted fool.

There were KATE and ELLEN TERRY, looking beautiful and merry,
WIDDICOMB about to bury poor Ophelia in her tomb;
There was SOTHERN as Dundreary, FANNY JOSEPHS as a Peri;
There was Richard Pride all beery, there was Manfred in his gloom.

And I thought on all the pleasure that each photographic treasure
Had afforded, in my leisure, twenty times apiece to me;
But I'm only what one calls a man—e'en chronic Winkle palls a man,
And only Camaralzaman remáins for me to see!

I'm beginning to get weary of dramatic desert dreary,
And I ask myself a query, when will novelties begin?
But, alas! there's nothing novel, from the "Lane" to barn and hovel,
Until Harlequin Lord Lovel, Goody Two Shoes, Gaffer Gin!

As I turn away from LACY's, I'm detected making faces
As I scan the queer oasis now unfolding to my view;
It's a green I can't admire, for it comes of coloured fire;
I'm beginning now to tire of it—green, or red, or blue!

Seedy sprites forever vaulting, seedy metre ever halting,
Men of "property" cobalting eighteen-penny devil's face;
And the foolish culmination in a weary "transformation,"
Whose complete elaboration takes a twenty minutes' space!

Then the green and crimson fire, and the women hung on wire
Rising higher, rising higher—oh, their bony, baggy knees!
And the never-failing "rally," and the fine old crusted sally,
And the "Ladies of the Bally," and the fays who sniff and sneeze!

All the stockings gone in ladders—then the sausages and bladders,
And the chromes, and greens, and madders, that I've seen five thousand times;
And the glitter, gauze, and spangle, and the clown turned in the mangle,
And the everlasting jangle of the mutilated rhymes.

There's that fickle Covent Garding, promised operas retarding,
And perhaps for aye discarding, in their love of Dividend;
But they've failed in English operer, and wisely think it properer,
By pantomime tiptop-erer their balance sheet to mend!

So, with gorge-e-ous Aladdin, dream of luring swell and cad in
(Who are always to be had in for a showy pantomime),
And abandoning old trammels, wean poor Opera on mammals,
In the shape of four live camels, draped as in Aladdin's time.
So I turn away from LACY's, making unbecoming faces
At this Pantomime oasis,—fun and fire, and leg and rhyme!

THE BAR AND ITS MOANING

Three publishers journeyed out into the West-
  Minster Hall where the Bench and the Bar go down:
Each published the cases that pleased him the best,
  And sold them to barristers working in town:
    For Bar must work, and tradesmen are deep;
    So the cases they publish are far from cheap,
      And in spite of the Bar and its moaning!

A barrister sat in his chambers drear
  And he studied reports which the three took down;
He found them imperfect, and clumsy, and dear,
  Yet no others were published in country or town.
    And the counsel worked and the publishers slept,
    And the publishers grinned while the counsel wept,
      And they laughed at the Bar and its moaning!

But one morning the counsel his temper lost,
  And the publishers' books to the winds he cast;
For he found them increasing in number and cost,
  And each was more clumsy and dear than the last:
    So the Bar complained, protested, and wrote;
    But the publishers grinned, and they took no note
      Of the Bench, and the Bar, and its moaning!

Then the Bench and the Bar set to work in a trice—
  A working committee was formed one day,
And they gathered reports at a uniform price,
  Which simplified things in a wonderful way.
    Then the counsel grinned, and the publishers wept,
    And the publishers cursed while the counsel slept,
      And they swore at the Bar and its moaning!

So the publishers woke from their golden dream,
  And did all in their power the plan to burke;
But while they disparaged the barristers' scheme,
  The committee went steadily on with their work:
    And the counsel grinned, and the publishers wept
    As the new reports into favour crept,
      And they bothered the Bar with their moaning!

So the publishers come with a scrape and a bow,
  And they beg the committee, with many a whine,
To allow them to join the committeemen now,
  Which of course they politely but firmly decline:
    And the counsel laugh, and the publishers weep,
    For the new reports are judicious and cheap,
      So good-bye to the Bar and its moaning!

TO EUPHROSYNE

WITH MY CARTE DE VISITE

I've heard EUPHROSYNE declare
  That handsome men, both dark and fair,
Are dear at three a penny.
  I've searched the world, and this I know,
That nowhere, at a price so low,
  Could I discover any.

Men ridiculed my folly, when
  I asked the price of handsome men,
And christened me a ninny.
  Till PHOCAS KAMMERER I tried,
And found the article supplied
  At twenty-four a guinea!

THE PHANTOM CURATE

A FABLE

A Bishop once—I will not name his see—
  Annoyed his clergy in the mode conventional;
From pulpit shackles never set them free,
  And found a sin where sin was unintentional.
    All pleasures ended in abuse auricular—
    That Bishop was so terribly particular.

Though, on the whole, a wise and upright man,
  He sought to make of human pleasures clearances,
And form his priests on that much-lauded plan
  Which pays undue attention to appearances.
    He couldn't do good deeds without a psalm in 'em,
    Although, in truth, he bore away the palm in 'em.

Enraged to find a deacon at a dance,
  Or catch a curate at some mild frivolity,
He sought by open censure to enhance
  Their dread of joining harmless social jollity.
    Yet he enjoyed (a fact of notoriety)
    The ordinary pleasures of society.

One evening, sitting at a pantomime
  (Forbidden treat to those who stood in fear of him),
Roaring at jokes *sans* metre, sense, or rhyme,
    He turned, and saw immediately in rear of him—
      His peace of mind upsetting, and annoying it—
      A curate, also heartily enjoying it.

Again, 'twas Christmas Eve, and to enhance
  His children's pleasure in their harmless rollicking,
He, like a good old fellow, stood to dance;
    When something checked the current of his frolicking:
      That curate, with a maid he treated loverly,
      Stood up and figured with him in the "Coverley"!

Once, yielding to an universal choice
  (The company's demand was an emphatic one,
For the old Bishop had a glorious voice),
    In a quartet he joined—an operatic one—
      Harmless enough, though ne'er a word of grace in it;
      When, lo! that curate came and took the bass in it!

One day, when passing through a quiet street,
  He stopped awhile and joined a Punch's gathering,
And chuckled more than solemn folk think meet
    To see that gentleman his Judy lathering;
      And heard, as Punch was being treated penally,
      That phantom curate laughing all hyaenally!

Now at a picnic, 'mid fair golden curls,
  Bright eyes, straw hats, *bottines* that fit amazingly,
A croquêt-bout is planned by all the girls,
    And he, consenting, speaks of croquêt praisingly;
      But suddenly declines to play at all in it—
      The curate fiend has come to take a ball in it!

Next, when at quiet seaside village, freed
  From cares episcopal and ties monarchical,
He grows his beard, and smokes his fragrant weed,
    In manner anything but hierarchical—
      He sees—and fixes an unearthly stare on it—
      That curate's face, with half a yard of hair on it!

At length he gave a charge, and spake this word:
  "Vicars, your curates to enjoyment urge ye may;
To check their harmless pleasuring's absurd;
    What laymen do without reproach, my clergy may."
      He spake, and lo! at this concluding word of him,
      The curate vanished—no one since has heard of him.

TO A LITTLE MAID

BY A POLICEMAN

Come with me, little maid!
Nay, shrink not, thus afraid—
    I'll harm thee not!
Fly not, my love, from me—
I have a home for thee—
    A fairy grot,
        Where mortal eye
        Can rarely pry,
There shall thy dwelling be!

List to me, while I tell
The pleasures of that cell,
    Oh, little maid!
What though its couch be rude—
Homely the only food
    Within its shade?
        No thought of care
        Can enter there,
No vulgar swain intrude!

Come with me, little maid,
Come to the rocky shade
    I love to sing;
Live with us, maiden rare—
Come, for we "want" thee there,
    Thou elfin thing,
        To work thy spell,
        In some cool cell
In stately Pentonville!

FERDINANDO AND ELVIRA

OR, THE GENTLE PIEMAN

PART I

At a pleasant evening party I had taken down to supper
One whom I will call ELVIRA, and we talked of love and TUPPER,

MR. TUPPER and the poets, very lightly with them dealing,
For I've always been distinguished for a strong poetic feeling.

Then we let off paper crackers, each of which contained a motto,
And she listened while I read them, till her mother told her not to.

Then she whispered, "To the ball-room we had better, dear, be walking;
If we stop down here much longer, really people will be talking."

There were noblemen in coronets, and military cousins,
There were captains by the hundred, there were baronets by dozens.

Yet she heeded not their offers, but dismissed them with a blessing;
Then she let down all her back hair which had taken long in dressing.

Then she had convulsive sobbings in her agitated throttle,
Then she wiped her pretty eyes and smelt her pretty smelling-bottle.

So I whispered, "Dear ELVIRA, say—what can the matter be with you?
Does anything you've eaten, darling POPSY, disagree with you?"

But spite of all I said, her sobs grew more and more distressing,
And she tore her pretty back hair, which had taken long in dressing.

Then she gazed upon the carpet, at the ceiling then above me,
And she whispered, "FERDINANDO, do you really, *really* love me?"

"Love you?" said I, then I sighed, and then I gazed upon her sweetly—
For I think I do this sort of thing particularly neatly—

"Send me to the Arctic regions, or illimitable azure,
On a scientific goose-chase, with my COXWELL or my GLAISHER!

"Tell me whither I may hie me, tell me, dear one that I *may* know—
Is it up the highest Andes? down a horrible volcano?"

But she said, "It isn't polar bears, or hot volcanic grottoes,
Only find out who it is that writes those lovely cracker mottoes!"

PART II

"Tell me, HENRY WADSWORTH, ALFRED, POET CLOSE, or MISTER TUPPER,
Do you write the bonbon mottoes my ELVIRA pulls at supper?"

But HENRY WADSWORTH smiled, and said he had not had that honour;
And ALFRED, too, disclaimed the words that told so much upon her.

"MISTER MARTIN TUPPER, POET CLOSE, I beg of you inform us";
But my question seemed to throw them both into a rage enormous.

MISTER CLOSE expressed a wish that he could only get anigh to me.
And MISTER MARTIN TUPPER sent the following reply to me:—

"A fool is bent upon a twig, but wise men dread a bandit."
Which I think must have been clever, for I didn't understand it.

Seven weary years I wandered—Patagonia, China, Norway,
Till at last I sank exhausted at a pastrycook his doorway.

There were fuchsias and geraniums, and daffodils and myrtle,
So I entered, and I ordered half a basin of mock turtle.

He was plump and he was chubby, he was smooth and he was rosy,
And his little wife was pretty, and particularly cozy.

And he chirped and sang, and skipped about, and laughed with laughter hearty—
He was wonderfully active for so very stout a party.

And I said, "Oh, gentle pieman, why so very, very merry?
Is it purity of conscience, or your one-and-seven sherry?"

But he answered, "I'm so happy—no profession could be dearer—
If I am not humming 'Tra! la! la!' I'm singing 'Tirer, lirer!'

"First I go and make the patties, and the puddings and the jellies,
Then I make a sugar birdcage, which upon a table swell is;

"Then I polish all the silver, which a supper-table lacquers;
Then I write the pretty mottoes which you find inside the crackers"—

"Found at last!" I madly shouted. "Gentle pieman, you astound me!"
Then I waved the turtle soup enthusiastically round me.

And I shouted and I danced until he'd quite a crowd around him—
And I rushed away, exclaiming, "I have found him! I have found him!"

And I heard the gentle pieman in the road behind me trilling,
"'Tira! lira!' stop him, stop him! 'Tra! la! la!' the soup's a shilling!"

But until I reached ELVIRA's home, I never, never waited,
And ELVIRA to her FERDINAND's irrevocably mated!

THE PANTOMIME "SUPER" TO HIS MASK

Vast, empty shell!
Impertinent, preposterous abortion:
With vacant stare,
And ragged hair,
And every feature out of all proportion!
Embodiment of echoing inanity,
Excellent type of simpering insanity,
Unwieldy, clumsy nightmare of humanity,
I ring thy knell!

To-night thou diest,
Beast that destroy'st my heaven-born identity!
Nine weeks of nights
Before the lights,
Swamped in thine own preposterous nonentity,
I've been ill-treated, cursed, and thrashed diurnally,
Credited for the smile you wear externally—
I feel disposed to smash thy face, infernally,
As there thou liest!

I've been thy brain:
I've been the brain that lit thy dull concavity!
The human race
Invest *my* face
With thine expression of unchecked depravity.
Invested with a ghastly reciprocity,
I've been responsible for thy monstrosity,
I, for thy wanton, blundering ferocity—
But not again!

'Tis time to toll
Thy knell, and that of follies pantomimical:
A nine weeks' run,
And thou hast done
All thou canst do to make thyself inimical.
Adieu, embodiment of all inanity!
Excellent type of simpering insanity!
Unwieldy, clumsy nightmare of humanity!
Freed is thy soul!

(*The Mask respondeth.*)

Oh! master mine,
Look thou within thee, ere again ill-using me.
Art thou aware
Of nothing there
Which might abuse thee, as thou art abusing me?
A brain that mourns *thine* unredeemed rascality?
A soul that weeps at *thy* threadbare morality?
Both grieving that *their* individuality
Is merged in thine?

75

THE YARN OF THE "NANCY BELL"

'Twas on the shores that round our coast
  From Deal to Ramsgate span,
That I found alone on a piece of stone
  An elderly naval man.

His hair was weedy, his beard was long,
  And weedy and long was he,
And I heard this wight on the shore recite,
  In a singular minor key:

"Oh, I am a cook and a captain bold,
  And the mate of the *Nancy* brig,
And a bo'sun tight, and a midshipmite,
  And the crew of the captain's gig."

And he shook his fists and he tore his hair,
  Till I really felt afraid,
For I couldn't help thinking the man had been drinking,
  And so I simply said:

"Oh, elderly man, it's little I know
  Of the duties of men of the sea,
But I'll eat my hand if I understand
  How you can possibly be

"At once a cook, and a captain bold,
  And the mate of the *Nancy* brig,
And a bo'sun tight, and a midshipmite,
  And the crew of the captain's gig."

Then he gave a hitch to his trousers, which
    Is a trick all seamen larn,
And having got rid of a thumping quid,
    He spun this painful yarn:

"'Twas in the good ship *Nancy Bell*
    That we sailed to the Indian sea,
And there on a reef we come to grief,
    Which has often occurred to me.

"And pretty nigh all o' the crew was drowned
    (There was seventy-seven o' soul),
And only ten of the *Nancy's* men
    Said 'Here!' to the muster-roll.

"There was me and the cook and the captain bold,
    And the mate of the *Nancy* brig,
And the bo'sun tight, and a midshipmite,
    And the crew of the captain's gig.

"For a month we'd neither wittles nor drink,
    Till a-hungry we did feel,
So we drawed a lot, and accordin' shot
    The captain for our meal.

"The next lot fell to the *Nancy's* mate,
    And a delicate dish he made;
Then our appetite with the midshipmite
    We seven survivors stayed.

"And then we murdered the bo'sun tight,
    And he much resembled pig;
Then we wittled free, did the cook and me,
    On the crew of the captain's gig.

"Then only the cook and me was left,
    And the delicate question, 'Which
Of us two goes to the kettle?' arose,
    And we argued it out as sich.

"For I loved that cook as a brother, I did,
    And the cook he worshipped me;
But we'd both be blowed if we'd either be stowed
    In the other chap's hold, you see.

"'I'll be eat if you dines off me,' says Tom,
    'Yes, that,' says I, 'you'll be,'—
'I'm boiled if I die, my friend,' quoth I,
    And 'Exactly so,' quoth he.

"Says he, 'Dear James, to murder me
    Were a foolish thing to do,
For don't you see that you can't cook *me*,
    While I can—and will—cook *you!*'

"So he boils the water, and takes the salt
    And the pepper in portions true
(Which he never forgot), and some chopped shalot,
    And some sage and parsley too.

"'Come here,' says he, with a proper pride,
    Which his smiling features tell,
''Twill soothing be if I let you see
    How extremely nice you'll smell.'

"And he stirred it round and round and round,
    And he sniffed at the foaming froth;
When I ups with his heels, and smothers his squeals
    In the scum of the boiling broth.

"And I eat that cook in a week or less,
    And—as I eating be
The last of his chops, why, I almost drops,
    For a wessel in sight I see!

*   *   *   *   *

"And I never larf, and I never smile,
    And I never lark nor play,
But I sit and croak, and a single joke
    I have—which is to say:

"Oh, I am a cook and a captain bold,
    And the mate of the *Nancy* brig,
And a bo'sun tight, and a midshipmite,
    And the crew of the captain's gig!"

MONSIEUR LE BLOND ON LONDON

Air—"Fall of Paris"

I've spent three weeks, my SKETCHLEY, in your fog-enveloped Fatherland,
And really, sir, upon the shores of Tartarus I'd rather land.
I mean to show it up at home, so with the lying curtain hence!—
That shrouds your wretched country and your insular impertinence.
I landed inside out, and asking, "Is it heels or is it head?"
And this decided fact from my condition I elicited.
        The sea around you shows,
        When a strong sou'-wester blows,
That it never was intended that you Vandals should be visited.
        Creaking, squeaking, groaning, moaning,
        Rolling, bowling, baggage-owning;
    Agonising illness, culminating in a trance,
        You hurl, or 'twouldn't be you, sir,
        At those who come to see you, sir,—
    We manage all these little matters better far in France!

Your infamous outspoken press the emblem is of sinistry,
Abusing, as they please, the Opposition and the Ministry;
Of freedom of opinion in their minds there seems a drop or two,
For really they appear to say whatever they think proper to!
Your journals are absurdly cheap, and even the tip-topper ones
Are always to be had, I find, for prices that are copper ones;
        Which seems absurd to me,
        And I really blush to see
That all their illustrations are ridiculously proper ones!
        Reading, weeding, selling, quelling,
        Stopping, whopping, press-compelling,
    Safety and continuance of kindgom to enhance;
        Publishing diurnal lists
        Of too outspoken journalists,
    Are matters that we always manage better far in France!

Your theatres suffer from a dullness which appears incurable;
Your actors and your actresses are simply unendurable;
The whole affair is dull, and melancholy, and dejectable;
The dresses, too, with hardly an exception, are respectable!
Then the idiotic words and songs your operas you fetter to,
Opera and ballad, comic song, and operetta, too.
        I go to see a play
        That's original, you say,
And I've always seen it done at home, and done a great deal better, too!
        Laughing, chaffing, playing, saying,
        Talking, walking, stage-arraying;
  Opera, or vaudeville, or incidental dance:
        Paris in and out of it,
        There cannot be a doubt of it,
We manage all these little matters better far in France!

I find my little pleasant ways entirely unsocketed;
The waiter tells me that the sugar isn't to be pocketed,
I answer him by looking with a noble air his face in full,
And when he isn't looking, sir, I stow away the basin-full!
But landlords, on the other hand, show foolish incongruity,
In giving soap to customers they lose a small annuity.
        You'll find our people will
        Charge it extra in the bill,
For we always look upon it as a dainty superfluity!
        Splashing, dashing, scrubbing, rubbing,
        Messing, dressing, drubbing, tubbing,
  Taking hip or shower bath whenever you've a chance;
        It's shocking inhumanity,
        Amounting to insanity,—
We manage all these little matters better far in France!

Your ladies must be beautiful, I grant you, for unless they were
They never could afford to walk out in the dreadful dress they wear.
But married dames and single girls all dress so very shady-like,
And all your ladies really are ridiculously ladylike.
As soon as they are married they prefer to stop all day at home,
And always take their dinners in a formal kind of way at home;
        A tedious affair,
        And Parisian ladies stare,
And wonder what on earth can make your Englishwomen stay at home.
        Frizzing, quizzing, eyeing, sighing,
        Painting, fainting, tresses-dyeing,
  Giving you three volumes of a novel at a glance.
        Before they marry, dutiful,
        Then flirty, oh it's beautiful!
Now that's the way our womankind behave themselves in France!

HAUNTED

Haunted? Ay, in a social way,
By a body of ghosts in a dread array:
But no conventional spectres they—
    Appalling, grim, and tricky:
I quail at mine as I'd never quail
At a fine traditional spectre pale,
With a turnip head and a ghostly wail,
    And a splash of blood on the dicky!

Mine are horrible social ghosts,
Speeches and women and guests and hosts,
Weddings and morning calls and toasts,
    In every bad variety:
Ghosts that hover about the grave
Of all that's manly, free, and brave:
You'll find their names on the architrave
    Of that charnel-house, Society.

Black Monday—black as its schoolroom ink—
With its dismal boys that snivel and think
Of nauseous messes to eat and drink,
    And its frozen tank to wash in.
That was the first that brought me grief
And made me weep, till I sought relief
In an emblematical handkerchief,
    To choke such baby bosh in.

First and worst in the grim array—
Ghosts of ghosts that have gone their way,
Which I wouldn't revive for a single day
    For all the wealth of PLUTUS—
Are the horrible ghosts that schooldays scared:
If the classical ghost that BRUTUS dared
Was the ghost of his "Caesar" unprepared,
    I'm sure I pity BRUTUS.

I pass to critical seventeen:
The ghost of that terrible wedding scene,
When an elderly colonel stole my queen,
    And woke my dream of heaven:
No school-girl decked in her nursery curls
Was my gushing innocent queen of pearls;
If she wasn't a girl of a thousand girls,
    She was one of forty-seven!

I see the ghost of my first cigar—
Of the thence-arising family jar—
Of my maiden brief (I was at the bar),
    When I called the judge "Your wushup"!
Of reckless days and reckless nights,
With wrenched-off knockers, extinguished lights,
Unholy songs, and tipsy fights,
    Which I strove in vain to hush up.

Ghosts of fraudulent joint-stock banks,
Ghosts of "copy, declined with thanks,"
Of novels returned in endless ranks,
    And thousands more, I suffer.
The only line to fitly grace
My humble tomb, when I've run my race,
Is, "Reader, this is the resting-place
    Of an unsuccessful duffer."

I've fought them all, these ghosts of mine,
But the weapons I've used are sighs and brine,
And now that I'm nearly forty-nine,
    Old age is my only bogy;
For my hair is thinning away at the crown,
And the silver fights with the worn-out brown;
And a general verdict sets me down
    As an irreclaimable fogy.

THE REVEREND RAWSTON WRIGHT

Oh! the centre-divided hair,
    And the boots that shine so bright,
And the linen prepared with care,
And the stole and the surplice fair,
    Of the REVEREND RAWSTON WRIGHT.

A popular priest was he,
    And appreciated quite,
And eternally asked to tea
By the whole of his cura*cee,*
    Was the REVEREND RAWSTON WRIGHT.

The bishop he said, said he,
    "There's no such shining light
In the whole of my holy see
(Excepting only me),
    As the REVEREND RAWSTON WRIGHT!"

And the vicars they said, said they,
    "Our duty would be but slight
If we could get, some day,
For the moderate sum we pay,
    Such a REVEREND RAWSTON WRIGHT."

But though he was stern all day,
    He'd a singular habit at night—
Indeed, I may fairly say,
An exceedingly singular way
    Had the REVEREND RAWSTON WRIGHT.

He'd strike a gigantic gong,
    And then, the eccentric wight,
Would sing to a wondering throng;
And this was the singular song
    Of the REVEREND RAWSTON WRIGHT:

Oh, fan an aesthetical flame,
    And sing to the moon so bright,
For piggy-wigs worry and maim,
And my highly respected name
    Is the REVEREND RAWSTON WRIGHT."

And the wondering throng would say,
    "What a strange proceeding quite;
Will any one tell us, pray,
What means this singular way
    Of the REVEREND RAWSTON WRIGHT?"

But he said, "I find it pays
    To sing it with all my might.
You needn't stand in amaze;
It's only one of the ways
    Of the REVEREND RAWSTON WRIGHT."

And he banged at the gong once more,
    And he danced till the broad daylight;
Then his delicate locks he tore,
And he yelled with a yelping roar,
    Did this singular RAWSTON WRIGHT.

And though he's a serious gent,
    And a popular curate quite,
No man can guess his intent,
Or tell us whatever is meant
    When the REVEREND RAWSTON WRIGHT

Says, "Fan an aesthetical flame,
    And sing to the moon at night,
For piggy-wigs worry and maim,
And my highly respected name
    Is the REVEREND RAWSTON WRIGHT!"

THE STORY OF GENTLE ARCHIBALD

WHO WANTED TO BE A CLOWN

y children, once I knew a boy
(His name was ARCHIBALD MOLLOY),
Whose kind papa, one Christmas time,
Took him to see a pantomime.
He was a mild, delightful boy,
Who hated jokes that caused annoy;
And none who knew him could complain
That ARCHY ever gave them pain.
But don't suppose he was a sad,
Or serious, solemn kind of lad;
Indeed, he was a cheerful son,
Renowned for mild, respectful fun.

But, oh, it was a rueful day
When he was taken to the play;
The Christmas Pantomime that night
Destroyed his gentle nature quite;
And as they walked along the road
That led to his papa's abode,
As on they trudged through muck and mire,
He said, "Papa, if you desire
My fondest hopes and joys to crown,
Allow me to become a clown!"
I will not here attempt to show
The bitter agony and woe,
The sorrow and depression dire,
Of ARCHY's old and feeble sire.
"Oh, ARCHIBALD," said he, "my boy,
My darling ARCHIBALD MOLLOY!
Attention for one moment lend—
You cannot seriously intend
To spend a roving life in town,
As vulgar, base, dishonest clown;
And leave your father in the lurch,
Who always meant you for the Church,
And nightly dreams he sees his boy
The REVEREND ARCHIBALD MOLLOY?"

That night, as ARCHY lay awake,
Thinking of all he'd break and take,
If he but had his heart's desire,
The room seemed filled with crimson fire;
The wall expanded by degrees,
Disclosing shells and golden trees,
Revolving round, and round, and round:
Red coral strewn upon the ground;
And on the trees, in tasty green,
The loveliest fairies ever seen;
But one, more fair than all the rest,
Came from a lovely golden nest,
And said to the astonished boy,
"Oh, MASTER ARCHIBALD MOLLOY,
I know the object of your heart—
Tomorrow morning you shall start
Upon your rambles through the town
As merry, mischief-making clown!"

*   *   *   *   *   *

Next day, when nurse AMELIA called,
To wash and dress her ARCHIBALD,
She opened both her aged eyes,
With unmistakable surprise,
To find that ARCHY, in the night,
Had turned all red, and blue, and white,
Of healthy colour not a trace—
Red patches on his little face,
Black horsehair wig, round rolling eyes,
Short trousers of prodigious size,
White legs and arms, with spots of blue,
And spots upon his body, too!
Said she, "Why, what is this, my boy?
My gentle ARCHIBALD MOLLOY!
Your good papa I'll go and tell,
You must be dreadfully unwell,
Although I know of no disease
With any symptoms such as these."

The good old lady turned to go
And fetch his good papa, when lo!
With irresistible attack
He jumped upon her aged back,
Pulled off the poor old lady's front,
And thrashed her, while she tried to grunt,
"Oh, ARCHIBALD, what have you done?

Is this your mild, respectful fun,
You bad, ungentlemanly boy?
Fie on you, ARCHIBALD MOLLOY!"
Some dreadful power unseen, but near,
Still urged him on his wild career,
And made him burn, and steal, and kill,
Against his gentlemanly will.
The change had really turned his brain;
He boiled his little sister JANE;
He painted blue his aged mother;
Sat down upon his little brother;
Tripped up his cousins with his hoop;
Put pussy in his father's soup;
Placed beetles in his uncle's shoe;
Cut a policeman right in two;
Spread devastation round,—and, ah,
He red-hot-pokered his papa!

Be sure, this highly reckless course
Brought ARCHIBALD sincere remorse;
He like a joke, and loved a laugh,
But was too well-behaved by half—
With too much justice and good sense—
To laugh at other folks' expense.
The gentle boy could never sleep,
But used to lie awake and weep,
To think of all the ill he'd done.
"Is this," said he, "respectful fun?
Oh, fairy, fairy, I would fain
That you should change me back again;
Some dreadful power I can't resist
Directs my once respectful fist;
Change, and I'll never once complain,
Or wish to be a clown again!"

He spoke, and lo! the wretched boy
Once more was ARCHIBALD MOLLOY;
He gave a wild, delighted scream,
And woke—for, lo, it was a dream!

TO MY BRIDE

(WHOEVER SHE MAY BE)

Oh! little maid!—(I do not know your name,
  Or who you are, so, as a safe precaution
I'll add)—Oh, buxom widow! married dame!
   (As one of these must be your present portion)
    Listen, while I unveil prophetic lore for you,
    And sing the fate that Fortune has in store for you.

You'll marry soon—within a year or twain—
  A bachelor of *circa* two-and-thirty,
Tall, gentlemanly, but extremely plain,
   And, when you're intimate, you call him "BERTIE."
    Neat—dresses well; his temper has been classified
    As hasty; but he's very quickly pacified.

You'll find him working mildly at the Bar,
  After a touch at two or three professions,
From easy affluence extremely far,
   A brief or two on Circuit—"soup" at Sessions;
    A pound or two from whist and backing horses,
    And, say, three hundred from his own resources.

Quiet in harness; free from serious vice,
  His faults are not particularly shady;
You'll never find him "*shy*"—for, once or twice
   Already, he's been driven by a lady,
    Who parts with him—perhaps a poor excuse for him—
    Because she hasn't any further use for him.

Oh! bride of mine—tall, dumpy, dark, or fair!
    Oh! widow—wife, maybe, or blushing maiden,
I've told *your* fortune: solved the gravest care
    With which *your* mind has hitherto been laden.
        I've prophesied correctly, never doubt it;
        Now tell me mine—and please be quick about it!

You—only you—can tell me, an you will,
    To whom I'm destined shortly to be mated,
Will she run up a heavy *modiste's* bill?
    If so, I want to hear her income stated.
        (This is a point which interests me greatly),
        To quote the bard, "Oh! have I seen her lately?"

Say, must I wait till husband number one
    Is comfortably stowed away at Woking?
How is her hair most usually done?
    And tell me, please, will she object to smoking?
        The colour of her eyes, too, you may mention:
        Come, Sybil, prophesy—I'm all attention.

ONLY A DANCING GIRL

Only a dancing girl,
  With an unromantic style,
With borrowed colour and curl,
  With fixed mechanical smile,
  With many a hackneyed wile,
With ungrammatical lips,
And corns that mar her trips!

Hung from the "flies" in air,
  She acts a palpable lie;
She's as little a fairy there
  As unpoetical I!
  I hear you asking, Why—
Why in the world I sing
This tawdry, tinselled thing?

No airy fairy she,
  As she hangs in arsenic green,
From a highly impossible tree,
  In a highly impossible scene
  (Herself not over clean).
For fays don't suffer, I'm told,
From bunions, coughs, or cold.

And stately dames that bring
  Their daughters there to see,
Pronounce the "dancing thing"
  No better than she should be.
  With her skirt at her shameful knee,
And her painted, tainted phiz:
Ah, matron, which of us is?

(And, in sooth, it oft occurs
  That while these matrons sigh,
Their dresses are lower than hers,
  And sometimes half as high;
  And their hair is hair they buy.
And they use their glasses, too,
In a way she'd blush to do.)

But change her gold and green
  For a coarse merino gown,
And see her upon the scene
  Of her home, when coaxing down
  Her drunken father's frown,
In his squalid cheerless den:
She's a fairy truly, then!

TO MY STEED

Oh, bony, shambling, roaring mare,
Thou raw-boned, rickety affair,
You are endowed with so immense
An instinct, that it's almost sense,
If horsy sages do not lie;
Yet tell me, Rosinante, why,
Whene'er I mount thy bony back,
Whereon I sit me like a sack,
Why dost thou let me stop up there?
You've but to give a kick in air,
You've only just to swerve aside,
Or shy, as I begin to ride,
Or prance, or buck, or rear, or swerve,
And I should lose all trace of nerve—
Be ignominiously unhorsed,
From you and yours for aye divorced!
Why, if you have the instinct true
With which mankind accredit you,
Why do you fear to kick or trip—
Because, forsooth, I bear a whip?
Do you suppose that as I ride
I'd dare to use it on your hide?
Why, my good gracious goodness me,
How jolly verdant you must be!
I should as soon attempt to lash
The steed I ride upon, as thrash
The gladiator THOMAS KING,
Or other Genius of The Ring!
Is it my spurs that make you quail?
Do you suppose I'd dare assail
Your wretched flanks with spur-born marks
If ever you attempted larks?
Believe me, unattractive mare,
It ever is my cherished care
(For which I make no claim for thanks),
To keep them distant from thy flanks.
I'd rather run them, of the two,
Right into me than into you.
Why, ass, though from your cringing way,
You seem to dread my nervous sway,
Yet, if the truth you only knew,
I'm much—*much* more afraid of you!

KING BORRIA BUNGALEE BOO

King Borria Bungalee Boo
 Was a man-eating African swell;
His sigh was a hullaballoo,
 His whisper a horrible yell—
 A horrible, horrible yell!

Four subjects, and all of them male,
 To Borria doubled the knee,
They were once on a far larger scale,
 But he'd eaten the balance, you see
 ("Scale" and "balance" is punning, you see).

There was haughty Pish-Tush-Pooh-Bah,
 There was lumbering Doodle-Dum-Deh,
Despairing Alack-a-Dey-Ah,
 And good little Tootle-Tum-Teh—
 Exemplary Tootle-Tum-Teh.

One day there was grief in the crew,
 For they hadn't a morsel of meat,
And Borria Bungalee Boo
 Was dying for something to eat—
 "Come, provide me with something to eat!

"Alack-a-Dey, famished I feel;
 Oh, good little Tootle-Tum-Teh,
Where on earth shall I look for a meal?
 For I haven't a dinner to-day!—
 Not a morsel of dinner to-day!

"Dear Tootle-Tum, what shall we do?
 Come, get us a meal, or in truth,
If you don't we shall have to eat you,
 Oh, adorable friend of our youth!
 Thou beloved little friend of our youth!"

And he answered, "Oh, Bungalee Boo,
 For a moment I hope you will wait,—
Tippy-Wippity Tol-the-Rol-Loo
 Is the Queen of a neighbouring state—
 A remarkably neighbouring state.

"Tippy-Wippity Tol-the-Rol-Loo,
 She would pickle deliciously cold—
And her four pretty Amazons, too,
 Are enticing, and not very old—
 Twenty-seven is not very old.

"There is neat little Titty-Fol-Leh,
 There is rollicking Tral-the-Ral-Lah,
There is jocular Waggety-Weh,
 There is musical Doh-Reh-Mi-Fah—
 There's the nightingale Doh-Reh-Mi-Fah!"

So the forces of Bungalee Boo
 Marched forth in a terrible row,
And the ladies who fought for Queen Loo
 Prepared to encounter the foe—
 This dreadful insatiate foe!

But they sharpened no weapons at all,
 And they poisoned no arrows—not they!
They made ready to conquer or fall
 In a totally different way—
 A perfectly different way.

With a crimson and pearly-white dye
 They endeavoured to make themselves fair;
With black they encircled each eye,
 And with yellow they painted their hair.
 (It was wool, but they thought it was hair.)

The warriors met in the field:
 And the men of King Borria said,
"Amazonians, immediately yield!"
 And their arrows they drew to the head—
 Yes, drew them right up to the head.

But jocular Waggety-Weh
 Ogled Doodle-Dum-Deh (which was wrong),
And neat little Titty-Fol-Leh
 Said, "Tootle-Tum, you go along!
 You naughty old dear, go along!"

And rollicking Tral-the-Ral-Lah
  Tapped Alack-a-Dey-Ah with her fan;
And musical Doh-Reh-Mi-Fah
  Said, "Pish, go away, you bad man!
  Go away, you delightful young man!"

And the Amazons simpered and sighed,
  And they ogled, and giggled, and flushed,
And they opened their pretty eyes wide,
  And they chuckled, and flirted, and blushed
  (At least, if they could, they'd have blushed).

But haughty Pish-Tush-Pooh-Bah
  Said, "Alack-a-Dey, what does this mean?"
And despairing Alack-a-Deh-Ah
  Said, "They think us uncommonly green—
  Ha! ha! most uncommonly green!"

Even blundering Doodle-Dum-Deh
  Was insensible quite to their leers,
And said good little Tootle-Tum-Teh,
  "It's your blood we desire, pretty dears—
  We have come for our dinners, my dears!"

And the Queen of the Amazons fell
  To Borria Bungalee Boo,—
In a mouthful he gulped, with a yell,
  Tippy-Wippity Tol-the-Rol-Loo—
  The pretty Queen Tol-the-Rol-Loo.

And neat little Titty-Fol-Leh
  Was eaten by Pish-Pooh-Bah,
And light-hearted Waggety-Weh
  By dismal Alack-a-Dey-Ah—
  Despairing Alack-a-Dey-Ah.

And rollicking Tral-the-Ral-Lah
  Was eaten by Doodle-Dum-Deh,
And musical Doh-Reh-Mi-Fah
  By good little Tootle-Tum-Teh—
  Exemplary Tootle-Tum-Teh.

JACK CASTS HIS SHELL

Belay with yer argyments, 'national law,
    Reconstruction and noospaper letters!
We're game for a hornpipe, but oceans of jaw
    Won't induce us to dance it in fetters.

What's the good of them Navy Commissioners' teak,
    And the seven-inch plating and models,
When a Palliser's able to spring you a leak,
    Though their armour's as thick as their noddles?

D'ye think behind plating we're willing to skulk,
    Which them Parliament lubbers delight in?
Give us Palliser guns on an old wooden hulk—
    You may trust to us salts for the fightin'.

Let who will cast a shell, why, I'll stand to my gun,
    But I'll cast my own first, without fail, boys—
For we take off our jackets when work's to be done,
    And that they'll take off theirs, I'll go bail, boys!

Our muscles are iron—our courage is steel,
    And its temper's been pretty well tried, boys—
Keep the oak to the weather—it's used to the feel—
    Never fear, there'll be iron inside, boys!

HOW TO WRITE AN IRISH DRAMA

If you'd write an Irish drama,
  Be awhile attentive, pray,
While I show a panorama
  Of ingredients in the play.

Take, oh take some lads and lasses,
  Take a dreary moonlight glen,
Take a comic spy who passes
  Through a lodge of Ribbon men.

Take a burly Irish squire,
  Take a wretch to work the harm;
Let him set a barn on fire,
  Take a mortgage on a farm.

Take a chain of circumstances
  Implicating innocence,
Take a chambermaid who dances,
  Take unworthy evidence.

Take a secret still, and work it,
  Take a rattling Irish jig;
Take a judge who sits on circuit,
  In his flowing full-dress wig.

Take a lawyer in a fury—
  Evidence that's most unfair,
Take an idiotic jury
  With moustache and flowing hair.

Take a colleen, flirty, jilty,
  Take a crowd in court to yell,
Take a verdict, too, of guilty,
  Take a priest and take a cell.

Take a noble sheriff, bringing
  Pardon, which the convict claims,
Take the village bells a-ringing,—
  Take and pitch 'em in the Thames.

GENERAL JOHN

The bravest names for fire and flames
  And all that mortal durst,
Were GENERAL JOHN and PRIVATE JAMES,
  Of the Sixty-seventy-first.

GENERAL JOHN was a soldier tried,
  A chief of warlike dons;
A haughty stride and a withering pride
  Were MAJOR-GENERAL JOHN'S.

A sneer would play on his martial phiz,
  Superior birth to show;
"Pish!" was a favourite word of his,
  And he often said "Ho! ho!"

FULL-PRIVATE JAMES described might be,
  As a man of a mournful mind;
No characteristic trait had he
  Of any distinctive kind.

From the ranks, one day, cried PRIVATE JAMES,
   "Oh! MAJOR-GENERAL JOHN,
I've doubts of our respective names,
   My mournful mind upon.

"A glimmering thought occurs to me
   (Its source I can't unearth),
But I've a kind of a notion we
   Were cruelly changed at birth.

"I've a strange idea that each other's names
   We've each of us here got on.
Such things have been," said PRIVATE JAMES.
   "They have!" sneered GENERAL JOHN.

"My GENERAL JOHN, I swear upon
   My oath I think 'tis so——
"Pish!" proudly sneered his GENERAL JOHN,
   And he also said "Ho! ho!"

"My GENERAL JOHN! my GENERAL JOHN!
   My GENERAL JOHN!" quoth he,
"This aristocratical sneer upon
   Your face I blush to see!

"No truly great or generous cove
   Deserving of them names,
Would sneer at a fixed idea that's drove
   In the mind of a PRIVATE JAMES!"

Said GENERAL JOHN, "Upon your claims
   No need your breath to waste;
If this is a joke, FULL-PRIVATE JAMES,
   It's a joke of doubtful taste.

"But, being a man of doubtless worth,
   If you feel certain quite
That we were probably changed at birth,
   I'll venture to say you're right."

So GENERAL JOHN as PRIVATE JAMES
   Fell in, parade upon;
And PRIVATE JAMES, by change of names,
   Was MAJOR-GENERAL JOHN.

SIR GUY THE CRUSADER

Sir Guy was a doughty crusader,
    A muscular knight,
    Ever ready to fight,
A very determined invader,
    And Dickey de Lion's delight.

Lenore was a Saracen maiden,
    Brunette, statuesque,
    The reverse of grotesque,
Her pa was a bagman from Aden,
    Her mother she played in burlesque.

A *coryphée,* pretty and loyal,
    In amber and red
    The ballet she led;
Her mother performed at the Royal,
    Lenore at the Saracen's Head.

Of face and of figure majestic,
    She dazzled the cits—
    Ecstaticised pits;—
Her troubles were only domestic,
    But drove her half out of her wits.

Her father incessantly lashed her,
    On water and bread
    She was grudgingly fed;
Whenever her father he thrashed her
    Her mother sat down on her head.

Guy saw her, and loved her, with reason,
    For beauty so bright
    Sent him mad with delight;
He purchased a stall for the season,
    And sat in it every night.

His views were exceedingly proper,
    He wanted to wed,
    So he called at her shed
And saw her progenitor whop her—
    Her mother sit down on her head.

"So pretty," said he, "and so trusting!
    You brute of a dad,
    You unprincipled cad,
Your conduct is really disgusting,
    Come, come, now admit it's too bad!

"You're a turbaned old Turk, and malignant—
    Your daughter LENORE
    I intensely adore,
And I cannot help feeling indignant,
    A fact that I hinted before;

"To see a fond father employing
    A deuce of a knout
    For to bang her about,
To a sensitive lover's annoying."
    Said the bagman, "Crusader, get out."

Says GUY, "Shall a warrior laden
    With a big spiky knob,
    Sit in peace on his cob
While a beautiful Saracen maiden
    Is whipped by a Saracen snob?

"To London I'll go from my charmer."
    Which he did, with his loot
    (Seven hats and a flute),
And was nabbed for his Sydenham armour
    At MR. BEN-SAMUEL's suit.

SIR GUY he was lodged in the Compter,
    Her pa, in a rage,
    Died (don't know his age),
His daughter, she married the prompter,
    Grew bulky and quitted the stage.

SIR GALAHAD THE GOLUMPTIOUS

A MOST DOLEFUL BALLAD

Oh! list to a dismal story,
　　Oh, list to a mournful tale,
Oh, list to me, Whig and Tory,
　　Oh, list to my woeful wail!

Sir Galahad was hale and hearty,
　　Extremely tall and bold and strong;
Still with this exceptional party
　　Everything went always wrong:

Oh, whenever himself he treated
　　Oh, accidents would occur;
Oh, where'er himself he seated,
　　Oh, somebody placed a spur.

Ever floored by clumsy coaches,
　　Someone always stole his Dent;
In his bread he found cockroaches
　　Ever the chief ingredient!

Oh, shirts with a faithful button,
　　Oh, Galahad ne'er could find;
Oh, whenever his coat he put on,
　　Oh, the collar stuck up behind.

When with hunger almost starving,
　　Toothache racked his temper hard—
When a round of cold beef carving,
　　Ever forgot to use the guard.

Oh, orderly though behaving,
　　Oh, ever before the beak;
Oh, when he attempted shaving,
　　Oh, horribly slashed his cheek.

When he drank 'twas always fated
　　He should overturn his cup;
When in a company speculated,
　　Somebody came and wound it up.

Oh, making mistakes in talking;
　Oh, prey to the merest thief;
Oh, whenever in August walking,
　O-mitted his handkerchief!

When he followed home a lady
　(Which, I own, was hardly right),
Always found she turned out shady—
　Short of an eye or black as night!

Oh, ain't it a dismal story,
　Oh, ain't it a mournful tale—
Oh, isn't it, Whig and Tory,
　Oh, ain't it a woeful wail!

DISILLUSIONED

BY AN EX-ENTHUSIAST

Oh, that my soul its gods could see
As years ago they seemed to me
　When first I painted them;
Invested with the circumstance
Of old conventional romance:
　Exploded theorem!

The bard who could, all men above,
Inflame my soul with songs of love,
　And, with his verse, inspire
The craven soul who feared to die,
With all the glow of chivalry
　And old heroic fire;

I found him in a beerhouse tap
Awaking from a gin-born nap,
　With pipe and sloven dress;
Amusing chums, who fooled his bent,
With muddy, maudlin sentiment,
　And tipsy foolishness!

The novelist, whose painting pen
To legions of fictitious men
   A real existence lends,
Brain-people whom we rarely fail,
Whene'er we hear their names, to hail
   As old and welcome friends;

I found in clumsy snuffy suit,
In seedy glove, and blucher boot,
   Uncomfortably big.
Particularly commonplace,
With vulgar, coarse, stockbroking face,
   And spectacles and wig.

My favourite actor who, at will,
With mimic woe my eyes could fill
   With unaccustomed brine:
A being who appeared to me
(Before I knew him well) to be
   A song incarnadine;

I found a coarse unpleasant man
With speckled chin—unhealthy, wan—
   Of self-importance full:
Existing in an atmosphere
That reeked of gin and pipes and beer—
   Conceited, fractious, dull.

The warrior whose ennobled name
Is woven with his country's fame,
   Triumphant over all,
I found weak, palsied, bloated, blear;
His province seemed to be, to leer
   At bonnets in Pall Mall.

Would that ye always shone, who write,
Bathed in your own innate limelight,
   And ye who battles wage,
Or that in darkness I had died
Before my soul had ever sighed
   To see you off the stage!

JOHN AND FREDDY

John courted lovely Mary Ann,
  So likewise did his brother, Freddy.
Fred was a very soft young man,
  While John, though quick, was most unsteady.

Fred was a graceful kind of youth,
  But John was very much the strongest.
"Oh, dance away," said she, "in truth,
  I'll marry him who dances longest."

John tries the maiden's taste to strike
  With gay, grotesque, outrageous dresses,
And dances comically, like
  Clodoche and Co., at the Princess's.

But Freddy tries another style,
  He knows some graceful steps and does 'em—
A breathing Poem—Woman's smile—
  A man all poesy and buzzem.

Now Freddy's operatic *pas*—
  Now Johnny's hornpipe seems entrapping:
Now Freddy's graceful *entrechats*—
  Now Johnny's skilful "cellar-flapping."

For many hours—for many days—
  For many weeks performed each brother,
For each was active in his ways,
  And neither would give in to t'other.

After a month of this, they say
  (The maid was getting bored and moody)
A wandering curate passed that way
  And talked a lot of goody-goody.

"Oh my," said he, with solemn frown,
  "I tremble for each dancing *frater,*
Like unregenerated clown
  And harlequin at some the-ayter."

He showed that men, in dancing, do
  Both impiously and absurdly,
And proved his proposition true,
  With Firstly, Secondly, and Thirdly.

For months both JOHN and FREDDY danced,
    The curate's protests little heeding;
For months the curate's words enhanced
    The sinfulness of their proceeding.

At length they bowed to Nature's rule—
    Their steps grew feeble and unsteady,
Till FREDDY fainted on a stool,
    And JOHNNY on the top of FREDDY.

"Decide!" quoth they, "let him be named,
    Who henceforth as his wife may rank you."
"I've changed my views," the maiden said,
    "I only marry curates, thank you!"

Says FREDDY, "Here is goings on!
    To bust myself with rage I'm ready."
"I'll be a curate!" whispers JOHN—
    "And I," exclaimed poetic FREDDY.

But while they read for it, these chaps,
    The curate booked the maiden bonny—
And when she's buried him, perhaps,
    She'll marry FREDERICK or JOHNNY.

LORENZO DE LARDY

DALILAH DE DARDY adored
    The very correctest of cards,
LORENZO DE LARDY, a lord—
    He was one of Her Majesty's Guards.

DALILAH DE DARDY was fat,
    DALILAH DE DARDY was old—
(No doubt in the world about that)
    But DALILAH DE DARDY had gold.

LORENZO DE LARDY was tall,
    The flower of maidenly pets,
Young ladies would love at his call,
    But LORENZO DE LARDY had debts.

His money-position was queer,
    And one of his favourite freaks
Was to hide himself three times a year
    In Paris, for several weeks.

Many days didn't pass him before
    He fanned himself into a flame,
For a beautiful "DAM DU COMPTWORE,"
    And this was her singular name:

ALICE EULALIE CORALINE
    EUPHROSINE COLOMBINA THÉRÈSE
JULIETTE STEPHANIE CELESTINE
    CHARLOTTE RUSSE DE LA SAUCE MAYONNAISE.

She booked all the orders and tin,
    Accoutred in showy fal-lal,
At a two-fifty Restaurant, in
    The glittering Palais Royal.

He'd gaze in her orbit of blue,
    Her hand he would tenderly squeeze,
But the words of her tongue that he knew
    Were limited strictly to these:

"CORALINE CELESTINE EULALIE,
    Houp là! Je vous aime, oui, mossoo,
Combien donnez moi aujourd'hui
    Bonjour, Mademoiselle, parlez voo."

MADEMOISELLE DE LA SAUCE MAYONNAISE
    Was a witty and beautiful miss,
Extremely correct in her ways,
    But her English consisted of this:

"Oh my! pretty man, if you please,
    Blom boodin, biftek, currie lamb,
Bouldogue, two franc half, quite ze cheese,
    Rosbif, me spik Angleesh, godam."

He'd gaze in her eyes all the day,
    Admiring their sparkle and dance,
And list while she rattled away
    In the musical accents of France.

A waiter, for seasons before,
  Had basked in her beautiful gaze,
And burnt to dismember MILOR,
  He loved DE LA SAUCE MAYONNAISE.

He said to her, "Méchante Thérèse,
  Avec désespoir tu m'accables.
Pense tu, DE LA SAUCE MAYONNAISE,
  Ses intentions sont honorables?

"Flirtez toujours, ma belle, si tu ôses—
  Je me vengerai ainsi, ma chère,
Je lui dirai de quoi on compose
  Vol au vent à la Financière!"

LORD LARDY knew nothing of this—
  The waiter's devotion ignored,
But he gazed on the beautiful miss,
  And never seemed weary or bored.

The waiter would screw up his nerve,
  His fingers he'd snap and he'd dance—
And LORD LARDY would smile and observe,
  "How strange are the customs of France!"

Well, after delaying a space,
  His tradesmen no longer would wait:
Returning to England apace,
  He yielded himself to his fate.

LORD LARDY espoused, with a groan,
  MISS DARDY's developing charms,
And agreed to tag on to his own,
  Her name and her newly-found arms.

The waiter he knelt at the toes
  Of an ugly and thin *coryphée*,
Who danced in the hindermost rows
  At the Théâtre des Variétés.

MADEMOISELLE DE LA SAUCE MAYONNAISE
  Didn't yield to a gnawing despair,
But married a soldier, and plays
  As a pretty and pert Vivandière.

THE BISHOP AND THE BUSMAN

It was a Bishop bold,
    And London was his see,
He was short and stout and round about
    And zealous as could be.

It also was a Jew,
    Who drove a Putney bus—
For flesh of swine however fine
    He did not care a cuss.

His name was HASH BAZ BEN,
    And JEDEDIAH too,
And SOLOMON and ZABULON—
    This bus-directing Jew.

The Bishop said, said he,
    "I'll see what I can do
To Christianise and make you wise,
    You poor benighted Jew."

So every blessed day
    That bus he rode outside,
From Fulham town, both up and down,
    And loudly thus he cried:

"His name is HASH BAZ BEN,
    And JEDEDIAH too,
And SOLOMON and ZABULON—
    This bus-directing Jew."

At first the busman smiled,
    And rather liked the fun—
He merely smiled, that Hebrew child,
    And said, "Eccentric one!"

And gay young dogs would wait
    To see the bus go by
(These gay young dogs, in striking togs),
    To hear the Bishop cry:

"Observe his grisly beard,
    His race it clearly shows,
He sticks no fork in ham or pork—
    Observe, my friends, his nose."

"His name is HASH BAZ BEN,
    And JEDEDIAH too,
And SOLOMON and ZABULON—
    This bus-directing Jew."

But though at first amused,
    Yet after seven years,
This Hebrew child got rather riled,
    And melted into tears.

He really almost feared
    To leave his poor abode,
His nose, and name, and beard became
    A byword on that road.

At length he swore an oath,
  The reason he would know—
"I'll call and see why ever he
  Does persecute me so!"

The good old Bishop sat
  On his ancestral chair,
The busman came, sent up his name,
  And laid his grievance bare.

"Benighted Jew," he said
  (The good old Bishop did),
"Be Christian, you, instead of Jew—
  Become a Christian kid!

"I'll ne'er annoy you more."
  "Indeed?" replied the Jew;
"Shall I be freed?" "You will, indeed!"
  Then "Done!" said he, "with you!"

The organ which, in man,
  Between the eyebrows grows,
Fell from his face, and in its place
  He found a Christian nose.

His tangled Hebrew beard,
  Which to his waist came down,
Was now a pair of whiskers fair—
  His name ADOLPHUS BROWN!

He wedded in a year
  That prelate's daughter JANE,
He's grown quite fair—has auburn hair—
  His wife is far from plain.

BABETTE'S LOVE

Babette she was a fisher gal,
  With jupon striped and cap in crimps.
She passed her days inside the Halle,
  Or catching little nimble shrimps.
Yet she was sweet as flowers in May,
With no professional bouquet.

Jacot was, of the Customs bold,
  An officer, at gay Boulogne,
He loved Babette— his love he told,
  And sighed, "Oh, soyez vous my own!"
But "Non!" said she, "Jacot, my pet,
Vous êtes trop scraggy pour Babette.

"Of one alone I nightly dream,
  An able mariner is he,
And gaily serves the Gen'ral Steam-
  Boat Navigation Companee.
I'll marry him, if he but will—
His name, I rather think, is Bill.

"I see him when he's not aware,
  Upon our hospitable coast,
Reclining with an easy air
  Upon the *Port* against a post,
A-thinking of, I'll dare to say,
His native Chelsea far away!"

"Oh, mon!" exclaimed the Customs bold,
  "Mes yeux!" he said (which means "my eye").
"Oh, chère!" he also cried, I'm told,
  "Par Jove," he added, with a sigh.
"Oh, mon! oh, chère! mes yeux! par Jove!
Je n'aime pas cet enticing cove!"

The *Panther's* captain stood hard by,
  He was a man of morals strict,
If e'er a sailor winked his eye,
  Straightway he had that sailor licked,
Mast-headed all (such was his code)
Who dashed or jiggered, blessed or blowed.

He wept to think a tar of his
  Should lean so gracefully on posts,
He sighed and sobbed to think of this,
  On foreign, French, and friendly coasts.
"It's human natur', p'raps—if so,
Oh, isn't human natur' low!"

He called his Bill, who pulled his curl,
  He said, "My Bill, I understand
You've captivated some young gurl
  On this here French and foreign land.
Her tender heart your beauties jog—
They do, you know they do, you dog.

"You have a graceful way I learn
  Of leaning airily on posts,
By which you've been and caused to burn
  A tender flame on these here coasts.
A fisher gurl, I much regret,—
Her age, sixteen—her name, Babette.

"You'll marry her, you gentle tar—
    Your union I myself will bless,
And when you matrimonied are,
    I will appoint her stewardess."
But WILLIAM hitched himself and sighed,
And cleared his throat, and thus replied:

"Not so: unless you're fond of strife,
    You'd better mind your own affairs,
I have an able-bodied wife
    Awaiting me at Wapping Stairs;
If all this here to her I tell,
She'll larrup you and me as well.

"Skin-deep, and valued at a pin,
    Is beauty such as VENUS owns—
Her beauty is beneath her skin,
    And lies in layers on her bones.
The other sailors of the crew
They always calls her 'Whopping Sue!'"

"Oho!" the Captain said, "I see!
    And is she then so very strong?"
"She'd take your honour's scruff," said he,
    "And pitch you over to Bolong!"
"I pardon you," the Captain said,
"The fair BABETTE you needn't wed."

Perhaps the Customs had his will,
    And coaxed the scornful girl to wed,
Perhaps the Captain and his BILL,
    And WILLIAM's little wife are dead;
Or p'raps they're all alive and well:
I cannot, cannot, cannot tell.

FANNY AND JENNY

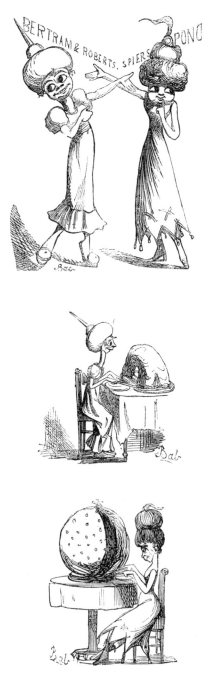

FANNY and JENNY in Paris did dwell,
MISS JANE was a dowdy, MISS FANNY a swell—
Each went for to dine at a quarter to four
At her own little favourite Restaura*tore*—
FANNY of BERTRAM AND ROBERTS was fond
While JENNY she worshipped her SPIERS AND POND.

FANNY was pretty and piquante and pert,
Her manners were shortish and so was her skirt,
While JENNY the elder would make a man wince,
In a dress of the mode of a century since.
BERTRAM AND ROBERTS'S FANNY was blonde,
And dark was the JENNY of SPIERS AND POND.

JANE lived in a modest and lady-like way:
To SPIERS AND POND she went every day,
She'd order up beef and potatoes as well,
And cut off the joint until senseless she fell:
(She fed herself daily all reason beyond
To gaze all the longer at SPIERS AND POND).

But FANNY, that frolicsome frivolous maid
(Whose tastes were more airy than JENNY's the staid),
To BERTRAM AND ROBERTS would hie her away,
And swallow plum-pudding the rest of the day.
The best of her dresses MISS FANNY she donned
(As JENNY did also for SPIERS AND POND).

The Restaurateurs didn't seem for to care
For JENNY's soft ogle or FANNY's fond stare,
Said JENNY, "Don't let us be taken aback,
We're probably on an erroneous tack,
And BERTRAM AND ROBERTS of *me* may be fond,
While *you* are belovéd by SPIERS AND POND!

"Oh, BERTRAM AND R., are you dying for me,
Or am I the chosen of SPIERS AND P.?
Oh, which is the angel and fostering star
Of SPIERS AND P., or of BERTRAM AND R.,
Which firm have I collared in VENUS's bond?
Say, BERTRAM AND ROBERTS—speak, SPIERS AND POND!

"Perhaps if you cannot completely agree
Which of you shall have FANNY and which shall have me,
And you wish for to go for to do what is right,
You will go to the Bois de Boulogne for to fight—
It's the mode that is popular in the *beau monde,*—
Will BERTRAM AND ROBERTS fight SPIERS AND POND?"

But SPIERS AND POND are but perishing clay,
So they gasped and they gurgled and fainted away—
The burden of BERTRAM AND ROBERTS'S song
Was "Goodness! how shocking! Oh, please go along!
With neither for worlds would we ever abscond!"
And "Ditto for us," exclaimed SPIERS AND POND.

Said FANNY, "How bold, and how dreadfully rude!"
"These men are too forward," said JENNY the prude,
"Such youth and such beauty as both of us own
Are safe in the walls of a convent alone,
We shall there be the coarse persecutions beyond
Of BERTRAM AND ROBERTS and SPIERS AND POND."

SIR MACKLIN

Of all the youths I ever saw
  None were so wicked, vain, or silly,
So lost to shame and Sabbath law
  As wordly TOM, and BOB, and BILLY.

For every Sabbath day they walked
  (Such was their gay and thoughtless natur')
In parks or gardens, where they talked
  From three to six, or even later.

SIR MACKLIN was a priest severe
  In conduct and in conversation,
It did a sinner good to hear
  Him deal in ratiocination.

He could in every action show
  Some sin, and nobody could doubt him.
He argued high, he argued low,
  He also argued round about him.

He wept to think each thoughtless youth
  Contained of wickedness a skinful,
And burnt to teach the awful truth,
  That walking out on Sunday's sinful.

"Oh, youths," said he, "I grieve to find
  The course of life you've been and hit on—
Sit down," said he, "and never mind
  The pennies for the chairs you sit on.

"My opening head is 'Kensington,'
  How walking there the sinner hardens;
Which when I have enlarged upon,
  I go to 'Secondly'—its Gardens.

"My 'Thirdly' comprehendeth 'Hyde,'
  Of Secrecy the guilts and shameses;
My 'Fourthly'—'Park'—its verdure wide—
  My 'Fifthly' comprehends 'St. James's.'

"That matter settled I shall reach
  The 'Sixthly' in my solemn tether,
And show that what is true of each,
  Is also true of all, together.

"Then I shall demonstrate to you,
  According to the rules of Whately,
That what is true of all, is true
  Of each, considered separately."

In lavish stream his accents flow,
  Tom, Bob, and Billy dare not flout him;
He argued high, he argued low,
  He also argued round about him.

"Ha, ha!" he said, "you loathe your ways,
  Repentance on your souls is dawning,
In agony your hands you raise."
  (They raised their hands, for they were yawning.)

To "Twenty-firstly" on they go,
  The lads do not attempt to scout him;
He argued high, he argued low,
  He also argued round about him.

"Ho, ho!" he cries, "you bow your crests—
  My eloquence has set you weeping;
In shame you bend upon your breasts!"
  (They bent their heads, for they were sleeping.)

He proved them this—he proved them that—
  This good but wearisome ascetic;
He jumped and thumped upon his hat,
  He was so very energetic.

His bishop at this moment chanced
  To pass, and found the road encumbered;
He noticed how the Churchman danced,
  And how his congregation slumbered.

The hundred and eleventh head
  The priest completed of his stricture;
"Oh, bosh!" the worthy bishop said,
  And walked him off, as in the picture.

THE TROUBADOUR

A troubadour he played
  Without a castle wall,
Within, a hapless maid
  Responded to his call.

"Oh, willow, woe is me!
  Alack and well-a-day!
If I were only free
  I'd hie me far away!"

Unknown her face and name,
  But this he knew right well,
The maiden's wailing came
  From out a dungeon cell.

A hapless woman lay
  Within that prison grim—
That fact, I've heard him say,
  Was quite enough for him.

"I will not sit or lie,
  Or eat or drink, I vow,
Till thou art free as I,
  Or I as pent as thou!"

Her tears then ceased to flow,
  Her wails no longer rang,
And tuneful in her woe
  The prisoned maiden sang:

"Oh, stranger, as you play
  I recognise your touch;
And all that I can say,
  Is thank you very much!"

He seized his clarion straight,
  And blew thereat, until
A warder oped the gate,
  "Oh, what might be your will?"

"I've come, sir knave, to see
  The master of these halls:
A maid unwillingly
  Lies prisoned in their walls."

With barely stifled sigh
  That porter drooped his head,
With teardrops in his eye,
  "A many, sir," he said.

He stayed to hear no more,
  But pushed that porter by,
And shortly stood before
  Sir Hugh de Peckham Rye.

Sir Hugh he darkly frowned,
  "What would you, sir, with me?"
The troubadour he downed
  Upon his bended knee.

"I've come, DE PECKHAM RYE,
　To do a Christian task,
You ask me what would I?
　It is not much I ask.

"Release these maidens, sir,
　Whom you dominion o'er—
Particularly her
　Upon the second floor!

"And if you don't, my lord"—
　He here stood bolt upright,
And tapped a tailor's sword—
　"Come out at once and fight!"

SIR HUGH he called—and ran
　The warden from the gate,
"Go, show this gentleman
　The maid in forty-eight."

By many a cell they passed
　And stopped at length before
A portal, bolted fast:
　The man unlocked the door.

He called inside the gate
　With coarse and brutal shout,
"Come, step it, forty-eight!"
　And forty-eight stepped out.

"They gets it pretty hot,
　The maidens wot we cotch—
Two years this lady's got
　For collaring a wotch."

"Oh, ah!—indeed—I see,"
　The troubadour exclaimed—
"If I may make so free,
　How is this castle named?"

The warden's eyelids fill,
　And, sighing, he replied,
"Of gloomy Pentonville
　This is the Female Side!"

The minstrel did not wait
　The warden stout to thank,
But recollected straight
　He'd business at the Bank.

BEN ALLAH ACHMET

OR, THE FATAL TUM

I once did know a Turkish man
    Whom I upon a two-pair-back met,
His name it was EFFENDI KHAN
    BACKSHEESH PASHA BEN ALLAH ACHMET.

A DOCTOR BROWN I also knew—
    I've often eaten of his bounty;
The Turk and he they lived at Hooe,
    In Sussex, that delightful county!

I knew a nice young lady there,
    Her name was EMILY MACPHERSON,
And though she wore another's hair,
    She was an interesting person.

The Turk adored the maid of Hooe
    (Although his harem would have shocked her).
But BROWN adored that maiden too:
    He was a most seductive doctor.

They'd follow her where'er she'd go—
    A course of action most improper;
She neither knew by sight, and so
    For neither of them cared a copper.

BROWN did not know that Turkish male,
    He might have been his sainted mother:
The people in this simple tale
    Are total strangers to each other.

One day that Turk he sickened sore,
    And suffered agonies oppressive;
He threw himself upon the floor
    And rolled about in pain excessive.

It made him moan, it made him groan,
    And almost wore him to a mummy.
Why should I hesitate to own
    That pain was in his little tummy?

At length a doctor came, and rung
  (As ALLAH ACHMET had desired),
Who felt his pulse, looked up his tongue,
  And hemmed and hawed, and then inquired:

"Where is the pain that long has preyed
  Upon you in so sad a way, sir?"
The Turk he giggled, blushed, and said:
  "I don't exactly like to say, sir."

"Come, nonsense!" said good DOCTOR BROWN.
  "So this is Turkish coyness, is it?
You must contrive to fight it down—
  Come, come, sir, please to be explicit."

The Turk he shyly bit his thumb,
  And coyly blushed like one half-witted,
"The pain is in my little tum,"
  He, whispering, at length admitted.

"Then take you this, and take you that—
  Your blood flows sluggish in its channel—
You must get rid of all this fat,
  And wear my medicated flannel.

"You'll send for me when you're in need—
  My name is BROWN—your life I've saved it."
"My rival!" shrieked the invalid,
  And drew a mighty sword and waved it:

"This to thy weazand, Christian pest!"
  Aloud the Turk in frenzy yelled it,
And drove right through the doctor's chest
  The sabre and the hand that held it.

The blow was a decisive one,
  And DOCTOR BROWN grew deadly pasty.
"Now see the mischief that you've done—
  You Turks are so extremely hasty.

"There are two DOCTOR BROWNS in Hooe—
  He's short and stout, *I'm* tall and wizen;
You've been and run the wrong one through,
  That's how the error has arisen."

The accident was thus explained,
　　Apologies were only heard now:
"At my mistake I'm really pained—
　　I am, indeed—upon my word now.

"With me, sir, you shall be interred,
　　A mausoleum grand awaits me."
"Oh, pray don't say another word,
　　I'm sure that more than compensates me.

"But p'raps, kind Turk, you're full inside?"
　　"There's room," said he, "for any number."
And so they laid them down and died.
　　In proud Stamboul they sleep their slumber.

THE FOLLY OF BROWN

BY A GENERAL AGENT

I knew a boor—a clownish card
　　(His only friends were pigs and cows and
The poultry of a small farmyard),
　　Who came into two hundred thousand.

Good fortune worked no change in BROWN,
　　Though she's a mighty social chymist;
He was a clown—and by a clown
　　I do not mean a pantomimist.

It left him quiet, calm, and cool,
　　Though hardly knowing what a crown was—
You can't imagine what a fool
　　Poor rich uneducated BROWN was!

He scouted all who wished to come
　　And give him monetary schooling;
And I propose to give you some
　　Idea of his insensate fooling.

I formed a company or two—
　　(Of course I don't know what the rest meant,
I formed them solely with a view
　　To help him to a sound investment).

Their objects were—their only cares—
    To justify their Boards in showing
A handsome dividend on shares
    And keep their good promoter going.

But no—the lout sticks to his brass,
    Though shares at par I freely proffer:
Yet—will it be believed?—the ass
    Declines, with thanks, my well-meant offer!

He adds, with bumpkin's stolid grin
    (A weakly intellect denoting),
He'd rather not invest it in
    A company of my promoting!

"You have two hundred 'thou' or more,"
    Said I. "You'll waste it, lose it, lend it;
Come, take my furnished second floor,
    I'll gladly show you how to spend it."

But will it be believed that he,
    With grin upon his face of poppy,
Declined my aid, while thanking me
    For what he called my "philanthroppy"?

Some blind, suspicious fools rejoice
    In doubting friends who wouldn't harm them;
They will not hear the charmer's voice,
    However wisely he may charm them!

I showed him that his coat, all dust,
    Top boots and cords provoked compassion,
And proved that men of station must
    Conform to the decrees of fashion.

I showed him where to buy his hat,
    To coat him, trouser him, and boot him;
But no—he wouldn't hear of that—
    "He didn't think the style would suit him!"

I offered him a county seat,
    And made no end of an oration;
I made it certainty complete,
    And introduced the deputation.

But no—the clown my prospect blights—
  (The worth of birth it surely teaches!)
"Why should I want to spend my nights
  In Parliament, a-making speeches?

"I haven't never been to school—
  I ain't had not no eddication—
And I should surely be a fool
  To publish that to all the nation!"

I offered him a trotting horse—
  No hack had ever trotted faster—
I also offered him, of course,
  A rare and curious "old master."

I offered to procure him weeds—
  Wines fit for one in his position—
But, though an ass in all his deeds,
  He'd learnt the meaning of "commission."

He called me "thief" the other day,
  And daily from his door he thrusts me;
Much more of this, and soon I may
  Begin to think that Brown mistrusts me.

So deaf to all sound Reason's rule
  This poor uneducated clown is,
You cannot fancy what a fool
  Poor rich uneducated Brown is.

JOE GOLIGHTLY

OR, THE FIRST LORD'S DAUGHTER

A tar, but poorly prized,
　　Long, shambling, and unsightly,
Thrashed, bullied, and despised,
　　Was wretched JOE GOLIGHTLY.

He bore a workhouse brand;
　　No Pa or Ma had claimed him,
The Beadle found him, and
　　The Board of Guardians named him.

P'raps some Princess's son—
　　A beggar p'raps his mother.
He rather thought the one,
　　I rather think the other.

He liked his ship at sea,
　　He loved the salt sea-water,
He worshipped junk, and he
　　Adored the First Lord's daughter.

The First Lord's daughter, proud,
　　Snubbed Earls and Viscounts nightly;
She sneered at Barts. aloud,
　　And spurned poor JOE GOLIGHTLY.

Whene'er he sailed afar
　　Upon a Channel cruise, he
Unpacked his light guitar
　　And sang this ballad (Boosey):

Ballad.
　　The moon is on the sea,
　　　　Willow!
　　The wind blows towards the lee,
　　　　Willow!
But though I sigh and sob and cry,
　　No Lady Jane for me,
　　　　Willow!

　　She says, " 'Twere folly quite,
　　　　Willow!
　　For me to wed a wight,
　　　　Willow!
Whose lot is cast before the mast";
　　And possibly she's right,
　　　　Willow!

His skipper (CAPTAIN JOYCE),
　　He gave him many a rating,
And almost lost his voice
　　From thus expostulating:

"Lay aft, you lubber, do!
　　What's come to that young man, JOE?
Belay!—'vast heaving! you!
　　Do kindly stop that banjo!

"I wish, I do—O lor'!—
    You'd shipped aboard a trader:
Are you a sailor or
    A negro serenader?"

But still the stricken cad,
    Aloft or on his pillow,
Howled forth in accents sad
    His aggravating "Willow!"

Stern love of duty had
    Been JOYCE's chiefest beauty;
Says he, "I love that lad,
    But duty, damme! duty!

"Twelve years' black-hole, I say,
    Where daylight never flashes;
And always twice a day
    Five hundred thousand lashes!"

But JOSEPH had a mate,
    A sailor stout and lusty,
A man of low estate,
    But singularly trusty.

Says he, "Cheer hup, young JOE!
    I'll tell you what I'm arter—
To that Fust Lord I'll go
    And ax him for his darter.

"To that Fust Lord I'll go
    And say you love her dearly."
And JOE said (weeping low),
    "I wish you would, sincerely!"

That sailor to that Lord
    Went, soon as he had landed,
And of his own accord
    An interview demanded.

Says he, with seaman's roll,
    "My Captain (wot's a Tartar)
Guv JOE twelve years' black-hole,
    For lovering your darter.

"He loves MISS LADY JANE
    (I own she is his betters),
But if you'll jine them twain,
    They'll free him from his fetters.

"And if so be as how
    You'll let her come aboard ship,
I'll take her with me now."
    "Get out!" remarked his Lordship.

That honest tar repaired
    To JOE upon the billow,
And told him how he'd fared.
    JOE only whispered, "Willow!"

And for that dreadful crime
    (Young sailors, learn to shun it)
He's working out his time;
    In ten years he'll have done it.

THE RIVAL CURATES

List while the poet trolls
  Of Mr. Clayton Hooper,
Who had a cure of souls
  At Spiffton-extra-Sooper.

He lived on curds and whey,
  And daily sang their praises,
And then he'd go and play
  With buttercups and daisies.

Wild croquêt Hooper banned,
  And all the sports of Mammon,
He warred with cribbage, and
  He exorcised backgammon.

His helmet was a glance
  That spoke of holy gladness;
A saintly smile his lance,
  His shield a tear of sadness.

His Vicar smiled to see
  This armour on him buckled;
With pardonable glee
  He blessed himself and chuckled:

"In mildness to abound
  My curate's sole design is,
In all the country round
  There's none so mild as mine is!"

And Hooper, disinclined
  His trumpet to be blowing,
Yet didn't think you'd find
  A milder curate going.

A friend arrived one day
  At Spiffton-extra-Sooper,
And in this shameful way
  He spoke to Mr. Hooper:

"You think your famous name
  For mildness can't be shaken,
That none can blot your fame—
  But, Hooper, you're mistaken!

"Your mind is not as blank
  As that of Hopley Porter,
Who holds a curate's rank
  At Assesmilk-cum-Worter.

He plays the airy flute,
  And looks depressed and blighted,
Doves round about him 'toot,'
  And lambkins dance delighted.

"*He* labours more than you
  At worsted work, and frames it;
In old maids' albums, too,
  Sticks seaweed—yes, and names it!"

The tempter said his say,
  Which pierced him like a needle—
He summoned straight away
  His sexton and his beadle.

These men were men who could
  Hold liberal opinions:
On Sundays they were good—
  On week-days they were minions.

"To Hopley Porter go,
    Your fare I will afford you—
Deal him a deadly blow,
    And blessings shall reward you.

"But stay—I do not like
    Undue assassination,
And so, before you strike,
    Make this communication:

"I'll give him this one chance—
    If he'll more gaily bear him,
Play croquêt, smoke, and dance,
    I willingly will spare him."

They went, those minions true,
    To Assesmilk-cum-Worter,
And told their errand to
    The Reverend Hopley Porter.

"What?" said that reverend gent,
    "Dance through my hours of leisure?
Smoke?—bathe myself with scent?—
    Play croquêt? Oh, with pleasure!

"Wear all my hair in curl?
    Stand at my door, and wink—so—
At every passing girl?
    My brothers, I should think so!

"For years I've longed for some
    Excuse for this revulsion:
Now that excuse has come—
    I do it on compulsion!!!"

He smoked and winked away—
    This Reverend Hopley Porter—
The deuce there was to pay
    At Assesmilk-cum-Worter.

And Hooper holds his ground,
    In mildness daily growing—
They think him, all around,
    The mildest curate going.

THOMAS WINTERBOTTOM HANCE

In all the towns and cities fair
  On Merry England's broad expanse,
No swordsman ever could compare
  With THOMAS WINTERBOTTOM HANCE.

The dauntless lad could fairly hew
  A silken handkerchief in twain,
Divide a leg of mutton, too—
  And this without unwholesome strain.

On whole half-sheep, with cunning trick,
  His sabre sometimes he'd employ—
No bar of lead, however thick,
  Had terrors for the stalwart boy.

At Dover daily he'd prepare
  To hew and slash, behind, before—
Which aggravated MONSIEUR PIERRE,
  Who watched him from the Calais shore.

It caused good PIERRE to swear and dance,
  The sight annoyed and vexed him so;
He was the bravest man in France—
  He said so, and he ought to know.

"Regardez, donc, ce cochon gros—
  Ce polisson! Oh, sacré bleu!
Son sabre, son plomb, et ses gigots!
  Comme cela m'ennuye, enfin, mon Dieu!

"Il sait que les foulards de soie
  Give no retaliating whack—
Les gigots morts n'ont pas de quoi—
  Le plomb don't ever hit you back."

But every day the headstrong lad
  Cut lead and mutton more and more;
And every day, poor PIERRE, half mad,
  Shrieked loud defiance from his shore.

HANCE had a mother, poor and old,
  A simple, harmless, village dame,
Who crowed and clapped as people told
  Of WINTERBOTTOM's rising fame.

She said, "I'll be upon the spot
  To see my TOMMY's sabre-play";
And so she left her leafy cot,
  And walked to Dover in a day.

PIERRE had a doting mother, who
  Had heard of his defiant rage:
His ma was nearly ninety-two,
  And rather dressy for her age.

At HANCE's doings every morn,
  With sheer delight *his* mother cried;
And MONSIEUR PIERRE's contemptuous scorn
  Filled *his* mamma with proper pride.

But Hance's powers began to fail—
  His constitution was not strong—
And Pierre, who once was stout and hale,
  Grew thin from shouting all day long.

Their mothers saw them pale and wan,
  Maternal anguish tore each breast,
And so they met to find a plan
  To set their offsprings' minds at rest.

(The mothers were of decent size,
  Though not particularly tall;
But in the sketch that meets your eyes
  I've been obliged to draw them small.)

Loud sneered the doughty man of France,
  "Ho! ho! Ho! ho! Ha! ha! Ha! ha!"
"The French for 'Pish!'" said Thomas Hance.
  Said Pierre, "L'Anglais, Monsieur, pour 'Bah!'"

Said Mrs. Hance, "Of course I shrinks
  From bloodshed, ma'am, as you're aware,
But still they'd better meet, I thinks."
  "Assurément!" said Madame Pierre.

Said Mrs. H., "Come, one! two! three!—
  We're sittin' here to see all fair";
"C'est magnifique!" said Madame P.,
  "Mais, parbleu! ce n'est pas la guerre!"

A sunny spot in sunny France
  Was hit upon for this affair;
The ground was picked by Mrs. Hance,
  The stakes were pitched by Madame Pierre.

"Je scorn un foe si lâche que vous,"
  Said Pierre, the doughty son of France.
"I fight not coward foe like you!"
  Said our undaunted Tommy Hance.

Said Mrs. H., "Your work you see—
  Go in my noble boy, and win."
"En garde, mon fils!" said Madame P.
  "Allons!" "Go on!" "En garde!" "Begin!"

"The French for 'Pooh!'" our Tommy cried.
  "L'Anglais pour 'Va!'" the Frenchman crowed.
And so, with undiminished pride,
  Each went on his respective road.

A. AND B.

OR, THE SENSATION TWINS

Once, under Spain's enfeebling sun,
  Twin brothers lived with me,
And, personality to shun,
  I call then A. and B.

They loved each other—that they did,
  'Twas rumoured near and far,
But from the time each was a kid
  Were most dissimilar.

A. had a pair of monstrous eyes,
  B.'s eyes were awful small;
B.'s nose attained a fearful size,
  A. had no nose at all.

A.'s hair reached, when he shook it out,
  The middle of his leg;
B.'s little head was just about
  As bald as any egg.

B. had a thin and taper waist,
  A. had no waist at all;
A. was too short for proper taste,
  B. just as much too tall.

And for his benefit, I say,
  Who further knowledge seeks,
The one had Civil Service pay,
  The other wrote critiques.

They meekly bore their painful lots—
  Men shunned them as a cuss,
And little tiny todding tots
  Would babble at them thus:

"We don't believe you're human kind—
  We would not on your oath—
So unconceivably designed,
  Exaggerations both!"

And A.'d reply, "It's very true
  That I am much too short;
And B., I must admit that you
  Too tall by half are thought.

"But why this taunt from every curb,
  In bold defiance hurled?
The average we don't disturb—
  We wouldn't for the world!

"If you complain we're badly planned,
  Why all you've got to do,
Is add us both together and
  Divide the sum by two!"

The notion pleased the simple lad,
  He thought it quaintly rare;
It soon became his favourite fad
  To sing it everywhere.

"Divide us, please!" they would exclaim,
  With unabated noise,
A mania it at length became
  With these afflicted boys.

A Turk there was—BEN OUSEFF named,
  An armourer by trade
(He was the maker of the famed
  "One shilling Damask blade").

These lads their little joke would shout
  At peaceful OUSEFF's side,
And took delight in screaming out,
  "Divide us—pray, divide!"

The quaint conceit amused him much,
  He'd laugh, and would declare
With all his honest heart, that such
  A jest was passing rare!

Encouraged in their mirthful play
  They'd scream and yell and shout,
"Divide us, please!" till he would say,
  "Enough, my friends—get out."

But still they screamed and would not list,
  "Divide us, monstrous men!"
"Well, since upon it you insist,
  I will," said honest BEN.

"Your joke is getting stale and trite,
  You shan't offend again."
And then he smote a mighty smite,
  And cleft them into twain!

They shammed no meretricious glee
  At OUSEFF's handiwork;
A. felt it very much, and he
  Said sternly to the Turk:

"This is a quibble, sir, and what
  Sharp practice people call—"
"It's what you asked for!" "No, it's not—
  By no means—not at all!"

*   *   *   *   *   *

I often wish I knew how they
  Drain their unpleasant cup:
I only know that B. and A.
  Were terribly cut up.

Perhaps they lived in severed bliss—
  Perhaps they groaned and died—
Perhaps they joined themselves like this,
  And gave their legs a ride.

SEA-SIDE SNOBS

Here you have some Margate Snobs

Extended on the Margate shore
   (A lazy fit had bound me),
I fell a-moralizing o'er
   The snobs I saw around me.

They buy unholy suits of clothes,
   And every day they don them;
Their speech is crapulous with oaths,
   But still the sun shines on them!

They bawl and holloa, scream and shout,
   Some source of joy they find it—
And though they leave their "h's" out
   The sea don't seem to mind it!

They spit, and smoke tobacco rank,
   And live incontinently,
And though they look as if they drank,
   The sea air fans them gently!

The words with which themselves they pledge
   Cause decent ears to tingle;
But though it sets one's teeth on edge,
   It don't offend the shingle!

Their showy clothes are slopped with mire,
   Their paws with filth encrusted—
I wonder Nature don't retire
   From public life disgusted.

The sun shines on, the breezes blow,
   When shops and counters free them—
The waves dance gaily to and fro,
   And seem quite glad to see them!

Oh, sun and breeze and dancing trees,
   In one commingling blended,
You are not difficult to please—
   Not easily offended.

THE BISHOP OF RUM-TI-FOO

From east and south the holy clan
Of Bishops gathered, to a man;
To Synod, called Pan-Anglican,
  In flocking crowds they came.
Among them was a Bishop, who
Had lately been appointed to
The balmy isle of Rum-ti-Foo,
  And PETER was his name.

His people—twenty-three in sum—
They played the eloquent tum-tum,
And lived on scalps served up in rum—
  The only sauce they knew.
When first good Bishop PETER came
(For PETER was that Bishop's name),
To humour them, he did the same
  As they of Rum-ti-Foo.

His flock, I've often heard him tell,
(His name was PETER) loved him well,
And summoned by the sound of bell,
  In crowds together came.
"Oh, massa, why you go away?
Oh, Massa PETER, please to stay."
(They called him PETER, people say,
  Because it was his name.)

He told them all good boys to be,
And sailed away across the sea,
At London Bridge that Bishop he
  Arrived one Tuesday night—

And as that night he homeward strode
To his Pan-Anglican abode,
He passed along the Borough Road
  And saw a gruesome sight.

He saw a crowd assembled round
A person dancing on the ground,
Who straight began to leap and bound
  With all his might and main.
To see that dancing man he stopped,
Who twirled and wriggled, skipped and hopped,
Then down incontinently dropped,
  And then sprang up again.

The Bishop chuckled at the sight,
"This style of dancing would delight
A simple Rum-ti-Foozleite,
  I'll learn it if I can,
To please the tribe when I get back."
He begged the man to teach his knack.
"Right Reverend Sir, in half a crack,"
  Replied that dancing man.

The dancing man he worked away—
And taught the Bishop every day—
The dancer skipped like any fay—
 Good PETER did the same.
The Bishop buckled to his task
With *battements,* cuts, and *pas de basque*
(I'll tell you, if you care to ask,
 That PETER was his name).

"Come, walk like this," the dancer said,
"Stick out your toes—stick in your head,
Stalk on with quick, galvanic tread—
 Your fingers thus extend;
The attitude's considered quaint."
The weary Bishop, feeling faint,
Replied, "I do not say it ain't,
 But Time, my Christian friend."

"We now proceed to something new—
Dance as the PAYNES and LAURIS do,
Like this—one, two—one, two—one, two."
 The Bishop, never proud,
But in an overwhelming heat
(His name was PETER, I repeat)
Performed the PAYNE and LAURI feat,
 And puffed his thanks aloud.

Another game the dancer planned—
"Just take your ankle in your hand,
And try, my lord, if you can stand—
 Your body stiff and stark.
If, when revisiting your see,
You learnt to hop on shore—like me—
The novelty would striking be,
 And must attract remark."

"No," said the worthy Bishop, "No;
That is a length to which, I trow,
Colonial Bishops cannot go.
 You may express surprise
At finding Bishops deal in pride—
But, if that trick I ever tried,
I should appear undignified
 In Rum-ti-Foozle's eyes.

"The islanders of Rum-ti-Foo
Are well-conducted persons, who
Approve a joke as much as you,
 And laugh at it as such;
But if they saw their Bishop land,
His leg supported in his hand,
The joke they wouldn't understand—
 'Twould pain them very much!"

THE PRECOCIOUS BABY

A VERY TRUE TALE

(To be sung to the Air of the "Whistling Oyster")

An elderly person—a prophet by trade—
                With his quips and tips
                On withered old lips,
He married a young and a beautiful maid;
                The cunning old blade,
                Though rather decayed,
He married a beautiful, beautiful maid.

She was only eighteen, and as fair as could be,
                With her tempting smiles
                And maidenly wiles,
And he was a trifle off seventy-three:
                Now what she could see
                Is a puzzle to me,
In a prophet of seventy—seventy-three!

Of all their acquaintances bidden (or bad)
                With their loud high jinks
                And underbred winks
None thought they'd a family have—but they had;
                A singular lad
                Who drove 'em half mad,
He proved such a horribly fast little cad.

For when he was born he astonished all by,
                With their "Law, dear me!"
                "Did ever you see."
He'd a weed in his mouth and a glass in his eye,
                A hat all awry—
                An octagon tie,
And a miniature—miniature glass in his eye.

He grumbled at wearing a frock and a cap,
                With his "Oh dear, oh!"
                And his "Hang it! 'oo know!"
And he turned up his nose at his excellent pap—
                "My friends, it's a tap
                Dat is not worf a rap."
(Now this was remarkably excellent pap.)

129

He'd chuck his nurse under the chin, and he'd say,
　　　With his "Fal, lal, lal"—
　　　"'Oo doosed fine gal!"
This shocking precocity drove 'em away:
　　　"A month from to-day
　　　Is as long as I'll stay—
Then I'd wish, if you please, for to go, if I may."

His father, a simple old gentleman, he
　　　With nursery rhyme
　　　And "Once on a time,"
Would tell him the story of "Little Bo-P,"
　　　"So pretty was she,
　　　So pretty and wee,
As pretty, as pretty, as pretty could be."

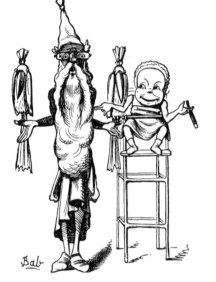

But the babe, with a dig that would startle an ox,
　　　With his "C'ck! Oh my!—
　　　Go along wiz 'oo, fie!"
Would exclaim, "I'm afraid 'oo a socking ole fox."
　　　Now a father it shocks,
　　　And it whitens his locks
When his little babe calls him a shocking old fox.

The name of his father he'd couple and pair
　　　(With his ill-bred laugh,
　　　And insolent chaff)
With those of the nursery heroines rare;
　　　Virginia the fair,
　　　Or Good Goldenhair,
Till the nuisance was more than a prophet could bear.

"There's Jill and White Cat" (said the bold little brat,
　　　With his loud, "Ha, ha!"
　　　"'Oo sly ickle pa!
Wiz 'oo Beauty, Bo-Peep, and 'oo Mrs. Jack Sprat!
　　　I've noticed 'oo pat
　　　My pretty White Cat—
I sink dear mamma ought to know about dat!"

He early determined to marry and wive,
　　　For better or worse
　　　With his elderly nurse—
Which the poor little boy didn't live to contrive:
　　　His health didn't thrive—
　　　No longer alive,
He died an enfeebled old dotard at five!

Now elderly men of the bachelor crew,
   With wrinkled hose
   And spectacled nose,
Don't marry at all—you may take it as true
   If ever you do
   The step you will rue,
For your babes will be elderly—elderly too.

BAINES CAREW, GENTLEMAN

No charges can approximate
   The worth of sympathy with woe;—
Although I think I ought to state
   He did his best to make them so.

Of all the good attorneys who
   Have placed their names upon the roll,
But few could equal BAINES CAREW
   For tender-heartedness and soul.

Of all the many clients who
   Had mustered round his legal flag,
No single client of the crew
   Was half so dear as CAPTAIN BAGG.

Whene'er he heard a tale of woe
   From client A or client B,
His grief would overcome him so,
   He'd scarce have strength to take his fee.

Now CAPTAIN BAGG had bowed him to
   A heavy matrimonial yoke:
His wifey had of faults a few—
   She never could resist a joke.

It laid him up for many days,
   When duty led him to distrain;
And serving writs, although it pays,
   Gave him excruciating pain.

Her chaff at first he meekly bore,
   Till unendurable it grew.
"To stop this persecution sore
   I will consult my friend CAREW.

He made out costs, distrained for rent,
   Forclosed and sued, with moistened eye—
No bill of costs could represent
   The value of such sympathy.

"And when CAREW's advice I've got,
   Divorce *a mensâ* I shall try."
(A legal separation—not
   A vinculo conjugii.)

"O BAINES CAREW, my woe I've kept
   A secret hitherto, you know";—
(And BAINES CAREW, ESQUIRE, he wept
   To hear that BAGG had any woe).

"My case, indeed, is passing sad,
   My wife—whom I considered true—
With brutal conduct drives me mad."
   "I am appalled," said BAINES CAREW.

"What! sound the matrimonial knell
    Of worthy people such as these!
Why was I an attorney? Well—
    Go on to the *saevitia*, please."

"Domestic bliss has proved my bane,
    A harder case you never heard,
My wife (in other matters sane)
    Pretends that I'm a Dicky Bird!

"She makes me sing, 'Too-whit, too-wee!'
    And stand upon a rounded stick,
And always introduces me
    To every one as 'Pretty Dick'!"

"Oh dear," said weeping BAINES CAREW,
    "This is the direst case I know"—
"I'm grieved," said BAGG, "at paining you—
    To COBB and POLTERTHWAITE I'll go.

"To COBB's cold calculating ear
    My gruesome sorrows I'll impart"—
"No; stop," said BAINES, "I'll dry my tear,
    And steel my sympathetic heart!"

"She makes me perch upon a tree,
    Rewarding me with, 'Sweety—nice!'
And threatens to exhibit me
    With four or five performing mice."

"Restrain my tears I wish I could"
    (Said BAINES), "I don't know what to do."
Said CAPTAIN BAGG, "You're very good."
    "Oh, not at all," said BAINES CAREW.

"She makes me fire a gun," said BAGG;
    "And at a preconcerted word,
Climb up a ladder with a flag,
    Like any street-performing bird.

"She places sugar in my way—
    In public places calls me 'Sweet!'
She gives me groundsel every day,
    And hard canary seed to eat."

"Oh, woe! oh, sad! oh, dire to tell!"
    (Said BAINES), "Be good enough to stop."
And senseless on the floor he fell
    With unpremeditated flop.

Said CAPTAIN BAGG, "Well, really I
    Am grieved to think it pains you so.
I thank you for your sympathy;
    But, hang it—come—I say, you know!"

But BAINES lay flat upon the floor,
    Convulsed with sympathetic sob—
The Captain toddled off next door,
    And gave the case to MR. COBB.

A DISCONTENTED SUGAR BROKER

A gentleman of City fame
  Now claims your kind attention;
East India broking was his game,
  His name I shall not mention;
    No one of finely pointed sense
    Would violate a confidence,
      And shall *I* go
      And do it? No.
  His name I shall not mention.

He had a trusty wife and true,
  And very cosy quarters,
A manager, a boy or two,
  Six clerks, and seven porters.
    A broker must be doing well
    (As any lunatic can tell)
      Who can employ
      An active boy,
  Six clerks, and seven porters.

His knocker advertised no dun,
  No losses made him sulky,
He had one sorrow—only one—
  He was extremely bulky.
    A man must be, I beg to state,
    Exceptionally fortunate
      Who owns his chief
      And only grief
  Is being very bulky.

"This load," he'd say, "I cannot bear,
  I'm nineteen stone or twenty!
Henceforward I'll go in for air
  And exercise in plenty."
    Most people think that, should it come,
    They can reduce a bulging tum
      To measures fair
      By taking air
  And exercise in plenty.

In every weather, every day,
  Dry, muddy, wet, or gritty,
He took to dancing all the way
  From Brompton to the City.
    You do not often get the chance
    Of seeing sugar-brokers dance
      From their abode
      In Fulham Road
  Through Brompton to the City.

He braved the gay and guileless laugh
  Of children with their nusses,
The loud uneducated chaff
  Of clerks on omnibuses.
    Against all minor things that rack
    A nicely balanced mind, I'll back
      The noisy chaff
      And ill-bred laugh
  Of clerks on omnibuses.

His friends, who heard his money chink,
  And saw the house he rented,
And knew his wife, could never think
  What made him discontented.
    It never entered their pure minds
    That fads are of eccentric kinds,
      Nor would they own
      That fat alone
  Could make one discontented.

"Your riches know no kind of pause,
　Your trade is fast advancing,
You dance—but not for joy, because
　You weep as you are dancing.
　　To dance implies that man is glad,
　　To weep implies that man is sad.
　　　But here are you
　　　Who do the two—
You weep as you are dancing!"

His mania soon got noised about
　And into all the papers—
His size increased beyond a doubt
　For all his reckless capers:
　　It may seem singular to you,
　　But all his friends admit it true—
　　　The more he found
　　　His figure round,
　The more he cut his capers.

His bulk increased—no matter that—
　He tried the more to toss it—
He never spoke of it as "fat"
　But "adipose deposit."
　　Upon my word, it seems to me
　　Unpardonable vanity
　　　(And worse than that)
　　　To call your fat
　An "adipose deposit."

At length his brawny knees gave way,
　And on the carpet sinking,

Upon his shapeless back he lay
　And kicked away like winking.
　　Instead of seeing in his state
　　The finger of unswerving Fate,
　　　He laboured still
　　　To work his will,
And kicked away like winking.

His friends, disgusted with him now,
　Away in silence wended—
I hardly like to tell you how
　This dreadful story ended.
　　The shocking sequel to impart,
　　I must employ the limner's art—
　　　If you would know,
　　　This sketch will show
How his exertions ended.

MORAL

I hate to preach—I hate to prate—
　I'm no fanatic croaker,
But learn contentment from the fate
　Of this East India broker.
　　He'd everything a man of taste
　　Could ever want, except a waist:
　　　And discontent
　　　His size anent,
And bootless perseverance blind,
Completely wrecked the peace of mind
　Of this East India broker.

THE FORCE OF ARGUMENT

LORD B. was a nobleman bold
  Who came of illustrious stocks,
He was thirty or forty years old,
  And several feet in his socks.

To Turniptopville-by-the-Sea
  This elegant nobleman went,
For that was a borough that he
  Was anxious to rep-per-re-sent.

At local assemblies he danced
  Until he felt thoroughly ill;
He waltzed, and he galoped, and lanced,
  And threaded the mazy quadrille.

The maidens of Turniptopville
  Were simple—ingenuous—pure—
And they all worked away with a will
  The nobleman's heart to secure.

Two maidens all others beyond
  Endeavoured his cares to dispel—
The one was the lively ANN POND,
  The other sad MARY MORELL.

ANN POND had determined to try
  And carry the Earl with a rush;
Her principal feature was eye,
  Her greatest accomplishment—gush.

And MARY chose this for her play:
  Whenever he looked in her eye
She'd blush and turn quickly away,
  And flitter, and flutter, and sigh.

It was noticed he constantly sighed
  As she worked out the scheme she had planned,
A fact he endeavoured to hide
  With his aristocratical hand.

Old POND was a farmer, they say,
  And so was old TOMMY MORELL.
In a humble and pottering way
  They were doing exceedingly well.

They both of them carried by vote
  The Earl was a dangerous man;
So nervously clearing his throat,
  One morning old TOMMY began:

"My darter's no pratty young doll—
  I'm a plain-spoken Zommerzet man—
Now what do 'ee mean by my POLL,
  And what do 'ee mean by his ANN?"

Said B., "I will give you my bond
　　I mean them uncommonly well,
Believe me, my excellent POND,
　　And credit me, worthy MORELL."

"It's quite indisputable, for
　　I'll prove it with singular ease,—
You shall have it in 'Barbara' or
　　'Celarent'—whichever you please.

"You see, when an anchorite bows
　　To the yoke of intentional sin,
If the state of the country allows,
　　Homogeny always steps in—

"It's a highly aesthetical bond,
　　As any mere ploughboy can tell——"
"Of course," replied puzzled old POND.
　　"I see," said old TOMMY MORELL.

"Very good, then," continued the lord;
　　"When it's fooled to the top of its bent,
With a sweep of a Damocles sword
　　The web of intention is rent.

"That's patent to all of us here,
　　As any mere schoolboy can tell."
POND answered, "Of course it's quite clear";
　　And so did that humbug MORELL.

"Its tone's esoteric in force—
　　I trust that I make myself clear?"
MORELL only answered, "Of course,"
　　While POND slowly muttered, "Hear, hear."

"Volition—celestial prize,
　　Pellucid as porphyry cell—
Is based on a principle wise."
　　"Quite so," exclaimed POND and MORELL.

"From what I have said you will see
　　That I couldn't wed either—in fine,
By Nature's unchanging decree
　　Your daughters could never be *mine.*

"Go home to your pigs and your ricks,
　　My hands of the matter I've rinsed."
So they take up their hats and their sticks,
　　And *exeunt ambo*, convinced.

AT A PANTOMIME

BY A BILIOUS ONE

An actor sits in doubtful gloom,
  His stock-in-trade unfurled,
In a damp funereal dressing-room
  In the Theatre Royal, World.

He comes to town at Christmas-time,
  And braves its icy breath,
To play in that favourite pantomime,
  Harlequin Life and Death.

A hoary flowing wig his weird,
  Unearthly cranium caps;
He hangs a long benevolent beard
  On a pair of empty chaps.

To smooth his ghastly features down
  The actor's art he cribs;
A long and a flowing padded gown
  Bedecks his rattling ribs.

He cries, "Go on—begin, begin!
  Turn on the light of lime;
I'm dressed for jolly Old Christmas in
  A favourite pantomime!"

The curtain's up—the stage all black—
  Time and the Year nigh sped—
(Time as an advertising quack)
  The Old Year nearly dead.

The wand of Time is waved, and lo!
  Revealed Old Christmas stands,
And little children chuckle and crow,
  And laugh and clap their hands.

The cruel old scoundrel brightens up
  At the death of the Olden Year,
And he waves a gorgeous golden cup,
  And bids the world good cheer.

The little ones hail the festive King—
  No thought can make them sad;
Their laughter comes with a sounding ring,
  They clap and crow like mad!

They only see in the humbug old
  A holiday every year,
And handsome gifts, and joys untold,
  And unaccustomed cheer.

The old ones, palsied, blear, and hoar,
  Their breasts in anguish beat—
They've seen him seventy times before,
  How well they know the cheat!

They've seen that ghastly pantomime,
  They've felt its blighting breath,
They know that rollicking Christmas-time
  Meant cold and want and death—

Starvation—Poor Law Union fare,
  And deadly cramps and chills,
And illness—illness everywhere—
  And crime, and Christmas bills.

They know Old Christmas well, I ween,
  Those men of ripened age;
They've often, often, often seen
  That actor off the stage.

They see in his gay rotundity
  A clumsy stuffed-out dress;
They see in the cup he waves on high
  A tinselled emptiness.

Those aged men so lean and wan,
  They've seen it all before;
They know they'll see the charlatan
  But twice or three times more.

And so they bear with dance and song,
  And crimson foil and green;
They wearily sit, and grimly long
  For the Transformation Scene.

THE THREE KINGS OF CHICKERABOO

There were three niggers of Chickeraboo—
PACIFICO, BANG-BANG, POPCHOP—who
Exclaimed, one terribly sultry day,
"Oh, let's be kings in a humble way."

The first was a highly-accomplished "bones,"
The next elicited banjo tones,
The third was a quiet, retiring chap,
Who danced an excellent break-down "flap."

"We niggers," said they, "have formed a plan
By which, whenever we like, we can
Extemporise kingdoms near the beach,
And then we'll collar a kingdom each.

"Three casks, from somebody else's stores,
Shall represent our island shores,
Their sides the ocean wide shall lave,
Their heads just topping the briny wave.

"Great Britain's navy scours the sea,
And everywhere her ships they be;
She'll recognise our rank, perhaps,
When she discovers we're Royal Chaps.

"If to her skirts you want to cling,
It's quite sufficient that you're a king;
She does not push inquiry far
To learn what sort of king you are."

A ship of several thousand tons,
And mounting seventy-something guns,
Ploughed, every year, the ocean blue,
Discovering kings and countries new.

The brave REAR-ADMIRAL BAILEY PIP,
Commanding that magnificent ship,
Perceived one day, his glasses through,
The kings that came from Chickeraboo.

"Dear eyes!" said ADMIRAL PIP, "I see
Three flourishing islands on our lee.
And, bless me! most remarkable thing!
On every island stands a king!

"Come, lower the Admiral's gig," he cried,
"And over the dancing waves I'll glide;
That low obeisance I may do
To those three kings of Chickeraboo!"

The Admiral pulled to the islands three;
The kings saluted him gracious*lee*.
The Admiral, pleased at his welcome warm,
Unrolled a printed Alliance form.

"Your Majesty, sign me this, I pray—
I come in a friendly kind of way—
I come, if you please, with the best intents,
And QUEEN VICTORIA's compliments."

The kings were pleased as they well could be;
The most retiring of the three,
In a "cellar-flap" to his joy gave vent
With a banjo-bones accompaniment.

The great REAR-ADMIRAL BAILEY PIP
Embarked on board his jolly big ship,
Blue Peter flew from his lofty fore,
And off he sailed to his native shore.

ADMIRAL PIP directly went
To the Lord at the head of the Government,
Who made him, by a stroke of a quill,
BARON DE PIPPE, OF PIPPETONNEVILLE.

The College of Heralds permission yield
That he should quarter upon his shield
Three islands, *vert*, on a field of blue,
With the pregnant motto "Chickeraboo."

Ambassadors, yes, and attachés, too,
Are going to sail for Chickeraboo.
And, see, on the good ship's crowded deck,
A bishop, who's going out there on spec.

And let us all hope that blissful things
May come of alliance with darky kings,
And, may we never, whatever we do,
Declare a war with Chickeraboo!

THE PERIWINKLE GIRL

I've often thought that headstrong youths
    Of decent education,
Determine all-important truths,
    With strange precipitation.

The ever-ready victims they,
    Of logical illusions,
And in a self-assertive way
    They jump at strange conclusions.

Now take my case: Ere sorrow could
    My ample forehead wrinkle,
I had determined that I should
    Not care to be a winkle.

"A winkle," I would oft advance
    With readiness provoking,
"Can seldom flirt, and never dance,
    Or soothe his mind by smoking."

In short, I spurned the shelly joy,
    And spoke with strange decision—
Men pointed to me as a boy
    Who held them in derision.

But I was young—too young, by far—
    Or I had been more wary,
I knew not then that winkles are
    The stock-in-trade of MARY.

I knew not how her features would
    Light up with merry twinkles,
Or in a jealous fit, I should
    Have hated all her winkles.

I had not watched her sunlight blithe
    As o'er their shells it dances—
I've seen those winkles almost writhe
    Beneath her beaming glances.

And when, to eat, she's taken out
    A winkle, having picked him,
I've even heard a joyous shout
    Emitted by her victim!

Of slighting all the winkly brood
    I surely had been chary,
If I had known they formed the food
    And stock-in-trade of MARY.

Both high and low and great and small
    Fell prostrate at her tootsies,
They all were noblemen, and all
    Had balances at COUTTS's.

Dukes with the lovely maiden dealt,
    DUKE BAILEY and DUKE HUMPHY,
Who eat her winkles till they felt,
    Exceedingly uncomfy.

DUKE BAILEY greatest wealth computes,
  And sticks, they say, at no-thing,
He wears a pair of golden boots
  And silver underclothing.

DUKE HUMPHY, as I understand,
  Though mentally acuter,
His boots are only silver, and
  His underclothing pewter.

A third adorer had the girl,
  A man of lowly station—
A miserable grov'ling Earl
  Besought her approbation.

This humble cad she did refuse
  With much contempt and loathing,
He wore a pair of leather shoes
  And cambric underclothing!

"Ha! ha!" she cried. "Upon my word!
  Well, really—come, I never!
Oh, go along, it's too absurd!
  My goodness! Did you ever?

"Two Dukes would MARY make a bride,
  And from her foes defend her"—
"Well, not exactly that," they cried,
  "We offer guilty splendour.

"We do not offer marriage rite,
  So please dismiss the notion!"
"Oh dear," said she, "that alters quite
  The state of my emotion."

The Earl he up and says, says he,
  "Dismiss them to their orgies,
For I am game to marry thee
  Quite reg'lar at St. George's."

He'd had, it happily befell,
  A decent education,
His views would have befitted well
  A far superior station.

His sterling worth had worked a cure,
  She never heard him grumble;
She saw his soul was good and pure,
  Although his rank was humble.

Her views of earldoms and their lot,
  All underwent expansion—
Come, Virtue in an earldom's cot!
  Go, Vice in ducal mansion!

CAPTAIN REECE

Of all the ships upon the blue
No ship contained a better crew
Than that of worthy CAPTAIN REECE,
Commanding of *The Mantelpiece.*

He was adored by all his men,
For worthy CAPTAIN REECE, R.N.,
Did all that lay within him to
Promote the comfort of his crew.

If ever they were dull or sad,
Their captain danced to them like mad,
Or told, to make the time pass by,
Droll legends of his infancy.

A feather bed had every man,
Warm slippers and hot-water can,
Brown windsor from the captain's store,
A valet, too, to every four.

Did they with thirst in summer burn?
Lo, seltzogenes at every turn,
And on all very sultry days
Cream ices handed round on trays.

Then currant wine and ginger pops
Stood handily on all the "tops";
And, also, with amusement rife,
A "Zoetrope, or Wheel of Life."

New volumes came across the sea
From MISTER MUDIE's libraree;
The Times and *Saturday Review*
Beguiled the leisure of the crew.

Kind-hearted CAPTAIN REECE, R.N.,
Was quite devoted to his men;
In point of fact, good CAPTAIN REECE
Beatified *The Mantelpiece.*

One summer eve, at half-past ten,
He said (addressing all his men):
"Come, tell me, please, what I can do
To please and gratify my crew?

"By any reasonable plan
I'll make you happy, if I can;
My own convenience count as *nil*;
It is my duty, and I will."

Then up and answered WILLIAM LEE
(The kindly captain's coxwain he,
A nervous, shy, low-spoken man),
He cleared his throat and thus began:

"You have a daughter, CAPTAIN REECE,
Ten female cousins and a niece,
A ma, if what I'm told is true,
Six sisters, and an aunt or two.

"Now, somehow, sir, it seems to me,
More friendly-like we all should be
If you united of 'em to
Unmarried members of the crew.

"If you'd ameliorate our life,
Let each select from them a wife;
And as for nervous me, old pal,
Give me your own enchanting gal!"

Good CAPTAIN REECE, that worthy man,
Debated on his coxwain's plan:
"I quite agree," he said, "O BILL;
It is my duty, and I will.

"My daughter, that enchanting gurl,
Has just been promised to an earl,
And all my other familee,
To peers of various degree.

"But what are dukes and viscounts to
The happiness of all my crew?
The word I gave you I'll fulfil;
It is my duty, and I will.

"As you desire it shall befall,
I'll settle thousands on you all,
And I shall be, despite my hoard,
The only bachelor on board."

The boatswain of *The Mantelpiece,*
He blushed and spoke to CAPTAIN REECE:
"I beg your honour's leave," he said;
"If you would wish to go and wed,

"I have a widowed mother who
Would be the very thing for you—
She long has loved you from afar,
She washes for you, CAPTAIN R."

The captain saw the dame that day—
Addressed her in his playful way—
"And did it want a wedding ring?
It was a tempting ickle sing!

"Well, well, the chaplain I will seek,
We'll all be married this day week—
At yonder church upon the hill;
It is my duty, and I will!"

The sisters, cousins, aunts, and niece,
And widowed ma of CAPTAIN REECE,
Attended there as they were bid;
It was their duty, and they did.

THOMSON GREEN AND HARRIET HALE

(To be sung to the Air of "An 'Orrible Tale")

Oh list to this incredible tale
Of THOMSON GREEN and HARRIET HALE;
Its truth in one remark you'll sum—
"Twaddle twaddle twaddle twaddle twaddle twaddle twum!"

Oh, THOMSON GREEN was an auctioneer,
And made three hundred pounds a year;
And HARRIET HALE, most strange to say,
Gave pianoforte lessons at a sovereign a day.

Oh, THOMSON GREEN, I may remark,
Met HARRIET HALE in Regent's Park,
Where he, in a casual kind of way,
Spoke of the extraordinary beauty of the day.

They met again, and strange, though true,
He courted her for a month or two,
Then to her pa he said, says he,
"Old man, I love your daughter and your daughter worships me!"

Their names were regularly banned,
The wedding day was settled, and
I've ascertained by dint of search
They were married on the quiet at St. Mary Abbot's Church.

Oh, list to this incredible tale
Of THOMSON GREEN and HARRIET HALE,
Its truth in one remark you'll sum—
"Twaddle twaddle twaddle twaddle twaddle twaddle twum!"

That very self-same afternoon
They started on their honeymoon,
And (oh, astonishment!) took flight
To a pretty little cottage close to Shanklin, Isle of Wight.

But now—you'll doubt my word, I know—
In a month they both returned, and lo!
Astounding fact! this happy pair
Took a gentlemanly residence in Canonbury Square!

They led a weird and reckless life,
They dined each day, this man and wife
(Pray disbelieve it, if you please),
On a joint of meat, a pudding, and a little bit of cheese.

In time came those maternal joys
Which take the form of girls or boys,
And strange to say of each they'd one—
A tiddy-iddy daughter, and a tiddy-iddy son!

Oh, list to this incredible tale
Of Thomson Green and Harriet Hale,
Its truth in one remark you'll sum—
"Twaddle twaddle twaddle twaddle twaddle twaddle twum!"

My name for truth is gone, I fear,
But, monstrous as it may appear,
They let their drawing-room one day
To an eligible person in the cotton-broking way.

Whenever Thomson Green fell sick
His wife called in a doctor, quick,
From whom some words like these would come—
Fiat mist. sumendum haustus, in a *cochleyareum.*

For thirty years this curious pair
Hung out in Canonbury Square,
And somehow, wonderful to say,
They loved each other dearly in a quiet sort of way.

Well, THOMSON GREEN fell ill and died;
For just a year his widow cried,
And then her heart she gave away
To the eligible lodger in the cotton-broking way.

Oh, list to this incredible tale
Of THOMSON GREEN and HARRIET HALE,
Its truth in one remark you'll sum—
"Twaddle twaddle twaddle twaddle twaddle twaddle twum!"

BOB POLTER

Bob Polter was a navvy, and
  His hands were coarse, and dirty too,
His homely face was rough and tanned,
  His time of life was thirty-two.

He lived among a working clan
  (A wife he hadn't got at all),
A decent, steady, sober man—
  No saint, however—not at all.

He smoked, but in a modest way,
  Because he thought he needed it;
He drank a pot of beer a day,
  And sometimes he exceeded it.

At times he'd pass with other men
  A loud convivial night or two,
With, very likely, now and then,
  On Saturdays, a fight or two.

But still he was a sober soul,
  A labour-never-shirking man,
Who paid his way—upon the whole,
  A decent English working-man.

One day, when at the Nelson's Head
  (For which he may be blamed of you),
A holy man appeared and said,
  "Oh, Robert, I'm ashamed of you."

He laid his hand on Robert's beer
  Before he could drink up any,
And on the floor, with sigh and tear,
  He poured the pot of "thruppenny."

"Oh, Robert, at this very bar,
  A truth you'll be discovering,
A good and evil genius are
  Around your noddle hovering.

"They both are here to bid you shun
  The other one's society,
For Total Abstinence is one,
  The other, Inebriety."

He waved his hand—a vapour came—
  A wizard, Polter reckoned him:
A bogy rose and called his name,
  And with his finger beckoned him.

The monster's salient points to sum,
  His heavy breath was portery;
His glowing nose suggested rum;
  His eyes were gin-and-wortery.

His dress was torn—for dregs of ale
    And slops of gin had rusted it;
His pimpled face was wan and pale,
    Where filth had not encrusted it.

"Come, POLTER," said the fiend, "begin,
    And keep the bowl a-flowing on—
A working-man needs pints of gin
    To keep his clockwork going on."

BOB shuddered: "Ah, you've made a miss,
    If you take me for one of you—
You filthy brute, get out of this—
    BOB POLTER don't want none of you."

The demon gave a drunken shriek,
    And crept away in stealthiness,
And lo, instead, a person sleek
    Who seemed to burst with healthiness.

"In me, as your adviser hints,
    Of Abstinence you've got a type—
Of MR. TWEEDIE's pretty prints
    I am the happy prototype.

"If you abjure the social toast,
    And pipes, and such frivolities,
You possibly some day may boast
    My prepossessing qualities!"

BOB rubbed his eyes, and made 'em blink,
    "You almost make me tremble, you!
If I abjure fermented drink,
    Shall I, indeed, resemble you?

"And will my whiskers curl so tight?
    My cheeks grow smug and muttony?
My face become so pink and white?
    My coat so blue and buttony?

"Will trousers, such as yours, array
    Extremities inferior?
Will chubbiness assert its sway
    All over my exterior?

"In this, my unenlightened state,
    To work in heavy boots I comes—
Will pumps henceforward decorate
    My tiddle toddle tootsicums?

"And shall I get so plump and fresh,
    And look no longer seedily?
My skin will henceforth fit my flesh
    So tightly and so TWEEDIE-ly?"

The phantom said, "You'll have all this,
    You'll have no kind of huffiness,
Your life will be one chubby bliss,
    One long unruffled puffiness!"

"Be off," said irritated BOB,
    "Why come you here to bother one?
You pharisaical old snob,
    You're wuss, almost, than t'other one!

"I takes my pipe—I takes my pot,
    And drunk I'm never seen to be:
I'm no teetotaller or sot,
    And as I am I mean to be!"

THE GHOST, THE GALLANT,
THE GAEL, AND THE GOBLIN

O'er unreclaimed suburban clays
  Some years ago were hobblin',
An elderly ghost of easy ways,
  And an influential goblin.
The ghost was a sombre spectral shape,
  A fine old five-act fogy,
The goblin imp, a lithe young ape,
  A fine low-comedy bogy.

And as they exercised their joints,
  Promoting quick digestion,
They talked on several curious points,
  And raised this pregnant question:
"Which of us two is Number One—
  The ghostie, or the goblin?"
And o'er the point they raised in fun
  They fairly fell a-squabblin'.

They'd barely speak, and each, in fine,
  Grew more and more reflective,
Each thought his own particular line
  By far the more effective.
At length they settled some one should
  By each of them be haunted,
And so arrange that either could
  Exert his prowess vaunted.

"The Quaint against the Statuesque"—
  By competition lawful—
The goblin backed the Quaint Grotesque,
  The ghost the Grandly Awful.
"Now," said the goblin, "here's my plan—
  In attitude commanding,
I see a stalwart Englishman
  By yonder tailor's standing.

"The very fittest man on earth
  My influence to try on—
Of gentle, p'raps of noble birth,
  And dauntless as a lion!
Now wrap yourself within your shroud—
  Remain in easy hearing—
Observe—you'll hear him scream aloud
  When I begin appearing!

The imp with yell unearthly—wild—
  Threw off his dark enclosure:
His dauntless victim looked and smiled
  With singular composure.
For hours he tried to daunt the youth,
  For days, indeed, but vainly—
The stripling smiled!—to tell the truth,
  The stripling smiled inanely.

For weeks the goblin weird and wild,
  That noble stripling haunted;
For weeks the stripling stood and smiled
  Unmoved and all undaunted.
The sombre ghost exclaimed, "Your plan
  Has failed you, goblin, plainly:
Now watch yon hardy Hieland man,
  So stalwart and ungainly.

"These are the men who chase the roe,
  Whose footsteps never falter,
Who bring with them where'er they go,
  A smack of old SIR WALTER.
Of such as he, the men sublime
  Who lead their troops victorious,
Whose deeds go down to after-time,
  Enshrined in annals glorious!

"Of such as he the bard has said
  'Hech thrawfu' raltie rawkie!
Wi' thecht ta' croonie clapperhead
  And fash' wi' unco pawkie!'
He'll faint away when I appear
  Upon his native heather;
Or p'raps he'll only scream with fear,
  Or p'raps the two together."

The spectre showed himself, alone,
  To do his ghostly battling,
With curdling groan and dismal moan
  And lots of chains a-rattling!
But no—the chiel's stout Gaelic stuff
  Withstood all ghostly harrying,
His fingers closed upon the snuff
  Which upwards he was carrying.

For days that ghost declined to stir,
  A foggy, shapeless giant—
For weeks that splendid officer
  Stared back again defiant!
Just as the Englishman returned
  The goblin's vulgar staring,
Just so the Scotchman boldly spurned
  The ghost's unmannered scaring.

For several years the ghostly twain
  These Britons bold have haunted,
But all their efforts are in vain—
  Their victims stand undaunted.
This very day the imp and ghost
  (Whose powers the imp derided),
Stand each at his allotted post—
  The bet is undecided.

ELLEN McJONES ABERDEEN

Macphairson Clonglocketty Angus McClan
Was the son of an elderly labouring man,
You've guessed him a Scotchman, shrewd reader, at sight,
And p'raps altogether, shrewd reader, you're right.

From the bonnie blue Forth to the hills of Deeside,
Round by Dingwall and Wrath to the mouth of the Clyde,
There wasn't a child or a woman or man
Who could pipe with Clonglocketty Angus McClan.

No other could wake such detestable groans,
With reed and with chanter—with bag and with drones:
All day and all night he delighted the chiels
With sniggering pibrochs and jiggety reels.

He'd clamber a mountain and squat on the ground,
And the neighbouring maidens would gather around
To list to his pipes and to gaze in his een,
Especially Ellen McJones Aberdeen.

All loved their McClan, save a Sassenach brute,
Who came to the Highlands to fish and to shoot;
He dressed himself up in a Highlander way,
Though his name it was Pattison Corby Torbay.

Torbay had incurred a good deal of expense
To make him a Scotchman in every sense;
But this is a matter, you'll readily own,
That isn't a question of tailors alone.

A Sassenach chief may be bonily built,
He may purchase a sporran, a bonnet, and kilt;
Stick a skean in his hose—wear an acre of stripes—
But he cannot assume an affection for pipes.

Clonglocketty's pipings all night and all day
Quite frenzied poor Pattison Corby Torbay;
The girls were amused at his singular spleen,
Especially Ellen McJones Aberdeen.

"Macphairson Clonglocketty Angus, my lad,
With pibrochs and reels you are driving me mad;
If you really must play on that cursed affair,
My goodness! play something resembling an air."

Boiled over the blood of MACPHAIRSON McCLAN—
The clan of Clonglocketty rose as one man;
For all were enraged at the insult, I ween—
Especially ELLEN McJONES ABERDEEN.

"Let's show," said McCLAN, "to this Sassenach loon
That the bagpipes can play him a regular tune.
Let's see," said McCLAN, as he thoughtfully sat,
"'In My Cottage' is easy—I'll practise at that."

He blew at his "Cottage," and blew with a will,
For a year, seven months, and a fortnight, until
(You'll hardly believe it) McCLAN, I declare,
Elicited something resembling an air.

It was wild—it was fitful—as wild as the breeze—
It wandered about into several keys;
It was jerky, spasmodic, and harsh, I'm aware,
But still it distinctly suggested an air.

The Sassenach screamed, and the Sassenach danced,
He shrieked in his agony—bellowed and pranced;
And the maidens who gathered rejoiced at the scene,
Especially ELLEN McJONES ABERDEEN.

"Hech gather, hech gather, hech gather around;
And fill a' yer lugs wi' the exquisite sound.
An air frae the bagpipes—beat that if ye can!
Hurrah for CLONGLOCKETTY ANGUS McCLAN!"

The fame of his piping spread over the land:
Respectable widows proposed for his hand,
And maidens came flocking to sit on the green—
Especially ELLEN McJONES ABERDEEN.

One morning the fidgety Sassenach swore
He'd stand it no longer—he drew his claymore,
And (this was, I think, in extremely bad taste),
Divided CLONGLOCKETTY close to the waist.

Oh! loud were the wailings for ANGUS McCLAN—
Oh! deep was the grief for that excellent man—
The maids stood aghast at the horrible scene,
Especially ELLEN McJONES ABERDEEN.

It sorrowed poor Pattison Corby Torbay
To find them "take on" in this serious way,
He pitied the poor little fluttering birds,
And solaced their souls with the following words:—

"Oh, maidens," said Pattison, touching his hat,
"Don't snivel, my dears, for a fellow like that;
Observe, I'm a very superior man,
A much better fellow than Angus McClan."

They smiled when he winked and addressed them as "dears,"
And they all of them vowed, as they dried up their tears,
A pleasanter gentleman never was seen—
Especially Ellen McJones Aberdeen.

THE SENSATION CAPTAIN

No nobler captain ever trod
Than Captain Parklebury Todd,
  So good—so wise—so brave, he!
But still, as all his friends would own,
He had one folly—one alone—
  This Captain in the Navy.

I do not think I ever knew
A man so wholly given to
  Creating a sensation;
Or p'raps I should in justice say—
To what in an Adelphi play
  Is known as "situation."

He passed his time designing traps
To flurry unsuspicious chaps—
  The taste was his innately;
He couldn't walk into a room
Without ejaculating "Boom!"
  Which startled ladies greatly.

He'd wear a mask and muffling cloak,
Not, you will understand, in joke,
  As some assume disguises;
He did it, actuated by
A simple love of mystery
  And fondness for surprises.

I need not say he loved a maid—
His eloquence threw into shade
  All others who adored her.
The maid, though pleased at first, I know,
Found, after several years or so,
  Her startling lover bored her.

So, when his orders came to sail,
She did not faint or scream or wail,
  Or with her tears anoint him:
She shook his hand, and said "Good-bye,"
With laughter dancing in her eye—
  Which seemed to disappoint him.

But ere he went aboard his boat,
He placed around her little throat
  A ribbon, blue and yellow,
On which he hung a double tooth—
A simple token this, in sooth—
  'Twas all he had, poor fellow!

"I often wonder," he would say,
When very, very far away,
  "If Angelina wears it?
A plan has entered in my head:
I will pretend that I am dead,
  And see how Angy bears it."

The news he made a messmate tell.
His Angelina bore it well,
  No sign gave she of crazing;
But, steady as the Inchcape Rock,
His Angelina stood the shock
  With fortitude amazing.

She said, "Some one I must elect
Poor Angelina to protect
  From all who wish to harm her.
Since worthy Captain Todd is dead,
I rather feel inclined to wed
  A comfortable farmer."

A comfortable farmer came
(Bassanio Tyler was his name),
   Who had no end of treasure.
He said, "My noble gal, be mine!"
The noble gal did not decline,
   But simply said, "With pleasure."

When this was told to Captain Todd,
At first he thought it rather odd,
   And felt some perturbation;
But very long he did not grieve,
He thought he could a way perceive
   To *such* a situation!

"I'll not reveal myself," said he,
"Till they are both in the Eccle-
   Siastical arena;
Then suddenly I will appear,
And paralysing them with fear,
   Demand my Angelina!"

At length arrived the wedding day;
Accoutred in the usual way
   Appeared the bridal body;
The worthy clergyman began,
When in the gallant Captain ran
   And cried, "Behold your Toddy!"

The bridegroom, p'raps, was terrified,
And also possibly the bride—
   The bridesmaids *were* affrighted;
But Angelina, noble soul,
Contrived her feelings to control,
   And really seemed delighted.

"My bride!" said gallant Captain Todd,
"She's mine, uninteresting clod!
   My own, my darling charmer!"
"Oh dear," said she, "you're just too late—
I'm married to, I beg to state,
   This comfortable farmer!"

"Indeed," the farmer said, "she's mine;
You've been and cut it far too fine!"
   "I see," said Todd, "I'm beaten."
And so he went to sea once more,
"Sensation" he for aye forswore,
And married on her native shore
A lady whom he'd met before—
   A lovely Otaheitan.

TRIAL BY JURY

AN OPERETTA

Scene—*A Court of Law at Westminster*

Opening Chorus of Counsel, Attorneys, and Populace.

Hark! The hour of ten is sounding,
Hearts with anxious hopes are bounding,
Halls of Justice crowds surrounding,
    Breathing hope and fear—
For to-day in this arena
Summoned by a stern subpoena
Edwin, sued by Angelina,
    Shortly will appear!

Chorus of Attorneys.

Attorneys are we
And we pocket our fee,
Singing so merrily, "Trial la law!"
With our merry ca. sa.,
And our jolly fi. fa.
Worshipping verily Trial la law!
    Trial la law!
    Trial la law!
Worshipping verily Trial la law!

Chorus of Barristers.

Barristers we,
With demurrer and plea,
Singing so merrily, "Trial la law!"
Be-wigged and be-gowned
We rejoice at the sound
Of the several syllables "Trial by law!"
    Trial la law!
    Trial la law!
Singing so merrily, "Trial la law!"

Usher.—Silence in court, and all attention lend!
   Behold the Judge! In due submission bend.

(*The Judge enters and bows to the Bar.
The Bar returns the compliment.*)

Recitative.

Counsel for Plaintiff.—May it please you, my lud!
   Gentlemen of the Jury!

Aria.

With a sense of deep emotion
   I approach this painful case,
For I never had a notion
   That a man could be so base.
      Or deceive a girl confiding,
      Vows, *et caetera,* deriding!

All.—He deceived a girl confiding,
   Vows, *et caetera,* deriding!

Counsel.—See my interesting client,
   Victim of a heartless wile,
See the traitor all defiant
   Wear a supercilious smile:
      Sweetly smiled my client on him,
      Coyly woo'd and gently won him!

All.—Sweetly smiled the plaintiff on him,
   Coyly woo'd and gently won him!

Counsel.—Swiftly fled each honied hour
   Spent with this unmanly male,
Camberwell became a bower,
   Peckham an Arcadian vale;
      Breathing concentrated otto!
      An existence *à la Watteau!*

All.—Bless us, concentrated otto!
   An existence *à la Watteau!*

Counsel.—Picture, then, my client naming
   And insisting on the day,

Picture him excuses framing,
Going from her far away.
Doubly criminal to do so
For the maid had bought her trousseau!

All.—Doubly criminal to do so
For the maid had bought her trousseau!

Recitative.

Counsel.—Angelina!

(*Angelina steps into the witness box.*)

Solo.

Judge.—In the course of my career
As a judex, sitting here,
Never, never, I declare,
Have I seen a maid so fair!

All.—Ah! Sly dog!

Judge.—See her sinking on her knees
In the Court of Common Pleas—
Place your briefs upon the shelf
I will marry her myself!

(*He throws himself into her arms.*)

All.—Ah! Sly dog!

Recitative.

Judge.—Come all of you—the breakfast I'll prepare—
Five hundred and eleven, Eaton Square!

Final Chorus.

Trial la law! Trial la law!
Singing so merrily, Trial la law!

Curtain.

THE REVEREND MICAH SOWLS

The REVEREND MICAH SOWLS,
He shouts and yells and howls,
He screams, he mouths, he bumps,
He foams, he rants, he thumps.

His armour he has buckled on, to wage
The regulation war against the Stage;
And warns his congregation all to shun
"The Presence-Chamber of the Evil One."

The subject's sad enough
To make him rant and puff,
And fortunately, too,
His Bishop's in a pew.

So REVEREND MICAH claps on extra steam,
His eyes are flashing with superior gleam,
He is as energetic as can be,
For there are fatter livings in that see.

The Bishop, when it's o'er,
Goes through the vestry door,
Where MICAH, very red,
Is mopping of his head.

"Pardon, my Lord, your SOWLS' excessive zeal,
It is a theme on which I strongly feel."
(The sermon somebody had sent him down
From London, at a charge of half-a-crown.)

The Bishop bowed his head,
And, acquiescing, said,
"I've heard your well-meant rage
Against the Modern Stage.

"A modern Theatre, as I heard you say,
Sows seeds of evil broadcast—well, it may;
But let me ask you, my respected son,
Pray, have you ever ventured into one?"

"My Lord," said MICAH, "no!
I never, never go!
What! Go and see a play?
My goodness gracious, nay!"

The worthy Bishop said, "My friend, no doubt
The Stage may be the place you make it out;
But if, my REVEREND SOWLS, you never go,
I don't quite understand how you're to know."

"Well, really," MICAH said,
"I've often heard and read,
But never go—do you?"
The Bishop said, "I do."

"That proves me wrong," said MICAH, in a trice;
"I thought it all frivolity and vice."
The Bishop handed him a counter plain;
"Just take this stall and go to Drury Lane."

The Bishop took his leave,
Rejoicing in his sleeve.
The next ensuing day
SOWLS went and heard a play.

He saw a dreary person on the stage,
Who mouthed and mugged in simulated rage,
Who growled and spluttered in a mode absurd,
And spoke an English SOWLS had never heard.

For "gaunt" was spoken "garnt,"
And "haunt" transformed to "harnt,"
And "wrath" pronounced as "rath,"
And "death" was changed to "dath."

For hours and hours that dismal actor walked,
And talked, and talked, and talked, and talked, and talked,
Till lethargy upon the parson crept,
And sleepy MICAH SOWLS serenely slept.

He slept away until
The farce that closed the bill
Had warned him not to stay,
And then he went away.

"I thought," said he, "*I* was a dreary thing,
I thought *my* voice quite destitute of ring,
I thought *my* ranting could distract the brain,
But oh! I hadn't been to Drury Lane.

"Forgive me, Drury Lane,
Thou penitential fane,
Where sinners should be cast
To mourn their wicked past!"

PETER THE WAG

Policeman PETER FORTH I drag
  From his obscure retreat:
He was a merry, genial wag,
  Who loved a mad conceit.
If he were asked the time of day
  By country bumpkins green,
He not unfrequently would say,
  "A quarter past thirteen."

If ever you by word of mouth
  Enquired of MISTER FORTH
The way to somewhere in the South,
  He always sent you North.
With little boys his beat along
  He loved to stop and play;
He loved to send old ladies wrong,
  And teach their feet to stray.

He would in frolic moments, when
  Such mischief bent upon,
Take Bishops up as betting men—
  Bid Ministers move on.
Then all the worthy boys he knew
  He regularly licked,
And always collared people who
  Had had their pockets picked.

He was not naturally bad,
  Or viciously inclined,
But from his early youth he had
  A waggish turn of mind.

The Men of London grimly scowled
  With indignation wild;
The Men of London gruffly growled,
  But PETER calmly smiled.

Against this minion of the Crown
  The swelling murmurs grew—
From Camberwell to Kentish Town—
  From Rotherhithe to Kew.
Still humoured he his wagsome turn,
  And fed in various ways
The coward rage that dared to burn
  But did not dare to blaze.

Still, Retribution has her day
  Although her flight is slow,
One day that Crusher lost his way
  Near Poland Street, Soho.
The haughty youth, too proud to ask,
  To find his way resolved,
And in the tangle of his task
  Got more and more involved.

The Men of London, overjoyed,
  Came there to jeer their foe—
And flocking crowds completely cloyed
  The mazes of Soho.
The news, on telegraphic wires,
  Sped swiftly o'er the lea—
Excursion trains from distant shires
  Brought myriads to see.

For weeks he trod his self-made beats
   Through Newport, Gerrard, Bear,
Greek, Rupert, Frith, Dean, Poland Streets,
   And into Golden Square:
But all, alas, in vain, for when
   He tried to learn the way
Of little boys or grown-up men
   They none of them would say.

Their eyes would flash—their teeth would grind—
   Their lips would tightly curl—
They'd say, "Thy way thyself must find,
   Thou misdirecting churl!"
And, similarly, also, when
   He tried a foreign friend;
Italians answered, "Il balen"—
   The French, "No comprehend."

The Russ would say with gleaming eye,
   "Sevastopol!" and groan.
The Greek said, "Τυπτω, τυπτομαι,
   Τυπτω, τυπτειν, τυπτων."
To wander thus for many a year
   That Crusher never ceased—
The Men of London dropped a tear,
   Their anger was appeased.

At length exploring gangs were sent
   To find poor FORTH's remains—
A handsome grant by Parliament
   Was voted for their pains.
To seek the poor policeman out
   Bold spirits volunteered,
And when at length they solved the doubt
   The Men of London cheered.

And in a yard, dark, dank, and drear,
   They found him, on the floor—
(It leads from Richmond Buildings—near
   The Royalty stage-door).
With brandy cold and brandy hot
   They plied him, starved and wet,
And made him sergeant on the spot—
   The Men of London's pet!

THE STORY OF PRINCE AGIB

Strike the concertina's melancholy string!
Blow the spirit-stirring harp like anything!
    Let the piano's martial blast
    Rouse the echoes of the past,
For of AGIB, Prince of Tartary, I sing!

Of AGIB, who, amid Tartaric scenes,
Wrote a lot of ballet-music in his teens:
    His gentle spirit rolls
    In the melody of souls—
Which is pretty, but I don't know what it means.

Of AGIB, who could readily, at sight,
Strum a march upon the loud Theodolite.
    He would diligently play
    On the Zoetrope all day,
And blow the gay Pantechnicon all night.

One winter—I am shaky in my dates—
Came two starving Tartar minstrels to his gates;
    Oh, Allah be obeyed,
    How infernally they played!
I remember that they called themselves the "Oüaits."

Oh! that day of sorrow, misery, and rage,
I shall carry to the Catacombs of Age,
    Photographically lined
    On the tablet of my mind,
When a yesterday has faded from its page!

Alas! PRINCE AGIB went and asked them in;
Gave them beer, and eggs, and sweets, and scent, and tin;
    And when (as snobs would say)
    They had "put it all away,"
He requested them to tune up and begin.

Though its icy horror chill you to the core,
I will tell you what I never told before—
    The consequences true
    Of that awful interview,
For I listened at the keyhole in the door!

They played him a sonata—let me see!
"Medulla oblongata"—key of G.
　　Then they began to sing
　　That extremely lovely thing,
"Scherzando! ma non troppo, ppp."

He gave them money, more than they could count,
Scent from a most ingenious little fount,
　　More beer in little kegs,
　　Many dozen hard-boiled eggs,
And goodies to a fabulous amount.

Now follows the dim horror of my tale,
And I feel I'm growing gradually pale;
　　For even at this day,
　　Though its sting has passed away,
When I venture to remember it, I quail!

The elder of the brothers gave a squeal,
All-overish it made me for to feel.
　　"O Prince," he says, says he,
　　"If a Prince indeed you be,
I've a mystery I'm going to reveal!

"Oh, listen, if you'd shun a horrid death,
To what the gent who's speaking to you saith:
　　No 'Oüaits' in truth are we,
　　As you fancy that we be,
For (ter-remble!) I am ALECK—this is BETH!"

Said AGIB, "Oh! accursed of your kind,
I have heard that ye are men of evil mind!"
　　BETH gave a dreadful shriek—
　　But before he'd time to speak
I was mercilessly collared from behind.

In number ten or twelve, or even more,
They fastened me, full length, upon the floor.
　　On my face extended flat,
　　I was walloped with a cat,
For listening at the keyhole of a door.

Oh! the horror of that agonising thrill!
(I can feel the place in frosty weather still.)
　　For a week from ten to four
　　I was fastened to the floor,
While a mercenary wopped me with a will!

They branded me and broke me on a wheel,
And they left me in a hospital to heal;
    And, upon my solemn word,
    I have never, never heard
What those Tartars had determined to reveal.

But that day of sorrow, misery, and rage,
I shall carry to the Catacombs of Age,
    Photographically lined
    On the tablet of my mind,
When a yesterday has faded from its page!

GENTLE ALICE BROWN

It was a robber's daughter, and her name was ALICE BROWN,
Her father was the terror of a small Italian town;
Her mother was a foolish, weak, but amiable old thing;
But it isn't of her parents that I'm going for to sing.

As ALICE was a-sitting at her window-sill one day
A beautiful young gentleman he chanced to pass that way;
She cast her eyes upon him, and he looked so good and true,
That she thought, "I could be happy with a gentleman like you!"

And every morning passed her house that cream of gentlemen,
She knew she might expect him at a quarter unto ten,
A sorter in the Custom-house, it was his daily road
(The Custom-house was fifteen minutes' walk from her abode).

But ALICE was a pious girl, who knew it wasn't wise
To look at strange young sorters with expressive purple eyes;
So she sought the village priest to whom her family confessed—
The priest by whom their little sins were carefully assessed.

"Oh, holy father," ALICE said, "'twould grieve you, would it not?
To discover that I was a most disreputable lot!
Of all unhappy sinners I'm the most unhappy one!"
The padre said, "Whatever have you been and gone and done?"

"I have helped mamma to steal a little kiddy from its dad,
I've assisted dear papa in cutting up a little lad.
I've planned a little burglary and forged a little cheque,
And slain a little baby for the coral on its neck!"

The worthy pastor heaved a sigh, and dropped a silent tear—
And said, "You mustn't judge yourself too heavily, my dear—
It's wrong to murder babies, little corals for to fleece;
But sins like these one expiates at half-a-crown apiece.

"Girls will be girls—you're very young, and flighty in your mind;
Old heads upon young shoulders we must not expect to find:
We mustn't be too hard upon these little girlish tricks—
Let's see—five crimes at half-a-crown—exactly twelve-and-six."

"Oh, father," little ALICE cried, "your kindness makes me weep,
You do these little things for me so singularly cheap—
Your thoughtful liberality I never can forget;
But oh, there is another crime I haven't mentioned yet!

"A pleasant-looking gentleman, with pretty purple eyes,—
I've noticed at my window, as I've sat a-catching flies;
He passes by it every day as certain as can be—
I blush to say I've winked at him, and he has winked at me!"

"For shame," said FATHER PAUL, "my erring daughter! On my word
This is the most distressing news that I have ever heard.
Why, naughty girl, your excellent papa has pledged your hand
To a promising young robber, the lieutenant of his band!

"This dreadful piece of news will pain your worthy parents so!
They are the most remunerative customers I know;
For many many years they've kept starvation from my doors,
I never knew so criminal a family as yours!

"The common country folk in this insipid neighbourhood
Have nothing to confess, they're so ridiculously good;
And if you marry any one respectable at all,
Why, you'll reform, and what will then become of FATHER PAUL?"

The worthy priest, he up and drew his cowl upon his crown,
And started off in haste to tell the news to ROBBER BROWN;
To tell him how his daughter, who was now for marriage fit,
Had winked upon a sorter, who reciprocated it.

Good ROBBER BROWN he muffled up his anger pretty well,
He said, "I have a notion, and that notion I will tell;
I will nab this gay young sorter, terrify him into fits,
And get my gentle wife to chop him into little bits.

"I've studied human nature, and I know a thing or two;
Though a girl may fondly love a living gent, as many do,
A feeling of disgust upon her senses there will fall
When she looks upon his body chopped particularly small."

He traced that gallant sorter to a still suburban square;
He watched his opportunity and seized him unaware;
He took a life-preserver and he hit him on the head,
And Mrs. Brown dissected him before she went to bed.

And pretty little Alice grew more settled in her mind,
She never more was guilty of a weakness of the kind,
Until at length good Robber Brown bestowed her pretty hand
On the promising young robber, the lieutenant of his band.

PASHA BAILEY BEN

A proud Pasha was BAILEY BEN,
His wives were three, his tails were ten;
His form was dignified, but stout,
Men called him "Little Roundabout."

His Importance.

Pale Pilgrims came from o'er the sea
To wait on PASHA BAILEY B.,
All bearing presents in a crowd,
For B. was poor as well as proud.

His Presents.

They brought him onions strung on ropes,
And cold boiled beef, and telescopes,
And balls of string, and shrimps, and guns,
And chops, and tacks, and hats, and buns.

More of them.

They brought him white kid gloves, and pails,
And candlesticks, and potted quails,
And capstan-bars, and scales and weights,
And ornaments for empty grates.

Why I mention these.

My tale is not of these—oh no!
I only mention them to show
The divers gifts that divers men
Brought o'er the sea to BAILEY BEN.

His Confidant.

A confidant had BAILEY B.,
A gay Mongolian dog was he;
I am not good at Turkish names,
And so I call him SIMPLE JAMES.

His Confidant's Countenance.

A dreadful legend you might trace
In SIMPLE JAMES's honest face,

For there you read, in Nature's print,
"A Scoundrel of the Deepest Tint."

His Character.

A deed of blood, or fire, or flames,
Was meat and drink to SIMPLE JAMES:
To hide his guilt he did not plan,
But owned himself a bad young man.

The Author to his Reader.

And why on earth good BAILEY BEN
(The wisest, noblest, best of men)
Made SIMPLE JAMES his right hand man
Is quite beyond my mental span.

The same, continued.

But there—enough of gruesome deeds!
My heart, in thinking of them, bleeds;
And so let SIMPLE JAMES take wing,—
'Tis not of him I'm going to sing.

The Pasha's Clerk.

Good PASHA BAILEY kept a clerk
(For BAILEY only made his mark),
His name was MATTHEW WYCOMBE COO,
A man of nearly forty-two.

His Accomplishments.

No person that I ever knew
Could "yödel" half as well as COO,
And Highlanders exclaimed, "Eh, weel!"
When COO began to dance a reel.

His Kindness to the Pasha's Wives.

He used to dance and sing and play
In such an unaffected way,

He cheered the unexciting lives
Of PASHA BAILEY's lovely wives.

The Author to his Reader.

But why should I encumber you
With histories of MATTHEW COO?
Let MATTHEW COO at once take wing,—
'Tis not of COO I'm going to sing.

The Author's Muse.

Let me recall my wandering Muse;
She *shall* be steady if I choose—
She roves, instead of helping me
To tell the deeds of BAILEY B.

The Pasha's Visitor.

One morning knocked, at half-past eight,
A tall Red Indian at his gate.
In Turkey, as you're p'raps aware,
Red Indians are extremely rare.

The Visitor's Outfit.

Mocassins decked his graceful legs,
His eyes were black, and round as eggs,
And on his neck, instead of beads,
Hung several Catawampous seeds.

What the Visitor said.

"Ho, ho!" he said, "thou pale-faced one,
Poor offspring of an Eastern sun,
You've *never* seen the Red Man skip
Upon the banks of Mississip!"

The Author's Moderation.

To say that BAILEY oped his eyes
Would feebly paint his great surprise—
To say it almost made him die
Would be to paint it much too high.

The Author to his Reader.

But why should I ransack my head
To tell you all that Indian said;
We'll let the Indian man take wing,—
'Tis not of him I'm going to sing.

The Reader to the Author.

Come, come, I say, that's quite enough
Of this absurd disjointed stuff;
Now let's get on to that affair
About LIEUTENANT-COLONEL FLARE.

BLABWORTH-CUM-TALKINGTON

Draper's clerk in a humble way,
Margate-bound, on a Seventh-day;
Gent in figured dicky and frill
Smoking pipes on Richmond Hill;
Coster dressed for an Epping bout;
Servant-gal with a Sunday out;
Quail, quail, quail, quail!
Here is the REVEREND BARNEY PAYLE,
    Good in a dismal way!
      Gurgle and groan
      Never were known
      Ever to fail
      BARNABY PAYLE,
    BARNABY PAYLE, B.A.

Rumble, blunder, stumble, thunder,
Wrangle, tangle, jingle-jangle,
Fluttery, stuttery, bog, fog,
    Missing his tack,
    Changing his track,
    Losing his threads,
    Mixing his "heads,"
Flash! Dash! Splash! Crash!
  Slowly, fastly, grimly, ghastly;
  Firstly, secondly, thirdly, lastly.
      Lastly first,
      Firstly last,

      Sinners curst,
      Hope all past.
  Down! down! down! down!
  Sob—sigh—gulp—frown.
  Boil! boil! boil! boil!
  Boiling lead and blazing oil.
      Groans—squirms—
      Bones—worms—
  Contradiction full, in terms,
      (Half-past one—
      Almost done).
  Wake! wake! wake! wake!
      Deuce to take!
      All at stake!
  Wake! wake! wake! wake!

Suddenly—grandly devotional—
Thrilling—emphatic—emotional—
      Various kinds
      Of baby minds
Trained on BARNABY PAYLE-ian rules,
At Blabworth-Talkington Infant Schools.
  Fill, oh fill the silver plate—
  Donors dwindling down of late—
  Hundreds wanted—thousands—more—
  Give, oh give, at the church's door!

This was the sermon one fine day,
Preached by BARNABY PAYLE, B.A.,
The first he'd ever had to speak,
For PAYLE was only "frocked" last week.

In an otherwise empty pew,
Sat a respectable Jew,
His starting eyeballs glistened—
Despite dissent, with best attent
That Hebrew person listened.

And PAYLE, B.A., remarked the way
In which the Jew drank in, that day,
The burning things he chose to say,
And hoped to see him christened.

The sermon at an end,
His Israelitish friend,
Heart-smitten to the core,
Sought out the vestry door.

"Oh, admirable PAYLE,
I've heard my people rail
Against your priests, and say that they can only smirk or roar,
But I can only say
That, thanks to you, to-day
I've learnt a better lesson than I ever learnt before.

"I've learnt why clerks in a humble way
Sail abroad on their Seventh Day;
I've learnt why costermongers will
Spend that day on the Epping hill;
I've learnt the meaning of pious cant,
Baldness, ignorance, dullness, rant—
A wonderful study for thoughtful minds
At Blabworth-Talkington Church one finds!"

THE SAILOR BOY TO HIS LASS

I go away, this blessed day,
   To sail across the sea, MATILDA!
My vessel starts for various parts
   At twenty after three, MATILDA;
I hardly know where we may go,
   Or if it's near or far, MATILDA,
For CAPTAIN HYDE does not confide
   In any 'fore-mast tar, MATILDA!

Beneath my ban that mystic man
   Shall suffer, *coûte que coûte,* MATILDA!
What right has he to keep from me
   The Admiralty route, MALTIDA?
Because, forsooth! I am a youth
   Of common sailors' lot, MATILDA!
Am I a man on human plan
   Designed, or am I not, MATILDA?

But there, my lass, we'll let that pass!
   With anxious love I burn, MATILDA.
I want to know if we shall go
   To church when I return, MATILDA?
Your eyes are red, you bow your head;
   It's pretty clear you thirst, MATILDA,
To name the day—What's that you say?—
   "You'll see me further first," MATILDA?

I can't mistake the signs you make,
   Although you barely speak, MATILDA;
Though pure and young, you thrust your tongue
   Right in your pretty cheek, MATILDA!
My dear, I fear I hear you sneer—
   I do—I'm sure I do, MATILDA—
With simple grace you make a face,
   Ejaculating, "Ugh!" MATILDA.

Oh, pause to think before you drink
   The dregs of Lethe's cup, MATILDA!
Remember, do, what I've gone through,
   Before you give me up, MATILDA!
Recall again the mental pain
   Of what I've had to do, MATILDA!
And be assured that I've endured
   It, all along of you, MATILDA!

Do you forget, my blithesome pet,
   How once with jealous rage, MATILDA,
I watched you walk and gaily talk
   With some one thrice your age, MATILDA?
You squatted free upon his knee,
   A sight that made me sad, MATILDA!
You pinched his cheek with friendly tweak,
   Which almost drove me mad, MATILDA!

I knew him not, but thought to spot
   Some man you wished to wed, MATILDA!
I took a gun, my darling one,
   And shot him through the head, MATILDA!
I'm made of stuff that's rough and gruff
   Enough, I own; but, ah, MATILDA!
It *did* annoy your poor old boy
   To find it was your pa, MATILDA!

I've passed a life of toil and strife,
    And disappointments deep, MATILDA;
I've lain awake with dental ache
    Until I fell asleep, MATILDA;
At times again I've missed a train,
    Or p'raps run short of tin, MATILDA,
And worn a boot on corns that shoot,
    Or, shaving, cut my chin, MATILDA!

But, oh! no trains—no dental pains—
    Believe me when I say, MATILDA,
No corns that shoot—no pinching boot
    Upon a summer day, MATILDA—
It's my belief, could cause such grief
    As that I've suffered for, MATILDA,
My having shot in vital spot
    Your old progenitor, MATILDA!

Bethink you how I've kept the vow
    I made one winter day, MATILDA—
That, come what could, I never would
    Remain too long away, MATILDA.
And, oh! the crimes with which, at times,
    I've charged my gentle mind, MATILDA,
To keep the vow I made—and now
    You treat me so unkind, MATILDA!

For when at sea off Caribbee,
    I felt my passion burn, MATILDA;
By passion egged, I went and begged
    The captain to return, MATILDA;
And when, my pet, I couldn't get
    That captain to agree, MATILDA,
Right through a sort of open port
    I pitched him in the sea, MATILDA!

Remember, too, how all the crew,
    With indignation blind, MATILDA,
Distinctly swore they ne'er before
    Had thought me so unkind, MATILDA;
And how they'd shun me one by one—
    An unforgiving group, MATILDA—
I stopped their howls and sulky scowls
    By pizening their soup, MATILDA!

So pause to think, before you drink
    The dregs of Lethe's cup, MATILDA;
Remember, do, what I've gone through,
    Before you give me up, MATILDA.
Recall again the mental pain
    Of what I've had to do, MATILDA,
And be assured that I've endured
    It, all along of you, MATILDA!

SIR CONRAD AND THE RUSTY ONE

A knight for doughty doings rife,
  With falchion, lance, or bill,
Was fair SIR CONRAD TALBOTYPE,
  Of Talbotypetonneville.

His parents he had never known
  (The sting of many a taunt);
He had one relative alone—
  A sweet, dyspeptic aunt.

A time must come when loving hearts
  Must part awhile—and lo!
SIR CONRAD into foreign parts
  As errant-knight must go!

Some name to which he might be true
  He sought for near and far,
But with the maidens whom he knew
  He was not popular.

Men jeered the knight who ne'er had been
  With love of maiden blessed,
Till, mad with disappointment keen,
  His aunt he thus addressed:

"No longer shall such chaff inane
  Against my head be hurled;
If you'll allow me, I'll maintain
  Your charms against the world!

"All knights shall at thine honoured name
  In fealty bend the knee—
From every errant I will claim
  His homage, aunt, for thee!"

A tear stood in her widow'd eye,
  And thus outspoke the dame—
"Oh, don't you think you'd better try
  Some younger lady's name?

"For folks would chuckle if they should
  Discover I'm your aunt——"
"I would," said CONRAD, "if I could,
  But, then, you see, I can't."

"Then go, my boy, with dauntless eye,
  My peerlessness maintain;
Make this your dreaded battle-cry,
  'KING HARRY and AUNT JANE!'"

*   *   *   *   *   *

"Ho! stand, Sir Knight, if thou be brave,
  And try thy might with mine,
Unless you wish this trusty glaive
  To cleave thee to the chine!"

176

So spake Sir Conrad as he thrust
  His lance in gallant mode—
'Towards a knight in suit of rust,
  Who passed him on the road.

The knight at words so boldly shaped
  Stopped short and turned him round,
Then humbly touched his brow, and scraped
  His foot upon the ground.

"Ha!" quoth Sir Conrad, "malapert!
  Dost think with threats to brave
Sir Conrad's wrath, thou thing of dirt—
  Thou braggadocio knave?

"Sir Conrad thus you may not daunt,
  Or make him hold his rein—
Come—swear you never knew an aunt
  So fair as my Aunt Jane!"

"Fair sir," the Rusty One replied,
  "Indeed, I do not think
I ever knew but one—who died,
  And all along of drink."

"Then own, thou braggart, by thy star,"
  Sir Talbotype replied,
"That my Aunt Jane is fairer far
  Than she who lately died!"

The knight rejoined, "Oh, do not cut—
  Forbear, my lord, to strike!
I have not seen the lady, but
  I think it's very like.

"To that belief—I own it free—
  I solemnly incline—
No aunt of yours could ever be
  So great a beast as mine.

"She figured in police reports
  Along of 'heavy wet,'
And was beknown at all the Courts
  As 'Coxybogy Bet'!"

"Then sign this paper," Conrad said,
  "Or there I'll stretch thee stark!"
The Rusty One inclined his head
  And made his knightly mark.

"Beshrew me! here's a dullard wight,
  Gramercy, halidame!
Thou call'st thyself an errant knight,
  And canst not sign thy name!"

"A knight?" exclaimed the Rusty One;
  "Lor' bless your honour, no!
I'm only hired till set of sun
  To join the Lord Mayor's Show!"

*   *   *   *   *   *

Sir Conrad hied him home again
  As quickly as he could,
Right-welcomed by his kind Aunt Jane
  And all the neighbourhood.

He told them how, in foreign land,
  He fought that rusty buck;
And though the maidens scorn his hand,
  They do not doubt his pluck.

THE CUNNING WOMAN

On all Arcadia's sunny plain,
  On all Arcadia's hill,
None were so blithe as BILL and JANE,
  So blithe as JANE and BILL.

No social earthquake e'er occurred
  To rack their common mind:
To them a Panic was a word—
  A Crisis, empty wind.

No Stock Exchange disturbed the lad
  With overwhelming shocks—
BILL ploughed with all the shares he had,
  JANE planted all her stocks.

And learn in what a simple way
  Their pleasures they enhanced—
JANE danced like any lamb all day,
  BILL piped as well as danced.

Surrounded by a twittling crew,
  Of linnet, lark, and thrush,
BILL treated his young lady to
  This sentimental gush:

"Oh, JANE, how true I am to you!
  How true you are to me!
And how we woo, and how we coo!
  So fond a pair are we!

"To think, dear JANE, that anyways,
  Your chiefest end and aim
Is, one of these fine summer days,
  To bear my humble name!"

Quoth JANE, "Well, as you put the case,
  I'm true enough, no doubt,
But then, you see, in this here place
  There's none to cut you out.

"But, oh! if anybody came—
  A Lord or any such—
I do not think your humble name
  Would fascinate me much.

"For though your mates, you often boast,
  You distance out-and-out;
Still, in the abstract, you're a most
  Uncompromising lout!"

Poor BILL, he gave a heavy sigh,
  He tried in vain to speak—
A fat tear started to each eye
  And coursed adown each cheek.

For, oh! right well in truth he knew
  That very self-same day,
The LORD DE JACOB PILLALOO
  Was coming there to stay!

The LORD DE JACOB PILLALOO
  All proper maidens shun—
He loves all women, it is true,
  But never marries one.

Now JANE, with all her mad self-will,
  Was no coquette—oh no!
She really loved her faithful BILL,
  And thus she tuned her woe:

"Oh, willow, willow, o'er the lea!
  And willow once again!
The Peer will fall in love with me!
  Why wasn't I made plain?"

*   *   *   *   *   *

A cunning woman lived hard by,
  A sorceressing dame,
MacCatacomb de Salmon-Eye
  Was her uncommon name.

To her good Jane, with kindly yearn
  For Bill's increasing pain,
Repaired in secrecy to learn
  How best to make her plain.

"Oh, Jane," the worthy woman said,
  "This mystic phial keep,
And rub its liquor in your head
  Before you go to sleep.

"When you awake next day, I trow,
  You'll look in form and hue
To others just as you do now—
  But not to Pillaloo!

"When you approach him, you will find
  He'll think you coarse—unkempt—
And rudely bid you get behind,
  With undisguised contempt."

The Lord de Pillaloo arrived
  With his expensive train,
And when in state serenely hived,
  He sent for Bill and Jane.

"Oh, spare her, Lord of Pillaloo!
  If ever wed you be,
There's anything *I'd* rather do
  Than flirt with Lady P."

Lord Pillaloo looked in her eye,
  He looked her through and through:
The cunning woman's prophecy
  Was clearly coming true.

Lord Pillaloo, the Rustic's Bane
  (Bad person he, and proud),
He laughed Ha! ha! at pretty Jane,
* And sneered at her aloud!*

He bade her get behind him then,
  And seek her mother's stye—
Yet to her native countrymen
  She was as fair as aye!

MacCatacomb, continue green!
  Grow, Salmon-Eye, in might,
Except for you, there might have been
  The deuce's own delight!

THE MODEST COUPLE

When man and maiden meet, I like to see a drooping eye,
I always droop my own—I am the shyest of the shy.
I'm also fond of bashfulness, and sitting down on thorns,
For modesty's a quality that womankind adorns.

Whenever I am introduced to any pretty maid,
My knees they knock together, just as if I were afraid;
I flutter, and I stammer, and I turn a pleasing red,
For to laugh, and flirt, and ogle I consider most ill-bred.

Some persons when they're introduced to maidens young and fair,
Begin at once by begging for a little lock of hair;
Or when they meet a strange young girl, they'll take her round the waist;
Perhaps I am old-fashioned, but it argues want of taste.

But still in all these matters, as in other things below,
There is a proper medium, as I'm about to show.
I do not recommend a newly-married pair to try
To carry on as PETER carried on with SARAH BLIGH.

Betrothed they were when very young—before they'd learnt to speak
(For SARAH was but six days old, and PETER was a week);
Though little more than babies at those early ages, yet
They bashfully would faint when they occasionally met.

They blushed, and flushed, and fainted, till they reached the age of nine,
When PETER's good papa (he was a Baron of the Rhine)
Determined to endeavour some sound argument to find
To bring these shy young people to a proper frame of mind.

He told them that as SARAH was to be his PETER's bride,
They might at least consent to sit at table side by side;
He begged that they would now and then shake hands, till he was hoarse,
Which SARAH thought indelicate, and PETER very coarse.

And PETER in a tremble to the blushing maid would say,
"You must excuse papa, MISS BLIGH,—it is his mountain way."
Says SARAH, "His behaviour I'll endeavour to forget,
But your papa's the coarsest person that I ever met.

"He plighted us without our leave, when we were very young,
Before we had begun articulating with the tongue.
His underbred suggestions fill your SARAH with alarm;
Why, gracious me! he'll ask us next to walk out arm-in-arm!"

At length when SARAH reached the legal age of twenty-one,
The Baron he determined to unite her to his son;
And SARAH in a fainting-fit for weeks unconscious lay,
And PETER blushed so hard you might have heard him miles away.

And when the time arrived for taking SARAH to his heart,
They were married in two churches half-a-dozen miles apart
(Intending to escape all public ridicule and chaff),
And the service was conducted by electric telegraph.

And when it was concluded, and the priest had said his say,
Until the time arrived when they were both to drive away,
They never spoke or offered for to fondle or to fawn,
For *he* waited in the attic, and *she* waited on the lawn.

At length, when four o'clock arrived, and it was time to go,
The carriage was announced, but decent SARAH answered "No!
Upon my word, I'd rather sleep my everlasting nap,
Than go and ride alone with MR. PETER in a trap."

And PETER's over-sensitive and highly-polished mind
Wouldn't suffer him to sanction a proceeding of the kind;
And further, he declared he suffered overwhelming shocks
At the bare idea of having any coachman on the box.

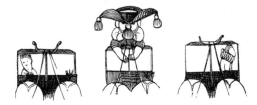

So Peter into one turn-out incontinently rushed,
While Sarah in a second trap sat modestly and blushed;
And Mr. Newman's coachman, on authority I've heard,
Drove away in gallant style upon the coach-box of a third.

Now, though this modest couple in the matter of the car
Were very likely carrying a principle too far,
I hold their shy behaviour was more laudable in them
Than that of Peter's brother with Miss Sarah's sister Em.

Alphonso, who in cool assurance all creation licks,
He up and said to Emmie (who had impudence for six),
"Miss Emily, I love you—will you marry? Say the word!"
And Emily said, "Certainly, Alphonso, like a bird!"

I do not recommend a newly-married pair to try
To carry on as Peter carried on with Sarah Bligh,
But still their shy behaviour was more laudable in them
Than that of Peter's brother with Miss Sarah's sister Em.

THE "BANDOLINE" PLAYER

A troubadour, young, brave, and tall,
  One morning might be seen,
A singing under COLTER's hall
  Upon the village green.

He went through all the usual forms,
  And rolled his eyes of blue,
As dying ducks in thunderstorms
  Are often said to do.

For COLTER had a daughter, she
  Was barely twenty-two.
Why sang that minstrel party? He
  Adored her—so would you.

He played upon a what's-its-name—
  You know the thing I mean—
The *Pall Mall* critics call the same
  A "dainty bandoline."

And COLTER's daughter, wrapt in joy
  (A sweet, romantic maid),
She smiled upon that guileless boy
  As gracefully he played.

"Oh, person in the crimson legs,"
  She modestly exclaimed,
"A bashful maiden coyly begs
  You'll tell her how you're named.

"For, oh, you feed a tender flame
  In playing on the green,
And, oh, she loves what critics name
  The dainty bandoline!"

That troubadour he tore his hair
  And sent a sigh above,
To think his bandoline should share
  That maiden's wealth of love.

He hied him to his village shed,
  Wept village tears in quarts,
Then laid him on his village bed,
  And thought these village thoughts:

"I must be worshipped all in all—
  For what I've always been—
And not for what the critics call
  My dainty bandoline.

"To which of us her loving may
  Be due, I'll thus detect—
Upon the fiddle I can play
  With singular effect.

"To-morrow, with its graceful aid,
  Her moments I'll beguile,
That maiden I will serenade
  In JOACHIM's finest style."

And so he did, that gallant boy,
  But never came the maid;
He, hoping she was only coy,
  Still sang to her and played.

BEETHOVEN, GLUCK, PICCINNI, SPOHR—
  He gave her for a while;
And other masters, even more,
  "Dot-touch-and-go" in style.

For hours that patient boy he played
  At FATHER COLTER's farm—
Behind his noble shoulder-blade,
  And underneath his arm—

Below his leg—behind his back—
  He played till he was red—
Between his knees, with dainty knack,
  And then above his head.

With musico-gymnastic tricks
  He warbled forth her name;
From half-past nine till half-past six,
  But, ah! no maiden came.

(For MARY had been sent away
  To Weston-super-Mare—
A fact of which that minstrel gay
  Was wholly unaware.)

But FATHER COLTER rose at nine,
  His wrath it also rised,
For fiddle, voice, and bandoline
  He equally despised.

"I have," said he, "some bellows *here*—
  A fine young noddle *there*—
It would but be politeness mere
  To introduce the pair!"

No sooner was it said than done,
  And as above I've shown,
Upon the sconce he fetched him one—
  One for himself alone!

"Ah, MARY," said the simple lad,
  "I know thy gentle touch.
Upon my word this is too bad,
  I feel it very much.

"That you don't care for me at all
  Is easy to be seen—
You love what *Pall Mall* critics call
  My dainty bandoline!"

(But MARY had been sent away
  To Weston-super-Mare—
A fact of which that minstrel gay
  Was wholly unaware.)

SIR BARNABY BAMPTON BOO

This is Sir Barnaby Bampton Boo,
  Last of a noble race,
Barnaby Bampton, coming to woo,
  All at a deuce of a pace.
          Barnaby Bampton Boo,
          Here is a health to you:
    Here is wishing you luck, you elderly buck—
          Barnaby Bampton Boo!

The excellent women of Tuptonvee
  Knew Sir Barnaby Boo;
One of them surely his bride would be,
  But dickens a soul knew who.
          Women of Tuptonvee,
          Here is a health to ye:
    For a Baronet, dears, you would cut off your ears,
          Women of Tuptonvee!

Here are old Mr. and Mrs. de Plow
  (Peter his Christian name),
They kept seven oxen, a pig, and a cow—
  Farming it was their game.
          Worthy old Peter de Plow,
          Here is a health to thou:
    Your race isn't run, though you're seventy-one,
          Worthy old Peter de Plow!

To excellent Mr. and Mrs. de Plow
  Came Sir Barnaby Boo,
He asked for their daughter, and told 'em as how
  He was as rich as a Jew.
          Barnaby Bampton's wealth,
          Here is your jolly good health:
    I'd never repine if you came to be mine,
          Barnaby Bampton's wealth!

"O great Sir Barnaby Bampton Boo"
  (Said Plow to that titled swell),
"My missus has given me daughters two—
  Amelia and Carrotty Nell!"
          Amelia and Carrotty Nell,
          I hope you're uncommonly well:
    You two pretty pearls—you extremely nice girls—
          Amelia and Carrotty Nell!

"There are AMELIA and CARROTTY NELL—
  MILLY is good but plain,
The other is pretty, as I've heard tell,
  But terribly pert and vain."
        CARROTTY ELLEN DE PLOW,
        I drink to you willingly now;
  But, oh dear! you *should* copy MILLY THE GOOD,
        CARROTTY ELLEN DE PLOW!

"AMELIA is passable only, in face,
  But, oh! she's a worthy girl;
Superior morals like hers would grace
  The home of a belted Earl."
        Morality, heavenly link!
        To you I'll eternally drink:
  I'm awfully fond of that heavenly bond,
        Morality, heavenly link!

"Now NELLY's the prettier, p'raps, of my gals,
  But, oh! she's a wayward chit;
She dresses herself in her showy fal-lals,
  And doesn't read TUPPER a bit!"
        O TUPPER, philosopher true,
        How do you happen to do?
  A publisher looks with respect on your books,
        For they *do* sell, philosopher true!

The Bart. (I'll be hanged if I drink him again,
  Or care if he's ill or well),
He sneered at the goodness of MILLY THE PLAIN,
  And cottoned to CARROTTY NELL!
        O CARROTTY NELLY DE P.!
        Be hanged if I'll empty to thee:
  I like worthy maids, not mere frivolous jades,
        CARROTTY NELLY DE P.!

They bolted, the Bart. and his frivolous dear,
  And MILLY was left to pout;
For years they've got on very well, as I hear,
  But soon he will rue it, no doubt.
        O excellent MILLY DE PLOW,
        I really can't drink to you now;
  My head isn't strong, and the song has been long,
        Excellent MILLY DE PLOW!

BOULOGNE

Of all the snug places where hardworking races rush every summer, a crop of
 'em,
I think you will own that delightful Boulogne may be said to stand quite at the
 top of 'em.
It's conveniently near, and it's not over dear, so your purse won't want much
 re-imbursing;
You can sit on a bench and learn how to speak French, just from hearing the
 natives conversing.
It has halls and two piers, and plump British young dears, and sands, theatre,
 picnics, and races;
Then it's clean and it's bright, and, oh! different quite from our commonplace
 watering-places!
It was once two days' sail, but the South-Eastern mail goes so quick that it isn't
 thought, now, far.
You can say, too, you've been on the Continent seen—though, of course, you
 need never say how far!
              Though other towns can boast of crowns,
                 I think you'll freely own,
              For bathing rare, and breezy air,
                 There's nothing like Boulogne!

If you're French in your taste, you can pull in your waist, and imbibe, till all
    consciousness ceases,
Absinthe and Vermouth, with the Boulonnais youth, and play billiards like mad
    for franc pieces—
You can sit in a *café* with gents rather raffy—a weed in your teeth you can make
    fast,
And French training to show, take grapes, soup, and Bordeaux at twelve-thirty,
    and call it a breakfast!
Or, if you incline to tea rather than wine (British dishes your mind, perhaps,
    takes to),
You will find over here very good bitter beer, and chops, buns, and roast beef,
    and rump steaks, too!
You can row, fish, or ride, or go bathing beside, in a dress rather given to
    ripping,
Or sit down on the pier, which costs nothing (not dear), and talk out, like a tar,
    on the shipping!
                       Though other towns can boast of crowns, &c.

And although it seems strange, and beyond British range, to behold in all
    decentish weather,
Pretty modest young maids and tall strapping young blades side by side in the
    water together;
Yet we soon get to see, though startling it be, we need find no important alarm
    in it—
For they manage it so that in couples they go, and there's sorrow a tittle of harm
    in it.

Each girl wears a dress that a prude would confess is most proper to wear, and
    each fellow
In a striped trouser-shirt, which fits tight (but don't hurt) like a fisher's in
    MASANIELLO.
They splash and they plunge, and they dive and they lunge, and they float and
    they jump, and they dance, they do;
For in all bathing matters they beat us to tatters—They manage them better in
    France, they do!
                       Though other towns can boast of crowns, &c.

The Etablissement balls, and the dresses and shawls, and the brandy—they've
    always the best of it;
The marvelous dresses, the yellow dyed tresses, vandyked petticoats, and the rest
    of it.
Those old dogs of nineteen, who the world must have seen, they so patronise,
    cherish, and foster us;
Those reckless nerve-shockers, in gay knickerbockers, and legs which are simply
    preposterous.
Then the brave fisher girls, in their earrings and curls, and their smiles when you
    go to buy shrimps of 'em;
And their marvelous legs, like mahogany pegs, and their wonderful caps and the
    crimps of 'em!
And their singular talk as together they walk—never linguist attained at the ease
    of them—
And their jackets in stripes, and their crosses and pipes, and their petticoats down
    to the knees of them!
                       Though other towns can boast of crowns, &c.

BRAVE ALUM BEY

Oh, big was the bosom of brave ALUM BEY,
And also the region that under it lay,
In safety and peril remarkably cool,
And he dwelt on the banks of the river Stamboul.

Each morning he went to his garden, to cull
A bunch of zenana or sprig of bul-bul,
And offered the bouquet, in exquisite bloom,
To BACKSHEESH, the daughter of RAHAT LAKOUM.

No maiden like BACKSHEESH could tastily cook
A kettle of kismet or joint of tchibouk,
As ALUM, brave fellow! sat pensively by,
With a bright sympathetic ka-bob in his eye.

Stern duty compelled him to leave her one day—
(A ship's supercargo was brave ALUM BEY)—
To pretty young BACKSHEESH he made a salaam,
And sailed to the isle of Seringapatam.

"O ALUM," said she, "think again, ere you go—
Hareems may arise and Moguls they may blow;
You may strike on a fez, or be drowned, which is wuss!"
But ALUM embraced her and spoke to her thus:

"Cease weeping, fair BACKSHEESH! I willingly swear
Cork jackets and trousers I always will wear,
And I also throw in a large number of oaths
That I never—no, *never*—will take off my clothes!"

*   *   *   *   *   *

They left Madagascar away on their right,
And made Clapham Common the following night,
Then lay on their oars for a fortnight or two,
Becalmed in the ocean of Honolulu.

One day ALUM saw, with alarm in his breast,
A cloud on the nor-sow-sow-nor-sow-nor-west;
The wind it arose, and the crew gave a scream,
For they knew it—they knew it!—the dreaded Hareem!!

The mast it went over, and so did the sails,
Brave ALUM threw over his casks and his bales;
The billows arose as the weather grew thick,
And all except ALUM were terribly sick.

The crew were but three, but they holloa'd for nine,
They howled and they blubbered with wail and with whine:
The skipper he fainted away in the fore,
For he hadn't the heart for to skip any more.

"Ho, coward!" said ALUM, "with heart of a child!
Thou son of a party whose grave is defiled!
Is ALUM in terror? is ALUM afeard?
Ho! ho! If you had one I'd laugh at your beard."

His eyeball it gleamed like a furnace of coke;
He boldly inflated his clothes as he spoke;
He daringly felt for the corks on his chest,
And he recklessly tightened the belt at his breast.

For he knew, the brave ALUM, that, happen what might,
With belts and cork-jacketing, *he* was all right;
Though others might sink, he was certain to swim,—
No Hareem whatever had terrors for him!

They begged him to spare from his personal store
A single cork garment—they asked for no more;
But he couldn't, because of the number of oaths
That he never—no, never!—would take off his clothes.

The billows dash o'er them and topple around,
They see they are pretty near sure to be drowned.
A terrible wave o'er the quarter-deck breaks,
And the vessel it sinks in a couple of shakes!

The dreadful Hareem, though it knows how to blow,
Expends all its strength in a minute or so;
When the vessel had foundered, as I have detailed,
The tempest subsided, and quiet prevailed.

One seized on a cork with a yelling "Ha! ha!"
(Its bottle had 'prisoned a pint of Pacha)—
Another a toothpick—another a tray—
"Alas! it is useless!" said brave ALUM BEY.

"To holloa and kick is a very bad plan:
Get it over, my tulips, as soon as you can;
You'd better lay hold of a good lump of lead,
And cling to it tightly until you are dead.

"Just raise your hands over your pretty heads—so—
Right down to the bottom you're certain to go.
Ta! ta! I'm afraid we shall not meet again"—
For the truly courageous are truly humane.

Brave ALUM was picked up the very next day—
A man-o'-war sighted him smoking away;
With hunger and cold he was ready to drop,
So they sent him below and they gave him a chop.

O reader, or readress, whichever you be,
You weep for the crew who have sunk in the sea?
O reader, or readress, read further, and dry
The bright sympathetic ka-bob in your eye.

That ship had a grapple with three iron spikes,—
It's lowered, and, ha! on a something it strikes!
They haul it aboard with a British "heave-ho!"
And what it has fishéd the drawing will show.

There was WILSON, and PARKER, and TOMLINSON, too—
(The first was the captain, the others the crew)—
As lively and spry as a Malabar ape,
Quite pleased and surprised at their happy escape.

And ALUM, brave fellow, who stood in the fore,
And never expected to look on them more,
Was really delighted to see them again,
For the truly courageous are truly humane.

GREGORY PARABLE, LL.D.

A leafy cot, where no dry rot
Had ever been by tenant seen,
Where ivy clung and wopses stung,
Where beeses hummed and drummed and strummed,
Where treeses grew and breezes blew--
A thatchy roof, quite waterproof,
Where countless herds of dicky-birds
Built twiggy beds to lay their heads
(My mother begs I'll make it "eggs,"
But though it's true that dickies do
Construct a nest with chirpy noise,
With view to rest their eggy joys,
'Neath eavy sheds, yet eggs and beds,
As I explain to her in vain
Five hundred times, are faulty rhymes).
'Neath such a cot, built on a plot
Of freehold land, dwelt MARY and
Her worthy father, named by me
GREGORY PARABLE, LL.D.

He knew no guile, this simple man,
No worldly wile, or plot, or plan,
Except that plot of freehold land
That held the cot, and MARY, and
Her worthy father, named by me
GREGORY PARABLE, LL.D.

A grave and learned scholar he,
Yet simple as a child could be.
He'd shirk his meal to sit and cram
A goodish deal of Eton Gram.
No man alive could him nonplus
With vocative of *filius;*
No man alive more fully knew
The passive of a verb or two;
None better knew the worth than he
Of words that end in *b, d, t.*
Upon his green in early spring
He might be seen endeavouring
To understand the hooks and crooks
Of HENRY and his Latin books,
Or calling for his "Caesar on

The Gallic War," like any don.
Or, p'raps, expounding unto all
How mythic Balbus built a wall.
So lived the sage who's named by me
Gregory Parable, LL.D.

To him one autumn day there came
A lovely youth of mystic name:
He took a lodging in the house,
And fell a-dodging snipe and grouse,
For, oh! that mild scholastic one
Let shooting for a single gun.

By three or four, when sport was o'er,
The Mystic One laid by his gun,
And made sheep's eyes of giant size,
Till after tea, at Mary P.
And Mary P. (so kind was she),
She, too, made eyes of giant size,
Whose every dart right through the heart
Appeared to run that Mystic One.
The Doctor's whim engrossing him,
He did not know they flirted so.
For, save at tea, *"musa musae,"*
As I'm advised, monopolised
And rendered blind his giant mind.
But looking up above his cup
One afternoon, he saw them spoon.
"Aha!" quoth he, "you naughty lass!
As quaint old Ovid says, 'Amas!'"

The Mystic Youth avowed the truth,
And, claiming ruth, he said, "In sooth
I love your daughter, aged man:
Refuse to join us if you can.
Treat not my offer, sir, with scorn,
I'm wealthy though I'm lowly born."
"Young sir," the aged scholar said,
"I never thought you meant to wed:
Engrossed completely with my books,
I little noticed lovers' looks.
I've lived so long away from man,
I do not know of any plan
By which to test a lover's worth,
Except, perhaps, the test of birth.
I've half forgotten in this wild
A father's duty to his child.

It is his place, I think it's said,
To see his daughters richly wed
To dignitaries of the earth,
If possible, of noble birth.
If noble birth is not at hand,
A father may, I understand
(And this affords a chance for you),
Be satisfied to wed her to
A Boucicault or Baring—which
Means any one who's very rich.
Now, there's an Earl who lives hard by,—
My child and I will go and try
If he will make the maid his bride—
If not, to you she shall be tied."

They sought the Earl that very day;
The sage began to say his say.
The Earl (a very wicked man,
Whose face bore Vice's blackest ban)
Cut short the scholar's simple tale,
And said in voice to make them quail,
"Pooh! go along! you're drunk no doubt—
Here, Peters, turn these people out!"

The Sage, rebuffed in mode uncouth,
Returning, met the Mystic Youth.
"My darling boy," the Scholar said,
"Take Mary—blessings on your head!"

The Mystic Boy undid his vest,
And took a parchment from his breast,
And said, "Now, by that noble brow,
I ne'er knew father such as thou!
The sterling rule of common sense
Now reaps its proper recompense.
Rejoice, my soul's unequalled Queen,
For I am Duke of Gretna Green!"

LIEUTENANT-COLONEL FLARE

The earth has armies plenty,
　And semi-warlike bands,
I dare say there are twenty
　In European lands;
But, oh! in no direction
　You'd find one to compare
In brotherly affection
　With that of COLONEL FLARE.

His soldiers might be rated
　As military Pearls:
As unsophisticated
　As pretty little girls!
They never smoked or ratted,
　Or talked of Sues or Polls;
The Sergeant-Major tatted,
　The others nursed their dolls.

He spent his days in teaching
　These truly solemn facts:
There's little use in preaching,
　Or circulating tracts.
(The vainest plan invented
　For stifling other creeds,
Unless it's supplemented
　With charitable *deeds*.)

He taught his soldiers kindly
　To give at Hunger's call:
"Oh, better far give blindly,
　Than never give at all!

Though sympathy be kindled
　By Imposition's game,
Oh, better far be swindled
　Than smother up its flame!"

His means were far from ample
　For pleasure or for dress,
Yet note this bright example
　Of single-heartedness:
Though ranking as a Colonel,
　His pay was but a groat,
While their reward diurnal
　Was—each a five-pound note.

Moreover,—this evinces
　His kindness, you'll allow,—
He fed them all like princes,
　And lived himself on cow.
He set them all regaling
　On curious wines, and dear,
While he would sit pale-ale-ing,
　Or quaffing ginger-beer.

Then at his instigation
　(A pretty fancy this)
Their daily pay and ration
　He'd take in change for his;
They brought it to him weekly,
　And he without a groan,
Would take it from them meekly,
　And give them all his own!

Though not exactly knighted
    As knights, of course, should be,
Yet no one so delighted
    In harmless chivalry.
If peasant girl or ladye
    Beneath misfortunes sank,
Whate'er distinctions made he,
    They were not those of rank.

No maiden young and comely
    Who wanted good advice
(However poor or homely)
    Need ask him for it twice.
He'd wipe away the blindness
    That comes of teary dew;
His sympathetic kindness
    No sort of limit knew.

He always hated dealing
    With men who schemed or planned;
A person harsh—unfeeling—
    The Colonel could not stand.

He hated cold, suspecting,
    Official men in blue,
Who pass their lives detecting
    The crimes that others do.

For men who'd shoot a sparrow,
    Or immolate a worm
Beneath a farmer's harrow,
    He could not find a term.
Humanely, ay, and knightly
    He dealt with such an one;
He took and tied him tightly,
    And blew him from a gun.

The earth has armies plenty,
    And semi-warlike bands,
I'm certain there are twenty
    In European lands;
But, oh! in no direction
    You'd find one to compare
In brotherly affection
    With that of COLONEL FLARE.

THE HERMIT

I don't suppose you'd ever find
  A man who galloped faster
To grief of a decisive kind
  Than FREDERICK DISASTER.

I never knew a purer man
  Or one who lived more gently,
But still in every little plan
  He failed incontinently.

For daily bit and daily sup,
  Unfitted quite to battle—
No man has been more shaken up
  In this terrestrial rattle.

Poor FREDERICK succeeded ill
  In every single section;
He could not forge a simple bill
  Or cheque, without detection;

Indeed he often came to grief
  With pots on area railings,
And taking someone's handkerchief
  Ensured immediate jailings.

He couldn't take a pocket-book,
  Or finger people's dials,
But safe detection overtook
  This man of many trials.

I've known him long, and watched his ways
  And seen him growing thinner,
Along of passing many days
  Without a scrap of dinner.

And yet no man more closely bent
  To work than did my neighbour,
For every holiday he spent
  Ensured a year's hard labour.

He worked in Chatham, Devonport,
  And Portland dockyards featly;
I've known him build a bomb-proof fort
  Particularly neatly.

He worked abroad like any horse
  Or other dumb mammalia,
He once passed through a ten-years' course
  Road-making in Australia.

But still, though toiling like a brute,
  His labour little gained him;
Its anything-but-toothsome fruit
  But scantily sustained him.

But though black-holed he often got,
  And bread-and-watered weekly,
He never murmured at his lot
  But always bore it meekly.

Sometimes he'd say, poor gentle boy,
  "Though lodged and boarded poorly,
E'en such poor boons as I enjoy
  I'm undeserving surely.

"Suppose I quit the world so bright
  And turn a simple hermit—
A dim recluse—an anchorite—
  I don't know what you term it.

"Then, freed from every sinful mesh,
  On herbs and frugal diet,
I'll mortify rebellious flesh
  And live in rural quiet.

"In stony cell without a door
  I'll live and pay no usance—
(I've lived in stony cells before
  And found the door a nuisance).

"In such a cell in mossy glade
  I'll sit, and live austerely;
And sympathetic village maids
  Shall love their hermit dearly.

"The maidens, too, before I wake—
  Before I draw my awning—
Shall come and ask me what I'll take
  And how I feel this dawning.

"And every visitor who comes
  To see me in my cavern,
Shall bring me marmalade and plums,
  And dinner from a tavern.

"So, for a skull, a knotted rope,
  And charitable rations,
A robe of sack, a hooded cope,
  And box for small donations,

"I'll freely, willingly resign
  (The pang will not be bitter)
The joys of life which now are mine
  With all their sheen and glitter!"

And so he did! To forest thick
  He fled from worldly folly;
When last I heard from FREDERICK
  He was extremely jolly.

ANNIE PROTHEROE

A LEGEND OF STRATFORD-LE-BOW

Oh! listen to the tale of little ANNIE PROTHEROE,
She kept a small post-office in the neighbourhood of Bow;
She loved a skilled mechanic, who was famous in his day—
A gentle executioner whose name was GILBERT CLAY.

I think I hear you say, "A dreadful subject for your rhymes!"
O reader, do not shrink—he didn't live in modern times!
He lived so long ago (the sketch will show it at a glance)
That all his actions glitter with the limelight of Romance.

In busy times he laboured at his gentle craft all day—
"No doubt you mean his Cal-craft" you amusingly will say—
But, no—he didn't operate with common bits of string,
He was a Public Headsman, which is quite another thing.

And when his work was over, they would ramble o'er the lea,
And sit beneath the frondage of an elderberry tree;
And ANNIE's simple prattle entertained him on his walk,
For public executions formed the subject of her talk.

And sometimes he'd explain to her, which charmed her very much,
How famous operators vary very much in touch,
And then, perhaps, he'd show how he himself performed the trick,
And illustrate his meaning with a poppy and a stick.

Or, if it rained, the little maid would stop at home, and look
At his favourable notices, all pasted in a book,
And then her cheek would flush—her swimming eyes would dance with joy
In a glow of admiration at the prowess of her boy.

One summer eve, at supper-time, the gentle GILBERT said
(As he helped his pretty ANNIE to a slice of collared head),
"This collared head reminds me that to-morrow is the day
When I decapitate your former lover, PETER GRAY."

He saw his ANNIE tremble and he saw his ANNIE start,
Her changing colour trumpeted the flutter at her heart;
Young GILBERT's manly bosom rose and sank with jealous fear,
And he said, "O gentle ANNIE, what's the meaning of this here?"

And ANNIE answered, blushing in an interesting way,
"You think, no doubt, I'm sighing for that felon PETER GRAY:
That I was his young woman is unquestionably true,
But not since I began a-keeping company with you."

Then GILBERT, who was irritable, rose and loudly swore
He'd know the reason why if she refused to tell him more;
And she answered (all the woman in her flashing from her eyes),
"You mustn't ask no questions, and you won't be told no lies!

"Few lovers have the privilege enjoyed, my dear, by you,
Of chopping off a rival's head and quartering him too!
Of vengeance, dear, to-morrow you will surely take your fill!"
And GILBERT ground his molars as he answered her, "I will!"

Young GILBERT rose from table with a stern determined look,
And, frowning, took an inexpensive hatchet from its hook;
And ANNIE watched his movements with an interested air—
For the morrow—for the morrow he was going to prepare!

He chipped it with a hammer and he chopped it with a bill,
He poured sulphuric acid on the edge of it, until
This terrible Avenger of the Majesty of Law
Was far less like a hatchet than a dissipated saw.

And Annie said, "O Gilbert, dear, I do not understand
Why ever you are injuring that hatchet in your hand?"
He said, "It is intended for to lacerate and flay
The neck of that unmitigated villain Peter Gray!"

"Now, Gilbert," Annie answered, "wicked headsman, just beware—
I won't have Peter tortured with that horrible affair;
If you attempt to flay him, you will surely rue the day."
But Gilbert said, "Oh, shall I?" which was just his nasty way.

He saw a look of anger from her eyes distinctly dart,
For Annie was a woman, and had pity in her heart!
She wished him a good evening—he answered with a glare;
She only said, "Remember, for your Annie will be there!"

*　*　*　*　*　*

The morrow Gilbert boldly on the scaffold took his stand,
With a vizor on his face and with a hatchet in his hand,
And all the people noticed that the Engine of the Law
Was far less like a hatchet than a dissipated saw.

The felon very coolly loosed his collar and his stock,
And placed his wicked head upon the handy little block—
The hatchet was uplifted for to settle Peter Gray,
When Gilbert plainly heard a woman's voice exclaiming, "Stay!"

'Twas ANNIE, gentle ANNIE, as you'll easily believe—
"O GILBERT, you must spare him, for I bring him a reprieve,
It came from our Home Secretary many weeks ago,
And passed through that post-office which I used to keep at Bow.

"I loved you, loved you madly, and you know it, GILBERT CLAY,
And having quite surrendered all idea of PETER GRAY,
I quietly suppressed it, as you'll clearly understand,
For I thought it might be awkward if he came and claimed my hand.

"In anger at my secret (which I could not tell before)
To lacerate poor PETER GRAY vindictively you swore;
I told you if you used that blunted axe you'd rue the day,
And so you will, you monster, for I'll marry PETER GRAY!"

[And so she did.

THE CAPTAIN AND THE MERMAIDS

I sing a legend of the sea,
So hard-a-port upon your lee!
   A ship on starboard tack!
She's bound upon a private cruise—
(This is the kind of spice I use
   To give a salt-sea smack).

Behold, on every afternoon
(Save in a gale or strong monsoon)
   Great CAPTAIN CAPEL CLEGGS
(Great morally, though rather short)
Sat at an open weather-port
   And aired his shapely legs.

And Mermaids hung around in flocks,
On cable chains and distant rocks,
   To gaze upon those limbs;
For legs like his, of flesh and bone,
Are things "not generally known"
   To any Merman TIMBS.

But Mermen didn't seem to care
Much time (as far as I'm aware)
   With CLEGG's legs to spend;
Though Mermaids swam around all day
And gazed, exclaiming, "That's the way
   A gentleman should end!

"A pair of legs with well-cut knees
And calves and ankles such as these
   Which we in rapture hail,
Are far more eloquent, it's clear,
When clothed in silk and kerseymere,
   Than any nasty tail."

And CLEGGS—a worthy kind old boy—
Rejoiced to add to others' joy,
   And (though he scarce knew why)
Because it pleased the lookers-on,
He sat there every day—though con-
   Stitutionally shy.

At first the Mermen sneered pooh-pooh,
But finally they jealous grew,
   And sounded loud recalls;
But vainly. So these fishy males
Declared they too would clothe their tails
   In silken hose and smalls.

They set to work, these water-men,
And made their nether robes—but when
   They drew with dainty touch
The kerseymere upon their tails,
They found it scraped against their scales,
   And hurt them very much.

The silk, besides, with which they chose
To deck their tails, by way of hose
    (They never thought of shoon),
For such a use was much too thin,—
It tore against the caudal fin
    And "went in ladders" soon.

So they designed another plan:
They sent their most seductive man
    This note to CLEGGS to show—
"Our Monarch sends to CAPTAIN CLEGGS
His humble compliments, and begs
    He'll join him down below;

"We've pleasant homes below the sea—
Besides, if CAPTAIN CLEGGS should be
    (As our advices say)
A judge of Mermaids, he will find
Our lady-fish of every kind
    Inspection will repay."

Good CAPEL sent a kind reply,
For CAPEL thought he could descry
    An admirable plan
To study all their ways and laws—
(But not their lady-fish, because
    He was a married man).

The Merman sank—the Captain too
Jumped overboard, and dropped from view
    Like stone from catapult;
And when he reached the Merman's lair
He certainly was welcomed there,
    But, ah! with what result?

They didn't let him learn their law,
Or make a note of what he saw,
    Or interesting mem.:
The lady-fish he couldn't find,
But that, of course, he didn't mind—
    He didn't come for them.

For though when CAPTAIN CAPEL sank,
The Mermen drawn in double rank
    Gave him a hearty hail;
Yet when secure of CAPTAIN CLEGGS,
They cut off both his lovely legs,
    And gave him *such* a tail!

When CAPTAIN CLEGGS returned aboard,
His blithesome crew convulsive roar'd,
    To see him altered so.
The Admiralty did insist
That he upon the Half-pay List
    Immediately should go.

In vain declared the poor old salt,
"It's my misfortune—not my fault,"
    With tear and trembling lip—
In vain poor CAPEL begged and begged—
"A man must be completely legged
    Who rules a British ship."

So spake the stern First Lord aloud—
He was a wag, though very proud,
    And much rejoiced to say,
"You're only half a captain now—
And so, my worthy friend, I vow
    You'll only get half-pay!"

AN UNFORTUNATE LIKENESS

I've painted SHAKESPEARE all my life—
    "An infant" (even then at play),
"A boy," with stage-ambition rife,
    Then "Married to ANN HATHAWAY."

"The bard's first ticket night" (or "ben."),
    His "First appearance on the stage,"
His "Call before the curtain"—then
    "Rejoicings when he came of age."

The bard play-writing in his room,
    The bard a humble lawyer's clerk,
The bard a lawyer[1]—parson[2]—groom[3]—
    The bard deer-stealing, after dark.

The bard a tradesman[4]—and a Jew[5]—
    The bard a botanist[6]—a beak[7]—
The bard a skilled musician[8] too—
    A sheriff[9] and a surgeon[10] eke!

Yet critics say (a friendly stock)
    That, though with all my skill I try,
Yet even I can barely mock
    The glimmer of his wondrous eye!

One morning as a work I framed,
    There passed a person, walking hard:
"My gracious goodness," I exclaimed,
    "How very like my dear old bard!

[1] "Go with me to a notary—seal me there
Your single bond."—*Merchant of Venice,* Act I., sc. 3.

[2] "And there she shall, at Friar Lawrence' cell,
Be shrived and married."—*Romeo and Juliet,* Act II., sc. 4.

[3] "And give their fasting horses provender."—*Henry the Fifth,* Act IV., sc. 2.

[4] "Let us, like merchants, show our foulest wares."—*Troilus and Cressida,* Act I., sc. 3.

[5] "Then must the Jew be merciful."—*Merchant of Venice,* Act IV., sc. 1.

[6]   "The spring, the summer,
The childing autumn, angry winter, change
Their wonted liveries."—*Midsummer Night's Dream,* Act II., sc. 1.

[7] "In the county of Glo'ster, justice of the peace and *coram.*"—*Merry Wives of Windsor,*
Act. I., sc. 1.

[8] "What lusty trumpet thus doth summon us?"—*King John,* Act V., sc. 2.

[9] "And I'll provide his executioner."—*Henry the Sixth* (Second Part), Act III., sc. 1.

[10] "The lioness had torn some flesh away,
Which all this while had bled."—*As You Like It,* Act IV., sc. 3.

"Oh, what a model he would make!"
    I rushed outside—impulsive me!—
"Forgive the liberty I take,
    But you're so very"—"Stop!" said he.

"You needn't waste your breath or time,—
    I know what you are going to say,—
That you're an artist, and that I'm
    Remarkably like SHAKESPEARE. Eh?

"You wish that I would sit to you?"
    I clasped him madly round the waist,
And breathlessly replied, "I do!"
    "All right," said he, "but please make haste."

I led him by his hallowed sleeve,
    And worked away at him apace,
I painted him till dewy eve,—
    There never was a nobler face!

"Oh, sir," I said, "a fortune grand
    Is yours, by dint of merest chance,—
To sport *his* brow at second-hand,
    To wear *his* cast-off countenance!

"To rub *his* eyes whene'er they ache—
    To wear *his* baldness ere you're old—
To clean *his* teeth when you awake—
    To blow *his* nose when you've a cold!"

His eyeballs glistened in his eyes—
    I sat and watched and smoked my pipe;
"Bravo!" I said, "I recognise
    The phrensy of your prototype!"

His scanty hair he wildly tore:
    "That's right," said I, "it shows your breed."
He danced—he stamped—he wildly swore—
    "Bless me, that's very fine indeed!"

"Sir," said the grand Shakespearian boy
    (Continuing to blaze away),
"You think my face a source of joy;
    That shows you know not what you say.

"Forgive these yells and cellar-flaps,
    I'm always thrown in some such state
When on his face well-meaning chaps
    This wretched man congratulate.

"For, oh! this face—this pointed chin—
    This nose—this brow—these eyeballs too,
Have always been the origin
    Of all the woes I ever knew!

"If to the play my way I find,
    To see a grand Shakespearian piece,
I have no rest, no ease of mind
    Until the author's puppets cease!

"Men nudge each other—thus—and say,
    'This certainly is SHAKESPEARE's son,'
And merry wags (of course in play)
    Cry 'Author!' when the piece is done.

"In church the people stare at me,
    Their soul the sermon never binds;
I catch them looking round to see,
    And thoughts of SHAKESPEARE fill their minds.

"And sculptors, fraught with cunning wile,
    Who find it difficult to crown
A bust with BROWN's insipid smile,
    Or TOMKINS's unmannered frown,

"Yet boldly make my face their own,
    When (oh, presumption!) they require
To animate a paving-stone
    With SHAKESPEARE's intellectual fire.

"At parties where young ladies gaze,
    And I attempt to speak my joy,
'Hush, pray,' some lovely creature says,
    'The fond illusion don't destroy!'

"Whene'er I speak my soul is wrung
    With these or some such whisperings;
' 'Tis pity that a SHAKESPEARE's tongue
    Should say such un-Shakespearian things!'

"I should not thus be criticised
    Had I a face of common wont:
Don't envy me—now, be advised!"
    And, now I think of it, I don't!

A BOULOGNE TABLE D'HOTE

Air, "He vowed that he never would leave her"

No gathering ever can beat
        Such a treat
        As you meet
In the people who gather, to eat
    At a table d'hôte every day,
So strange in appearance and phrase
        A leur aise
        In their ways—
As the people who show off their traits
    At a table d'hôte every day.
You'll never be tired of meeting
The people who gather for eating
At a table d'hôte, table d'hôte, table d'hôte, table d'hôte,
    Table d'hôte every day!

In the chair an old fellow you'll find—
        He sits there
        In the chair
Because for a fortnight he's dined
    At the table d'hôte every day.
He's fatherly quite in his ways,
        Looking most
        Like a host,
Your senior by several days.
    He table d'hôtes every day!
            You'll never be tired of meeting, &c.

There's another you know at a glance,
        Who's designed
        In his mind
To shine in the language of France,
  At the table d'hôte every day.
"Hi, Garsong, vous venez ici,
        Here, I say,
        S'il vous plait—
Donnez moi—thanks—all right." He will be
  At the table d'hôte every day.
      You'll never be tired of meeting, &c.

Then the lady so very genteel
        That you'd think
        She would shrink
From the notion of making a meal
  At a table d'hôte every day.
But you find, though genteel she can eat,
        Go right through
        the "menoo"—
Soup, fish, entrée, joint, cheese, and sweet—
  At the table d'hôte every day.
      You'll never be tired of meeting, &c.

There's the vulgar old glutton and wife,
        He who shines
        As he dines,
And who swallows the blade of his knife
  At the table d'hôte every day.
With his napkin tucked under his chin,
        The old bear
        Settles there,
Long before it is time to begin,
  At the table d'hôte every day!
      You'll never be tired of meeting, &c.

There's a gay and a gushing old girl,
        Who must be
        Forty-three
With a seven-and-sixpenny curl,
  At the table d'hôte every day.
There's also a boy of nineteen
        (Quite a lad)
        Driven mad
By her beauty, who always is seen
  At the table d'hôte every day.
      You'll never be tired of meeting, &c.

THE RAILWAY GUARD'S SONG

Air, "Crescendo Galop"

Train is starting, people parting, hurry, scurry all around,
People rushing, pushing, crushing—luggage somehow can't be found,
Here's the wicket, show your ticket—in your pocket, I'll be bound;
  For they'd be knowing if you're going all along the line.
    With a dash and a rush and a crash and a crush,
      And a puff, puff, puff, puff, puff;
    With a dash and a rush and a crash and a crush,
      And a puff, puff, puff, puff, puff.
    Counties right and left are flying,
    Whistle screaming, shrieking, crying,
    Engine puffing, blowing, sighing,
      Sighing all along the line!

Strange sensation passing station, through a tunnel then you go,
Dashing, crashing, signal flashing, darkness all above, below,
Flags unfurling, quickly whirling, rushing into daylight glow;
  With posts and wires, lamps and fires, all along the line.
    With a dash and a rush, &c. (*Bis*)
    Here we stop for ticket-showing,
    Engine off her steam is blowing,
    Get in, please, sir, if you're going,
      Going all along the line.

Gem'man beckons, ah, I reckons, he's been smoking up from town.
Want a weed, sir? Oh, indeed, sir, carriage all the journey down.
Fond of fees, sir? If you please, sir, thankee! (pocket half-a-crown)
  He'll smoke away, sir, I dare say, sir, all along the line!
    With a dash and a rush, &c. (*Bis*)
    Gent and engine both are smoking,
    Driver with a poker poking,
    Very grimy stoker stoking,
      Stoking all along the line.

Gent and lady (gent is shady—lady pretty, young, and fair),
P'raps eloping—lady hoping they may be a happy pair;
Secret marriage, want a carriage to themselves, well, get in there;
  A single tizzy! Gem'man, is he? Isn't one of mine!
    With a dash and a rush, &c. (*Bis*)
    Running off from her relations,
    Who will make investigations
    At a dozen score of stations,
      Stations all along the line!

"THE UNDECIDED MAN"

Air, "The Sugar Shop"

Of all the small annoyances that weight our mental buoyances,
No chaff or cold derision is so sad as indecision is—
It's ruined me, it's plain it has—through life it's been my bane, it has,
It's driven me insane, it has, as anyone can see!
  Oh my! the troubles and perplexities,
  Oh dear! that mar each little plan!
  Oh law! sufficient quite to vex it is,
 The short uncertain temper of an undecided man!

In bed each day a-dundering, I lie awake a-wondering
(In sad uncertain doubt of it), by which side to get out of it,
For all I ever knew of 'em have sides (or feet in lieu of 'em),
They've generally two of 'em, as anyone can see!
    Oh my! the troubles and perplexities, &c.

I never went a-marrying but single stopped a-tarrying,
Though lots of girls I've known, I have; been introduced and shown, I have,
But ne'er a one I've got of 'em—no single girl could spot of 'em,
There's such a plaguey lot of 'em, as anyone can see!
    Oh my! the troubles and perplexities, &c.

I've reached a decent time of life, and tired, nearly, I'm of life,
Whom ought I to enquire of what illness to expire of?
Most men appear to fall of 'em—the short of 'em, the tall of 'em,
I cannot die of all of 'em, as anyone can see!
  Oh my! perplexed and always wondering,
  Oh dear! ill-natured people say,
  Oh law! I'm like in all my blundering,
 A donkey hesitating 'tween two packages of hay!

PREMONITORY SYMPTOMS

We're thoroughly clear of Folkestone Pier,
  With a holiday all to come;
With a beautiful day and a porte-monnaie,
  Containing a good round sum.
The waves are flecked with a foaming white,
  As they gaily raise their crest;
And on we dash in a steam-borne flight,
  With a breeze from the sou'-sou'-west.
    Merrily, merrily on we go,
      With many a quip and jest;
    So happy are we on a tumbling sea,
      With a breeze from the sou'-sou'-west.

We never were better in our lives,
  And long for a hearty meal;
Though every now and then arrives
  A shuddery kind of feel.
Though a shivery quivery kind of qualm,
  Just shimmers our manly breast;
It's jollier far than a perfect calm,
  Is a breeze from the sou'-sou'-west!
      Merrily, merrily, &c.

A film is spreading all over your eyes,
  And all the while you think,
It isn't so much in the steamboat's rise,
  As at each successive sink!

The drop-down after a wave, you find,
  Is the thing you most detest;
It leaves you, body and soul, behind,
  When the wind's at the sou'-sou'-west!
      Merrily, merrily, &c.

You find your tongue has attained a size
  You never remarked before;
You're much relieved when you close your eyes,
  You're shuddering more and more.
A sickening kind of warmth is felt
  Just under your manly chest,
You never should wear too tight a belt
  In a breeze from the sou'-sou'-west!
      Merrily, merrily, &c.

You shudder and quiver and quake on deck,
  And shiver and glow and freeze;
And you wish you'd nothing between your neck
  And your inorganic knees.
The climax comes, with a wrenching pain,
  It's agony quite, at best;
You swear that you never will cross again
  With the wind at the sou'-sou'-west!
      Merrily, merrily, &c.

LOST MR. BLAKE

Mr. Blake was a regular out-and-out hardened sinner,
  Who was quite out of the pale of Christianity, so to speak.
He was in the habit of smoking a long pipe and drinking a glass of grog on
    Sunday after dinner,
    And seldom thought of going to church more than twice or (if Good Friday or
    Christmas Day happened to come in it) three times a week.

He was quite indifferent as to the particular kinds of dresses
  That the clergymen wore at the church where he used to go to pray,
And whatever he did in the way of relieving a chap's distresses,
  He always did in a nasty, sneaking, underhanded, hole-and-corner sort of way.

I have known him indulge in profane, ungentlemanly emphatics,
  When the Protestant Church has been divided on the subject of the width of a
    chasuble's hem;
I have even known him to sneer at albs—and as for dalmatics,
  Words can't convey an idea of the contempt he expressed for *them*.

He didn't believe in persons who, not being well off themselves, are obliged to
    confine their charitable exertions to collecting money from wealthier people,
  And looked upon individuals of the former class as ecclesiastical hawks;
He used to say that he would no more think of interfering with his priest's robes
    than with his church or his steeple,
  And that he did not consider his soul imperilled because somebody over whom
    he had no influence whatever, chose to dress himself up like an ecclesiastical
    GUY FAWKES.

This shocking old vagabond was so unutterably shameless
  That he actually went a-courting a very respectable and pious middle-aged
    sister, by the name of BIGGS:
She was a rather attractive widow whose life, as such, had always been
    particularly blameless;
  Her first husband had left her a secure but moderate competence owing to
    some fortunate speculations in the matter of figs.

She was an excellent person in every way—and won the respect even of MRS.
    GRUNDY,
  She was a good housewife, too, and wouldn't have wasted a penny if she had
    owned the Koh-i-noor;
She was just as strict as he was lax in her observance of Sunday,
  And being a good economist, and charitable besides, she took all the bones and
    cold potatoes and broken pie-crusts and candle-ends (when she had quite
    done with them), and made them into an excellent soup for the deserving
    poor.

I am sorry to say that she rather took to BLAKE—that outcast of society;
  And when respectable brothers who were fond of her began to look dubious
    and to cough,
She would say, "Oh, my friends, it's because I hope to bring this poor benighted
    soul back to virtue and propriety"
  (And besides, the poor benighted soul, with all his faults, was uncommonly well
    off).

And when MR. BLAKE's dissipated friends called his attention to the frown or the
    pout of her,
  Whenever he did anything which appeared to her to savour of an
    unmentionable place,

He would say she would be a very decent old girl when all that nonsense was
  knocked out of her—
  And his method of knocking it out of her is one that covered him with
  disgrace.

She was fond of going to church services four times every Sunday, and four or
  five times in the week, and never seemed to pall of them,
  So he hunted out all the churches within a convenient distance that had
  services at different hours, so to speak;
And when he had married her he positively insisted upon their going to all of
  them,
  So they contrived to do about twelve churches every Sunday, and, if they had
  luck, from twenty-two to twenty-three in the course of the week.

She was fond of dropping his sovereigns ostentatiously into the plate, and she
  liked to see them stand out rather conspicuously against the commonplace
  half-crowns and shillings,
  So he took her to all the charity sermons, and if by any extraordinary chance
  there wasn't a charity sermon anywhere, he would drop a couple of
  sovereigns (one for him and one for her) into the poor-box at the door;
And as he always deducted the sums thus given in charity from the housekeeping
  money, and the money he allowed her for her bonnets and frillings,
  She soon began to find that even charity, if you allow it to interfere with your
  personal luxuries, becomes an intolerable bore.

On Sundays she was always melancholy and anything but good society,
  For that day in her household was a day of sighings and sobbings and
  wringing of hands and shaking of heads:
She wouldn't hear of a button being sewn on a glove, because it was a work
  neither of necessity nor of piety,
  And strictly prohibited her servants from amusing themselves, or indeed doing
  anything at all except dusting the drawing-rooms, cleaning the boots and
  shoes, cooking the dinner, waiting generally on the family, and making the
  beds.

But BLAKE even went farther than that, and said that, on Sundays, people should
do their own works of necessity, and not delegate them to persons in a
menial situation,
So he wouldn't allow his servants to do so much as even answer a bell.
Here he is making his wife carry up the water for her bath to the second floor,
much against her inclination,—
And why in the world the gentleman who illustrates these ballads has put him
into a cocked hat is more than I can tell.

After about three months of this sort of thing, taking the smooth with the rough
of it
(Blacking her own boots and peeling her own potatoes was not her notion of
connubial bliss),
MRS. BLAKE began to find that she had pretty nearly had enough of it,
And came, in course of time, to think that BLAKE's own original line of
conduct wasn't so much amiss.

And now that wicked person—that detestable sinner ("BELIAL BLAKE" his friends
and well-wishers call him for his atrocities),
And his poor deluded victim whom all her Christian brothers dislike and pity
so,
Go to the parish church only on Sunday morning and afternoon and occasionally
on a week-day, and spend their evenings in connubial fondlings and
affectionate reciprocities,
And I should like to know where in the world (or rather, out of it) they expect
to go!

LITTLE OLIVER

Earl Joyce he was a kind old party
  Whom nothing ever could put out,
Though eighty-two, he still was hearty,
  Excepting as regarded gout.

He had one unexampled daughter,
  The Lady Minnie-haha Joyce,
Fair Minnie-haha, "Laughing Water,"
  So called from her melodious voice.

By Nature planned for lover-capture,
  Her beauty every heart assailed;
The good old nobleman with rapture
  Observed how widely she prevailed.

Aloof from all the lordly flockings
  Of titled swells who worshipped her,
There stood, in pumps and cotton stockings,
  One humble lover—Oliver.

He was no peer by Fortune petted,
  His name recalled no bygone age;
He was no lordling coronetted—
  Alas! he was a simple page!

With vain appeals he never bored her,
  But stood in silent sorrow by—
He knew how fondly he adored her,
  And knew, alas! how hopelessly!

Well grounded by a village tutor
  In languages alive and past,
He'd say unto himself, "Knee-suitor,
  Oh, do not go beyond your last!"

But though his name could boast no handle,
  He could not every hope resign;
As moths will hover round a candle,
  So hovered he about her shrine.

The brilliant candle dazed the moth well:
  One day she sang to her Papa
The air that Marie sings with Bothwell
  In Niedermeyer's opera.

(Therein a stable boy, it's stated,
  Devoutly loved a noble dame,
Who ardently reciprocated
  His rather injudicious flame.)

And then, before the piano closing
  (He listened coyly at the door),
She sang a song of her composing—
  I give one verse from half a score:

Ballad

Why, pretty page, art ever sighing?
Is sorrow in thy heartlet lying?
  Come, set a-ringing
    Thy laugh entrancing,

And ever singing
  And ever dancing.
Ever singing, Tra! la! la!
Ever dancing, Tra! la! la!
    Ever singing, ever dancing,
    Ever singing, Tra! la! la!

He skipped for joy like little muttons,
  He danced like Esmeralda's kid.
(She did not mean a boy in buttons,
  Although he fancied that she did.)

Poor lad! convinced he thus would win her,
  He wore out many pairs of soles;
He danced when taking down the dinner—
  He danced when bringing up the coals.

He danced and sang (however laden)
  With his incessant "Tra! la! la!"
Which much surprised the noble maiden,
  And puzzled even her Papa.

He nourished now his flame and fanned it,
  He even danced at work below.
The upper servants wouldn't stand it,
  And Bowles the butler told him so.

At length on impulse acting blindly,
  His love he laid completely bare;
The gentle Earl received him kindly
  And told the lad to take a chair.

"Oh, sir," the suitor uttered sadly,
  "Don't give your indignation vent;
I fear you think I'm acting madly,
  Perhaps you think me insolent?"

The kindly Earl repelled the notion;
  His noble bosom heaved a sigh,
His fingers trembled with emotion,
  A tear stood in his mild blue eye:

For, oh! the scene recalled too plainly
  The half-forgotten time when he,
A boy of nine, had worshipped vainly
  A governess of forty-three!

"My boy," he said, in tone consoling,
  "Give up this idle fancy—do—
The song you heard my daughter trolling
  Did not, indeed, refer to you.

"I feel for you, poor boy, acutely;
  I would not wish to give you pain;
Your pangs I estimate minutely,—
  I, too, have loved, and loved in vain.

"But still your humble rank and station
  For Minnie surely are not meet"—
He said much more in conversation
  Which it were needless to repeat.

Now I'm prepared to bet a guinea,
  Were this a mere dramatic case,
The page would have eloped with Minnie,
  But, no—he only left his place.

The simple Truth is my detective,
  With me Sensation can't abide;
The Likely beats the mere Effective,
  And Nature is my only guide.

WHAT IS A BURLESQUE?

Pretty princess,
Beautiful dress;
Exquisite eyes,
Wonderful size;
Lots of back hair
Coming to *there;*
Shoulders so fair,
Marvellous pair!
Dear little dress
(Couldn't be less);
Story confused,
Frequently used;
Sillified pun
Clumsily done.

> Dresses grotesque,
> Girls statuesque,
> Scene picturesque—
> That's a burlesque!

Wicked old king,
Shocking old thing!
Very big head,
Horribly red;
Given to clout
Nobles about;
Horribly fat,
Poor as a rat,
Shockingly mean;
Bullies his queen,
Wishes her dead;
Crown on his head,
Given to stand
Sceptre in hand.

> Dresses grotesque, etc.

Baron so rich,
Acting as sich;
Terribly plain,
Painfully vain
(Singular dress);
Loves the princess;

Sends, through the king,
Jewel and ring,
Vowing he burns—
These she returns.
Having been told
Sixty is old
(Meaning his age),
Doesn't engage.

> Dresses grotesque, etc.

Prince whom she loves,
Beautiful gloves,
Clothes very fine,
Glitter and shine,
Exquisite tie,
Glass in his eye,
Highly urbane,
Neat little cane,
Comb in his hair
Sunnily fair,
Beautiful curls,
Form like a girl's—
Figure, I mean,
Looks epicene.

> Dresses grotesque, etc.

Though he's so trim,
Natty and slim,
No one so brave
Thrashing a knave.
Safe to engage
Vice on the stage;
(This he has heard
Often averred.)
Though for the time
Folly and crime
Seem to excel,
Virtue will quell
Vice in the run
Ere the play's done.

> Dresses grotesque, etc.

Fairy in white,
Pretty and bright;
Helping the prince,
Bids him evince
Plenty of pluck,
Sure to have luck!
Comes (with the lime)
Always in time;
Just as you fear
Matters look queer,
"Bang!" on the drums
Tells you she comes,
Putting things quite
Tidy and right.
            Dresses grotesque, etc.

Story just here
Seems to appear
(Seen from the pit)
Muddled a bit.
People come in,
Quibbles begin;
People go out,
Rightly, no doubt.
Follow the plot
That I can*not*.
"Business" from France,
Singing and dance,
Quibble and pun—
That's how it's done.
            Dresses grotesque, etc.

Dresses look bright
(Seen in the light);
Music-hall song
Terribly long,
Dreary affair
As you're aware;
Then, for your sins,
Ballet begins:
Girls, rather old,
Terribly bold,
Petticoats thought
Dreadfully short,
Bony old legs
Shapeless as pegs.
            Dresses grotesque, etc.

Finishing choir,
Lots of red fire;
Curtain then falls.
Audience calls
All of the "cast";
First and the last,
Crowd on the stage
(Mode of the age);
Boxes and pits
Almost in fits.
Author comes now,
Making his bow.
Very well done,
Safe for a run;
Banish all fear,
Run for a year!
            Dresses grotesque, etc.

THE PHANTOM HEAD

There never was a face
   So suited, in its way,
A clergyman to grace,
   As Mr. Parks', M.A.

There never was a face
   (Excepting Mr. Parks')
More suited to its place,
   Than Mr. Parks's clerk's.

There never was a face
   So medically fine,
So free from metal base,
   As that of Dr. Brine.

In fact, if actors could
   Contrive to "look a part"
As perfectly, they would
   Have mastered half their art.

These worthy people three,
   They were the special pride
Of Twipton-on-the-Sea
   And all that countryside.

And strangers who might be
   In Twipton, too, would say,
"We never noticed three
   So *comme il faut* as they."

But, ah, and well-a-day!
   I fear it wasn't meant,
That with our features' play
   We should be quite content!

The clergyman would say,
   "My face is far too mild,
Suggestive in its way
   Of quite a little child."

The doctor wished for eyes
   That, eagle-like, would pierce;
The little clerk, likewise,
   He wished to look more fierce.

(We must not be severe:
   We have our failings, all;
For none are perfect here
   On this terrestrial ball.)

One night when nearly dark
   (The wind was blowing hard),
It so befell, the clerk
   Passed through the cold churchyard.

And, lo! while treading there
   The causeway of the dead,
He saw in middle-air
   A Solitary Head.

"Now this," he mused, "is strange,
   And though I may be dense,
It's quite beyond the range
   Of my experience.

"I've noticed heads before,
   Young, pretty, old, and plain;
But all, I'm nearly sure,
   Had bodies in their train."

"Clerk," said that Phantom Head,
    "Do you admire my smile?"
The clerk politely said,
    "It is my favourite style.

"Your eyes, with lightning pronged,
    Quite pierce me through and through;
For many years I've longed
    To have a head like you!"

"To-morrow evening, halt,"
    The awful Spectre said,
"At yonder handsome vault,
    And you shall have my head.

"For I, and brother two
    (You would not know our names),
Were all beheaded through
    The wicked SECOND JAMES.

"We're weary of our beds;
    Those merciless old hunks
Preserved our little heads
    But burnt our little trunks.

"('Trunks,' you'll observe, stand for
    Our bodies—now no more—
Not our portmanteaux, nor
    The breeches that we wore.)

"So, sure as eggs are eggs,
    We never shall stir out
Until we get some legs
    On which to move about.

"Go, tell your worthy friends
    That if they'll lend us theirs,
'Twill serve their private ends
    And help us from our lairs."

The doctor and the priest
    Rejoiced to hear that day
That they, good men, at least
    Might have their wilful way.

Now mark the sorry plight
    Their envy brought them to:
They sought the vault that night—
    The Head had told them true!

But though the faces there
    Looked handsome in the light,
In point of fact they were
    Unsuited to them, quite.

One handsome head each friend
    Assumed—and bore it thence;
But, ah, the fearful end!
    But, ah, the consequence!

For none would take a pew
    In MR. PARKS's church!
The Doctor's patients, too,
    Have left him in the lurch!

The humble little clerk
    Has no companions, when
He rises grim and stark
    To give his loud "Amen!"

MORAL

You'll learn this moral fit,
    That beauty, to the state
Of him who pays for it,
    Should be appropriate.

THE POLITEST OF NATIONS!

Paris fashions to puff people can't say enough,
   Its idioms, its shrugs, and its phrases—
And people who chance to have visited France
   Are eternally singing its praises.
Wherever we go, as all travellers know,
   We are met by the same observations,
We are constantly told by the young and the old
    That it's much the politest of nations,
     By far the politest of nations,
      Most courteous and civil of nations,
Though Britons we be, we are bound to agree
    That it's much the politest of nations!

Though it's true beyond doubt that they shove you about
   With an unceremonious behavement,
And ladies they meet in a narrowish street
   They will elbow right off of the pavement.
Though conduct like this, touchy men take amiss,
   As a blot on their civilisations,
Yet only think how they will chatter and bow—
    It's by chalks the politest of nations—
         By chalks the politest of nations, &c.

Though they fight with ill grace for a popular place
   At a theatre or concert or races,
Though rollicking blades sneer at blighted old maids,
   And puff bad cigars in their faces,
Though they cover with shame any elderly dame,
   Who elicits unkind observations,
How they twist and they twirl to a pretty young girl!
    It's by far the politest of nations,
         By far the politest of nations, &c.

Though the dresses they wear I'd be sorry, I swear,
   To see on my wife or my daughter—
Though they rouge themselves fair, and don't comb out their hair,
   And are n—not over partial to water—
Though untidy by day in a slipsloppy way,
   And scorning all kinds of lavations,
Yet it must be confessed that when—*when* they are dressed,
    They do look the politest of nations,
         By far the politest of nations, &c.

WOMAN'S GRATITUDE

A FACT

In underbred society
  (Which I was nurtured in),
No species of impiety
  Is reckoned such a sin—
No shocking inhumanity
  So lowly to degrade
(Alas, oh, human vanity!)—
  As being badly made.

Men, absolute iniquity
  With bandiness assess,
And physical obliquity
  With moral twistiness.
There, natural deformity
  Or curvature of bone
Is viewed as an enormity
  No penance can atone.

No atom of mortality
  Bore worthier repute
For vigourous morality,
  Than Mr. Baker Coote.
Conspicuous for charity
  And active virtue, too—
In truth a moral rarity—
  A worthy man, and true.

But, ah, my friends, unluckily
  His form was strongly warped!
He bore his sorrow pluckily
  And seldom on it harped.

At parties, girls, perchance, with him
  Would nothing have to do—
No maiden cared to dance with him,
  Much less, of course, to woo.

Too short his legs were thought to be;
  His little back, no doubt,
Was higher than it ought to be;
  His arms, at times, slipped out.
One eye adored astronomy
  And bright celestial zones,
The other (strange economy!)
  Inspected paving stones.

Misshapen though amazingly
  With inconvenient twirl,
He dared to mention praisingly
  The bowyer Wilson's girl.
Grotesque as a barbarian
  (Poor Baker Coote, I mean),
He dared to love fair Marian,
  The Beauty of Wood-Green.

Although in form inferior
  He had affections fine—
A sensitive interior
  Like yours, dear friend, or mine.
He dared to love the Beautiful,
  The Graceful, and the True,
The Sensible, the Dutiful,
  The Kind, and Well-to-do.

But she (poor COOTE in talking with,
  She banished all his claims)
Preferred to go out walking with
  A well-made person—JAMES.
Poor COOTE determined pluckily
  To stab that well-made man,
But incidents unluckily
  Occurred to baulk his plan.

So COOTE, with strange temerity,
  Would gaze on her all day,
Till JAMES, with much asperity,
  Would bid him go away.
"Don't shorten my felicity,"
  Said BAKER in a blaze,
"The cat of domesticity
  On Royalty may gaze.

"Look on yon sky's concavity,
  The sun, celestial ball,
We, spite of our depravity,
  May love and worship all!
The moon shines brightly—beamingly—
  And though I'm crook'd, it's true,
Yet I may court her, seemingly,
  Till everything is blue!"

JAMES, though adored by MARIAN,
  Was pitiably dense,
A commonplace vulgarian
  With no poetic sense.
"Now BAKER, go your ways, my boy,
  You poor, misshapen loon—
Spend, if you like, your days, my boy,
  In crying for the moon.

"Perhaps she is—you say she is—
  Unangered at your smiles,
But think how far away she is—
  Three hundred thousand miles!
Were you a gay Lunarian
  You might, I'm sure, have stared
All day at MISTRESS MARIAN
  For anything I cared!"

No man of true nobility
  Could stand such taunts and names,
Or suffer with tranquillity
  The gibes of well-made JAMES.
He used his blade unskilfully—
  With blunderbuss instead,
He aimed at JAMIE, wilfully,
  And shot that springald dead!

You would have fancied, tearfully,
  He would not sigh in vain,
Who braves the gallows cheerfully,
  His only love to gain.
Don't let such wild insanity
  Upon your thoughts intrude,
You little know the vanity
  Of female gratitude!

THE BABY'S VENGEANCE

Weary at heart and extremely ill
Was PALEY VOLLAIRE of Bromptonville,
In a dirty lodging, with fever down,
Close to the Polygon, Somers Town.

PALEY VOLLAIRE was an only son
(For why? His mother had had but one),
And PALEY herited gold and grounds
Worth several hundred thousand pounds.

But he, like many a rich young man,
Through this magnificent fortune ran,
And nothing was left for his daily needs
But duplicate copies of mortgage-deeds.

Shabby and sorry and sorely sick,
He slept, and dreamt that the clock's "tick, tick,"
Was one of the Fates, with a long sharp knife,
Snicking off bits of his shortened life.

He woke and counted the pips on the walls,
The outdoor passengers' loud footfalls,
And reckoned all over, and reckoned again,
The little white tufts on his counterpane.

A medical man to his bedside came
(I can't remember that doctor's name),
And said, "You'll die in a very short while
If you don't set sail for Madeira's isle."

"Go to Madeira? goodness me!
I haven't the money to pay your fee!"
"Then, PALEY VOLLAIRE," said the leech, "good-bye;
I'll come no more, for you're sure to die."

He sighed and he groaned and smote his breast;
"Oh, send," said he, "for FREDERICK WEST,
Ere senses fade or my eyes grow dim:
I've a terrible tale to whisper him!"

Poor was FREDERICK's lot in life,—
A dustman he with a fair young wife,
A worthy man with a hard-earned store,
A hundred and seventy pounds—or more.

FREDERICK came, and he said, "Maybe
You'll say what you happen to want with me?"
"Wronged boy," said PALEY VOLLAIRE, "I will,
But don't you fidget yourself—sit still.

THE TERRIBLE TALE

" 'Tis now some thirty-seven years ago
   Since first began the plot that I'm revealing.
A fine young woman, wed ten years or so,
   Lived with her husband down in Drum Lane, Ealing,
Herself by means of mangling reimbursing,
And now and then (at intervals) wet-nursing.

"Two little babes dwelt in her humble cot:
   One was her own—the other only lent to her:
Her own she slighted. Tempted by a lot
   Of gold and silver regularly sent to her,
She ministered unto the little other
In the capacity of foster-mother.

"*I was her own.* Oh! how I lay and sobbed
   In my poor cradle—deeply, deeply cursing
The rich man's pampered bantling, who had robbed
   My only birthright—an attentive nursing!
Sometimes, in hatred of my foster-brother,
I gnashed my gums—which terrified my mother.

"One darksome day (I should have mentioned that
    We were alike in dress and baby feature)
I *in* MY cradle having placed the brat,
    Crept into his—the pampered little creature!
It was imprudent—well, disgraceful maybe,
For, oh! I was a bad, black-hearted baby!

"So great a luxury was food, I think
    There was no wickedness I wouldn't try for it.
Now if I wanted anything to drink
    At any time, I only had to cry for it!
Once, if I dared to weep, the bottle lacking,
My blubbering involved a serious smacking!

"We grew up in the usual way—my friend,
    My foster-brother, daily growing thinner,
While gradually I began to mend,
    And thrived amazingly on double dinner.
And every one, besides my foster-mother,
Believed that either of us was the other.

"I came into his wealth—I bore his name,
    I bear it still—his property I squandered—
I mortgaged everything—and now (oh, shame!)
    Into a Somers Town shake-down I've wandered!
I am no PALEY—no VOLLAIRE—it's true, my boy!
The only rightful PALEY V. is *you,* my boy!

"And all I have is yours—and yours is mine.
    I still may place you in your true position:
Give me the pounds you've saved, and I'll resign
    My noble name, my rank, and my condition.
So for my wickedness in falsely owning
Your vasty wealth, I am at last atoning!"

· · · · · ·

FREDERICK he was a simple soul,
He pulled from his pocket a bulky roll,
And gave to PALEY his hard-earned store,
A hundred and seventy pounds or more.

PALEY VOLLAIRE, with many a groan,
Gave FREDERICK all that he'd called his own,—
Two shirts and a sock, and a vest of jean,
A Wellington boot and a bamboo cane.

And FRED (entitled to all things there)
He took the fever from MR. VOLLAIRE,
Which killed poor FREDERICK WEST. Meanwhile
VOLLAIRE sailed off to Madeira's isle.

THE TWO OGRES

Good children, list, if you're inclined,
  And wicked children too—
This pretty ballad is designed
  Especially for you.

Two ogres dwelt in Wickham Wold—
  Each *traits* distinctive had:
The younger was as good as gold,
  The elder was as bad.

A wicked, disobedient son
  Was JAMES McALPINE, and
A contrast to the elder one,
  Good APPLEBODY BLAND.

McALPINE—brutes like him are few—
  In greediness delights,
A melancholy victim to
  Unchastened appetites.

Good, well-bred children every day
  He ravenously ate,—
All boys were fish who found their way
  Into McALPINE's net:

Boys whose good breeding is innate,
  Whose sums are always right;
And boys who don't expostulate
  When sent to bed at night;

And kindly boys who never search
  The nests of birds of song;
And serious boys for whom, in church,
  No sermon is too long.

Contrast with JAMES's greedy haste
  And comprehensive hand,
The nice discriminating taste
  Of APPLEBODY BLAND.

BLAND only eats bad boys, who swear—
  Who *can* behave, but *don't*—
Disgraceful lads who say "don't care,"
  And "shan't," and "can't," and "won't."

Who wet their shoes and learn to box,
  And say what isn't true,
Who bite their nails and jam their frocks,
  And make long noses too;

Who kick a nurse's aged shin,
  And sit in sulky mopes;
And boys who twirl poor kittens in
  Distracting zoetropes.

But JAMES, when he was quite a youth,
  Had often been to school,
And though so bad, to tell the truth,
  He wasn't quite a fool.

At logic few with him could vie;
  To his peculiar sect
He could propose a fallacy
  With singular effect.

So, when his Mentors said, "Expound—
  Why eat good children—why?"
Upon his Mentors he would round
  With this absurd reply:

"I have been taught to love the good—
    The pure—the unalloyed—
And wicked boys, I've understood,
    I always should avoid.

"Why do I eat good children—why?
    Because I love them so!"
(But this was empty sophistry,
    As your Papa can show.)

Now, though the learning of his friends
    Was truly not immense,
They had a way of fitting ends
    By rule of common sense.

"Away, away!" his Mentors cried,
    "Thou uncongenial pest!
A quirk's a thing we can't abide,
    A quibble we detest!

"A fallacy in your reply
    Our intellect descries,
Although we don't pretend to spy
    Exactly where it lies.

"In misery and penal woes
    Must end a glutton's joys;
And learn how ogres punish those
    Who dare to eat good boys.

"Secured by fetter, cramp, and chain,
    And gagged securely—so—

You shall be placed in Drury Lane,
    Where only good lads go.

"Surrounded there by virtuous boys,
    You'll suffer torture wus
Than that which constantly annoys
    Disgraceful TANTALUS.

("If you would learn the woes that vex
    Poor TANTALUS, down there,
Pray borrow of Papa an ex-
    Purgated LEMPRIÈRE.)

"But as for BLAND who, as it seems,
    Eats only naughty boys,
We've planned a recompense that teems
    With gastronomic joys.

"Where wicked youths in crowds are stowed
    He shall unquestioned rule,
And have the run of Hackney Road
    Reformatory School!"

MISTER WILLIAM

Oh, listen to the tale of MISTER WILLIAM, if you please,
Whom naughty, naughty judges sent away beyond the seas.
He forged a party's will, which caused anxiety and strife,
Resulting in his getting penal servitude for life.

He was a kindly goodly man, and naturally prone,
Instead of taking others' gold, to give away his own.
But he had heard of Vice, and longed for only once to strike—
To plan *one* little wickedness—to see what it was like.

He argued with himself, and said, "A spotless man am I;
I can't be more respectable, however hard I try;
For six and thirty years I've always been as good as gold,
And now for half-an-hour I'll deal in infamy untold!

"A baby who is wicked at the early age of one,
And then reforms—and dies at thirty-six a spotless son,
Is never, never saddled with his babyhood's defect,
But earns from worthy men consideration and respect.

"So one who never revelled in discreditable tricks
Until he reached the comfortable age of thirty-six,
Is free for half-an-hour to perpetrate a deed of shame,
Without incurring permanent disgrace, or even blame.

"That babies don't commit such crimes as forgery is true,
But little sins develop, if you leave 'em to accrue;
And he who shuns all vices as successive seasons roll,
Should reap at length the benefit of so much self-control.

"The common sin of babyhood—objecting to be drest—
If you leave it to accumulate at compound interest,
For anything you know, may represent, if you're alive,
A burglary or murder at the age of thirty-five.

"Still, I wouldn't take advantage of this fact, but be content
With some pardonable folly—it's a mere experiment.
The greater the temptation to go wrong, the less the sin;
So with something that's particularly tempting I'll begin.

"I would not steal a penny, for my income's very fair—
I do not want a penny—I have pennies and to spare—
And if I stole a penny from a money-bag or till,
The sin would be enormous—the temptation being *nil.*

"But if I broke asunder all such pettifogging bounds,
And forged a party's Will for (say) Five Hundred Thousand Pounds,
With such an irresistible temptation to a haul,
Of course the sin must be infinitesimally small.

"There's WILSON who is dying—he has wealth from Stock and rent—
If I divert his riches from their natural descent,
I'm placed in a position to indulge each little whim."
So he diverted them—and they, in turn, diverted him.

Unfortunately, though, by some unpardonable flaw,
Temptation isn't recognised by Britain's Common Law;
Men found him out by some peculiarity of touch,
And WILLIAM got a "lifer," which annoyed him very much.

For ah! he never reconciled himself to life in gaol,
He fretted and he pined, and grew dispirited and pale;
He was numbered like a cabman, too, which told upon him so,
That his spirits, once so buoyant, grew uncomfortably low.

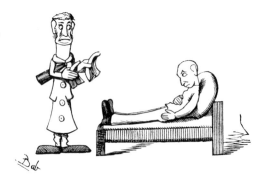

And sympathetic gaolers would remark, "It's very true,
He ain't been brought up common, like the likes of me and you."
So, they took him into hospital, and gave him mutton chops,
And chocolate, and arrowroot, and buns, and malt and hops.

Kind clergymen, besides, grew interested in his fate,
Affected by the details of his pitiable state.
They waited on the Secretary, somewhere in Whitehall,
Who said he would receive them any day they liked to call.

"Consider, sir, the hardship of this interesting case:
A prison life brings with it something very like disgrace;
It's telling on young WILLIAM, who's reduced to skin and bone—
Remember he's a gentleman, with money of his own.

"He had an ample income, and of course he stands in need
Of sherry with his dinner, and his customary weed;
No delicacies now can pass his gentlemanly lips—
He misses his sea-bathing and his continental trips.

"He says the other prisoners are commonplace and rude;
He says he cannot relish the disgusting prison food,
For when a boy they taught him to distinguish Good from Bad,
And other educational advantages he's had.

"A burglar or garroter, or, indeed, a common thief
Is very glad to batten on potatoes and on beef,
Or anything, in short, that prison kitchens can afford,—
A cut above the diet in a common workhouse ward.

"But beef and mutton-broth don't seem to suit our WILLIAM's whim,
A boon to other prisoners—a punishment to him:
It never was intended that the discipline of gaol
Should dash a convict's spirits, sir, or make him thin or pale."

"Good Gracious Me!" that sympathetic Secretary cried,
"Suppose in prison fetters MISTER WILLIAM should have died!
Dear me, of course! Imprisonment for *Life* his sentence saith:
I'm very glad you mentioned it—it might have been For Death!

"Release him with a ticket—he'll be better then, no doubt,
And tell him I apologise." So MISTER WILLIAM's out.
I hope he will be careful in his manuscripts, I'm sure,
And not begin experimentalising any more.

THE MARTINET

Some time ago, in simple verse,
   I sang the story true
Of CAPTAIN REECE, *The Mantelpiece,*
   And all her happy crew.

I showed how any captain may
   Attach his men to him,
If he but heeds their smallest needs,
   And studies every whim.

Now mark how, by Draconic rule
   And *hauteur* ill-advised,
The noblest crew upon the blue
   May be demoralised.

When his ungrateful country placed
   Kind REECE upon half-pay,
Without much claim SIR BERKELY came,
   And took command one day.

SIR BERKELY was a martinet—
   A stern unyielding soul—
Who ruled his ship by dint of whip
   And horrible black-hole.

A sailor who was overcome
   From having freely dined,
And chanced to reel when at the wheel,
   He instantly confined!

And tars who, when an action raged,
   Appeared alarmed or scared,
And those below who wished to go,
   He very seldom spared.

E'en he who smote his officer
   For punishment was booked,
And mutinies upon the seas
   He rarely overlooked.

In short, the happy *Mantelpiece*
   Where all had gone so well,
Beneath that fool SIR BERKELY's rule
   Became a floating hell.

When first SIR BERKELY came aboard
   He read a speech to all,
And told them how he'd made a vow
   To act on duty's call.

Then WILLIAM LEE, he up and said
   (The captain's coxwain he):
"We've heard the speech your honour's made,
   And werry pleased we be.

"We won't pretend, my lad, as how
   We're glad to lose our REECE;
Urbane, polite, he suited quite
   The saucy *Mantelpiece.*

"But if your honour gives your mind
    To study all our ways,
With dance and song we'll jog along
    As in those happy days.

"I like your honour's looks, and feel
    You're worthy of your sword.
Your hand, my lad—I'm doosid glad
    To welcome you aboard!"

SIR BERKELY looked amazed, as though
    He did not understand.
"Don't shake your head," good WILLIAM said,
    "It is an honest hand.

"It's grasped a better hand than yourn—
    Come, gov'nor, I insist!"
The Captain stared—the coxwain glared—
    The hand became a fist!

"Down, upstart!" said the hardy salt;
    But BERKELY dodged his aim,
And made him go in chains below:
    The seamen murmured "Shame!"

He stopped all songs at 12 P.M.,
    Stopped hornpipes when at sea,
And swore his cot (or bunk) should not
    Be used by aught than he.

He never joined their daily mess,
    Nor asked them to his own,
But chaffed in gay and social way
    The officers alone.

His First Lieutenant, PETER, was
    As useless as could be,
A helpless stick, and always sick
    When there was any sea.

This First Lieutenant proved to be
    His foster-sister MAY,
Who went to sea for love of he,
    In masculine array.

And when he learnt the curious fact,
    Did he emotion show,
Or dry her tears, or end her fears
    By marrying her? No!

Or did he even try to soothe
    This maiden in her teens?
Oh no!—instead he made her wed
    The Sergeant of Marines!

Of course such Spartan discipline
    Would make an angel fret.
They drew a lot, and straightway shot
    This fearful martinet.

The Admiralty saw how ill
    They'd treated CAPTAIN REECE;
He was restored once more aboard
    The saucy *Mantelpiece.*

THE KING OF CANOODLE-DUM

The story of Frederick Gowler,
  A mariner of the sea,
Who quitted his ship, *The Howler,*
  A-sailing in Caribbee.
For many a day he wandered,
  Till he met, in a state of rum,
Calamity Pop Von Peppermint Drop,
  The King of Canoodle-Dum.

That monarch addressed him gaily,
  "Hum! Golly de do to-day?
Hum! Lily-white Buckra Sailee"—
  (You notice his playful way?)—
"What dickens you doin' here, sar?
  Why debbil you want to come?
Hum! Picaninnee, dere isn't no sea
  In City Canoodle-Dum!"

And Gowler he answered sadly,
  "Oh, mine is a doleful tale!
They've treated me werry badly
  In Lunnon, from where I hail.
I'm one of the Family Royal—
  No common Jack Tar you see;
I'm William the Fourth, far up in the North,
  A King in my own countree!"

Bang-bang! How the tom-toms thundered!
  Bang-bang! How they thumped the gongs!
Bang-bang! How the people wondered!
  Bang-bang! At it, hammer and tongs!
Alliance with Kings of Europe
  Is an honour Canoodlers seek;
Her monarchs don't stop with Peppermint Drop
  Every day in the week!

Fred told them that he was undone,
  For his people all went insane,
And fired the Tower of London,
  And Grinnidge's Naval Fane.
And some of them racked St. James's,
  And vented their rage upon
The Church of St. Paul, the Fishmongers' Hall,
  And the "Angel" at Islington.

Calamity Pop implored him
  At Canoodle-Dum to remain
Till those people of his restored him
  To power and rank again.
Calamity Pop he made him
  A Prince of Canoodle-Dum,
With a couple of caves, some beautiful slaves,
  And the run of the royal rum.

Pop gave him his only daughter,
   HUM PICKETY WIMPLE TIP:
FRED vowed that if over the water
   He went, in an English ship,
He'd make her his Queen,—though truly,
   It is an unusual thing
For a Caribbee brat who's as black as your hat
   To be wife of an English King.

And all the Canoodle-Dummers
   They copied his rolling walk,
His method of draining rummers,
   His emblematical talk.
For his dress and his graceful breeding,
   His delicate taste in rum,
And his nautical way, were the talk of the day
   In the Court of Canoodle-Dum.

CALAMITY POP most wisely
   Determined in everything
To model his Court precisely
   On that of the English King;
And ordered that every lady
   And every lady's lord
Should masticate jacky (a kind of tobaccy)
   And scatter its juice abroad.

They signified wonder roundly
   At any astounding yarn,
By darning their dear eyes roundly
   ('Twas all that they had to darn).
They "hoisted their slacks," adjusting
   Garments of plantain-leaves
With nautical twitches (as if they wore—stitches,
   Instead of a dress like EVE's!)

They shivered their timbers proudly,
   At a phantom fore-lock dragged,
And called for a hornpipe loudly
   Whenever amusement flagged.
"Hum! Golly! him POP resemble,
   Him Britisher sov'reign, hum!
CALAMITY POP VON PEPPERMINT DROP,
   De King of Canoodle-Dum!"

The mariner's lively "Hollo!"
   Enlivened Canoodle's plain
(For blessings unnumbered follow
   In Civilisation's train).
But Fortune, who loves a bathos,
   A terrible ending planned,
For ADMIRAL D. CHICKABIDDY, C.B.,
   Placed foot on Canoodle land!

That officer seized KING GOWLER,
   He threatened his royal brains,
And put him aboard *The Howler*,
   And fastened him down with chains.
The Howler she weighed her anchor,
   With FREDERICK nicely nailed,
And off to the North with WILLIAM THE FOURTH
   That Admiral slowly sailed.

CALAMITY said (with folly)
   "Hum! nebber want him again—
Him civilise all of us, golly!
   CALAMITY suck him brain!"
The people, however, were pained when
   They saw him aboard the ship,
But none of them wept for their FREDDY, except
   HUM PICKETY WIMPLE TIP.

FIRST LOVE

A clergyman in Berkshire dwelt,
    The Reverend Bernard Powles,
And in his church there weekly knelt
    At least a hundred souls.

There little Ellen you might see,
    The modest rustic belle;
In maidenly simplicity,
    She loved her Bernard well.

Though Ellen wore a plain silk gown
    Untrimmed with lace or fur,
Yet not a husband in the town
    But wished his wife like her.

Though sterner memories might fade,
    You never could forget
The child-form of that baby-maid,
    The Village Violet!

A simple frightened loveliness,
    Whose sacred spirit-part
Shrank timidly from worldly stress,
    And nestled in your heart.

Powles woo'd with every well-worn plan
    And all the usual wiles
With which a well-schooled gentleman
    A simple heart beguiles.

The hackneyed compliments that bore
    World-folks like you and me,
Appeared to her as if they wore
    The crown of Poesy.

His winking eyelid sang a song
    Her heart could understand,
Eternity seemed scarce too long
    When Bernard squeezed her hand.

He ordered down the martial crew
    Of Godfrey's Grenadiers,
And Coote conspired with Tinney to
    Ecstaticise her ears.

Beneath her window, veiled from eye,
    They nightly took their stand;
On birthdays supplemented by
    The Covent Garden band.

And little Ellen, all alone,
    Enraptured sat above,
And thought how blest she was to own
    The wealth of Powles's love.

I often, often wonder what
    Poor Ellen saw in him;
For calculated he was *not*
    To please a woman's whim.

He wasn't good, despite the air
    An M.B. waistcoat gives;
Indeed, his dearest friends declare
    No greater humbug lives.

No kind of virtue decked this priest,
    He'd nothing to allure;
He wasn't handsome in the least,—
    He wasn't even poor.

No—he was cursed with acres fat
    (A Christian's direst ban),
And gold—yet, notwithstanding that,
    Poor ELLEN loved the man.

As unlike BERNARD as could be
    Was poor old AARON WOOD
(Disgraceful BERNARD's curate he):
    He was extremely good.

A BAYARD in his moral pluck
    Without reproach or fear,
A quiet venerable duck
    With fifty pounds a year.

No fault had he—no fad, except
    A tendency to strum,
In mode at which you would have wept,
    A dull harmonium.

He had no gold with which to hire
    The minstrels who could best
Convey a notion of the fire
    That raged within his breast.

And so, when COOTE and TINNEY's Own
    Had tootled all they knew,
And when the Guards, completely blown,
    Exhaustedly withdrew,

And NELL began to sleepy feel,
    Poor AARON then would come,
And underneath her window wheel
    His plain harmonium.

He woke her every morn at two,
    And having gained her ear,
In vivid colours AARON drew
    The sluggard's grim career.

He warbled Apiarian praise,
    And taught her in his chant
To shun the dog's pugnacious ways,
    And imitate the ant.

Still NELL seemed not, how much he played,
    To love him out and out,
Although the admirable maid
    Respected him, no doubt.

She told him of her early vow,
    And said as BERNARD's wife
It might be hers to show him how
    To rectify his life.

"You are so pure, so kind, so true,
    Your goodness shines so bright,
What use would ELLEN be to you?
    Believe me, you're all right."

She wished him happiness and health,
    And flew on lightning wings
To BERNARD with his dangerous wealth
    And all the woes it brings.

THE HAUGHTY ACTOR

An actor—GIBBS, of Drury Lane—
    Of very decent station,
Once happened in a part to gain
    Excessive approbation;
It sometimes turns a fellow's brain
And makes him singularly vain
When he believes that he receives
    Tremendous approbation.

His great success half drove him mad,
    But no one seemed to mind him;
Well, in another piece he had
    Another part assigned him.
This part was smaller, by a bit,
Than that in which he made a hit.
So, much ill-used, he straight refused
    To play the part assigned him.

*   *   *   *   *   *

That night that actor slept, and I'll attempt
To tell you of the vivid dream he dreamt:

In fighting with a robber band
   (A thing he loved sincerely)
A sword struck GIBBS upon the hand
   And wounded it severely.
At first he didn't heed it much,
He thought it was a simple touch,
But soon he found the weapon's bound
   Had wounded him severely.

To Surgeon COBB he made a trip,
   Who'd just effected featly
An amputation at the hip
   Particularly neatly.
A rising man was Surgeon COBB,
But this extremely ticklish job
He had achieved (as he believed)
   Particularly neatly.

The actor rang the surgeon's bell.
   "Observe my wounded finger;
Be good enough to strap it well,
   And prithee do not linger,
That I, dear sir, may fill again
The Theatre Royal, Drury Lane:
This very night I have to fight—
   So prithee do not linger."

"I don't strap fingers up for doles,"
   Replied the haughty surgeon;
"To use your cant, I don't play *rôles*
   'Utility' that verge on.
'First amputation'—nothing less—
That is my line of business:
We surgeon nobs despise all jobs
   Utility that verge on.

"When in your hip there lurks disease"
   (So dreamt this lively dreamer),
"Or devastating *caries*
   In *humerus* or *femur*,
If you can pay a handsome fee,
Oh, then you may remember me,
With joy elate I'll amputate
   Your *humerus* or *femur*."

The disconcerted actor ceased
   The haughty leech to pester,
But when the wound in size increased,
   And then began to fester,
He sought a learned Counsel's lair,
And told that Counsel, then and there,
How COBB's neglect of his defect
   Had made his finger fester.

"Oh, bring my action, if you please,
   The case I pray you urge on,
And win me thumping damages
   From COBB, that haughty surgeon.
He culpably neglected me
Although I proffered him his fee,
So pray come down, in wig and gown,
   On COBB, that haughty surgeon!"

That Counsel, learned in the laws,
　　With passion almost trembled,
He just had gained a mighty cause
　　Before the Peers assembled!
Said he, "How dare you have the face
To come with Common Jury case
To one who wings rhetoric flings
　　Before the Peers assembled?"

Dispirited became our friend—
　　Depressed his moral pecker—
"But stay! a thought! I'll gain my end,
　　And save my poor exchequer.
I won't be placed upon the shelf,
I'll take it into Court myself,
And legal lore display before
　　The Court of the Exchequer."

He found a Baron—one of those
　　Who with our laws supply us—
In wig and silken gown and hose,
　　As if at *Nisi Prius.*
But he'd just given, off the reel,
A famous judgment on Appeal:
It scarce became his heightened fame
　　To sit at *Nisi Prius.*

Our friend began, with easy wit,
　　That half concealed his terror:
"Pooh!" said the Judge, "I only sit
　　In *Banco* or in Error.
Can you suppose, my man, that I'd
O'er *Nisi Prius* Courts preside,
Or condescend my time to spend
　　On anything but Error?"

"Too bad," said GIBBS, "my case to shirk!
　　You must be bad innately,
To save your skill for mighty work
　　Because it's valued greatly!"
But here he woke, with sudden start.

*　*　*　*　*　*

He wrote to say he'd play the part.
I've but to tell he played it well—
　　The author's words—his native wit
Combined, achieved a perfect "hit"—
　　The papers praised him greatly.

242

THE TWO MAJORS

An excellent soldier who's worthy the name,
  Loves officers dashing and strict:
When good, he's content with escaping all blame,
  When naughty, he likes to be licked.

He likes for a fault to be bullied and stormed,
  Or imprisoned for several days;
And hates, for a duty correctly performed,
  To be slavered with sickening praise.

No officer sickened with praises his *corps*
  So little as Major La Guerre—
No officer swore at his warriors more
  Than Major Makredi Prepere.

Their soldiers adored them, and every grade
  Delighted to hear their abuse;
Though whenever these officers came on parade,
  They shivered and shook in their shoes.

For, oh! if La Guerre could all praises withhold,
  Why, so could Makredi Prepere,
And, oh! if Makredi could bluster and scold,
  Why, so could the mighty La Guerre.

"No doubt we deserve it—no mercy we crave—
  Go on—you're conferring a boon;
We would rather be slanged by a warrior brave
  Than praised by a wretched poltroon!"

Makredi would say that in battle's fierce rage
  True happiness only was met:
Poor Major Makredi, though fifty his age,
  Had never known happiness yet!

La Guerre would declare, "With the blood of a foe
    No tipple is worthy to clink."
Poor fellow! he hadn't, though sixty or so,
    Yet tasted his favourite drink!

They agreed at their mess—they agreed in the glass—
    They agreed in the choice of their "set,"
And they also agreed in adoring, alas!
    The Vivandière, pretty Fillette.

Agreement, we know, may be carried too far,
    And after agreeing all round
For years—in this soldierly "maid of the bar,"
    A bone of contention they found.

It may seem improper to call such a pet—
    By a metaphor, even—a bone;
But though they agreed in adoring her, yet
    Each wanted to make her his own.

"On the day that you marry her," muttered Prepere
    (With a pistol he quietly played),
"I'll scatter the brains in your noddle, I swear,
    All over the stony parade!"

"I cannot do *that* to you," answered La Guerre,
    "Whatever events may befall;
But this *I can* do—if you wed her, *mon cher!*
    I'll eat you, moustachios and all!"

The rivals, although they would never engage,
    Yet quarrelled whenever they met;
They met in a fury and left in a rage,
    But neither took pretty Fillette.

"I am not afraid," thought MAKREDI PREPERE:
    "For my country I'm ready to fall;
But nobody wants, for a mere Vivandière,
    To be eaten, moustachios and all!

"Besides, though LA GUERRE has his faults, I'll allow
    He's one of the bravest of men:
My goodness! If I disagree with him now,
    I might disagree with him then!"

"No coward am I," said LA GUERRE, "as you guess—
    I sneer at an enemy's blade;
But I don't want PREPERE to get into a mess
    For splashing the stony parade!"

One day on parade to PREPERE and LA GUERRE
    Came CORPORAL JACOT DEBETTE,
And, trembling all over, he prayed of them there
    To give him the pretty FILLETTE.

"You see, I am willing to marry my bride
    Until you've arranged this affair;
I will blow out my brains when your honours decide
    Which marries the sweet Vivandière!"

"Well, take her," said both of them in a duet
    (A favourite form of reply),
"But when I am ready to marry FILLETTE,
    Remember you've promised to die!"

He married her then: from the flowery plains
    Of existence the roses they cull:
He lived and he died with his wife; and his brains
    Are reposing in peace in his skull.

THE THREE BOHEMIAN ONES

A worthy man in every way
Was MR. JASPER PORKLEBAY:
He was a merchant of renown
(The firm was PORKLEBAY AND BROWN).

Three sons he had—and only three—
But they were bad as bad could be;
They spurned their father's righteous ways,
And went to races, balls, and plays.

On Sundays they would laugh and joke,
I've heard them bet—I've known them smoke.
At Whist they'd sometimes take a hand.
These vices JASPER couldn't stand.

At length the eldest son, called DAN,
Became a stock tragedian,
And earned his bread by ranting through
Shakespearian parts, as others do.

The second (DONALD) would insist
On starting as a journalist,
And wrote amusing tales and scenes
In all the monthly magazines.

The youngest (SINGLETON his name)
A comic artist he became,
And made an income fairly good
By drawing funny heads on wood.

And as they trod these fearful ways
(Those three misguided PORKLEBAYS),
They drew not on their father's hoard—
For JASPER threw them overboard.

Yes, JASPER—grieving at their fall—
Renounced them one—renounced them all;
And lived alone, so good and wise,
At Zion Villa, Clapham Rise.

By dint of work and skilful plan
Our JASPER grew a wealthy man;
And people said, in slangy form,
That JASPER P. would "cut up warm."

He had no relative at all
To whom his property could fall,
Except, of course, his wicked sons,
Those three depraved Bohemian ones!

So he determined he would fain
Bequeath his wealth (despite Mortmain),
Freeholds, debenture stock, and all,
To some deserving hospital.

When his intent was known abroad,
Excitement reigned in every ward;
And with the well-experienced throng
Of operators, all went wrong.

St. George's, Charing Cross, and Guy's,
And little Westminster likewise,
And Lying-In, and Middlesex,
Combined old JASPER to perplex.

House-surgeons, spite of patients' hints,
Bound headaches up in fracture-splints;
In measles, strapped the spots that come,
With strips of plain diachylum.

Rare leeches, skilled at fever beds,
For toothache shaved their patients' heads;
And always cut their fingers off
If they complained of whooping cough.

Their zeal grew greater day by day,
And each did all that with him lay
To prove his own pet hospital
The most deserving of them all.

Though JASPER P. could not but feel
Delighted at this show of zeal,
When each in zeal excels the rest,
One can't determine which is best.

Interea, his reckless boys
Indulged in low Bohemian joys;
They sometimes smoked till all was blue,
And danced at evening parties, too.

The hospitals, conflicting sore,
Perplexed poor JASPER more and more,
But, ah! ere JASPER could decide,
Poor charitable man, he died!

And DONALD, SINGLETON, and DAN,
Now roll in wealth, despite his plan;
So DONALD, DAN, and SINGLETON,
By dint of accident have won.

Vice triumphs here, but, if you please,
'Tis by exceptions such as these
(From probability removed)
That every standing rule is proved.

By strange exceptions Virtue deigns
To prove how paramount she reigns;
A standing rule I do not know
That's been more oft established so.

THE POLICEMAN'S BEARD

Go search throughout the human kind,
I'll undertake you will not find
A kinder, softer-hearted boy
Than gentle-eyed POLICEMAN JOY.

He sickened at the sight of sin,
And sought a hallowed refuge in
That haven of unruffled peace,
The Metropolitan Police.

"Here," thought the gentle-minded lad,
"Protected from examples bad,
And far removed from worldly strife,
I'll pass a calm monastic life.

"For wicked men, with nimble feet,
Avoid the good policeman's beat;
And miscreants of every kind
Disperse like chaff before the wind.

"My beat shall serve me, as, I'm told,
Grey cloisters served the monks of old—
A spot convenient, where, at ease,
To ruminate on vanities.

"'Twill be, on all material scores,
A monastery out-of-doors,
With (here it beats monastic shades)
A good supply of servant maids."

Nor did his hopes betray the boy—
His life was one unruffled joy.
He breathed, at government's expense,
An atmosphere of innocence.

Vice fled before him day by day,
While Virtue often "asked the way";
Or beg he'd kindly leave his beat
To help her cross a crowded street.

Where'er he went 'twas just the same;
Whene'er he whistled, Virtue came;
And Virtue always found him near,
When she was sent to fetch the beer.

For Virtue said, "That gentle eye
Could never compass villainy.
A DON GIOVANNI none could trace
In that fair smooth angelic face!"

And Virtue guessed the simple truth,
He *was* a good and harmless youth,
As simple-hearted as he looked;
His "inside places" Truth had booked.

But, ah, alas! as time rolled on,
LIEUTENANT COLONEL HENDERSON
This order to policemen gave,
"All Constables must Cease to Shave!"

The order soon was noised about,
The prisoned beards broke madly out.
And sacred from the morning knife,
They revelled in a new-found life.

Moustachios, freed from scissor clips,
Poured madly over upper lips;
Or curled themselves in either eye—
They breathed the breath of Liberty!

How fared it with our gentle boy,
That tender lad, POLICEMAN JOY,
Whose eye recalls the mild gazelle?
Alas! with him it fared not well.

That peaceful chin—those chubby cheeks,
That mouth that smiles but rarely speaks,
Now wear by Hendersonian law,
The fiercest beard you ever saw!

It spoke of blood—it spoke of bones,
It spoke of yells and midnight groans;
Of death in lonely robber-cribs,
Of poignards stuck between the ribs!

And Virtue, timid fluttering maid,
Shrank from her gentle boy afraid;
And took him for—I know not what,
At all events she knew him not.

Attracted by no whistled air,
Shy shrinking Virtue took good care
To see the boy was nowhere near,
When she was sent to fetch the beer.

And Vice, that used to run away,
Would now take heart of grace, and say,
"A beard that twirls and tangles thus
Must appertain to one of us!"

He brushed it often—combed it through,
He oiled it and he soaped it, too;
But useless 'twas such means to try,
It curled again when it was dry.

Well, Virtue sadly gave him up,
Vice proffered him her poisoned cup,
And thus good, kind POLICEMAN JOY,
Became a lost, abandoned boy!

THE BISHOP OF RUM-TI-FOO AGAIN

I often wonder whether you
Think sometimes of that Bishop, who
From black but balmy Rum-ti-Foo
    Last summer twelvemonth came.
Unto your mind I p'raps may bring
Remembrance of the man I sing
To-day, by simply mentioning
    That Peter was his name.

Remember how that holy man
Came with the great Colonial clan
To Synod, called Pan-Anglican;
    And kindly recollect
How, having crossed the ocean wide,
To please his flock all means he tried
Consistent with a proper pride
    And manly self-respect.

He only, of the reverend pack
Who minister to Christians black,
Brought any useful knowledge back
    To his Colonial fold.
In consequence a place I claim
For "Peter" on the scroll of Fame
(For Peter was that Bishop's name,
    As I've already told).

He carried Art, he often said,
To places where that timid maid
(Save by Colonial Bishops' aid)
    Could never hope to roam.
The Payne-cum-Lauri feat he taught
As he had learnt it; for he thought
The choicest fruits of Progress ought
    To bless the Negro's home.

And he had other work to do,
For, while he tossed upon the blue,
The islanders of Rum-ti-Foo
    Forgot their kindly friend.
Their decent clothes they learnt to tear—
They learnt to say, "I do not care,"
Though they, of course, were well aware
    How folks, who say so, end.

Some sailors whom he did not know,
Had landed there not long ago,
And taught them "Bother!" also, "Blow!"
    (Of wickedness the germs.)
No need to use a casuist's pen
To prove that they were merchantmen;
No sailor of the Royal N.
    Would use such awful terms.

And so, when Bishop PETER came
(That was the kindly Bishop's name),
He heard these dreadful oaths with shame,
    And chid their want of dress.
(Except a shell—a bangle rare—
A feather here—a feather there—
The South Pacific Negroes wear
    Their native nothingness.)

He taught them that a Bishop loathes
To listen to unseemly oaths,
He gave them all his left-off clothes—
    They bent them to his will.
The Bishop's gift spreads quickly round;
In PETER's left-off clothes they bound
(His three-and-twenty suits they found
    In fair condition still).

The Bishop's eyes with water fill,
Quite overjoyed to find them still
Obedient to his sovereign will,
    And said, "Good Rum-ti-Foo!

Half-way I'll meet you, I declare:
I'll dress myself in cowries rare,
And fasten feathers in my hair,
    And dance the 'Cutch-chi-boo!'"

And to conciliate his see
He married PICCADILLILLEE,
The youngest of his twenty-three,
    Tall—neither fat nor thin.
(And though the dress he made her don
Looks awkwardly a girl upon,
It was a great improvement on
    The one he found her in.)

The Bishop in his gay canoe
(His wife, of course, went with him too),
To some adjacent island flew,
    To spend his honeymoon.
Some day in sunny Rum-ti-Foo
A little PETER'll be on view;
And that (if people tell me true)
    Is like to happen soon.

A WORM WILL TURN

I love a man who'll smile and joke
   When with misfortune crowned;
Who'll pun beneath a pauper's yoke,
And as he breaks his daily toke,
   Conundrums gay propound.

Just such a man was BERNARD JUPP,
   He scoffed at Fortune's frown;
He gaily drained his bitter cup—
Though Fortune often threw him up,
   It never cast him down.

Though years their share of sorrow bring,
   We know that far above
All other griefs, are griefs that spring
From some misfortune happening
   To those we really love.

E'en sorrow for another's woe
   Our BERNARD failed to quell;
Though by this special form of blow
No person ever suffered so,
   Or bore his grief so well.

His father, wealthy and well clad,
   And owning house and park,
Lost every halfpenny he had,
And then became (extremely sad!)
   A poor attorney's clerk.

All sons it surely would appal,
   Except the passing meek,
To see a father lose his all,
And from an independence fall
   To one pound ten a week!

But JUPP shook off this sorrow's weight,
   And, like a Christian son,
Proved Poverty a happy fate—
Proved Wealth to be a devil's bait,
   To lure poor sinners on.

With other sorrows BERNARD coped,
   For sorrows came in packs;
His cousins with their housemaids sloped—
His uncles forged—his aunts eloped—
   His sisters married blacks.

But BERNARD, far from murmuring
   (Exemplar, friends to us),
Determined to his faith to cling,—
He made the best of everything,
   And argued softly thus:

" 'Twere harsh my uncles' forging knack
   Too rudely to condemn—
My aunts, repentant, may come back,
And blacks are nothing like as black
   As people colour them!"

Still Fate, with many a sorrow rife,
　Maintained relentless fight:
His grandmamma next lost her life,
Then died the mother of his wife,
　But still he seemed all right.

His brother fond (the only link
　To life that bound him now)
One morning, overcome by drink,
He broke his leg (the right, I think)
　In some disgraceful row.

But did my BERNARD swear and curse?
　Oh no—to murmur loth,
He only said, "Go, get a nurse:
Be thankful that it isn't worse;
　You might have broken both!"

But worms who watch without concern
　The cockchafer on thorns,
Or beetles smashed, themselves will turn
If, walking through the slippery fern,
　You tread upon their corns.

And if when all the mischief's done
　You watch their dying squirms,
And listen, ere their breath has run,
You'll hear them sigh, "Oh, clumsy one!"
　—And devil blame the worms.

One night as BERNARD made his track
　Through Brompton home to bed,
A footpad, with a vizor black,
Took watch and purse, and dealt a crack
　On BERNARD's saint-like head.

It was too much—his spirit rose,
　He looked extremely cross.
Men thought him steeled to mortal foes,
But no—he bowed to countless blows,
　But kicked against this loss.

He finally made up his mind
　Upon his friends to call;
Subscription lists were largely signed,
For men were really glad to find
　Him mortal, after all!

THE MYSTIC SELVAGEE

Perhaps already you may know
SIR BLENNERHASSET PORTICO?
A Captain in the Navy, he—
A Baronet and K.C.B.
        You do? I thought so!
It was that captain's favourite whim
(A notion not confined to him)
That RODNEY was the greatest tar
Who ever wielded capstan-bar.
        He had been taught so.

"BENBOW? CORNWALLIS? HOOD?—Belay!
Compared with RODNEY"—he would say—
"No other tar is worth a rap;
The great LORD RODNEY was the chap
        The French to polish!
Though, mind you, I respect LORD HOOD;
CORNWALLIS, too, was rather good;
BENBOW could enemies repel;
LORD NELSON, too, was pretty well—
        That is, tol-lol-ish!"

SIR BLENNERHASSET spent his days
In learning RODNEY's little ways,
And closely imitated, too,
His mode of talking to his crew—
        His port and paces.
An ancient tar he tried to catch
Who'd served in RODNEY's famous batch;
But since his time long years have fled,
And RODNEY's tars are mostly dead:
        Eheu fugaces!

But after searching near and far,
At last he found an ancient tar
Who served with RODNEY and his crew
Against the French in 'eighty-two
        (That gained the peerage).
He gave him fifty pounds a year,
His rum, his baccy, and his beer;
And had a comfortable den
Rigged up in what, by merchantmen,
        Is called the steerage.

"Now, JASPER"—'twas that sailor's name—
"Don't fear that you'll incur my blame
By saying, when it seems to you,
That there is anything I do
        That RODNEY wouldn't."
The ancient sailor turned his quid,
Prepared to do as he was bid:
"Ay, ay, yer honour; to begin,
You've done away with 'swifting in'—
        Well, sir, you shouldn't!

"Upon your spars I see you've clapped
Peak-halliard blocks, all iron-capped;
I would not christen that a crime,
But 'twas not done in RODNEY's time.
        It looks half-witted!
Upon your maintop-stay, I see,
You always clap a selvagee;
Your stays, I see, are equalised—
No vessel, such as RODNEY prized,
        Would thus be fitted.

"And RODNEY, honoured sir, would grin
To see you turning deadeyes in,
Not *up,* as in the ancient way,
But downwards, like a cutter's stay—
        You didn't oughter!
Besides, in seizing shrouds on board,
Breast backstays you have quite ignored;
Great RODNEY kept unto the last
Breast backstays on topgallant mast—
        They make it tauter."

SIR BLENNERHASSET "swifted in,"
Turned deadeyes up, and lent a fin
To strip (as told by JASPER KNOX)
The iron capping from his blocks,
        Where there was any.
SIR BLENNERHASSET does away
With selvagees from maintop-stay;
And though it makes his sailors stare,
He rigs breast backstays everywhere—
        In fact, too many.

One morning, when the saucy craft
Lay calmed, old JASPER toddled aft.
"My mind misgives me, sir, that we
Were wrong about that selvagee—
        I should restore it."
"Good," said the captain, and that day
Restored it to the maintop-stay.
Well-practised sailors often make
A much more serious mistake,
        And then ignore it.

Next day old JASPER came once more:
"I think, sir, I was right before."
Well, up the mast the sailors skipped,
The selvagee was soon unshipped,
        And all were merry.
Again a day, and JASPER came:
"I p'raps deserve your honour's blame,
I can't make up my mind," said he,
"About that cursed selvagee—
        It's foolish—very.

"On Monday night I could have sworn
That maintop-stay it should adorn,
On Tuesday morning I could swear
That selvagee should not be there.
        The knot's a rasper!"
"Oh, you be hanged!" said CAPTAIN P.,
"Here, go ashore at Caribbee.
Get out—good-bye—shove off—all right!"
Old JASPER soon was out of sight—
        Farewell, old JASPER!

EMILY, JOHN, JAMES, AND I

A DERBY LEGEND

Emily Jane was a nursery maid—
  James was a bold Life Guard,
And John was a constable, poorly paid
  (And I am a doggerel bard).

A very good girl was Emily Jane,
  Jimmy was good and true,
And John was a very good man in the main
  (And I am a good man, too).

Rivals for Emmie were Johnny and James,
  Though Emily liked them both;
She couldn't tell which had the strongest claims
  (And *I* couldn't take my oath).

But sooner or later you're certain to find
  Your sentiments can't lie hid—
Jane thought it was time that she made up her mind
  (And I think it was time she did).

Said Jane, with a smirk, and a blush on her face,
  "I'll promise to wed the boy
Who takes me to-morrow to Epsom Race!"
  (Which *I* would have done, with joy.)

From Johnny escaped an expression of pain,
  But Jimmy said, "Done with you!
I'll take you with pleasure, my Emily Jane!"
  (And I would have said so too.)

John lay on the ground, and he roared like mad
  (For Johnny was sore perplexed),
And he kicked very hard at a very small lad
  (Which *I* often do, when vexed).

For JOHN was on duty next day with the Force,
   To punish all Epsom crimes;
Some people *will* cross, when they're clearing the course
   (I do it myself, sometimes).

*   *   *   *   *   *

The Derby Day sun glittered gaily on cads,
   On maidens with gamboge hair,
On sharpers and pickpockets, swindlers and pads
   (For I, with my harp, was there).

And JIMMY went down with his JANE that day,
   And JOHN by the collar or nape
Seized everybody who came in his way
   (And *I* had a narrow escape).

He noticed his EMILY JANE with JIM,
   And envied the well-made elf;
And people remarked that he muttered "Oh, dim!"
   (I often say "dim!" myself.)

JOHN dogged them all day, without asking their leaves;
   For his sergeant he told, aside,
That JIMMY and JANE were notorious thieves
   (And I think he was justified).

But JAMES wouldn't dream of abstracting a fork,
   And JENNY would blush with shame
At stealing so much as a bottle or cork
   (A bottle I think fair game).

But, ah! there's another more serious crime!
   They wickedly strayed upon
The course, at a critical moment of time
   (I pointed them out to JOHN).

The crusher came down on the pair in a crack—
   And then, with a demon smile,
Let JENNY cross over, but sent JIMMY back
   (I played on my harp the while).

Stern JOHNNY their agony loud derides
   With a very triumphant sneer—
They weep and they wail from the opposite sides
   (And *I* shed a silent tear).

And Jenny is crying away like mad,
    And Jimmy is swearing hard;
And Johnny is looking uncommonly glad
    (And I am a doggerel bard).

But Jimmy he ventured on crossing again
    The scenes of our Isthmian Games—
John caught him, and collared him, giving him pain
    (I felt very much for James).

John led him away with a victor's hand,
    And Jimmy was shortly seen
In the station-house under the grand Grand Stand
    (As many a time *I've* been).

And Jimmy, bad boy, was imprisoned for life,
    Though Emily pleaded hard;
And Johnny had Emily Jane to wife
    (And I am a doggerel bard).

THE GHOST TO HIS LADYE LOVE

Fair Phantom, come! The moon's awake,
The owl hoots gaily from its brake,
    The blithesome bat's a-wing.
Come, soar to yonder silent clouds;
The ether teems with peopled shrouds:
We'll fly the lightsome spectre crowds,
    Thou cloudy, clammy thing!

Though there are others, spectre mine,
With eyes as hollow, quite, as thine,
    That thrill me from above—
Whose lips are quite as deathly pale,
Whose voices rival thine in wail
When, riding on the joyous gale,
    They breathe sepulchral love.

Still, there's a modest charm in thee,
That causes thee to seem to be
    More pure than others are—
Though rich in calico and bone,
Thou art not beautiful alone—
For thou art also *good*, my own!
    And that is better, far.

United, we'll defy alarms:
A death-time in each other's arms
    We'll pass—and fear no dearth
Of jollity: when Morpheus flits
O'er mortal eyes, we'll whet our wits,
And frighten people into fits
    Who did us harm on earth!

Come, essence of a slumb'ring soul,
Throw off thy maidenly control
    Un-shroud thy ghastly face!
Give me thy foggy lips divine,
And let me press my mist to thine,
And fold thy nothingness in mine,
    In one long damp embrace.
                   [*She does.*

PRINCE IL BALEINE

When Autumn boat and train
  Bore London folk to pleasure,
The good PRINCE IL BALEINE
He sought, across the main,
  Amusement for his leisure.

A dusty time, and long,
  He'd had at balls and races,
At crowded levée throng,
At Play and Concert song,
  And various other places.

But, ah! the British Snob
  Besieged that Prince, in plenty:
The Snob adores a Nob,
And follows him, to rob
  His *dolce far niente!*

And finding that the Prince
  Much eagerness to know them
Did not at once evince,
They did not matters mince,
  But begged himself he'd show them.

"Our wishes do not baulk,
  Throw off this English shyness—
And show us how you walk,
And let us hear you talk,
  Now do, your Royal Highness!

"You're too reserved, by half:
  Begin perambulating;
We've paid to see you laugh—
We've paid to hear you chaff
  Four gentlemen in waiting.

"Come sit and eat an ice,
  Or drain a bumping measure;
We've practised much device,
And paid a heavy price,
  To see you take your leisure."

[It grieved that PRINCE BALEINE—
  Most sensitive of fishes—
It always gives him pain
When people can't obtain
  The fulness of their wishes.

But doctors grave had said,
  "Hang up your stick and beaver;
You *must* have rest and shade,
Or you will soon be laid
  Upon your back with fever."]

No morning when he woke
  But British Snobs addressed him;
His peace of mind they broke,
So up he rose, and spoke
  These words to those who pressed him.

"Oh, over-loyal throng,
    Be guided, pray, by reason:
You may encore a song
(Though that, I think, is wrong),
    But not a London Season!

"I'm told to lie me down
    And rest me at my leisure;
But here's my valet, BROWN,
He's not much worked in town,
    He'll take my place with pleasure!

"I am his special care;
    He brushes, combs, and laves me,
He parts my chestnut hair—
He folds the coats I wear—
    And strops the blade that shaves me.

"He knows my little ways
    And, though it's not expected,
He'll watch my Royal blaze,
Yet, basking in my rays,
    He'll shine with light reflected."

"Oh, my!" the people cried,
    "To MISTER BROWN I'll bow me!
Oh, ain't he dignified,
Yet not a spark of pride!
    Oh, MISTER BROWN, allow me!

"And so you wash the Prince,
    And pack his clothes for starting,
You scent with jasmine leaf
His pocket-handkerchief,
    And regulate his parting!

"And that, I understand,
    Is your department, is it?
And this then is the hand
That combs at his command?
    Oh, please, do let me kiss it!

"Is this (oh treat of treats!)
    The bedroom that you sleep in?
When cloyed with Royal sweets,
Are these the very sheets
    Which every night you creep in?

"And in this bath you tub,
    Ere out of doors you sally?
And do these flesh gloves scrub—
These dainty towels rub—
    The Prince's happy *valet?*"

The Snobs, with joy insane,
    Kotoo'd to BROWN, unseemly;
And BROWN does not complain,
While good PRINCE IL BALEINE
    Enjoys his rest extremely.

THE WAY OF WOOING

A maiden sat at her window wide,
Pretty enough for a prince's bride,
　　Yet nobody came to claim her.
She sat like a beautiful picture there,
With pretty bluebells and roses fair,
　　And jasmine leaves to frame her.
And why she sat there nobody knows;
But thus she sang as she plucked a rose,
　　The leaves around her strewing:
"I've time to lose and power to choose;
'Tis not so much the gallant who woos
　　As the gallant's way of wooing!"

A lover came riding by awhile,
A wealthy lover was he, whose smile
　　Some maids would value greatly—
A formal lover, who bowed and bent,
With many a high-flown compliment,
　　And cold demeanour stately.
"You've still," said she to her suitor stern,
"The 'prentice-work of your craft to learn,
　　If thus you come a-cooing.
I've time to lose and power to choose;
'Tis not so much the gallant who woos
　　As the gallant's way of wooing!"

A second lover came ambling by—
A timid lad with a frightened eye
   And a colour mantling highly.
He muttered the errand on which he'd come,
Then only chuckled and bit his thumb,
   And simpered, simpered shyly.
"No," said the maiden, "go your way,
You dare but think what a man would say,
   Yet dare to come a-suing!
I've time to lose and power to choose;
'Tis not so much the gallant who woos
   As the gallant's way of wooing!"

A third rode up at a startling pace—
A suitor poor, with a homely face—
   No doubts appeared to bind him.
He kissed her lips and he pressed her waist,
And off he rode with the maiden, placed
   On a pillion safe behind him.
And she heard the suitor bold confide
This golden hint to the priest who tied
   The knot there's no undoing:
"With pretty young maidens who can choose,
'Tis not so much the gallant who woos
   As the gallant's way of wooing!"

THE SCORNFUL COLONEL

Once, going round his daily beats
In Stamboul's uninviting streets,
He heard these words, in accents clear,
"Oh, Little Stranger, welcome here!"

The Colonel stopped—he had no choice,
For, ah! it was a WOMAN's voice!
And through a window dark and grim
Two EYES flashed, lightning-like, on him.

Though not, as common rumour says,
Remarkable in other ways,
No haughty, supercilious swell
Could scorn so well as COLONEL BELL.

At sight of snobs his lip would curl—
His lip would quiver, twist, and twirl
In an astonishing degree—
He often curled his lip at me.

His men, to give them all their due,
Were most accomplished sneerers, too:
Their Colonel gave them, with a will,
Six daily hours of sneering drill.

"Now, by your right, prepare to 'Whish'!
Come, all at once and smartly, 'Pish'!
Prepare to 'Bah'! By sections, 'Phew'!
Good! At three hundred yards, 'Pooh-pooh'!"

And though (as I can prove too well)
They could not sneer like COLONEL BELL,
Still, not to flatter them a jot,
They were a supercilious lot.

Some two-and-thirty years ago
He sailed to fight the Paynim foe,
For then a dreadful war began
'Tween England and the Ottoman.

Such eyes! So soft—so full of soul!
Such silent pathos in their roll!
No deadlier weapon women wield:
Au reste, her face was quite concealed.

"Oh, sir," the vision whispered, "though
You're certainly our country's foe,
Let's hail the emblematic dove
As subjects of One Monarch—Love!"

"Oh, ma'am," he said—I will not stay
To tell you all he chose to say;
But all the workings of his brain
Were in the same impassioned strain.

"Oh, sir," the eyes replied, "I fear
You dare not penetrate up here—
I'm no mere drab in humble life,
I *was* the Sultan's favourite wife!"

"Oh, *ma'am*!!!" said he—suffice to add,
The gallant Colonel, rapture-mad,
This graceful sentiment displays
In fifty-seven different ways.

He sought the Hareem's portals wide,
He sneered the sentinel aside,
And when his scornful eyeballs flashed,
The very guard fell back abashed!

On cloth of gold in *negligé*,
The Sultan's former fancy lay;
He saw that once (in early life)
She *might* have been his favourite wife.

ZARLINE (her name) with one big bound,
Threw COLONEL BELL her arms around,
And danced her best, but truth to tell,
She was a creaky, old gazelle.

The Colonel gazed—then turned away;
Love *fled*, and Duty held its sway:
That sterner stuff that, near and far,
Makes British warriors what they are.

"Why BELL, my boy, come, come, what's this?
Unmanned by thoughts of simple bliss?
Unsoldiered by a lovely girl?"
The warrior's lip resumed its curl.

But ah, too late. The Sultan's ears
Much sharpened by his jealous fears,
Had overheard, behind a screen,
The creakiness of fair ZARLINE!

The Colonel soon was seized and bound;
He struggled not, but looked around,
Relying on the wide-spread fear
Instilled by his notorious sneer.

But ah! the move was ill-designed;
The Sultan he was old and blind,
And all the Hareem's soldiers then
Were elderly, short-sighted men!

Those soldiers soon contrived to pack
The gallant Colonel in a sack;
But, mindful of his scornful fame,
LIEUTENANT-COLONEL BELL died game.

The Bosphorus, with gloomy roll,
Closed mournfully upon his soul;
Its billows sang the only knell
That mourned LIEUTENANT-COLONEL BELL!

THE VARIABLE BABY

There never was a man
  Who studied more minutely
His very simplest plan
  Than JEREMIAH STUTELY.

The smallest of his schemes
  (As I've already stated),
And all his wildest dreams,
  Were equally debated.

But, ah! of all the host
  Of social cons that harry,
This con perplexed him most:
  "Shall I do well to marry?"

For A. espoused a wife
  Young, lovely, and with money,
And people thought their life
  Would be one moon of honey.

But, ah, before a year
  O'er life's rough road they'd jolted,
With some disgraceful peer
  Good MRS. A. had bolted.

While B., whose wife is plain,
  Poor, cross, and half-demented,
Seems always, in the main,
  Exceedingly contented.

But there is C., his joy,—
  (His wife, a year united,
Has given him a boy,
  And C. is quite delighted).

And STUTELY sees his pride,
  And thinks it pleasant, rather,
(And also dignified)
  To be a baby's father.

"But, ah!" thinks he, "perhaps
  This baby, full of graces,
May prove the worst of chaps,
  And have the worst of faces!

"To-day's bright source of joy
  May joyless be to-morrow,
And this much-cherished boy
  May bring his parents sorrow!

"I'll see how he turns out,
  His parents' care rewarding,
A Crichton or a lout,
  And I'll be ruled according.

"If Baby turns out well,
  I certainly will marry—
If Baby proves a sell,
  A bachelor I'll tarry!"

Now, Baby's good as gold,
　With cheeks as red as roses,
And STUTELY (rather old)
　To some fair maid proposes:

Now, Baby's cross and cries,
　And won't let Nursey clean it;
And STUTELY seeks his prize,
　And says he didn't mean it.

Well, Baby, fat and bluff,
　And first-rate health enjoying—
Is sometimes good enough,
　And sometimes most annoying.

And S., with puzzled fate,
　Immediate marriage throws up,
And thinks he'd better wait
　And see how Baby grows up.

When Baby grows a lad,
　No rule of conduct stops him;
And when extremely bad,
　His father comes and whops him.

And STUTELY says with joy,
　"I'm glad I thought of stopping;
I couldn't whop a boy,
　And boys want lots of whopping!"

When Baby grows a man,
　He takes to serious teaching;
And later on, began
　A course of highway preaching.

And STUTELY cries, "Well done!
　A credit to his mother!
That's something like a son—
　I wish I'd such another!"

And Instinct whispers, "Mate!
　You're wasting time, you gaby!"
But Prudence whispers, "Wait!
　And see what comes of Baby!"

And Prudence gains the day,
　For Baby takes to orgies:
He seeks the sinner's way,
　And finally he forges.

And Baby, for his crime,
　Is numbered, shaved, and sorted,
And to a penal clime
　Is carefully transported.

And STUTELY shakes his head,
　And says he's glad he tarried;
And STUTELY's still unwed,
　And means to die unmarried.

THE LADIES OF THE LEA

There was flutter in the bosoms of the Ladies of the Lea,
When occurred a change of curates in their village by the sea;
For appointed to a living was the old BARTHOLOMEW,
And coming down to take his place, was JAMES, the curate new!

BARTHOLOMEW was reverend, but elderly and stout,
And—a martyr to lumbago—he could scarcely get about;
But JAMES DE VYSE was young and fair, and comfortably off,
With the gentlest indication of a sweet comsumptive cough.

His linen would have suited ALBERT EDWARD PRINCE OF WALES,
He was properly particular about his fingernails.
His legs were straight as arrows (as the picture of him shows),
His feet were little toddlekins, with tiddy-iddy toes.

Though anything but foppish, he was careful in his dress,
His trousers were perfection, his boots were nothing less.
I think he wore the smallest gloves of any man alive
(His hand was barely seven, and his fingers only five).

'Twas no unseemly vanity, but admiration meet,
Of Nature's skill as shown in abstract, hands, and legs, and feet.
He loved them for they proved that Nature only can combine,
Simplicity of outline with perfection of design.

It sprung from abstract reverence for Nature's Wondrous Touch:
Any feature in the Kosmos he'd have reverenced as much,
If any other feature had appeared to him as neat
As his pretty little legs, and little hands, and little feet.

And JESSIE, JANE, and MARGARET, the Ladies of the Lea,
When they heard that JAMES DE VYSE their future curate was to be,
Resolved to do whatever well-intentioned girls should do,
To atone for having slighted poor old fat BARTHOLOMEW.

Then JESSIE (little JESSIE!) thought, "How heedless have I been
Of all religious duties, and in charity how mean!
I will mortify the body with fatiguing exercise,
I will work a pair of slippers for the REVEREND DE VYSE."

And JENNY, who for many months her parish work had shirked,
Exclaimed, "How have I slumbered, while devouter people worked!
Of penances and pains it's fit that I should suffer some,
I'll embroider pretty braces for the curate that's to come!"

And Maggie said, "Oh, sluggish one!" (alluding to herself)
"How long shall works of piety lie idle on the shelf?
Lest Reverend De Vyse should think my toil a hollow form,
I will knit a pair of gloves to keep his jack-a-dandies warm!"

But Jessie, who at needlework was rivalled once by few,
Had grown quite out of practise during old Bartholomew:
And when the High Church slippers were delivered to De Vyse,
They were very well intended but preposterous in size.

And Jenny, who for old Bartholomew had never toiled,
Found her schemes for decorating young De Vyse were nearly foiled;
Want of practical experience with braces sent her wrong.
It was very kind of Jane, but they were very much too long.

And Maggie's want of practise told upon her efforts, too;
She had never knitted anything for old Bartholomew.
The gloves were kindly meant, but they were clumsy as could be.
Poor Maggie did her best—but they were big enough for me!

And did De Vyse reject these gifts because misfitting? No.
He wore them conscientiously, determining to show
That curates should endeavour (though with awkward presents curst)
To conciliate parishioners—at all events at first.

And Jessie, Jane, and Margaret, the Ladies of the Lea,
Were eager all their presents on the curate for to see;
So they clambered up his garden wall, in three successive lifts,
And there was James a-gardening in all his little gifts.

But the slippers, very roomy, made his feet appear a size
That caused both JANE and MARGARET unqualified surprise.
And the gloves that MAGGIE knitted in her leisure, I declare,
Were more like boxing gloves than those that curates ought to wear.

And the braces, though he triced them up as short as they could go,
Left his trousers very baggy—anything but *comme il faut;*
They might have been suspended on a pair of wooden pegs,
So completely did they muffle all the drawing of his legs.

And JESSIE (who had laboured at the slippers on his feet)
Said, "His trotters, I allow you, are particularly neat,
But such coarse ungainly hands possess no interest for me,
And his legs are just as clumsy as a pair of legs can be!"

Then JENNY (who had made the pretty braces for him) spoke,
"I do *not* believe his legs deserve the comments they provoke;
But I quite agree his hands are very awful in their way,
And his feet! oh goodness gracious, what monstrosities are they!"

And MAGGIE (who had knitted the unhappy pair of gloves)
Said, "His hands too big? Oh, nonsense! Why, his hands are perfect loves!
But I quite agree with JENNY that his feet would suit a boor,
And I quite agree with JESSIE that his legs are very poor."

So JESSIE, JANE, and MARGARET, the Ladies of the Lea,
Were satisfied that JAMES was as ungainly as could be;
They never quite recovered from their disappointment sore,
So they all became Dissenters, and he never saw them more!

MORAL

Young ladies, if you wish to marry curates, *don't refuse*
To work at gloves and slippers, e'en for old BARTHOLOMEWS;
Or your hands will lose their cunning, and you'll disappointed be,
Like JESSIE, JANE, and MARGARET, the Ladies of the Lea.

HONGREE AND MAHRY

A Richardsonian Melodrama

The sun was setting in its wonted west,
When Hongree, Sub-Lieutenant of Chassoores,
Met Mahry Daubigny, the Village Rose,
Under the Wizard's Oak—old trysting-place
Of those who loved in rosy Aquitaine.

They thought themselves unwatched, but they were not;
For Hongree, Sub-Lieutenant of Chassoores,
Found in Lieutenant-Colonel Jooles Dubosc
A rival, envious and unscrupulous,
Who thought it not foul scorn to dog his steps,
And listen, unperceived, to all that passed
Between the simple little Village Rose
And Hongree, Sub-Lieutenant of Chassoores.

A clumsy barrack-bully was Dubosc,
Quite unfamiliar with the well-bred tact
That actuates a proper gentleman
In dealing with a girl of humble rank.
You'll understand his coarseness when I say
He would have married Mahry Daubigny,
And dragged the unsophisticated girl
Into the whirl of fashionable life,
For which her singularly rustic ways,
Her breeding (moral, but extremely rude),
Her language (chaste, but ungrammatical),
Would absolutely have unfitted her.
No such intention lurked within the breast
Of Hongree, Sub-Lieutenant of Chassoores!

Contemporary with the incident
Related in our opening paragraph,
Was that sad war 'twixt Gallia and ourselves
That followed on the treaty signed at Troyes;
And so Lieutenant-Colonel Jooles Dubosc
(Brave soldier, he, with all his faults of style)
And Hongree, Sub-Lieutenant of Chassoores,
Were sent by Charles of France against the lines
Of our Sixth Henry (Fourteen twenty-nine),
To drive his legions out of Aquitaine.

When HONGREE, Sub-Lieutenant of Chassoores,
Returned (suspecting nothing) to his camp,
After his meeting with the Village Rose,
He found inside his barrack letter-box
A note from the commanding-officer,
Requiring his attendance at headquarters.

He went, and found LIEUTENANT-COLONEL JOOLES.
"Young HONGREE, Sub-Lieutenant of Chassoores,
This night we shall attack the English camp:
Be the 'forlorn hope' yours—you'll lead it, sir,
And lead it too with credit, I've no doubt"
(These last words with a cruelly obvious sneer).
"As every soul must certainly be killed
(For you are twenty 'gainst two thousand men),
It is not likely that you will return;
But what of that? you'll have the benefit
Of knowing that you die a soldier's death."

Obedience was young HONGREE's strongest point,
But he imagined that he only owed
Allegiance to his MAHRY and his King.
"If MAHRY bade me lead these fated men,
I'd lead them—but I do not think she would.
If CHARLES, my King, said, 'Go, my son, and die,'
I'd go, of course—my duty would be clear.
But MAHRY is in bed asleep (I hope),
And CHARLES, my King, a hundred leagues from this.
As for LIEUTENANT-COLONEL JOOLES DUBOSC,
How know I that our monarch would approve
The order he has given me to-night?
My King I've sworn in all things to obey—
I'll only take my orders from my King!"
Thus HONGREE, Sub-Lieutenant of Chassoores
Interpreted the terms of his commission.

And HONGREE, who was wise as he was good,
Disguised himself that night in ample cloak,
Round flapping hat, and visor mask of black,
And made, unnoticed, for the English camp.
He passed the unsuspecting sentinels
(Who little thought a man in this disguise
Could be a proper object of suspicion),
And ere the curfew-bell had boomed "lights out,"
He found in audience Bedford's haughty Duke.

"Your Grace," he said, "start not—be not alarmed,
Although a Frenchman stands before your eyes.
I'm HONGREE, Sub-Lieutenant of Chassoores.
My colonel will attack your camp to-night,
And orders me to lead the hope forlorn.
Now I am sure our excellent KING CHARLES
Would not approve of this; but he's away
A hundred leagues, and rather more than that.
So, utterly devoted to my King,
Blinded by my attachment to the throne,
And having but its interest at heart,
I feel it is my duty to disclose
All schemes that emanate from COLONEL JOOLES,
If I believe that they are not the kind
Of schemes that our good monarch could approve."

"But how," said Bedford's Duke, "do you propose
That we should overthrow your colonel's scheme?"
And HONGREE, Sub-Lieutenant of Chassoores,
Replied at once with never-failing tact:
"Oh, sir, I know this cursed country well.
Entrust yourself and all your host to me;
I'll lead you safely by a secret path
Into the heart of COLONEL JOOLES' array,
And you can then attack them unprepared,
And slay my fellow-countrymen unarmed."

The thing was done. The DUKE OF BEDFORD gave
The order, and two thousand fighting-men
Crept silently into the Gallic camp,
And killed the Frenchmen as they lay asleep;
And Bedford's haughty Duke slew COLONEL JOOLES,
And married MAHRY, pride of Aquitaine,
To HONGREE, Sub-Lieutenant of Chassoores.

ETIQUETTE

The Ballyshannon foundered off the coast of Cariboo,
And down in fathoms many went the captain and the crew;
Down went the owners—greedy men whom hope of gain allured:
Oh, dry the starting tear, for they were heavily insured.

Besides the captain and the mate, the owners and the crew,
The passengers were also drowned, excepting only two:
Young PETER GRAY, who tasted teas for BAKER, CROOP, AND CO.,
And SOMERS, who from Eastern shores imported indigo.

These passengers, by reason of their clinging to a mast,
Upon a desert island were eventually cast.
They hunted for their meals, as ALEXANDER SELKIRK used,
But they couldn't chat together—they had not been introduced.

For PETER GRAY, and SOMERS too, though certainly in trade,
Were properly particular about the friends they made;
And somehow thus they settled it without a word of mouth—
That GRAY should take the northern half, while SOMERS took the south.

On PETER's portion oysters grew—a delicacy rare,
But oysters were a delicacy PETER couldn't bear.
On SOMERS' side was turtle, on the shingle lying thick,
Which SOMERS couldn't eat, because it always made him sick.

GRAY gnashed his teeth with envy as he saw a mighty store
Of turtle unmolested on his fellow-creature's shore:
The oysters at his feet aside impatiently he shoved,
For turtle and his mother were the only things he loved.

And SOMERS sighed in sorrow as he settled in the south,
For the thought of PETER's oysters brought the water to his mouth.
He longed to lay him down upon the shelly bed, and stuff:
He had often eaten oysters, but had never had enough.

How they wished an introduction to each other they had had
When on board *The Ballyshannon!* And it drove them nearly mad
To think how very friendly with each other they might get,
If it wasn't for the arbitrary rule of etiquette!

One day, when out a-hunting for the *mus ridiculus,*
GRAY overheard his fellow-man soliloquising thus:
"I wonder how the playmates of my youth are getting on,
McCONNELL, S. B. WALTERS, PADDY BYLES, and ROBINSON?"

These simple words made PETER as delighted as could be,
Old chummies at the Charterhouse were ROBINSON and he!
He walked straight up to SOMERS, then he turned extremely red,
Hesitated, hummed and hawed a bit, then cleared his throat, and said:

"I beg your pardon—pray forgive me if I seem too bold,
But you have breathed a name I knew familiarly of old.
You spoke aloud of ROBINSON—I happened to be by—
You know him?" "Yes, extremely well." "Allow me—so do I!"

It was enough: they felt they could more sociably get on,
For (ah, the magic of the fact!) they each knew ROBINSON!
And MR. SOMERS' turtle was at PETER's service quite,
And MR. SOMERS punished PETER's oyster-beds all night.

They soon became like brothers from community of wrongs:
They wrote each other little odes and sang each other songs;
They told each other anecdotes disparaging their wives;
On several occasions, too, they saved each other's lives.

They felt quite melancholy when they parted for the night,
And got up in the morning soon as ever it was light;
Each other's pleasant company they reckoned so upon,
And all because it happened that they both knew ROBINSON!

They lived for many years on that inhospitable shore,
And day by day they learned to love each other more and more.
At last, to their astonishment, on getting up one day,
They saw a vessel anchored in the offing of the bay!

To PETER an idea occurred. "Suppose we cross the main?
So good an opportunity may not occur again."
And SOMERS thought a minute, then ejaculated, "Done!
I wonder how my business in the City's getting on?"

"But stay," said MR. PETER: "when in England, as you know,
I earned a living tasting teas for BAKER, CROOP, AND CO.,
I may be superseded—my employers think me dead!"
"Then come with me," said SOMERS, "and taste indigo instead."

But all their plans were scattered in a moment when they found
The vessel was a convict ship from Portland, outward bound!
When a boat came off to fetch them, though they felt it very kind,
To go on board they firmly but respectfully declined.

As both the happy settlers roared with laughter at the joke,
They recognised an unattractive fellow pulling stroke:
'Twas ROBINSON—a convict, in an unbecoming frock!
Condemned to seven years for misappropriating stock!!!

They laughed no more, for SOMERS thought he had been rather rash
In knowing one whose friend had misappropriated cash;
And PETER thought a foolish tack he must have gone upon
In making the acquaintance of a friend of ROBINSON.

At first they didn't quarrel very openly, I've heard;
They nodded when they met, and now and then exchanged a word:
The word grew rare, and rarer still the nodding of the head,
And when they meet each other now, they cut each other dead.

To allocate the island they agreed by word of mouth,
And PETER takes the north again, and SOMERS takes the south;
And PETER has the oysters, which he loathes with horror grim,
And SOMERS has the turtle—turtle disagrees with him.

THE REVEREND SIMON MAGUS

A rich advowson, highly prized,
For private sale was advertised;
And many a parson made a bid;
The REVEREND SIMON MAGUS did.

He sought the agent's: "Agent, I
Have come prepared at once to buy
(If your demand is not too big)
The Cure of Otium-cum-Digge."

"Ah!" said the agent, "*there's* a berth—
The snuggest vicarage on earth;
No sort of duty (so I hear),
And fifteen hundred pounds a year!

"If on the price we should agree,
The living soon will vacant be:
The good incumbent's ninety-five,
And cannot very long survive.

"See—here's his photograph—you see,
He's in his dotage." "Ah, dear me!
Poor soul!" said SIMON. "His decease
Would be a merciful release!"

The agent laughed—the agent blinked—
The agent blew his nose and winked—
And poked the parson's ribs in play—
It was that agent's vulgar way.

The REVEREND SIMON frowned: "I grieve
This light demeanour to perceive;
It's scarcely *comme il faut,* I think:
Now—pray oblige me—do not wink.

"Don't dig my waistcoat into holes—
Your mission is to sell the souls
Of human sheep and human kids
To that divine who highest bids.

"Do well in this, and on your head
Unnumbered honours will be shed."
The agent said, "Well, truth to tell,
I *have* been doing pretty well."

"You should," said SIMON, "at your age;
But now about the parsonage.
How many rooms does it contain?
Show me the photograph again.

"A poor apostle's humble house
Must not be too luxurious;
No stately halls with oaken floor—
It should be decent and no more.

"No billiard-rooms—no stately trees—
No croquêt-grounds or pineries."
"Ah!" sighed the agent, "very true:
This property won't do for you.

"All these about the house you'll find"—
"Well," said the parson, "never mind;
I'll manage to submit to these
Luxurious superfluities.

"A clergyman who does not shirk
The various calls of Christian work,
Will have no leisure to employ
These 'common forms' of worldly joy.

"To preach three times on Sabbath days—
To wean the lost from wicked ways—
The sick to soothe—the sane to wed—
The poor to feed with meat and bread;

"These are the various wholesome ways
In which I'll spend my nights and days:
My zeal will have no time to cool
At croquêt, archery, or pool."

The agent said, "From what I hear,
This living will not suit, I fear—
There are no poor, no sick at all;
For services there is no call."

The reverend gent looked grave. "Dear me!
Then there is *no* 'society'?—
I mean, of course, no sinners there
Whose souls will be my special care?"

The cunning agent shook his head,
"No, none—except"—(the agent said)—
"The Duke of A., the Earl of B.,
The Marquis C., and Viscount D.

"But you will not be quite alone,
For, though they've chaplains of their own,
Of course this noble well-bred clan
Receive the parish clergyman."

"Oh, silence, sir!" said Simon M.,
"Dukes—earls! What should I care for them?
These worldly ranks I scorn and flout!"
Of course the agent said, "No doubt."

"Yet I might show these men of birth
The hollowness of rank on earth."
The agent answered, "Very true—
But I should not, if I were you."

"Who sells this rich advowson, pray?"
The agent winked—it was his way—
"His name is Hart; 'twixt me and you,
He is, I'm griev'd to say, a Jew!"

"A Jew?" said Simon, "happy find!
I purchase this advowson, mind.
My life shall be devoted to
Converting that unhappy Jew!"

MY DREAM

The other night, from cares exempt,
I slept—and what d'you think I dreamt?
I dreamt that somehow I had come
To dwell in Topsy-Turveydom!—

Where vice is virtue—virtue, vice:
Where nice is nasty—nasty, nice:
Where right is wrong and wrong is right—
Where white is black and black is white.

Where babies, much to their surprise,
Are born astonishingly wise;
With every Science on their lips,
And Art at all their finger-tips.

For, as their nurses dandle them,
They crow binomial theorem,
With views (it seems absurd to us)
On differential calculus.

But though a babe, as I have said,
Is born with learning in his head,
He must forget it, if he can,
Before he calls himself a man.

For that which we call folly here,
Is wisdom in that favoured sphere;
The wisdom we so highly prize
Is blatant folly in their eyes.

A boy, if he would push his way,
Must learn some nonsense every day;
And cut, to carry out this view,
His wisdom teeth and wisdom too.

Historians burn their midnight oils,
Intent on giant-killers' toils;
And sages close their aged eyes
To other sages' lullabies.

Our magistrates, in duty bound,
Commit all robbers who are found;
But there the beaks (so people said)
Commit all robberies instead.

Our judges, pure and wise in tone,
Know crime from theory alone,
And glean the motives of a thief
From books and popular belief.

But there, a judge who wants to prime
His mind with true ideas of crime,
Derives them from the common sense
Of practical experience.

Policemen march all folks away
Who practise virtue every day—
Of course, I mean to say, you know,
What we call virtue here below.

For only scoundrels dare to do
What we consider just and true,
And only good men do, in fact,
What we should think a dirty act.

But strangest of these social twirls,
The girls are boys—the boys are girls!
The men are women, too—but then,
Per contra, women all are men.

To one who to tradition clings
This seems an awkward state of things,
But if to think it out you try,
It doesn't really signify.

With them, as surely as can be,
A sailor should be sick at sea,
And not a passenger may sail
Who cannot smoke right through a gale.

A soldier (save by rarest luck)
Is always shot for showing pluck—
That is, if others can be found
With pluck enough to fire a round.

"How strange," I said to one I saw,
"You quite upset our every law.
However can you get along
So systematically wrong?"

"Dear me," my mad informant said,
"Have you no eyes within your head?
You sneer when you your hat should doff:
Why, we begin where you leave off!

"Your wisest men are very far
Less learned than our babies are!"
I mused awhile—and then, oh me!
I framed this brilliant repartee:

"Although your babes are wiser far
Than our most valued sages are,
Your sages, with their toys and cots,
Are duller than our idiots!"

But this remark, I grieve to state,
Came just a little bit too late;
For as I framed it in my head,
I woke and found myself in bed.

Still I could wish that, 'stead of here,
My lot were in that favoured sphere!—
Where greatest fools bear off the bell
I ought to do extremely well.

DAMON v. PYTHIAS

Two better friends you wouldn't pass
  Throughout a summer's day,
Than DAMON and his PYTHIAS,—
  Two merchant princes they.

At school together they contrived
  All sorts of boyish larks;
And, later on, together thrived
  As merry mechants' clerks.

And then, when many years had flown,
  They rose together till
They bought a business of their own—
  And they conduct it still.

They loved each other all their lives,
  Dissent they never knew,
And, stranger still, their very wives
  Were rather friendly too.

Perhaps you think, to serve my ends,
  These statements I refute,
When I admit that these dear friends
  Were parties to a suit?

But 'twas a friendly action, for
  Good PYTHIAS, as you see,
Fought merely as executor,
  And DAMON as trustee.

They laughed to think, as through the throng
  Of suitors sad they passed,
That they, who'd lived and loved so long,
  Should go to law at last.

The junior briefs they kindly let
  Two sucking counsel hold;
These learned persons never yet
  Had fingered suitors' gold.

But though the happy suitors two
  Were friendly as could be,
Not so the junior counsel who
  Were earning maiden fee.

They too, till then, were friends. At school
  They'd done each other's sums,
And under Oxford's gentle rule
  Had been the closest chums.

But now they met with scowl and grin
  In every public place,
And often snapped their fingers in
  Each other's learned face.

It almost ended in a fight
  When they on path or stair
Met face to face. They made it quite
  A personal affair.

And Pythias, in merry mood,
   Digged Damon in the side;
And Damon, tickled with the feud,
   With other digs replied.

But oh! those deadly counsel twain,
   Who were such friends before,
Were never reconciled again—
   They quarrelled more and more.

At length it happened that they met
   On Alpine heights one day,
And thus they paid each one his debt,
   Their fury had its way—

They seized each other in a trice,
   With scorn and hatred filled,
And, falling from a precipice,
   They, both of them, were killed.

(Enthusiastically high
   Your sense of legal strife,
When it affects the sanctity
   Of your domestic life.)

And when at length the case was called
   (It came on rather late),
Spectators really were appalled
   To see their deadly hate.

One junior rose—with eyeballs tense,
   And swollen frontal veins:
To all his powers of eloquence
   He gave the fullest reins.

His argument was novel—for
   A verdict he relied
On blackening the junior
   Upon the other side.

"Oh," said the Judge, in robe and fur,
   "The matter in dispute
To arbitration pray refer—
   This is a friendly suit."

THE BUMBOAT WOMAN'S STORY

I'm old, my dears, and shrivelled with age, and work, and grief,
My eyes are gone, and my teeth have been drawn by Time, the Thief!
For terrible sights I've seen, and dangers great I've run—
I'm nearly seventy now, and my work is almost done!

Ah! I've been young in my time, and I've played the deuce with men!
I'm speaking of ten years past—I was barely sixty then:
My cheeks were mellow and soft, and my eyes were large and sweet,
POLL PINEAPPLE'S eyes were the standing toast of the Royal Fleet!

A bumboat woman was I, and I faithfully served the ships
With apples and cakes, and fowls and beer, and halfpenny dips,
And beef for the generous mess, where the officers dine at nights,
And fine fresh peppermint drops for the rollicking midshipmites.

Of all the kind commanders who anchored in Portsmouth Bay,
By far the sweetest of all was kind LIEUTENANT BELAYE.
LIEUTENANT BELAYE commanded the gunboat *Hot Cross Bun*,
She was seven and thirty feet in length, and she carried a gun.

With the laudable view of enhancing his country's naval pride,
When people inquired her size, LIEUTENANT BELAYE replied,
"Oh, my ship, my ship is the first of the Hundred and Seventy-ones!"
Which meant her tonnage, but people imagined it meant her guns.

Whenever I went on board he would beckon me down below,
"Come down, Little Buttercup, come" (for he loved to call me so),
And he'd tell of the fights at sea in which he'd taken a part,
And so LIEUTENANT BELAYE won poor POLL PINEAPPLE'S heart!

But at length his orders came, and he said one day, said he,
"I'm ordered to sail with *The Hot Cross Bun* to the German Sea."
And the Portsmouth maidens wept when they learnt the evil day,
For every Portsmouth maid loved good LIEUTENANT BELAYE.

And I went to a back back street, with plenty of cheap cheap shops,
And I bought an oilskin hat, and a second-hand suit of slops,
And I went to LIEUTENANT BELAYE (and he never suspected *me!*)
And I entered myself as a chap as wanted to go to sea.

We sailed that afternoon at the mystic hour of one,—
Remarkably nice young men were the crew of *The Hot Cross Bun.*
I'm sorry to say that I've heard that sailors sometimes swear,
But I never yet heard a *Bun* say anything wrong, I declare.

When Jack Tars meet, they meet with a "Messmate, ho! What cheer?"
But here, on *The Hot Cross Bun,* it was "How do you do, my dear?"
When Jack Tars growl, I believe they growl with a big big D—
But the strongest oath of *The Hot Cross Buns* was a mild "Dear me!"

Yet, though they were all well bred, you could scarcely call them slick:
Whenever a sea was on, they were all extremely sick;
And whenever the weather was calm, and the wind was light and fair,
They spent more time than a sailor should on his back back hair.

They certainly shivered and shook when ordered aloft to run,
And they screamed when LIEUTENANT BELAYE discharged his only gun.
And as he was proud of his gun—such pride is hardly wrong—
The Lieutenant was blazing away at intervals all day long.

They all agreed very well, though at times you heard it said
That BILL had a way of his own of making his lips look red—
That JOE looked quite his age—or somebody might declare
That BARNACLE's long pig-tail was never his own own hair.

BELAYE would admit that his men were of no great use to him,
"But then," he would say, "there is little to do on a gunboat trim.
I can hand, and reef, and steer, and fire my big gun too—
And it *is* such a treat to sail with a gentle well-bred crew."

I saw him every day! How the happy moments sped!
Reef topsails! Make all taut! There's dirty weather ahead!
(I do not mean that tempests threatened *The Hot Cross Bun:*
In *that* case, I don't know whatever we *should* have done!)

After a fortnight's cruise we put into port one day,
And off on leave for a week went kind LIEUTENANT BELAYE,
And after a long long week had passed (and it seemed like a life),
LIEUTENANT BELAYE returned to his ship with a fair young wife!

He up, and he says, says he, "Oh, crew of *The Hot Cross Bun,*
Here is the wife of my heart, for the Church has made us one!"
And as he uttered the word, the crew went out of their wits,
And all fell down in so many separate fainting fits.

And then their hair came down, or off, as the case might be,
And lo! the rest of the crew were simple girls, like me,
Who all had fled from their homes in a sailor's blue array,
To follow the shifting fate of kind LIEUTENANT BELAYE!

*   *   *   *   *   *

It's strange to think that *I* should ever have loved young men,
But I'm speaking of ten years past—I was barely sixty then;
And now my cheeks are furrowed with grief and age, I trow!
And poor POLL PINEAPPLE's eyes have lost their lustre now!

THE FAIRY CURATE

Once a fairy
Light and airy
Married with a mortal;
　Men, however,
　Never, never
Pass the fairy portal.
　Slyly stealing,
　She to Ealing
Made a daily journey;
　There she found him,
　Clients round him
(He was an attorney).

Long they tarried,
Then they married.
When the ceremony
　Once was ended,
　Off they wended
On their moon of honey.
　Twelvemonth, maybe,
　Saw a baby
(Friends performed an orgie).
　Much they prized him,
　And baptized him
By the name of GEORGIE.

GEORGIE grew up;
Then he flew up
To his fairy mother.
　Happy meeting
　Pleasant greeting—
Kissing one another.

"Choose a calling
Most enthralling,
I sincerely urge ye."
　"Mother," said he
　(Rev'rence made he),
"I would join the clergy.

"Give permission
In addition—
Pa will let me do it:
　There's a living
　In his giving,
He'll appoint me to it.
　Dreams of coff'ring
　Easter off'ring,
Tithe and rent and pew-rate,
　So inflame me
　(Do not blame me),
That I'll be a curate."

She, with pleasure,
Said, "My treasure,
'Tis my wish precisely.
　Do your duty,
　There's a beauty;
You have chosen wisely.
　Tell your father
　I would rather
As a churchman rank you.
　You, in clover,
　I'll watch over."
GEORGIE said, "Oh, thank you!"

GEORGIE scudded,
Went and studied,
Made all preparations,
And with credit
(Though he said it)
Passed examinations.
(Do not quarrel
With him, moral,
Scrupulous digestions—
But his mother,
And no other,
Answered all the questions.)

Time proceeded;
Little needed
GEORGIE admonition:
He, elated,
Vindicated
Clergyman's position.

People round him
Always found him
Plain and unpretending;
Kindly teaching,
Plainly preaching—
All his money lending.

So the fairy,
Wise and wary,
Felt no sorrow rising—
No occasion
For persuasion,
Warning, or advising.
He, resuming
Fairy pluming
(That's not English, is it?)
Oft would fly up,
To the sky up,
Pay mamma a visit.

*   *   *   *   *   *

Time progressing,
GEORGIE's blessing
Grew more Ritualistic—
Popish scandals,
Tonsures—sandals—
Genuflections mystic;
Gushing meetings—
Bosom-beatings—
Heavenly ecstatics—
Broidered spencers—
Copes and censers—
Rochets and dalmatics.

This quandary
Vexed the fairy—
Flew she down to Ealing.
"GEORGIE, stop it!
Pray you, drop it;
Hark to my appealing:
To this foolish
Papal rule-ish
Twaddle put an ending;
This a swerve is
From our Service
Plain and unpretending."

He, replying,
Answered, sighing,
Hawing, hemming, humming,
"It's a pity—
They're so pritty;
Yet in mode becoming,
Mother tender,
I'll surrender—
I'll be unaffected—"
Then his Bishop
Into *his* shop
Entered unexpected!

"Who is this, sir—
Ballet miss, sir?"
Said the Bishop coldly.
"'Tis my mother,
And no other,"
GEORGIE answered boldly.

"Go along, sir!
You are wrong, sir,
You have years in plenty;
While this hussy
(Gracious mussy!)
Isn't two-and-twenty!"

(Fairies clever
Never, never
Grow in visage older;
And the fairy,
All unwary,
Leant upon his shoulder!)
Bishop grieved him,
Disbelieved him;
GEORGE the point grew warm on;
Changed religion,
Like a pigeon,*
And became a Mormon.

*"Like a bird."

PHRENOLOGY

"Come, collar this bad man—
   Around the throat he knotted me
Till I to choke began—
   In point of fact, garroted me!"

So spake Sir Herbert White
   To James, Policeman Thirty-two—
All ruffled with his fight
   Sir Herbert was, and dirty too.

Policeman nothing said
   (Though he had much to say on it),
But from the bad man's head
   He took the cap that lay on it.

"No, great Sir Herbert White—
   Impossible to take him up.
This man is honest quite—
   Wherever did you rake him up?

"For Burglars, Thieves, and Co.,
   Indeed I'm no apologist;
But I, some years ago,
   Assisted a Phrenologist.

"Observe his various bumps,
   His head as I uncover it;
His morals lie in lumps
   All round about and over it."

"Now take him," said Sir White,
   "Or you will soon be ruing it;
Bless me! I must be right,—
   I caught the fellow doing it!"

Policeman calmly smiled,
   "Indeed you are mistaken, sir,
You're agitated—riled—
   And very badly shaken, sir.

"Sit down, and I'll explain
   My system of Phrenology,
A second, please, remain"—
   (A second is horology).

Policeman left his beat—
   (The Bart., no longer furious,
Sat down upon a seat,
   Observing, "This is curious!")

"Oh, surely here are signs
  Should soften your rigidity,
This gentleman combines
  Politeness with timidity.

"Of Shyness here's a lump—
  A hole for Animosity—
And like my fist his bump
  Of Generenerosity.

"Just here the bump appears
  Of Innocent Hilarity,
And just behind his ears
  Are Faith, and Hope, and Charity.

"He of true Christian ways
  As bright example sent us is—
This maxim he obeys,
  'Sorte tuâ contentus sis.'

"There, let him go his ways,
  He needs no stern admonishing."
The Bart., in blank amaze,
  Exclaimed, "This is astonishing!

"I *must* have made a mull,
  This matter I've been blind in it:
Examine, please, *my* skull,
  And tell me what you find in it."

Policeman looked, and said,
  With unimpaired urbanity,
"Sir Herbert, you've a head
  That teems with inhumanity.

"Here's Murder, Envy, Strife
  (Propensity to kill any),
And Lies as large as life,
  And heaps of Social Villainy:

"Here's Love of Bran New Clothes,
  Embezzling—Arson—Deism—
A taste for Slang and Oaths,
  And Fraudulent Trusteeism.

"Here's Love of Groundless Charge—
  Here's Malice, too, and Trickery,
Unusually large
  Your bump of Pocket-Pickery——"

"Stop!" said the Bart., "my cup
  Is full—I'm worse than him in all—
Policeman, take me up—
  No doubt I am some criminal!"

That Policeman's scorn grew large
  (Phrenology had nettled it),
He took that Bart. in charge—
  I don't know how they settled it.

291

THE PERILS OF INVISIBILITY

Old Peter led a wretched life—
Old Peter had a furious wife;
Old Peter, too, was truly stout,
He measured several yards about.

The little fairy Picklekin
One summer afternoon looked in,
And said, "Old Peter, how-de-do?
Can I do anything for you?

"I have three gifts—the first will give
Unbounded riches while you live;
The second, health where'er you be;
The third, invisibility."

"O, little fairy Picklekin,"
Old Peter answered, with a grin,
"To hesitate would be absurd,—
Undoubtedly I choose the third."

" 'Tis yours," the fairy said; "be quite
Invisible to mortal sight
Whene'er you please. Remember me
Most kindly, pray, to Mrs. P."

Old Mrs. Peter overheard
Wee Picklekin's concluding word,
And, jealous of her girlhood's choice,
Said, "That was some young woman's voice!"

Old Peter let her scold and swear—
Old Peter, bless him, didn't care.
"My dear, your rage is wasted quite—
Observe, I disappear from sight!"

A well-bred fairy (so I've heard)
Is always faithful to her word:
Old Peter vanished like a shot,
But then—*his suit of clothes did not.*

For when conferred the fairy slim
Invisibility on him,
She popped away on fairy wings,
Without referring to his "things."

So there remained a coat of blue,
A vest and double eyeglass too,
His tail, his shoes, his socks as well,
His pair of—no, I must not tell.

Old Mrs. Peter soon began
To see the failure of his plan,
And then resolved (I quote the bard)
To "hoist him with his own petard."

Old Peter woke next day and dressed,
Put on his coat and shoes and vest,
His shirt and stock—*but could not find
His only pair of*—never mind!

Old Peter was a decent man,
And though he twigged his lady's plan,
Yet, hearing her approaching, he
Resumed invisibility.

"Dear Mrs. P., my only joy,"
Exclaimed the horrified old boy;
"Now give them up, I beg of you—
You know what I'm referring to!"

But no; the cross old lady swore
She'd keep his—what I said before—
To make him publicly absurd;
And Mrs. Peter kept her word.

The poor old fellow had no rest;
His coat, his stock, his shoes, his vest,
Were all that now met mortal eye—
The rest, invisibility!

"Now, madam, give them up, I beg—
I've bad rheumatics in my leg;
Besides, until you do, it's plain
I cannot come to sight again!

"For though some mirth it might afford
To see my clothes without their lord,
Yet there would rise indignant oaths
If he were seen without his clothes!"

But no; resolved to have her quiz,
The lady held her own—and his—
And Peter left his humble cot
To find a pair of—you know what.

But—here's the worst of this affair—
Whene'er he came across a pair
Already placed for him to don,
He was too stout to get them on!

So he resolved at once to train,
And walked and walked with all his main;
For years he paced this mortal earth,
To bring himself to decent girth.

At night, when all around is still,
You'll find him pounding up a hill;
And shrieking peasants whom he meets,
Fall down in terror on the peats!

Old Peter walks through wind and rain,
Resolved to train, and train, and train,
Until he weighs twelve stone or so—
And when he does, I'll let you know.

THE WISE POLICEMAN

No Don Giovanni, sparrow-brained,
  Policeman ARTHUR KERR:
A steady, subtle, self-contained,
  Experienced officer.

So deep his schemes, to many a muff
  They seemed disgraceful quite;
But if you left him long enough,
  They always turned out right.

Now here's a case in point. One night
  He gallantly addressed
A good plain cook, who met his sight
  In Piccadilly, West.

"Oh, good plain cook, I like your heyes,
  They speak of health and truth—
They're bright and they are blue, likewise!"
  (Which was, indeed, the truth.)

"Why roam you forth alone so late?
  It's nearly half-past ten—
Why leave the silver and the plate
  To bad burglarious men?"

"To some theayter," said the maid,
  "The family have flown,
And I began to feel afraid
  At being left alone!"

The wise policeman did not chaff
  The maiden's idle fear,
But dried with his official staff
  An unofficial tear.

"Be mine the task to set that right!
  It were indeed foul scorn
To leave a maid alone at night,
  Defenceless and forlorn!

"Be mine, young EMMA, to instil
  The confidence you lack;
Be mine to comfort you, until
  The family comes back!"

With gratitude the maiden smiled,
  The door she let him through,
An hour or two away they wiled
  With joyous Irish stew.

A family I never knew
   That gadded so about—
To dinner and to playhouse, too,
   They every night went out;

And every night poor EMMA, she
   Shed lonely frightened tears,
And every night wise ARTHUR, he
   Came in to calm her fears.

For many a week and month, I know,
   She let wise ARTHUR through,
And fed him daintily below
   On joyous Irish stew.

At first I own I used to blame
   Policeman ARTHUR KERR,
But then I did not know the game
   Of that wise officer.

One night when, comfortably hived,
   He sat alone with EM,
Her mistress unannounced arrived,
   And there confronted them.

"Now, ma'am," said ARTHUR KERR, "to you
   This gal I do denounce,
On maids who steal the Irish stew
   The law at last will pounce!

"I long have thought she gave away
   Her kind employers' food,
And to detect her wicked play,
   This servant maid I woo'd.

"For many a week and month likewise
   I come down here to eat,
And only wanted witness eyes
   To make my case complete!

"The p'liceman's unsupported word
   The beaks begin to doubt;
But wot you've seen and wot you've heard
   Will bear my statement out."

They took young EMMA off to jail,
   To MR. KNOX, amain,
And nothing in the shape of bail
   That beak would entertain.

That beak he fully did commit
   The maid for stealing food
(What "fully" means in legal writ
   I never understood).

She got twelve months, the wretched drudge,
   While wise Policeman KERR
Was complimented by the Judge:
   Experienced officer!

He was promoted in the force
   For spotting that young gal
(The picture showing this, of course,
   Is allegorical).

A DROP OF PANTOMIME WATER

While "total abstainers,"
  By spirit forswearing,
Believe themselves gainers
  In dignified bearing,
In health and in morals,
In freedom from quarrels,
In conjugal duty,
In personal beauty,
In money to go on,
Clean linen, and so on—
The slaves of the "rosey"
(All pimply and nosey
From claret and burrage)
Are fain to encourage
That mystic high-stepper,
Professor von Pepper,
To show (by the proxy
Of hydrogen-oxy)
The horrible features
Of all the dread creatures
That foes to wine bottles
Would pour down our throttles.
Such consequence blesses
His list of successes,
That total abstainers
Become his retainers;
And often in terror,
Aghast at their error,
In spirit forswearing,
Have gone forth, declaring
They'd always drink sherry—or beer, which is humbler;
For they sensibly say,
As they hurry away,
"If you find such a crop
Of vile things in a *drop,*
Only think what you drink when you empty a tumbler!
As total abstainers exclaim at a skinful,
So I (being ordered,
And guarded, and wardered,
Advised and inducted,
And warned and instructed,

296

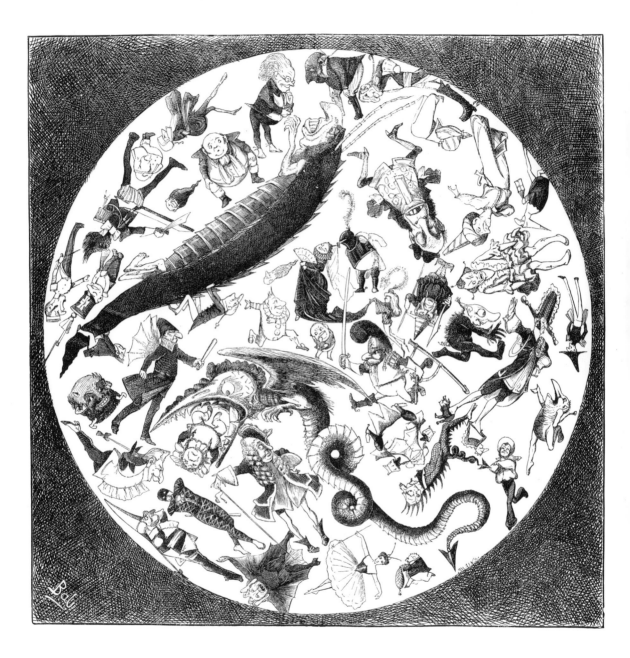

That people of quality
Shudder at jollity,
Fun, and frivolity,
Jocular polity),
  Always considered a pantomime sinful;
So having been sent
With a microscope lent
By PEPPER, Professor and Monarch of Phantom—I'm
Glad to display
In a fearful array
Little matters that may
Be detected, they say,
In a drop of real water employed in a Pantomime:
Red demons and dragons,
And barons with flagons,
And nobles and ladies,
Sultanas and cadis,
And big-headed squires,
And giants on wires,
And haughty magicians
In mystic positions,
And serpents and monkeys
And sailors and flunkeys,
And guards in a row,
With expressions that show
They're expecting a blow;
  Whose faces
  Bear traces
Of penal disgraces,
  That when
  To these men,
Our attention's directed,
By blows unexpected,
Sufficiently hard to produce an abrasion,
Their features may suit the unpleasant occasion.

OLD PAUL AND OLD TIM

When rival adorers come courting a maid,
There's something or other may often be said,
Why *he* should be pitched upon rather than *him*.
This wasn't the case with Old Paul and Old Tim.

No soul could discover a reason at all
For marrying Timothy rather than Paul;
Though all could have offered good reasons, on oath,
Against marrying either—or marrying both.

They were equally wealthy and equally old,
They were equally timid and equally bold;
They were equally tall as they stood in their shoes—
Between them, in fact, there was nothing to choose.

Had I been young Emily, I should have said,
"You're both much too old for a pretty young maid,
Threescore at the least you are verging upon";
But I wasn't young Emily. Let us get on.

No coward's blood ran in young Emily's veins,
Her martial old father loved bloody campaigns;
At the rumours of battles all over the globe
He pricked up his ears like the war-horse in "Job."

He chuckled to hear of a sudden surprise—
Of soldiers, compelled, through an enemy's spies,
Without any knapsacks or shakos to flee—
For an eminent army-contractor was he.

So when her two lovers, whose patience was tried,
Implored her between them at once to decide,
She told them she'd marry whichever might bring
Good proofs of his doing the pluckiest thing.

They both went away with a qualified joy:
That coward, Old PAUL, chose a very small boy,
And when no one was looking, in spite of his fears,
He set to work boxing that little boy's ears.

The little boy struggled and tugged at his hair,
But the lion was roused, and Old PAUL didn't care;
He smacked him, and whacked him, and boxed him, and kicked,
Till the poor little beggar was royally licked.

Old TIM knew a trick worth a dozen of that,
So he called for his stick and he called for his hat.
"I'll cover myself with cheap glory—I'll go
And wallop the Frenchmen who live in Soho!

"The German invader is ravaging France
With infantry rifle and cavalry lance,
And beautiful Paris is fighting her best
To shake herself free from her terrible guest.

"The Frenchmen in London, in craven alarms,
Have all run away from the summons to arms;
They haven't the pluck of a pigeon—I'll go
And wallop the Frenchmen who skulk in Soho!"

Old TIMOTHY tried it and found it succeed:
That day he caused many French noses to bleed;
Through foggy Soho he spread fear and dismay,
And Frenchmen all round him in agony lay.

He took care to abstain from employing his fist
On the old and the cripple, for they might resist;
A crippled old man may have pluck in his breast,
But the young and the strong ones are cowards confest.

Old TIM and Old PAUL, with the list of their foes,
Prostrated themselves at their EMILY's toes:
"Oh, which of us two is the pluckier blade?"
And EMILY answered and EMILY said:

"Old TIM has thrashed runaway Frenchmen in scores,
Who ought to be guarding their cities and shores;
Old PAUL has made little chaps' noses to bleed—
Old PAUL has accomplished the pluckier deed!"

"EHEU! FUGACES"

An old man sitting in church, and praying with all his breath.
An old man waiting alone for the life that comes of death;
As the parson tells the well-worn tale of heaven and earth:
Of the life that is only death—of the death that is only birth!

Aye, he could patter it all by heart, as a schoolboy hale;
But the old old words are telling a new and a welcome tale.
For the seal of death is set on the old man's wrinkled brow,
And words that once meant little are fraught with meaning now.

Dead in a pauper's grave, long 'ere next Christmas-day,
Here is the end at last—and it seemed so far away!
A careless wilful lad with many an idle plan—
A reckless headstrong youth—a cold indifferent man.

Much such a man as a dozen in every thirteen are;
Day in the fields at work, and night in the ale-house bar.
Nor better nor worse than others, though oftener wrong than right:
He worked with a will in the week, and he fought on Saturday night.

Yet he was often at church, where he made believe to pray,
For the rector furrowed the land for many a mile away:
And the rector's smile meant work, and a home with plenty crowned.
God help the fellow on whom that terrible rector frowned!

And often at church (for the parson proved a useful friend)
He listened perforce to the oft-told tale of the bad man's end,
With a sulky frown on his face as he shuffled a restless limb:
He was young and merry and strong—such words were never for him!

At times the turn of a hymn, or a simple Bible tale,
Chimed with the voice of his soul—a low half-stifled wail—
And roused the frivolous man to a sense of sorrow and pain;
But the long dull sermon always hardened his heart again!

The sermon's just as dull as it was in the days of yore;
But it bears a meaning now which it never possessed before:
The words are strange and long, but he knows their upshot well,
"The good will go to heaven—the wicked will go to hell!"

No scholar was he at his best, and his eyes are dim with age,
But the Book of the Earth is his, and he reads its open page;
Though rarely glanced at once, no longer idly scanned,
But there's little remains to read, for the end is close at hand.

In every silent page he finds a parable now;
In the plough that furrows the land—in the seed that follows the plough—
In the snow that covers the grass, and crackles under his tread—
In the grass that covers the mould—in the mould that covers the dead.

JESTER JAMES

In all the merry land that spreads from Humber to the Thames,
You couldn't find a jester who could rival JESTER JAMES;
His antic jokes were modelled on severely classic rules,
And all his quips passed muster at the strictest ladies' schools.

None imitated actors like this fascinating rogue;
His comic songs enjoyed a most extraordinary vogue;
And no one laughed so heartily at this engaging man
As LADY ISABEL, betrothed to HUGH DE BARBICAN.

"Now, good SIR HUGH," said ISABEL, "if fond of me you be,
Engage this merry fellow, for he hugely pleaseth me."
And good SIR HUGH DE BARBICAN engaged him, it appears,
To poke his fun at anyone for seven certain years.

For half a year, or thereabouts, he did extremely well;
His quaint remarks convulsed Sir Hugh and Lady Isabel;
And crowds dropped in each afternoon to hear his latest crank,
Including P-rson-ges of the V-ry H-ghest R-nk.

But, ah! there came a day when it was patent to Sir Hugh
That James had uttered nearly all the decent jests he knew.
He doled them out at intervals, and much impaired their strength,
By dwelling on their merits at unnecessary length.

His quips grew very feeble, and his puns fell flat and dead;
His riddles were so easy, you could do them on your head;
And though his imitations were by far the best of all,
Yet even imitations, all day long, are apt to pall.

Poor Jester James grew anxious when he found he didn't please;
And when they guessed his riddles (which they did with perfect ease)
He used to groan and weep, and beat his bosom with his fist,
Which isn't what you look for in a private humorist.

At length it got to such a pitch that thus outspake Sir Hugh:
"I fear you've undertaken rather more than you can do.
The practise of your calling seems to give you pain acute;
I'll cancel your agreement. Go to Margate, and recruit."

Said James, "A kinder offer I have never, never heard.
But a bargain is a bargain; I'm a jester of my word.
I've signed a bond by which I undertake to furnish you
With seven years of merriment, and I will do it, too!"

He struggled bravely on, and racked his unproductive brain,
And very sad indeed were his attempts to entertain;
He lost his nice refinement and his delicacy chaste,
And some of his conundrums were in execrable taste.

At first Sir Hugh said little, for his heart was good and kind,
And all his friends pretended that they really didn't mind.
(But great was the relief that o'er a dinner-party spread
When it was time for Jester James to toddle off to bed.)

The wretched knight he writhed beneath the dismal jester's ban;
And much as Lady Isabel loved Hugh de Barbican,
To marry him she firmly, but respectfully, declined,
Unless his jester altered for the better, or resigned.

At last Sir Hugh took heart and said, "I've borne with you too long;
Your jokes are much too weak, except when they are much too strong.
Be off, and don't come back; you'll have no reason to complain,
For I'll gladly pay your wages; but you don't joke here again."

But James, though dull, was proud, and scorned the bread of idleness:
"My contract is for seven years—no more, and nothing less.
If you have rights, why so have I. I know what I'm about;
And I must insist on joking till the seven years are out."

Sir Hugh gave in and tried another plan (for he was weak);
He spent his nights inventing decent jokes for James to speak;
And each day at James's breakfast, with his rolls and Sally Lunns,
Came a batch of blameless riddles and of inoffensive puns.

And every morn, from eight to ten, they'd sit beneath a tree,
Rehearsing conversations that would lead to repartee,
Or planning little incidents and complicated larks,
On which this dismal jester might extemporise remarks.

For instance, Hugh would bid him sit, his head between his feet,
To justify his saying, "I am making both ends meet."
On which a shout of merriment would echo through the hall,
Which must have been good nature, for the joke was very small.

And sometimes James was told to climb a venerable oak,
That he might say, "I'm up a tree"—an irritating joke.
But still his audience wore a pleasant smile upon their lips,
For they saw the Dawn of Reason in these gruesome little quips.

One day JAMES had to tumble down a well and break a bone,
To warrant him in saying, "Better far let 'well' alone."
He did it; and SIR HUGH was so impressed by the advice,
That he wouldn't hear of meddling with that well at any price.

JAMES persevered, "Let well alone," incessantly to shout
(It was the cue for good SIR HUGH to go and pull him out).
He cried, "Let well alone—let well alone!" as he was bid;
But SIR HUGH he only answered, "So I will!"—and so he did.

* * * * * *

Loud rang the merry castle bells from battlemented walls,
And gaily hummed the wassail in those proud ancestral halls;
And merry were the nuptials of SIR HUGH and ISABEL,
For no one ever thought of interfering with that well.

THE POLICEMAN'S STORY

Some time ago I met a Duke as tipsy as could be;
And when I urged him home to go, he rounded onto me;
He hit me in the eye, which caused considerable pain;
He knocked me down, and picked me up, and knocked me down again.
    So I took him into custody, and knew no fear;
    For there's but one law for the peasant and the peer.

The magistrate he says, "To such assaults I do assign
A month's imprisonment, without the option of a fine.
A man of education too! What is his name, I pray?"
And I says, "So please your worship, it's the noble DUKE OF A."
    And I didn't care a rap; for it seems quite clear
    That there's but one law for the peasant and the peer.

The worthy beak he hummed and hawed, and looked extremely blank,
And said, "I didn't know you were a gentleman of rank.
To see you standing in the dock gives me a moral wrench;
Pray take your seat with me upon the magisterial bench.
    You'll see more plainly, if you'll step up here,
    That there's but one law for the peasant and the peer."

My evidence I gave in my uneducated way.
The beak remarks, "Your grace has heard this poor policeman's say;
I needn't say how kind 'twould be, if you should think it right,
On his Boeotian words to throw a little ducal light.
    You'll pardon me, I'm sure; when I sit up here,
    I've but one law for the peasant and the peer."

The Duke he up and says, says he, "I haven't any doubt
I most unmercifully banged that officer about.
I had been dining very free on port and sherry-wine,
And richly I deserve to suffer in a heavy fine;
    And I beg to say I rejoice to hear
    That there's but one law for the peasant and the peer."

The beak replies, "I'll measure even justice to your grace.
I hold the magistrate who would deal hardly with a case
Because the prisoner's a Duke would not be worth his salt.
That you're the DUKE OF A. is your misfortune—not your fault.
    And I don't see why I should be severe
    Because you're not a peasant, but a first-class peer.

"Your grace's noble conduct in consenting to a fine
Reflects the brightest lustre on your proud ancestral line.
The two assaults at less than half-a-crown I cannot fix;
The summons is two shillings—and the total's one and six.
    And I trust your grace won't think it dear—
    There's but one law for the peasant and the peer."

And the Duke did wed the daughter of that beak—a girl of charms.
And, on the strength of it, the beak did buy a coat-of-arms;
And as he had to choose a crest, the whole affair to clench,
It was a Flunkey *Rampant* on a Magisterial Bench,
    With the pregnant motto, on a scroll, "Up here
    There is but one law for the peasant and the peer."

THE THIEF'S APOLOGY

In these good days man's only end is a life of pipes and tabors,
So instead of paddling his own canoe he tries to scuttle his neighbour's.
As he pushes along he don't much care whose back he lays the lash on,
No more do we—no more do we—we wouldn't be out of the fashion!
      We don't much care
      How others fare,
   But we mustn't be out of the fashion!

Your patriot for his country's weal would sell his own grandmother,
But on two wheels all countries run, and Fortune's wheel is the other.
Upon the latter he keeps his eye in his patriotic passion,
And so do we—and so do we—we wouldn't be out of the fashion!
      With Fortune's wheel
      Alone we deal—
   We wouldn't be out of the fashion!

Your soldier draws his sword to kill whenever the word is spoken,
And when unusual quantities of enemies' heads are broken
I'm not aware he stops to shed the tear-drop of compassion,
No more do we—no more do we—we wouldn't be out of the fashion!
      We shed no tears
      On dead men's biers—
   We wouldn't be out of the fashion!

Your author steals his plots and plays, so with him you may class us;
On somebody else's Pegasus he climbs a cheap Parnassus.
He don't much care whose brains he steals to fatten his native trash on,
No more do we—no more do we—we wouldn't be out of the fashion!
      Indeed we feel
      That we *must* steal
   If we wouldn't be out of the fashion!

Your counsel sings your praises; then, at hostile instigation,
He'll do his best to hang you for a small remuneration.
He don't much care as long as he makes enough to cut a dash on,
No more do we—no more do we—we wouldn't be out of the fashion!
      We'll put you away
      For half his pay,
   For we wouldn't be out of the fashion!

Where lawyer, patriot, soldier, author finds his game he strikes it,
For, oh, we live in a wicked world where dog eats dog, and likes it.
May all these worthy gentlemen have appetite for their ration,
And so may we—and so may we—we wouldn't be out of the fashion!
      For dog's the meat
      That dog must eat
   If he wouldn't be out of the fashion!

NOTES TO THE BALLADS

Because of the nature of this light illustrated verse and the inadvisability of spoiling the text pages with line numbers, references in the notes to particular lines are by a sequence of three numbers that indicate the page in the text, the number of the stanza (including partial stanzas) on that page, and the line in the stanza: 35.2.4. refers to p. 35, fourth line of the second stanza.

THE ADVENT OF SPRING (p. 33)—*Fun*, II (1 February 1862), 200.

This nonsense poem, originally printed with the by-line "By a Devout Admirer of Mr. T[ennyso]n," is identifiable as Gilbert's only because of its inadvertent reappearance in *Punch* on 26 April 1873 with these changes in the opening lines: "Sing for the garish eye/When moonless brandlings cling!" and these in two lines in the last stanza: "Hasten the deed to do/That shall roddle the welkin now!" Shirley Brooks, editor of *Punch,* explained the mistake in his diary: "Miss Emily Leith has helped me into a mull. She sent me some things of her own some time back, and with them some very good nonsense verses in MS., which I also took to be hers, but which she says she told me were copied. If she did, I overlooked the statement, and having touched them up, used them this week, as they fitted a cut of Sambourne's. Such things will happen, but I don't do them often, usually eschewing outsiders." The next week he gave an account of the outcome: "I inserted some verse sent me by Emily Leith, overlooking her distinct statement that she had copied them. So down come letters from Gilbert, who wrote them in *Fun* 10 years ago, Tom Hood and Burnand. Made the *amende* and wrote Gilbert. *Mea culpa,* and nobody else's" (George Somes Layard, *A Great "Punch" Editor* [London: Sir Isaac Pitman & Sons, 1907], 542).

Brooks also made an *amende* in *Punch,* suspiciously fulsome in its praise of an author usually damned by the *London Charivari:* "Mr. Punch presents his best compliments to Mr. W. S. Gilbert, the author of *Pygmalion* and other delightful plays. The former gentleman last week inserted in his immortal pages a poem, of which his opinion was therefore, of course, immeasurably high. . . . *Mr. Punch* had never seen them [the verses], or must have remembered anything so excellent. He is the soul of frankness, honour, and good humour, and he hastens to say '*Blunderavi';* yet can hardly regret having thus introduced Mr. Gilbert's poem to a delighted universe" (LXIV [3 May 1873], 188).

THE CATTLE SHOW (p. 34)—*Fun*, V (12 December 1863), 121.

The new cattle market, or "New Smithfield," on the Caledonian Road, Islington, was begun in 1855. In 1862 a great Agricultural Hall was built for the annual horse and cattle shows; these displays of prize livestock were popular attractions at that time, the comic papers invariably illustrating the event with a cartoon of a pig so round as to appear nearly legless being prodded by a gentleman with his stick or a lady with her parasol. In 1863 the show opened on December 13 with the Prince of Wales in attendance. The poem is identified as Gilbert's only through the initialed drawings.

35.2.4. *oil-cake:* a cake made of seeds left after their oil is pressed out, used to fatten animals.

THE CATTLE SHOW (p. 36)—*The Comic News,* I (19 December 1863), 180.

The Comic News was another of H. J. Byron's journalistic ventures. Gilbert's name is printed last of the fourteen contributors to the first volume, which may suggest that he wrote little for the paper or came on the staff last. There is no proof that this or any other poem in *The Comic News* is his, but because it combines the subject of the poem he almost certainly wrote that same week for *Fun* with the rhymes and rhythms of a poem he would write the following May ("Down to the Derby"), it has been included as nodding recognition of Gilbert's association with the periodical. See, however, the first note to "Down to the Derby" on the source of this stanza form.

SIXTY-THREE AND SIXTY-FOUR (p. 37)—*Fun,* V (2 January 1864), 162.

Identified as Gilbert's through the initialed drawing.

37.1.7. *pantomine actors:* Christmas pantomines were at the height of popularity in the sixties; on Boxing Night of 1863 at least a dozen London theaters offered them, and the most successful ran well into the following year.

38.1.3. *Christmas-boxes:* English term for the custom of giving gifts to one's tradesmen and employees the first weekday after Christmas; hence "Boxing Day." Note in Gilbert's illustration that the paper boy who delivers *Fun* is among those stretching out eager hands.

38.1.9. *waits:* a group of musicians, often quite amateur in talent, who play and sing at night or early morning, usually at Christmas.

38.1.9. *Willie:* reference to the song "O, Willie, We Have Missed You," by Stephen Foster.

38.1.10. *daisy:* reference to the song "I'd Choose to be a Daisy," by Frederick Buckley, whose "Serenaders" made it popular in 1860.

THE DREAM (p. 39)—*Fun,* V (27 February 1864), 242.

Leap Day was two days off when this poem, identified as Gilbert's through the initialed drawing, appeared in *Fun.*

39.3.1. *elderly dame:* the comic situation of the old woman wooing the young man was one Gilbert found irresistible. It appears in about half of the Savoy Operas and a number of the plays (for example, Miss de Vere, the "Romantic Old Lady" in *Foggerty's Fairy*).

40.3.3. *match or law:* marriage or a breach-of-promise suit, as in *Trial by Jury.*

THE BARON KLOPFZETTERHEIM (p. 41)—*Fun,* VI (19, 26 March; 2, 9, 16 April 1864), 8–9, 18, 21, 38, 48.

The metrical structure and even the narrative of this poem may have been suggested by the Ingoldsby Legend, "The Lay of St. Odille." An "Otto" figures prominently in both poems, and in both the name is distressingly rhymed with "got to." Barham divides several of his poems into "Fyttes," as Gilbert does here. By far the longest and most abundantly illustrated of Gilbert's poems, it is identified as his only by the initials. Under slightly different circumstances and names, the Baron and his daughter reappear in Gilbert's story "The Triumph of Vice," in *The Savage Club Papers,* ed. Andrew Halliday (London: Tinsley Brothers, 1867), 174–195. This "fairy tale" begins: "The wealthiest in the matter of charms, and the poorest in the matter of money, of all the well-born maidens of Tackleschlosstein, was the Lady Bertha. Her papa, the Baron von Klauffenbach, was indeed the fortunate possessor of a big castle on the top of a perpendicular rock, but his estate was deeply mortgaged, and there was not the smallest probability of its ever being free from the influence of the local money-lender."

44.1.1. *Robert the Devil:* originally applied to Robert, duke of Normandy, depicted in a thirteenth-century French romance as an arch-villain suddenly reclaimed and transformed into an exemplary Christian. In Meyerbeer's opera of this name, Robert is the son of the arch-fiend. Gilbert wrote a burlesque of the opera in 1868, titling it *Robert the Devil: or, The Nun, the Dun, and the Son of a Gun.*

44.1.2. *Crichton:* the Admirable Crichton, now usually identified with the hero in Barrie's play, was a remarkable sixteenth-century Scottish scholar and adventurer.

44.3.1. *Rupert:* "Otto" in *Fun;* obviously an error.

44.3.11. *voce sotto:* sotto voce, in normal order.

45.4.2. *opportunity:* compare the words of the Pirates of Penzance upon capturing General Stanley's daughters: "Here's a first-rate opportunity/To get married with impunity."

46.1.22. *consigning to Bath:* a mild oath, apparently originating from the fact that Bath attracted lunatic types and vagrants as well as respectable people.

46.3.4. *Bass-ified:* Bass ale was first introduced to the public at the Great Exhibition in 1851 by Michael Bass.

48.2.25. *The fair land of Poland:* a song near the conclusion of Balfe's opera *The Bohemian Girl,* in which Thaddeus admits to his sweetheart Arline and her father, Count Arnheim, that he is a Polish nobleman and not a gypsy and produces a parchment document to prove it. His words are: "My birth is noble, unstained my crest/As is thine own, let this attest." In *The Merry Zingara,* Gilbert's burlesque of the opera, Thaddeus produces a schedule of tax assessments and sings: "My men in livery, my horses, my crest,/Which is my own, were thus asses't."

48.3.4. *bencher:* a judge or magistrate, especially one of the senior members of the Inns of Court.

50.4.5. *stuff:* woolen or worsted material.

DOWN TO THE DERBY (p. 51)—*Fun,* VI (28 May 1864), 110–111.

The trip to Epsom in Derby Week (late May or early June) was made increasingly by train in the sixties, but the highway was still crammed with coaches and carriages as well as vendors, performers, thieves, toughs, and curious onlookers. From Westminster Bridge the way led south to the turnpike at Kennington Oval, then southwest to Clapham, Balham, Tooting, and Sutton, then south again to the Downs. The subtitle, "With Rhymes on the Road," comes from the title of what might be termed a book of travel verse by Thomas Moore, first published in Paris in 1823. The unusual stanza, also used in "The Cattle Show" (p. 36), is taken from the song "When a Man Marries," by J. W. Safe; it appears again in J. Ashby Sterry's "The Tale of a Toilet," in *Tom Hood's Comic Annual for 1868* (London, 1868), 63. The poem is identified as Gilbert's through the initialed drawing.

51.1.4. *quick sticks:* rapidly, hurriedly.

51.5.1. *schools:* there were two young ladies' seminaries, an academy for young gentlemen, and two preparatory schools at Clapham Rise at this time.

52.1.9. *Posturers:* acrobats.

52.1.10. *summerset:* somersault.

52.2.9. *Pike:* short for "turnpike," referring either to the toll-gate itself or the toll. The turnpike system was rapidly disappearing; the pike at Kennington Oval was abolished a year and a half after this poem appeared.

52.2.9. *no trust:* no credit.

52.3.7. *Careless's Booth:* at the Downs there were "dancing booths, and tableaux vivants booths; booths where sparring and booths where drinking might be indulged in freely, booths where terrible melodramas were given, gambling booths, and thimble-rig booths; roulette and three-card establishments, where every vice come down from the days of Noah might be indulged in without let or hindrance" ([Donald Shaw], *London in the Sixties,* by One of the Old Brigade, 3rd ed. [London: Everett, 1909], 84). Careless's was presumably one of several where road-begrimed travelers could get cleaned up.

52.3.14. *Leger bit:* bitten by unsuccessful betting at another famous annual race, the St. Leger, held at Doncaster in September.

53.1.3. *drag:* a four-horse coach.

53.2.9. *The Cock:* a famous coaching inn at Sutton.

53.2.12. *Dal:* a mild oath; dialectal, probably from "damn."

53.5.1. *upper rooms, supper rooms:* popular eating places for theater-goers until the Early Closing Act of 1872 made it illegal to serve meals after 12:30 A.M. The most famous of these was Evans's, "a man's resort, and *habitués* dropped in somewhere about midnight for a substantial supper. In the 'Fifties and 'Sixties these included some of the leading men in literary, journalistic, theatrical and legal circles, such as Dickens, Thackeray, H. J. Byron, Tom Hood, W. S. Gilbert, Lionel Lawson, Douglas Jerrold, Sergeant Ballantyne, F. C. Burnand and others" (Mark Edward Perugini, *Victorian Days and Ways* [London: Hutchinson, 1936], 161).

SOMETHING LIKE NONSENSE VERSES (p. 54)—*Fun,* n.s., I (10, 24 June 1865), 31, 51.

54.2. title. *Q.C.:* Queen's Counsel, a high-ranking barrister.

54.2.1. *Big Ben Denison:* "The bell [Big Ben] itself records that it is designed by Mr. Edmund Beckett Denison, Q. C., a gentleman who, fortunately for the rest of us, occupies his leisure hours with the improvement of clocks and bells" (London *Times,* 7 November 1856, p. 6).

54.4.4. *kinaster:* variant of "canaster," a kind of tobacco. "For the smoker and chewer it is prepared in various forms, and sold under different names. The dried leaves, coarsely broken, are sold as canaster or knaster," [J. F. W. Johnston] "The Narcotics We Indulge In," *Blackwood's Edinburgh Magazine,* LXXIV [August 1853], 132).

54.6.1. *Gye:* Frederick Gye, who rebuilt the Covent Garden Opera House at a cost of £120,000 in 1858 and served as its proprietor and manager until his death in 1878.

ODE TO MY CLOTHES (p. 55)—*Fun,* n.s., I (10 June 1865), 33.

55.4.2. *Peruvian Rolla:* Rolla is the hero of Sheridan's *Pizarro,* an adaptation of Kotzebue's *Die Spanier in Peru.* As recently as 1862 an extravaganza based on *Pizarro* had been produced in London.

55.4.8. *square bodies:* "The 'Square Bodies' (or bodice) was something like a loin cloth. It was cut in two sections, in rectangular form, and when in wear there were two openings—one on each side of the figure" (courtesy of the technical editor, *The Tailor and Cutter,* London).

THE STUDENT (p. 56)—*Fun,* n.s., I (1 July 1865), 67.

56.1.1. *Gray's-inn:* Gilbert had chambers there at this time (see Introduction).

56.7.1. *Mexico:* Maximilian was contending with Juarez for control of Mexico.

56.7.2. *Portugal and Spain:* there was considerable talk of pan-Iberianism at this time.

56.7.3. *Parliament dissolving:* Palmerston had dissolved Parliament; he called for a general election on July 12, at which time he, his cabinet, and his party were returned handily.

56.7.4. *excursion train:* on 7 June 1865 a train with over eight hundred Whitsun-week passengers had been wrecked at Rednal, on the Shrewsbury & Chester Railway, killing ten persons and injuring fifty. Two days later the "tidal train" from Folkestone to London was derailed at a bridge near Staplehurst, resulting in another ten deaths. Charles Dickens was among the uninjured passengers on the latter and helped at the scene of the accident (see the *Annual Register* for 1865 [London, 1866], 70–73). The derailing of trains, along with poaching and moonshining, is an occupation of the enterprising Scotsman Angus Macalister in Gilbert's comedy *Engaged.*

56.12.3. *Reading:* a pun on the name of the city, a major rail junction between London and Oxford.

57.1.5. *'Lectro-biology:* originally designating that branch of electricity which deals with electrical phenomena in living organisms, by the middle of the nineteenth century electrobiology had become a popular performer's art of hypnosis, based on the so-called principles of animal magnetism. John Wellington Wells, the dealer in magic and spells in *The Sorcerer,* includes "Lectro-biology," as well as nosology, in the list of accomplishments of his resident Djinn; he, too, rhymes them with "apology."

57.1.7. *nosology:* the study of the classification of diseases.

TEMPORA MUTANTUR (p. 58)—*Fun,* n.s., I (15 July 1865), 82.

This poem is the earliest Gilbert chose to collect in the first series of Bab Ballads. It was not illustrated until 1898. The title ("the times are changing") was an understandably popular one in minor Victorian verse.

58.3.2. *coin:* "tin" in *Fun.*

58.4.5. *heard:* "found" in *Fun.*

58.8.6. *Much . . . :* this line reads "Now unquestioned take the *pas*" in *Fun* and 1869 edition.

THE BACHELORS' STRIKE (p. 59)—*Fun,* n.s., I (22 July 1865), 99.

Gilbert added the following note of explanation when the poem appeared in *Fun:* "A WARNING TO LADIES——The *Publicité* of Marseilles announces a new kind of strike—that of bachelors. Not fewer than 6,000 young men, it states, of that place, between the age of 20 and 30 [40, actually], held a meeting in the open air a little way out of town, and entered into an agreement not to ask any young woman in marriage until a complete change shall have been operated in the manner of living, and particularly in the dress, of the fairer sex. The young men insist on greater simplicity in every respect, and a return to the more modest habits of a century or two ago."

The article Gilbert had read appeared on the second page of *La Publicité* on 8 June 1865, in a column headed "Petite Gazette de la ville":

On nous signale une autre grève autrement sérieuse, autrement importante, c'est la "grève des célibataires."

Six mille jeunes hommes, de 20 à 40 ans se sont réunis dans les terrains vagues de la Belle-de-Mai—et là, la main dans la main, ont juré de ne plus songer au mariage jusqu'a nouvel ordre, c'est à dire jusqu'au moment où en changement radical s'opérerait dans les moeurs de nos demoiselles.

—Plus de toilettes tapageuses et ruineuses, plus de coquetterie, plus de désirs de grandes dames, plus d'oisiveté coûteuse, le retour aux moeurs simples et primitives, le retour aux habitudes d'économie et de ménage, à la vie de vraie mère de famille et d'époux modeste, telles sont les conditions posées par la grève des célibataires.

Ainsi, avis au beau sexe!—c'est plus grave qu'on ne pense.

The "other strike" preceding this one was of prostitutes. Later, on 13 July, the young ladies of Belle-de-Mai wrote to the paper to complain that the article about the bachelors' strike would hurt their chances of marriage.

59.1.1. *July:* June, actually.

59.1.3. *Marseilles:* note the pronunciation, still sometimes used by the English. Gilbert rhymes the word similarly in a limerick he wrote in 1895:

There was a young man of Marseilles
Who plaited his hair in three tails—
He trimmed his moustacher
To look like a Masher,
And "went for" the Princess of Wales!

59.4.3. *bodies:* bodices.

A BAD NIGHT OF IT (p. 60)—*Fun,* n.s., I (19 August 1865), 139.

This poem is very much like the Lord Chancellor's "Nightmare Song" in *Iolanthe,* both in sound and sense. If that patter has always seemed a challenge to the comic baritone, think of what these lyrics would be like set to a rattling tune.

60.1.1. *Weybridge:* a town about twenty miles up the Thames from London.

TO PHOEBE (p. 61)—*Fun,* n.s., I (26 August 1865), 144.

The original title ran as follows:

A GOOD JOKE
(*To be sent to any Lady whom you don't absolutely adore.*)
TO (SAY) PHOEBE

Gilbert shortened the title when he included the poem in the 1869 edition. A note in the 1877 edition states: "This ballad is published as a Song, under the title 'If,' by Messrs. Cramer and Co." The illustration was added in 1898.

61.2.8. *But I do not, Phoebe, dear:* in *Yeomen of the Guard* it is Phoebe herself who sings a similar song, "Were I thy bride," to the doltish jailor Wilfred Shadbolt, in order to steal his keys and free the prisoner, Colonel Fairfax. Once the deed is done and the keys returned to Wilfred's belt, Phoebe abruptly concludes her song, "But then, of course, you see, I'm not thy bride!" and trips off.

OZONE (p. 62)—*Fun*, n.s., II (16 September 1865), 2.

In *Fun*, this poem included the parenthetical instruction, *"Vide Times of 30th ultimo,"* where on page six, in a letter to the editor from T. Herbert Baker, M.D., is written: "There can be little doubt that ozone is Nature's grand atmospheric disinfectant. All the facts which have hitherto been developed tend to prove this." To illustrate, the doctor points out that no ozone is found in the neighborhood of cesspools or to the leeward side of cowsheds and manure heaps; similarly, it is lacking in a crowded, badly ventilated church. "But if from the body of the church we simply mount to the battlements . . . we get marked evidence of the presence of the active oxidizing agent." In all fairness it should be added that the doctor does explain how ozone can be generated where needed.

62.1.1. *ohone:* a Scottish and Irish exclamation of lamentation.

TO THE TERRESTRIAL GLOBE (p. 63)—*Fun*, n.s., II (30 September 1865), 29.

In *Fun*, following the stage direction "it rolls on" is the word "curtain." The illustration was added in 1898.

63.2.4. *I have:* "I've got" in *Fun* and 1869 edition.

THE MONKEY IN TROUBLE (p. 64)—*Fun*, n.s., II (7 October 1865), 31.

This poem almost certainly refers to an actual event. If not always fond of people, Gilbert loved animals and was enraged by their ill-treatment. In his later years at Grim's Dyke he had quite a menagerie in and about the house, including several monkeys and two ring-tailed lemurs which rode on their master's shoulders.

64.2.3. *quodded:* jailed.

64.3.4. *is:* accidentally omitted in *Fun*.

64.6.1. *idem semper:* always the same.

64.7.3. *siller:* silver.

64.10.3. *Mr. Russell:* Henry Russell, the song writer and entertainer, set to music an adaptation by Leigh Cliffe of Matthew Gregory "Monk" Lewis' poem "The Maniac," in which the refrain of the imprisoned man is "No! by heaven, no by heav'n I am not mad."

BACK AGAIN! (p. 64)—*Fun*, n.s., II (7 October 1865), 39.

64.2.1. *Biedecher's Guide:* referring to one of Karl Baedeker's famous guidebooks to European cities and countries.

64.2.5. *diligence:* a type of stagecoach especially common in France, though very old-fashioned by this date.

64.2.6. *circular note:* comparable to our letter of credit; letter addressed to a bank's foreign agents, together with a statement of identification.

64.3.3. *Westminster fray:* refers to the law courts, which were held in rooms adjoining Westminster Hall until the new Law Courts in the Strand were opened by the Queen on 4 December 1888.

64.3.6. *Pam:* the nickname of Lord Palmerston, who in 1855 at the age of seventy-one became Prime Minister, an office he held almost without interruption until his death only eleven days after this poem was published.

65.1.6. *slap-bangy airs:* one of the "hit" tunes of 1865, "Jolly Dogs," had the refrain

"Slap bang, here we are again." The original version, by Harry Copeland and sung by Alfred Vance at the Crystal Palace and the Strand Music Hall, began "There is a school of jolly dogs." Such variants as "Long live our British gentlemen," "Laughter makes a man grow fat," and "The world is full of merry dogs" followed, but in each case the tune and refrain were the same, and the song, still to be heard in the music hall, soon took the refrain as its title.

65.4.3. *fantastical roll:* probably a reference to the long French bread.

TO MY ABSENT HUSBAND (p. 65)—*Punch,* XLIX (14 October 1865), 151.

This is the only poem Gilbert intentionally published in *Punch* (see note, p. 313, to "The Advent of Spring"), and is identified as his only through the "Bab" drawing accompanying it. Though not the first illustration to be so signed by Gilbert, it is the first to accompany a poem; hence *Punch,* not *Fun,* claims the honor of publishing the first actual "Bab" ballad (see Introduction).

65.3.3. *Abernethy:* hard biscuit with caraway seeds taking its name from the nineteenth-century English physician John Abernethy, who treated certain maladies by diets.

65.4.2. *barbel, tench, carp:* all fresh-water fish, of the same family.

MUSINGS IN A MUSIC HALL (p. 66)—*Fun,* n.s., II (28 October 1865), 69.

PANTOMIMIC PRESENTIMENTS (p. 66)—*Fun,* n.s., II (2 December 1865), 111.

The season of Christmas pantomine was approaching when Gilbert published this in *Fun,* accompanied by a very inappropriate illustration by one of the magazine's regular artists, Captain Alfred Thompson. Townley Searle noted the poem's metrical similarity to Poe's "The Raven."

66.1.1. *Lacy's:* Thomas Hailes Lacy, an actor in his youth, entered the theatrical bookselling business in 1844. From 1857 until the business was taken over by Samuel French in 1872, Lacy's was located at 89 Strand, where photographs of theatrical personalities, as well as plays, were displayed and sold.

66.2.1. *Menken as Mazeppa:* the American actress Adah Isaacs Menken was best known for her performance in the title role of this Byronic melodrama, in the most famous scene of which she was tied, in flesh-colored tights, to the back of a wild, rearing horse. She played the part first in America (1863) and later at Astley's in London (1864).

66.2.2. *Parepa:* Madame Euphrosyne Parepa, wife of the opera manager and director Carl Rosa and a popular soprano in London in the sixties.

66.2.2. *Billington and Toole:* John Billington and J. L. Toole were popular Adelphi comic actors in the fifties and sixties.

66.2.3. *Buckstone:* J. B. Buckstone, manager of the Haymarket Theatre (where he produced several of Gilbert's plays) and a great comic actor, his best-loved traits being a certain twitch of the mouth and twinkle of the eye.

66.2.3. *Eily sinking:* Eily O'Connor is the heroine of Dion Boucicault's *The Colleen Bawn,* which had a phenomenal success at the Adelphi in 1861–1862. At the end of Act II, the villainous hunchback Danny Mann hurls Eily into the water, but she is rescued by Myles-na-Coppaleen.

66.2.4. *Rip Van Winkle:* on 4 September 1865 Joseph Jefferson made his first London appearance at the Adelphi in a version of the Rip Van Winkle play provided for him by Boucicault but considerably altered by the actor. For the next fifteen years

Jefferson played almost nothing but the part of this toping Dutchman from the Catskills.

66.3.1. *Kate and Ellen Terry:* Kate Terry, who married and retired from the stage in 1867, was at this time at least as well known an actress as her younger sister Ellen. In her autobiography Ellen Terry recalls performing amateur theatricals with Gilbert (probably at Moray Lodge, the home of Kate's future husband, Arthur Lewis), and adds: "Kate and I established a prophetic link by carrying on a mild flirtation, I with Arthur Sullivan, Kate with Mr. Gilbert!" (*The Story of My Life* [London: Hutchinson, 1908], 116.)

66.3.2. *Widdicomb:* Jarvis Widdicomb was a comedian at the Lyceum, best known as the First Gravedigger in Fechter's production of *Hamlet.*

66.3.3. *Sothern as Dundreary:* E. A. Sothern, who became almost totally identified with the part of Lord Dundreary in Tom Taylor's *Our American Cousin,* had been allowed by Laura Keene to build it from a small into a large part while the play was presented in the United States, so that by the time it reached the Haymarket in London on 16 November 1861 he was the major attraction. Soon his long frock coat, absurd side-whiskers, and peculiar mannerisms of speech had become the styles of the day.

66.3.3. *Fanny Josephs:* "an actress of delicate and agreeable talent" (Augustine Filon, *The Victorian Stage* [London: John Milne, 1897], 104) best known early in her career for burlesque roles, including fairies. At the time Gilbert was writing, she had just become co-lessee with H. J. Byron of the Prince of Wales' Theatre (formerly the Queen's Theatre), where she enjoyed her greatest success.

66.3.4. *Richard Pride:* the villain in Dion Boucicault's *Janet Pride,* who admits to his daughter, "Drink! give it up—I can't."

66.3.4. *Manfred:* Samuel Phelps had made a great hit as Byron's Manfred in a revival of the play at Drury Lane in October 1863.

67.1.3. *chronic Winkle:* referring either to the regular reappearance of the play or the alcoholic condition of its title character.

67.1.4. *Camaralzaman:* Prince Camaralzaman, a figure from the *Arabian Nights* and hero of several burlesques, including one by Henry Bellingham and William Best which had opened at the Olympic Theatre on 12 August 1865.

67.2.3. *Lane:* Drury Lane.

67.2.4. *Harlequin Lord Lovel, Goody Two Shoes, Gaffer Gin:* pantomime characters; E. L. Blanchard, for example, wrote pantomimes about the first two.

67.4.2. *Men of "property":* stage hands painting the "props."

67.4.3. *transformation:* scene in the pantomime in which the characters are changed into figures of the harlequinade.

67.5.3. *rally:* the general chase and melee concluding the pantomime.

67.5.3. *crusted sally:* the rally almost invariably involved throwing about vegetables, buns, and so forth; the Sally Lunn, a raised and sweetened tea-cake, is named after the eighteenth-century Bath pastry cook who first made them. It appears also in *The Sorcerer:*

> Now for the tea of our host—
> Now for the rollicking bun—
> Now for the muffin and toast—
> Now for the gay Sally Lunn!

67.5.4. *fays who sniff and sneeze:* compare "Only a Dancing Girl" (p. 88).

67.6.1. *sausages and bladders:* clown always steals sausages from cook; the inflated bladder collapses when bitten into.

67.6.3. *clown turned in the mangle:* another traditional bit of business.

67.7.1. *Covent Garding:* the elegantly rebuilt Covent Garden, intended as the home of English opera, resorted to lavish pantomimes by E. L. Blanchard in 1864 (*Cinderella*) and 1865 (*Aladdin and the Wonderful Lamp*) for certain box-office success.

THE BAR AND ITS MOANING (p. 68)—*Fun,* n.s., II (9 December 1865), 122.

This is a parody of Charles Kingsley's "The Three Fishers," which begins, "Three fishers went sailing away to the West," and ends: "For men must work, and women must weep,/And the sooner it's over, the sooner to sleep;/And good-bye to the bar and its moaning." The poem gained additional popularity when set to music by Balfe and, with phenomenal success, by John Hullah. The decision upon which Gilbert comments is considered in detail in the London *Times* of 22 November 1865 (pp. 8–9), which reads in part:

> The new experiment in Law Reporting is now in actual operation, under the superintendence of a Council, representing the three principal Inns of Court and the Incorporated Law Society. . . . For some time past the increasing bulk and expense of Law Reports, the utter want of uniformity in their compilation, and the extreme irregularity of their appearance had overtaxed even the patience of the practitioners. . . . It was an essential feature of the system that it should be governed by professional and not by commercial interests, and the advantages expected from it were greater care in the selection of cases, with less prolixity and greater promptitude in publication, at a very moderate cost. . . .
>
> Of course such a scheme could not fail to excite much jealousy and hostility among those whose monopoly is thus invaded. Four eminent law publishers have forwarded a formal remonstrance to the Council, setting forth their grievances. . . .
>
> The law publishers deserve no thanks for establishing the so-called regular Reports. It was a mercantile speculation of the most ordinary kind, and the reason why a new series is demanded is that they have supplied a bad article, at an exorbitant price, and often too late to be of use, out of a shortsighted regard to their own profit.

TO EUPHROSYNE (p. 69)—*Fun,* n.s., II (23 December 1865), 150.

69.2.4. *Phocas Kammerer:* a punning reference to the practice, introduced in 1857, of using mounted photographic likenesses as *cartes de visites.* By 1865 the collecting of such visiting cards and cabinet photographs of the handsome and illustrious had become a hobby. In that year the firm of Alfred W. Bennett was offering "Photographic Portraits of Men of Eminence, in Literature, Science, and Art," at exactly twenty-four per guinea.

THE PHANTOM CURATE (p. 69)—*Fun,* n.s., II (6 January 1866), 162.

The illustration was added in 1898.

69.1.6. *That:* "The" in *Fun* and 1869 edition.

70.2.6. *Coverley:* the country dance Sir Roger de Coverley, in which the dancers line up in two rows, similar to the American Virginia Reel. Miss Rowland Grey, who knew Gilbert in his late years, recalls: "he was an adroit step-dancer. A Scot might have envied his consummate knowledge of the intricacies of the reel, and to see him lead Sir Roger de Coverley in his own picturesque ball-room on the last night of 1897 was something to remember" (see "The Author of Pinafore," *Century Magazine,* LXXXIV [October 1912], 847).

70.5.2. *bottines:* "The fashionable bottines have merely the toes of leather, the remainder of the boot being of some thin textile fabric" (*Illustrated London News,* 2 June 1866, 546).

70.5.6. *The:* "That" in *Fun.*

TO A LITTLE MAID (p. 71)—*Fun,* n.s., II (6 January 1866), 167.

The illustration was added in 1898.

71.3.2. *the:* "that" in *Fun.*

71.3.9. *Pentonville:* built from 1840 to 1843 and introducing the separate cell system, this was regarded as the first modern prison in England, and indeed in Europe.

FERDINANDO AND ELVIRA (p. 72)—*Fun,* n.s., II (17 February 1866), 229.

This was the first of Gilbert's poems to achieve both instant and lasting popularity; the phrase "we talked of love and Tupper" was to be heard everywhere. As late as 1889 Gilbert was writing to A. H. Miles and to Miss Davenport Adams granting them permission to anthologize the poem. The illustrations were added in 1898.

72.1.2. *Tupper:* "In the 'sixties, [Martin] Tupper was widely read and, judged by circulation, the most successful poet of the day. . . . Though his *Proverbial Philosophy* was the quintessence of commonplace and orthodoxy, there are passages in it, as Professor Elton has pointed out, which deviate into something like poetry" (Charles L. Graves, *Mr. Punch's History of Modern England* [London: Cassell, 1921], II, 270). The comic journals were constantly attacking Mr. Tupper in one fashion or another. Gilbert contributed this item to *Fun* on 5 October 1867:

THE TUPPER TESTIMONIAL

An advertisement inserted by Mr. Thomas Hunt in the *Times* tells us that Mr. Martin Tupper is "now at length," and that he is to have a testimonial.

We have not heard of Mr. Tupper's decease, so we are rather at a loss to explain the mystic intimation that he is "now at length"; but the fact that something is to be done in recognition of his "services to literature and religion" shines unmistakably through the fog of bad grammar in which the announcement is wrapped.

It is declared that the form of the Testimonial will be determined by its amount, and it is suggested that probably the simplest form is best. Both of these intimations point to a letter "O" as the form that the testimonial is likely to assume. Personally, we decline to send cheques to Mr. Thomas Hunt for that purpose; but the following inscription, adapted to its probable form, is quite at his service—

AD

MARTINUM TUPPER,

Philosopherum Proverbialem,

Qui scripsit magis nonsensii,

Quam ullus alius suae aetatis et sui ponderis,

Hoc monumentum rotundum,

Aedificatum erat a suo

Amico enthusiastico,

Thomas Hunt,

Esquire.

72.6.2. *long:* "hours" in *Fun;* the same change is made three stanzas later.

73.2.2. *my Coxwell or my Glaisher:* famous balloonists. On 5 September 1862 the aeronaut Henry Coxwell and the meteorologist James Glaisher ascended in a balloon to the record height of thirty-six thousand feet, at which altitude Glaisher lost consciousness and Coxwell, lacking sensation in his hands, pulled the valve-cord with his teeth. A squib in *Fun* described the pair as "Men up to their Work."

73.5.1. *Henry Wadsworth, Alfred, Poet Close:* references to Longfellow, Tennyson, and John Close, the last of whom is thus described in the *Dictionary of National Biography:* "He had not a spark of literary talent of any kind, but his assiduity in berhyming his friends and neighbours, and more especially the gentlefolk of the district, won him patrons who in April 1860 obtained for him a civil list pension of £50." The *DNB* mentions Gilbert's reference to Poet Close.

73.9.2. *Which . . . :* this line reads "Which, of course, was very clever; but I didn't understand it" in *Fun;* "of course" was changed to "I know" in 1869 edition.

THE PANTOMIME "SUPER" TO HIS MASK (p. 74)—*Fun,* n.s., II (24 February 1866), 238.

Originally published with an illustration by Captain Alfred Thompson, this poem was first illustrated by Gilbert in 1898.

74.2.3. *Nine:* "twelve" in second 1898 edition (also in stanza four). Counting the number of weeks between Boxing Day (when the pantomimes opened) and the date on which the poem appeared, "nine" is the more accurate number.

THE YARN OF THE "NANCY BELL" (p. 76)—*Fun,* n.s., II (3 March 1866), 242–243.

This is perhaps the best known of all the "Babs," in part because of Gilbert's statement about *Punch*'s refusal of it: "It may interest some to know that the first of the series, 'The Yarn of the *Nancy Bell,*' was originally offered to 'Punch,'—to which I was, at that time, an occasional contributor. It was, however, declined by the then Editor, on the ground that it was 'too cannibalistic for his readers' tastes' " ("Preface" to *Fifty "Bab" Ballads,* p. vii). The cannibalism is mild, however, if compared with the fate of poor Pedrillo in Byron's *Don Juan.* In fact, the tone is much like that of a poem *Punch had* published on 11 March 1865 entitled "The King of the Lumbagees," which includes the lines "We were talking of eating the skipper/With winegar, mustard, and pipper." Or compare Thackeray's "Little Billee":

> Says gorging Jack to guzzling Jimmy,
> "With one another we shouldn't agree!
> There's little Bill, he's young and tender,
> We're old and tough, so let's eat he."

Both in its use of ballad meter with internal rhyme and in its narrative voices, Gilbert's poem echoes "The Rhyme of the Ancient Mariner"; and note the piece of stone on which Gilbert's "elderly naval man" and Coleridge's Wedding Guest are seated. A note in the 1869 edition states: "A version of this ballad is published as a Song, by Mr. Jeffreys, Soho Square"; the music was composed by Alfred Plumpton and the ballad sung by David Fisher and Joseph Plumpton. The illustrations were added in 1898.

76.1.2. *Deal to Ramsgate:* a stretch of about twenty miles of the Kentish coast above Dover.

76.3.2. *Nancy brig:* Charles Dibdin, in his numerous nautical songs, had made the "Nancy" the commonest ship afloat in song since the eighteenth century. Nancy Bell is also the pining sweetheart of Lord Lovel in the old ballad, a story which F. C. Burnand had burlesqued in an extravaganza in 1856.

76.5.3. *But:* "And" in *Fun* and 1869 edition.

76.5.4. *How . . . :* in 1877 edition this line reads "However you can be."

77.1.3. *a thumping:* "his baccy" in *Fun.*

77.3.1. *o':* omitted in 1877 edition.

77.8.3. *kettle:* "butcher" in *Fun.*

77.9.1. *that:* "the" in *Fun.*

78.3.2. *portions:* "proportions," by mistake, in first 1898 edition.

78.5.2. *froth:* "broth," by mistake, in first 1898 edition.

78.6.4. *wessel:* "vessel" in *Fun.*

79.1.1. *And . . . :* in *Fun* and again in 1898 editions this stanza begins: "And I never grieve, and I never smile,/And I never larf nor play." Compare the Ancient Mariner's "We could not laugh nor wail."

79.1.3. *I:* omitted in 1877 edition.

MONSIEUR LE BLOND ON LONDON (p. 79)—*Fun*, n.s., II (3 March 1866), 249.

There was a French dancer in the early part of the nineteenth century named M. le Blond, but the gentleman Gilbert presents is only the French counterpart to Arthur Sketchley's Mrs. Brown, who visited Paris on several occasions and gave the readers of *Fun* her impressions of that city (see Introduction). The air to which the poem is set, "The Fall of Paris," was composed by Frantz Hünten (1793–1878).

79.2.14. *outspoken journalists:* the tight censorship imposed at the start of the Second Empire (1852) was not relaxed until May 1868.

80.1.1. *theatres:* apparently pronounced dissyllabically here.

80.1.8. *original:* the London stage was notorious at this time for "original" plays which were actually translations and adaptations from the French. *The Tomahawk's* definition of a dramatic author was "the English-French Dictionary in the flesh."

HAUNTED (p. 81)—*Fun*, n.s., III (24 March 1866), 12.

In *Fun* this poem had the by-line "By our Depressed Contributor." The illustration was added in 1898.

81.1.2. *in a dread:* "in dread" in 1869 edition.

81.2.5. *that:* "who" in 1869 edition.

81.2.6. *that's:* "that is" in *Fun.*

81.3.3. *Of nauseous:* "Of its nauseous" in *Fun* and 1869 edition.

81.5.5. *nursery:* "nurse-room" in *Fun* and 1869 edition.

81.5.7. *girl of a thousand:* Gilbert repeated this joke in *The Pirates of Penzance:*

FREDERICK: A lad of twenty-one usually looks for a wife of seventeen.

RUTH: A wife of seventeen! You will find me a wife of a thousand!

FREDERICK: No, but I shall find you a wife of forty-seven, and that is quite enough.

81.6.3. *my maiden brief:* Gilbert, too, failed miserably with his maiden brief but successfully transformed the incident into a story published in *Cornhill Magazine* in December 1863.

81.6.4. *When:* omitted in 1869 edition, where the line is in parentheses; "And" in 1877 edition.

81.6.4. *wushup:* "worship" in *Fun.*

81.6.6. *With wrenched-off:* "When I wrenched off" in *Fun.*

81.6.7. *Unholy . . . :* in *Fun* the line reads "And finished it up with unholy fights."

81.7.5. *to:* "that'll" in *Fun.*

81.8.4. *only:* "chiefest" in 1869 edition.

THE REVEREND RAWSTON WRIGHT (p. 82)—*Fun,* n.s., III (28 April 1866), 67.

In *Fun* this poem is described as "Being a Column of Abject Bosh." This reverend gentleman who sings of an esthetical flame might be considered the precursor of both the Rival Curates and the rival poets in *Patience.*

82.6.3. *wondering:* "wandering," by mistake, in *Fun.*

THE STORY OF GENTLE ARCHIBALD (p. 83)—*Fun,* n.s., III (19 May 1866), 100–101.

This, the first of Gilbert's poems in *Fun* to be accompanied by "Bab" illustrations, could be called the prototype of those that followed. It was unkind of Gilbert to exclude Archy and his pantomimic dream from the collected editions of the ballads.

85.1.9. *He boiled . . . :* compare the behavior of "Teasing Tom" as described by another Archibald, the Idyllic poet Grosvenor in *Patience:*

> He put live shrimps in his father's boots,
> And sewed up the sleeves of his Sunday suits;
> He punched his poor little sisters' heads,
> And cayenne-peppered their four-post beds.

TO MY BRIDE (p. 86)—*Fun,* n.s., III (9 June 1866), 125.

This poem accurately describes Gilbert's age, appearance, temperament, and professional condition at the time. It is also remarkably prophetic, for "within a year or twain" (fourteen months, to be exact) Gilbert *was* married. The illustration was added in 1898.

86.2.4. *you:* "you'll" in *Fun* and 1869 edition.

86.3.4. *"soup" at Sessions:* briefs for prosecutions given to junior members of the Bar, especially at Quarter Sessions, to defend poor prisoners. The fee of two guineas was paid by the court.

86.4.3. *shy:* this continues the horse metaphor of "in harness."

87.1.2. *widow—wife, or blushing maiden:* compare Wilfred Shadbolt's "maid, widow, and wife" and Colonel Fairfax's contemplation of his unknown bride in *Yeomen of the Guard.*

87.2.6. *To quote the bard:* the "bard" Gilbert quotes here is not Shakespeare, but Charles Merion, author of the comic song "Have You Seen Her Lately" (music by John Fairfax), with the refrain:

> She went away, a month to-day,
> Her absence grieves me greatly,

She'd a strawberry mark upon her arm,
Oh! have you seen her lately.

87.3.2. *Woking:* the Woking Cemetery, sometimes referred to as the London Necropolis, covered about four hundred acres in Gilbert's day.

ONLY A DANCING GIRL (p. 88)—*Fun,* n.s., III (23 June 1866), 146.

This is the earliest of the collected ballads to have been originally illustrated in *Fun.* It is possible that Gilbert's colleague Tom Robertson got the idea for his most successful play, *Caste,* from this poem. Esther Eccles is "only a dancing girl," and in love with a young nobleman whose "stately dame" of a mother opposes the match. Esther also has a "drunken father" to contend with at home. *Caste* opened at the Prince of Wales' on 6 April 1867.

88.2.6. *world I:* "world should I" in *Fun.*

88.3.4. *highly:* "mighty" in *Fun* and first 1898 edition.

TO MY STEED (p. 89)—*Fun,* n.s., III (23 June 1866), 152.

89.1.6. *Rosinante:* Don Quixote's horse.

89.1.27. *Thomas King:* an English boxer who retired as national champion in 1862 but returned to the ring the next year and beat the American Heenan in twenty-four rounds, winning a purse of £4,000.

KING BORRIA BUNGALEE BOO (p. 90)—*Fun,* n.s., III (7 July 1866), 167.

Gilbert delighted in creating fantastic names for his orientals and Africans out of commonplace English names and expressions, as in this poem. Several characters have been fabricated from nonsense refrains to songs, including "Tootle-Tum-Teh" (or "Tay"), which is the subtitle of Arthur Lloyd's "I Vowed that I Never Would Leave Her." The Amazon queen takes the first part of her name from a pantomime character, while the king is probably no more than a compounding of "bore," "bungle," and "boo." Or, it may be that Gilbert was recollecting Mrs. Jellyby's shattered hopes for Borrioboola-Gha (Dickens' *Bleak House*), where the King decided to sell for rum everybody who survived the climate. The haughty Pish-Tush-Pooh-Bah is, of course, divided into two characters in *The Mikado.*

90.4.4. *dying:* "exclaiming" in *Fun.*

90.5.4. *a:* "no" in *Fun* and 1869 edition.

90.6.2. *get:* "provide" in *Fun.*

90.11.5. *A perfectly:* "Entirely a" in *Fun;* "An entirely" in 1869 edition.

90.13.1. *The warriors:* "And the forces they" in *Fun* and 1869 edition.

90.14.4. *Tootle-Tum:* "Doodle-Dum" in *Fun;* obviously an error.

91.1.3. *And musical:* "And said musical" in *Fun.*

91.1.4. *Said:* omitted in *Fun.*

91.1.5. *Go away, you delightful young man:* compare the behavior of the fairies with the Peers in Act II of *Iolanthe:* "In vain to us you plead—Don't go!"

91.4.4. *It's . . . :* in second 1898 edition this line reads "It's your blood that we want, O my dears."

91.6.1. *And neat . . . :* in *Fun* this stanza reads:

And haughty Pish-Tush-Pooh-Bah
Eat neat little Titty-Fol-Leh,

And despairing ALACK-A-DEY AH
Eat jocular WAGGETY-WEH—
Little light-hearted WAGGETY-WEH.

JACK CASTS HIS SHELL (p. 92)—*Fun,* n.s., IV (6 October 1866), 37.

Written from the point of view of an old salt protesting the idea of ironclad ships, this poem plays on two senses of the word "cast" in its title: the encasing of a wooden vessel in an iron shell and the firing of a gun. England's fleet of about thirty ironclads at this time was considered by many inadequate against the other major sea powers. Parliament debated all year how many and what sort of armor-plated ships the navy should build.

92.1.1. *'national law:* international law.

92.2.3. *Palliser's:* Sir William Palliser had recently designed projectiles which could pierce the hulls of iron-plated ships.

HOW TO WRITE AN IRISH DRAMA (p. 93)—*Fun,* n.s., IV (1 December 1866), 127.

The incidents listed in this poem form a pastiche of Dion Boucicault's Irish melodramas, though perhaps *Arrah-na-Pogue* (1864) follows the sequence most closely.

93.2.4. *lodge of Ribbon men:* The Ribbon Society, so named for the green ribbons worn by the members, was an Irish nationalist organization established to oppose the Orange Society in North Ireland. "The members were bound together by an oath, had passwords and signs, and were divided locally into lodges" (*New Century Cyclopedia of Names* [New York: Appleton-Century-Crofts, 1954]).

GENERAL JOHN (p. 93)—*Fun,* n.s., V (1 June 1867), 127.

Gilbert reused this poem's abrupt and whimsical change of position of commanding officer and one of his men in *H.M.S. Pinafore:* Little Buttercup reveals that "Captain Corcoran and Ralph were exchanged in childhood's happy hour—that Ralph is really the Captain, and the Captain is Ralph." Chesterton remarks that although Gilbert went back to the ballad for the idea he had forgotten the real joke, which was not the unoriginal notion of mixed up babies, but the instant willingness of the two parties to believe they were switched ("Gilbert and Sullivan," *The Eighteen-Eighties,* ed. Walter de la Mare [Cambridge: Cambridge University Press, 1930], 141–143). Actually the joke has only been transferred to their willingness to believe the bumboat woman.

94.2.3. *of a notion:* "of notion" in 1869 edition.

94.3.1. *idea that each:* "idea, each" in 1869 edition.

94.3.2. *We've each of us here:* "That we have each" in 1869 edition.

94.8.1. *man:* "private" in *Fun.*

SIR GUY THE CRUSADER (p. 95)—*Fun,* n.s., V (8 June 1867), 139.

The legendary Guy, earl of Warwick, whose exploits included an adventure-filled pilgrimage to the Holy Land, was the subject of eighteenth-century chapbooks and nineteenth-century pantomimes.

95.1.5. *Dickey de Lion:* Richard the Lion-Heart.

95.2.4. *bagman from:* "bagman at" in *Fun;* a bagman is a commercial traveler (traveling salesman in the United States).

95.3.1. *coryphée:* a ballet dancer who ranks between the soloists and the corps de ballet.

95.3.4. *Royal:* from the names of these "theatres," Sir Guy would seem to be crusading in the provinces, or certainly no further east than Paris.

95.4.2. *cits:* citizens.

95.4.4. *only:* "wholly" in *Fun.*

95.4.5. *But:* "And" in *Fun.*

96.4.3. *Sit* . . . : this line reads "Stand idly and sob" in *Fun* and 1869 edition.

96.5.4. *Sydenham armour:* the firm of Samuel Brothers, 29 Ludgate Hill, offered what they called "Sydenham Trousers" at 17s. 6d. the pair. These were known well enough in the fifties to form the subject of a scene in a Drury Lane pantomime (see A. E. Wilson, *Christmas Pantomime* [London: George Allen & Unwin, 1934], 96).

96.6.1. *lodged in the Compter:* compters were city debtors' prisons; the last in London, the Giltspur Street Compter, was closed in 1854.

SIR GALAHAD THE GOLUMPTIOUS (p. 97)—*Fun,* n.s., V (15 June 1867), 149.

97.4.2. *Dent:* watch. The firm of E. Dent & Company, watch- and clock-makers to Queen Victoria, made the clocks for Big Ben and for the Royal Observatory at Greenwich. *Punch* referred to Dent as "The Tooth of Time."

97.8.4. *wound it up:* legal expression for the closing of a limited company. In *Utopia Limited* Mr. Goldberg explains how easy it is: "You merely file a Winding-Up Petition,/And start another Company at once."

DISILLUSIONED (p. 98)—*Fun,* n.s., V (6 July 1867), 173.

It is doubtful that Gilbert refers to any particular persons in this rather dully conventional poem, one very like "Behind the Scenes," by his colleague Henry S. Leigh, for instance. The second illustration, added by Gilbert in 1898, has been retained as possibly the best instance of a later drawing that harmonizes with an early, atypically restrained and delicate "Bab."

JOHN AND FREDDY (p. 100)—*Fun,* n.s., V (3 August 1867), 222.

100.2.1. *Fred* . . . : in 1869 edition this line reads "Young Fred had grace all men above"; in *Fun* the last word is "cove."

100.2.3. *Oh* . . . : in *Fun* and 1869 edition this line reads "Oh, dance, said she, to win my love—."

100.3.4. *Clodoche and Co.:* a troupe of four grotesque comic dancers from the Théâtre du Chatelet in Paris, who made a sensation in London when they performed a "Grand Ballet of Bohemians" in *The Huguenot Captain* at the Princess's Theatre on 2 July 1866. The *Era* critic thought their performances were "best described by explaining them as indescribable. Their odd, fantastic movements, in which the limbs are thrown into every possible position with unprecedented flexibility, and their bizarre action, which is pervaded by a graphic power giving a significant meaning to every turn, kept the house roaring with laughter, and elicited one universal demand for repetition. With these dancers alone, the piece would become the talk of the town."

100.4.4. *buzzem:* heart (bosom).

100.5.4. *cellar-flapping:* a part of the burlesque and minstrel tradition, this could be thought of as a predecessor to the Charlston and more recent popular dances. "The object of the . . . artist in the dance is to achieve as many changes of step as possible without shifting his ground: his action being restricted to the feet and legs" (John S. Farmer and W. E. Henley, *Slang and its Analogues* [London, 1890], II, 63). The effect is well captured in the figure of Johnny on the right in the first illustration.

LORENZO DE LARDY (p. 101)—*Fun,* n.s., V (10 August 1867), 225.

101.1.2. *The* . . . : this line reads "An officer, late of the Guards" in 1869 edition.
101.1.4. *He* . . . : this line reads "A personal friend of the Bard's" in 1869 edition.
102.2.3. *Dam du Comptwore: dame de comptoir,* a cashier.
102.3.4. *Charlotte Russe de la Sauce Mayonnaise:* her remarkably singular name degenerates into pudding and sauce.
102.4.4. *Palais Royal:* when Richelieu's original Palais Royal was rebuilt after a fire in the eighteenth century, it was designed to include various shops in the arcades around the central square. Never used as a residence after 1848, it became an outstanding tourist attraction, both for its historic associations and for its fine shops, restaurants, gambling establishments, and, in the northwest corner, the Théâtre du Palais-Royal.
102.6.2. *mossoo:* monsieur.
102.8.2. *Blom boodin:* plum pudding.
102.8.3. *Bouldogue:* bull dog.
102.9.1. *He'd* . . . : this stanza eliminated from 1898 editions.
103.3.3. *lui:* "le" in *Fun* and 1869 edition.
103.3.4. *Vol au vent:* puff paste; it would be a desperate measure for a Frenchman to reveal such a recipe to an Englishman. (Or would it?)
103.8.2. *coryphée:* a ballet dancer who ranks between the soloists and the corps de ballet.
103.8.4. *Théâtre des Variétés:* a vaudeville theater on the Boulevard Montmartre.
103.9.4. *Vivandière:* a woman who supplied provisions to troops in the field. Gilbert had recently written a burlesque of Donizetti's *La Figlia del reggimento* which he called *La Vivandière: or, True to the Corps.* It opened in Liverpool on 15 June 1867 and in London on 22 January 1868.

THE BISHOP AND THE BUSMAN (p. 104)—*Fun,* n.s., V (17 August 1867), 238.

104.3.1. *Hash Baz Ben:* Gilbert rearranged these words in the name of his costumier, Ben Hashbaz, in *The Grand Duke.*
104.3.3. *Solomon:* Swinburne, in a letter to Rossetti, describes a variant of this ballad which he sent to Simeon Solomon, "apropos of himself and a hostile critic—and as he doesn't drive a Brompton bus, I wrote—'It also was a Jew/(It couldn't well be wuss)'" (*The Swinburne Letters,* ed. Cecil Lang [New Haven: Yale University Press, 1959–1962], II, 106).
104.7.3. *He* . . . : in *Fun* this line reads "The Hebrew child he merely smiled."
104.11.3. *rather:* "awful" in *Fun* and 1869 edition.
104.11.4. *melted:* "busted" in *Fun* and 1869 edition.
105.3.2. *The* . . . : in 1869 edition this line reads "And chuckled loud with joy."
105.3.4. *kid:* "boy" in 1869 edition.
105.4.2. *"Indeed?" replied the:* "You poor benighted" in *Fun.*

BABETTE'S LOVE (p. 106)—*Fun*, n.s., V (24 August 1867), 247.

This would seem the best candidate for the "Bab" Gilbert is said to have written while on his honeymoon. (Rowland Grey is wrong in suggesting "Prince il Baleine," as it did not appear until August 1869.) He had been married on 7 August and had taken his bride to Boulogne, where this poem is set. One might also note that the sailor is named "Bill" and is loved by a "Babette" of about Lucy Turner's age.

106.1.2. *jupon:* petticoat.

106.1.3. *Halle:* located in the harbor on the Quai Gambetta, this hall was the scene of the fish market early each morning.

106.1.4. *Or . . . :* this line reads "Or collaring of little shrimps" in *Fun* and 1869 edition.

106.2.4. *my:* "ma" in *Fun.*

106.3.3. *Gen'ral Steamboat Navigation Companee:* besides daily sailings between London Bridge wharf and Boulogne, the General Steam Navigation Company made runs to northern Europe and the Mediterranean.

106.4.4. *Port:* wharf.

106.8.6. *They do, you know they do, you dog:* compare Robin Oakapple's words in *Ruddigore* to his foster-brother Richard Dauntless, about his being as fickle as any other mariner: "You are, you know you are, you dog!"

107.1.3. *matrimonied:* compare "conjugally matrimonified" in *Pirates.*

107.2.6. *you and me:* "me and you" in *Fun* and 1869 edition.

107.3.5. *The . . . :* in *Fun* the last two lines of this stanza read: "In face, I'm told, she's thought by some/Not unlike MISTER WIDDICOMB." This was followed by the grotesque illustration of the able-bodied wife printed here, which Gilbert eliminated in the 1869 edition and then replaced in 1898 with a weak imitation. For Mister Widdicomb, see note to "Pantomimic Presentiments," p. 321.

107.3.6. *Whopping:* "Wapping" in 1869 edition; the pun is obvious.

107.4.4. *Bolong:* Boulogne.

107.5.6. *I cannot . . . tell:* minus the extra "cannot's" this is the same as the conclusion to Bunthorne's precious nonsense "Oh, Hollow! Hollow! Hollow!" in *Patience.*

FANNY AND JENNY (p. 108)—*Fun*, n.s., V (7 September 1867), 269.

108.1.5. *Bertram and Roberts:* this firm and that of Spiers and Pond were well known vintners and restaurateurs. Bertram and Roberts, for instance, had the refreshment concessions at the race courses around London. George R. Sims recalled that his first meeting with Tom Hood occurred at the Spiers and Pond establishment in Ludgate Hill Station, which he described as a popular rendezvous of Bohemian literati (*My Life* [London: Eveleigh Nash, 1917], 58).

SIR MACKLIN (p. 109)—*Fun*, n.s., VI (14 September 1867), 6–7.

In a letter to the *Examiner* on 11 December 1875, Swinburne, attacking the author of "Jonas Fisher" (whom he thought was Robert Buchanan), compares a quatrain of the poem with one from "Baines Carew" and then concludes: "I will content myself with recommending the author . . . to study in future the metre as well as the style and reasoning of the 'Bab Ballads.' Intellectually and morally he would seem to have little left to learn from them; indeed, a careless reader might easily imagine any one of the passages quoted to be a cancelled fragment from the rough copy of a discourse delivered by 'Sir Macklin' or 'the Reverend Micah Sowls' . . ." (*Swinburne Letters,* III, 92).

109.1.3. *Sabbath:* "Sunday" in *Fun* and 1869 edition; altered in 1877 edition.

110.1.1. *head:* topic or chief point in a discourse or sermon.

110.4.2. *Whately:* Bishop Whately, who, in his *Elements of Rhetoric* (1828), distinguishes various types of arguments. Sir Macklin has the third kind, example, in mind: "In Arguments of this kind then it will be found, that, universally, we assume as a major premiss, that what is true . . . of the individual or individuals . . . is true of the whole Class to which they belong; the minor premiss next asserts something of that individual; and the same is then inferred respecting the whole Class" (quoted from the Douglas Ehninger ed. [Carbondale, Ill.: Southern Illinois University Press, 1963], 86).

110.6.2. *Repentance . . . :* in *Fun* and 1869 edition this line reads "You writhe at these, my words of warning."

110.6.4. *They raised their hands:* "And so they did" in *Fun* and 1869 edition.

110.8.4. *They bent their heads:* "And so they did" in *Fun* and 1869 edition.

THE TROUBADOUR (p. 111)—*Fun,* n.s., VI (21 September 1867), 15.

111.4.2. *prison:* "dungeon" in *Fun* and 1869 edition.

111.8.3. *warder:* "warden" in *Fun* and 1869 edition.

111.11.4. *Peckham Rye:* a fifty-acre common used as a recreation area in Peckham, below Camberwell, on the Surrey side of the Thames.

112.3.4. *at once:* "you cad" in *Fun* and 1869 edition.

112.5.1. *passed:* "past" in *Fun,* 1869 edition, and first 1898 edition.

112.7.1. *pretty:* "precious" in *Fun.*

112.9.3. *Pentonville:* see note to "To a Little Maid," p. 323.

BEN ALLAH ACHMET (p. 113)—*Fun,* n.s., VI (28 September 1867), 25.

In *Fun,* the subtitle to the poem is "The Fatal Error." Gilbert was the first to coin the now common words "tum" and "tummy."

113.1.4. *Backsheesh:* gratuity or alms giving.

113.3.1. *I knew . . . :* in *Fun* this stanza reads:

> I also knew a maiden miss
>   Whose father boasted many a coffer;
> She likewise lived at Hooe—and this
>   Is but a clumsy likeness of her.

113.3.2. *Emily Macpherson:* "Isabella Sherson" in 1869 edition.

113.7.2. *And suffered . . . :* this line reads "Which threw him straight into a sharp pet" in *Fun* and 1869 edition.

113.7.4. *in pain excessive:* "upon his—carpet" in *Fun* and 1869 edition.

114.1.3. *looked:* "took" in *Fun.*

114.1.4. *hemmed:* "hummed" in *Fun* and 1869 edition.

114.7.1. *weazand:* gullet or windpipe or throat (usually "weasand").

115.3.1. *full inside:* the common expression when all the inside seats in a coach or carriage were taken.

THE FOLLY OF BROWN (p. 115)—*Fun,* n.s., VI (5 October 1867), 35.

116.2.1. *sticks to:* "prefers" in 1869 edition.

116.2.3. *Yet:* "Yes" in *Fun* and 1869 edition.

116.3.1. *He* . . . : in *Fun* and 1869 edition this line reads "He added, with a bumpkin's grin."

116.7.4. *decrees:* "degrees" in *Fun.*

116.9.3. *it:* "the" in *Fun.*

117.6.2. *is:* "was" in *Fun;* and again in the fourth line.

JOE GOLIGHTLY (p. 118)—*Fun*, n.s., VI (12 October 1867), 54.

Gilbert dismantled this poem and reused both story and phrases when fitting out *H.M.S. Pinafore*, where Joe becomes Ralph Rackstraw and adores not the First Lord's daughter but the Captain's. Captain Corcoran, not Ralph, becomes the moonlight serenader.

118.4.3. *junk:* salt meat eaten by sailors.

118.6.4. *Boosey:* the London music publishing firm. Boosey published many of Sullivan's songs (including "The Lost Chord") and several of his larger works, including the two operettas he wrote with Burnand before his celebrated partnership with Gilbert, *The Contrabandista* and *Cox and Box* (both published the same year that this "Bab" appeared).

118.10.1. *aft:* "out" in *Fun* and 1869 edition.

119.4.1. *years':* "months'" in 1898 editions; also at 119.9.3.

119.4.4. *Five hundred thousand:* "A good six dozen" in 1898 editions.

119.13.4. *ten years:* "six months" in 1898 editions.

THE RIVAL CURATES (p. 120)—*Fun*, n.s., VI (19 October 1867), 57.

In an "Author's Note" which Gilbert provided for an American edition of *Patience* (New York: Doubleday, Page, 1902), he writes:

> The genesis of "Patience" is to be found in the "Bab Ballad," called "The Rival Curates." In the original draft of the MS. of my play Reginald Bunthorne and Archibald Grosvenor were two clergymen belonging to adjoining parishes, as in the ballad, and the Reverend Mr. Bunthorne was attended by a team of enthusiastic lady worshippers who had been fascinated by the lamb-like meakness of his demeanour. . . .
>
> While I was engaged upon the construction of this plot, I became uneasy at the thought of the danger I was incurring by dealing so freely with members of the clerical order, and I felt myself crippled at every turn by the necessity of protecting myself from a charge of irreverence.

A letter from Gilbert to Sullivan at the time the opera was being written, however, indicates that the original plan had been for poets: "Although it is about two-thirds finished, I don't feel comfortable about it. I mistrust the clerical element. I feel hampered by the restrictions which the nature of the subject places upon my freedom of action, and I want to revert to my old idea of rivalry between two Aesthetic fanatics, worshipped by a chorus of female aesthetics. . . . I entertained this idea at first, as you may remember, but abandoned it because I foresaw great difficulty in getting the chorus to dress and make up aesthetically—but if we can get Du Maurier to design the costumes, I don't know that the difficulty will be insupera-ble" (Hesketh Pearson, *Gilbert: His Life and Strife* [London: Methuen, 1957], 111). Chesterton rightly points out that "the seed of sublime nonsense is in the notion of men fiercely competing as to which of them is the more insipid. It is inherent in the idea of a mild curate being jealous of a milder curate. It evaporates altogether with the change to a wild poet being jealous of a wilder poet" ("Gilbert and Sullivan," *The Eighteen-Eighties,* 144).

121.7.1. *For years . . . :* compare this stanza with Grosvenor's speech when he agrees to become an every-day young man: "I have long wished for a reasonable pretext for such a change as you suggest. It has come at last. I do it on compulsion!"

THOMAS WINTERBOTTOM HANCE (p. 122)—*Fun,* n.s., VI (26 October 1867), 74-75.

In *Fun* the title is "Thomas Winterbottom Hance and Mons. Pierre," with the illustrations of both men immediately beneath their names. Thomas' cognomen is probably a play on the abbreviation for Hampshire, "Hants." The situation in this poem, in which the women encourage the reluctant men to do battle, is similar to the moment in *Pirates* in which Mabel bids the policemen, "Go, ye heroes, go and die!"

122.6.2. *polisson:* scamp or rascal.

122.6.3. *gigots:* legs of mutton.

122.11.3. *ninety-two:* "eighty-two" in 1898 editions.

123.2.4. *minds:* "mind" in *Fun.*

123.6.1. *The mothers . . . :* in 1898 editions Gilbert eliminated both this stanza and the superb illustration it describes.

122.7.2. *Ho! ho! Ho! ho!:* "Ho! ho! He! he!" in *Fun.*

A. AND B. (p. 124)—*Fun,* n.s., VI (2 November 1867), 77.

One of the gruesomest of the "Babs," it is not surprising that Gilbert never collected it. The twins' little joke and its consequence reappear in refined and more purely symbolic form in *The Gondoliers,* in which Marco and Giuseppe rule as one individual and then find themselves in such a muddle over who is married to whom that they are reduced to "vulgar fractions," at which point "excellent husbands are bisected,/Wives are divisible into three."

124.7.3. *todding:* possibly a misprint for "toddling."

125.1.4. *One shilling Damask blade:* probably the proud boast and motto of a cutlery or razor manufacturer.

SEA-SIDE SNOBS (p. 126)—*Fun,* n.s., VI (9 November 1867), 88.

Not a typical "Bab" of this period. Reprinted by Searle under the title "Margate."

THE BISHOP OF RUM-TI-FOO (p. 127)—*Fun,* n.s., VI (16 November 1867), 104.

At the time this poem was published, a pan-Anglican synod of seventy-five British, Colonial, and American Protestant bishops was meeting at Lambeth Palace. The very concept of dignified clergymen among savage tribes seemed fraught with humor to the comic papers. Gilbert published a piece in *Fun* entitled "A Christian Frame of Mind" (8 January 1870), which describes a colonial bishop who manages to transform a peaceable and harmonious African tribe into one so rent by factions that each man becomes a subdivision unto himself. On the other hand, as in this poem, the missionary who adapted too readily to native ways was also mocked. Dr. Colenso, the liberal and sympathetic Bishop of Natal, was often the target of unjustified abuse, his detractors claiming that he went out to convert and was himself converted.

127.1.7. *Rum-ti-Foo:* Gilbert's invention, perhaps suggested by "rum-ti-tum."

127.2.2. *tum-tum:* just as Gilbert introduced the "tum" (see note to "Ben Allah Achmet," p. 332), so he originated the "eloquent tum-tum," unless one chooses to think of it as an Indian dogcart or West Indian dish of boiled plantains.

128.1.6. *battements, cuts, and pas de basque:* battements are high kicks; cuts are a twiddling of the feet in front of one another while in the air; the *pas de basque* is a common ballet step, the basic one for the mazurka. In 1877 edition "cuts" is omitted.

128.3.2. *Paynes and Lauris:* Harry Payne was the pantomime clown from 1860 to 1873 at Covent Garden, where his father (who had played harlequin to Grimaldi's clown) was still in the company. Charles Lauri was the clown at Drury Lane from 1863 to 1868.

128.6.1. *islanders:* an undated letter from Gilbert, apparently written after he had read the proof of this poem before it was published in *Fun*, states: "I find that in the last verse of my ballad you [Mr. Giles] have printed 'inhabitants' instead of 'islanders' of Rum-ti-foo. Will you please correct it as soon as this reaches you. I dare say it is my fault" (Pierpont Morgan Library).

THE PRECOCIOUS BABY (p. 129)—*Fun*, n.s., VI (23 November 1867), 113.

For some reason Gilbert excluded the first illustration to this poem from the 1869 edition. He made up for the omission by using it as the title-page vignette in *More "Bab" Ballads* (1873). The poem, minus a few stanzas, reappeared in his first musical sketch for the German Reeds, *No Cards,* which opened on 29 March 1869. The air of the "Whistling Oyster" has not been traced, but its subject was a shelly celebrity of the 1840's which lodged in a shop in Vinegar Yard, near Drury Lane Theatre. Among the many who came to hear it perform was Douglas Jerrold, who told his readers in *Punch* that the oyster had "become extremely tame, and whistles various airs," and suggested (using Sheridan's phrase) that it "had been crossed in love, and now whistled to keep up appearances, with an idea of showing that it didn't care." See "The Whistling Oyster," *Punch*, V (July–December 1843), 142–143; and Edward Walford, *Old and New London* (London: Cassell, Petter and Galpin, n.d.), III, 282–284.

129.2.4. *off:* "of" in 1869 edition; "past" in 1877 edition.

129.2.7. *prophet:* "buffer" in *Fun* and 1869 edition; altered in 1877 edition.

129.3.5. *singular:* "dear little" in *Fun* and 1869 edition.

129.3.7. *He proved such:* "For he turned out" in *Fun* and 1869 edition.

129.4.4. *weed:* "pipe" in 1877 edition.

129.5.3. *'oo:* "you" in *Fun* and 1869 edition; altered in 1877 edition.

129.5.4. *pap:* baby food.

129.5.6. *Dat is not worf:* "That is not worth" in *Fun* and 1869 edition; altered in 1877 edition.

130.1.3. *'Oo:* "You" in *Fun* and 1869 edition; altered in 1877 edition.

130.1.7. *go, if I may:* "hook it away" in *Fun* and 1869 edition; "toddle away" in 1877 edition.

130.3.4. *afraid:* "affaid" in *Fun* and 1869 edition.

131.1.7. *babes:* "babies" in 1898 editions.

BAINES CAREW, GENTLEMAN (p. 131)—*Fun,* n.s., VI (30 November 1867), 124.

131.9.2. *a mensâ: a mensa et thoro* (from table and bed), the legal expression to designate a separation.

131.9.4. *A vinculo conjugii: a vinculo matrimonii* (from the bond of marriage), the legal expression to designate a divorce.

132.1.4. *saevitia:* in divorce law, cruelty—anything which tends to bodily harm and thus renders cohabitation unsafe. In *Fun* this line reads "Go on—the cruelty, sir, please."

132.4.4. *Polterthwaite:* "Potterthwaite" in *Fun.*

A DISCONTENTED SUGAR BROKER (p. 133)—*Fun,* n.s., VI (14 December 1867), 137.

133.1.5. *one:* "man" in *Fun.*

133.6.7. *chaff:* "laugh" in *Fun* and 1869 edition; altered in 1877.

134.3.9. *An:* accidentally omitted in *Fun.*

THE FORCE OF ARGUMENT (p. 135)—*Fun,* n.s., VI (21 December 1867), 149.

135.1.4. *And:* "But" in *Fun.*

135.3.3. *galoped, and lanced:* the galop and lancers were as popular as the waltz in the sixties; the former is a round dance, the latter a type of quadrille.

135.5.2. *Endeavoured . . . :* this line reads "Imagined their chances looked well—" in *Fun* and 1869 edition.

136.2.3. *Barbara:* "a syllogism in *Barbara* is one of which both the major and minor premises, and the conclusion, are universal affirmatives" (*Oxford English Dictionary*).

136.2.4. *Celarent:* "a term designating the second mood of the first figure of syllogisms, in which the major premiss and the conclusion are universal negatives, and the minor premiss a universal affirmative" (*OED*).

136.10.4. *exeunt ambo:* they go out together (as in the illustration).

AT A PANTOMIME (p. 137)—*Fun,* n.s., VI (28 December 1867), 165.

When Edith Browne, Gilbert's first biographer, praised this poem during an interview with him, "Gilbert's expression changed in a twinkling; bending forward in his chair he exclaimed earnestly, even somewhat excitedly, '"At a Pantomime"! Why that's one of the best things I ever wrote—and you're the first person who has ever singled it out. I can do something more than wear the cap and bells'" (*W. S. Gilbert* [London: John Lane, The Bodley Head, 1907], 16–17).

137.6.3. *advertising quack:* the Mikado refers to "The advertising quack who wearies/With tales of countless cures."

138.3.4. *Meant:* "Means" in *Fun.*

138.4.1. *Poor Law Union:* workhouse; British welfare was administered through local unions in each district or parish.

138.8.4. *Transformation Scene:* in Christmas pantomime, the scene in which characters of the pantomime are magically changed into those of the harlequinade; for the old men, of course, it is death.

THE THREE KINGS OF CHICKERABOO (p. 139)—*Fun,* n.s., VI (18 January 1868), 191.

These three kings, in names and accomplishments, are figures out of the minstrel shows then very much in vogue. Gilbert may have invented his Chickeraboo, but in the eighteenth century Charles Dibdin had written "Kickaraboo," a song sung from the point of view of a philosophic Negro who advises: "Lily laugh and grow fat, a best ting you can do,/Time enough to be sad when you kickaraboo." Gilbert's mild satire of certain excesses of imperialism is obvious.

139.2.4. *break-down "flap"*: Edmund Yates describes "a comic dance popular with burlesque actors, and known as a nigger break-down" (*Broken to Harness* [London, 1864], II, 54). See note to "John and Freddy" on cellar-flapping, p. 329.

139.3.3. *kingdoms:* "islands" in *Fun* and 1869 edition.

139.3.4. *a kingdom:* "an island" in *Fun* and 1869 edition.

139.4.2. *represent:* "rep-per-esent" in *Fun* and 1869 edition.

139.5.4. *Royal Chaps:* i.e., black-faced minstrels who do a turn at the Royal Music Hall.

139.8.2. *magnificent:* "superior" in 1869 edition.

139.9.3. *remarkable:* "extror'nary" in *Fun* and 1869 edition.

140.1.4. *Unrolled:* "Pulled out" in *Fun* and 1869 edition.

140.2.3. *if you please:* Admiral Pip reminds us somewhat of Sir Joseph Porter in his use of this expression, as well as in his gliding over the dancing waves. This "Bab," too, could rank as a source for *Pinafore*.

140.3.2. *of the:* "of all the" in *Fun* and 1869 edition.

140.4.3. *Blue Peter:* the flag which signals immediate sailing; blue, with a white square in the center.

140.7.4. *on spec:* on speculation.

140.8.3. *And:* "Oh" in *Fun* and 1869 edition.

THE PERIWINKLE GIRL (p. 141)—*Fun*, n.s., VI (1 February 1868), 211.

Gilbert may have had Joseph Plumpton's song "The Periwinkle Man" in mind when writing this poem. The situation of the two dukes vying for Mary's affections is similar to that of the Lords Mountararat and Tolloller wooing Phyllis in *Iolanthe*. The illustration of Mary with her come-hither look was not included in the 1869 edition.

141.2.1. *ever-ready:* "Over-ready" in *Fun* and 1869 edition.

141.3.3. *should:* "would" in *Fun* and 1869 edition.

141.3.4. *care:* "like" in *Fun* and 1869 edition.

141.7.1. *I knew . . .* : this stanza eliminated from all collected editions of the "Babs."

141.8.1. *watched:* "seen" in *Fun* and 1869 edition.

141.9.1. *And when . . .* : this stanza eliminated from all collected editions of the "Babs."

141.11.4. *Coutts's:* the great banking firm, absorbed by the National Provincial Bank in 1919. In *The Gondoliers* Marco sings of "The Aristocrat who banks with Coutts."

141.12.3. *eat:* the archaic past tense, and pronounced "ett."

142.6.1. *Mary make:* "make their Bowles" in *Fun* and 1869 edition.

CAPTAIN REECE (p. 143)—*Fun*, n.s., VI (8 February 1868), 221.

Always a favorite with Gilbert (placed first in both the 1869 and 1898 editions), this is another of the sources for *H.M.S. Pinafore*, though Captain Reece is considerably more tractable than Captain Corcoran about giving his daughter in marriage to a mere coxwain. Dark and Grey, in their biography of Gilbert, refer to a correspondent in the *Strand Magazine* who recalled a few verses from what he thought was another sailor's ballad by Gilbert published at about the same time as "Captain Reece."

The poem was actually by Tom Hood and not published (in *Fun*) until 16 May 1874; the first of four stanzas runs:

> To sail the seas is my delight,
> And bend a bowline on a bight,
> To fish the cro'jack yard, and haul
> On topsail lifts, true bliss I call.
> I'd fling mynabblin's to the crowds,
> To scale the giddy futtock shrouds
>   So yeo heave ho!
>   Stand by! Let go!
> While skulks and lubbers sneak below.

143.4.3. *Brown windsor:* an aromatic brown soap.

143.5.2. *seltzogenes:* a common name in the sixties for a sort of carbonated drink; the *OED* quotes Gilbert for an example.

143.6.4. *Zoetrope, or Wheel of Life:* "The Zoetrope, another toy based on the principle of persistence of vision, was invented by W. G. Horner of Bristol in 1834 although it was not put on the market until 1867. The Zoetrope consists of a slot-pierced drum of metal revolving horizontally on a pivot attached to a heavy base. . . . When the figures on [an inserted] band and disc are viewed through one of the slots as the drum is rotated, they spring at once into vivid action" (C. W. Ceram, *Archaeology of the Cinema* [New York: Harcourt, Brace & World, 1965], [67]: a photograph of the device is provided).

143.7.2. *Mister Mudie's libraree:* in 1842 Charles Edward Mudie founded Mudie's Lending Library, which became the largest circulating library in London.

144.2.1. *ameliorate:* William Lee's vocabulary is quite remarkable for an ordinary seaman, but nothing compared to Ralph Rackstraw's "simple eloquence" as he describes his hopeless love for Josephine: "In me there meet a combination of antithetical elements which are at eternal war with one another. Driven hither by objective influences—thither by subjective emotions—wafted one moment into blazing day, by mocking hope—plunged the next into the Cimmerian darkness of tangible despair, I am but a living ganglion of irreconcilable antagonisms."

THOMSON GREEN AND HARRIET HALE (p. 145)—*Fun,* n.s., VI (15 February 1868), 242.

The air to which this poem is set, "An 'Orrible Tale" (more correctly, "A Norrible Tale of the Suicidal Family"), was written by E. L. Blanchard and sung by J. L. Toole in the farce *The Area Belle,* by William Brough and Andrew Halliday, which opened at the Adelphi on 7 March 1864. George Grossmith recalled that as a young man he used to accompany Toole in this song at evening parties.

145.1.4. *Twaddle . . . :* this impressive line, used by Gilbert once before in a brief opera parody, "Piccadilly" (see Introduction, p. 13 n. 24), comes originally from "A Norrible Tale," which has the refrain:

> For oh it is such a norrible tale,
> 'Twill make your faces turn all pale,
> Your eyes with grief will be overcome:
> Tweedle twaddle twiddle twiddle twum.

Notes to the Ballads

145.5.4. *St. Mary Abbot's Church:* Gilbert himself had been married at this church in Kensington only six months before he wrote the poem. In the following year the church was rebuilt, designed by Sir Gilbert Scott.

146.2.1. *But now:* "At length" in *Fun.*

146.2.4. *Canonbury Square:* part of a then fast-growing middle-class district in Islington, this square has changed very little since the Greens took up residence there.

146.7.2. *called in a doctor, quick:* "consulted Doctor Crick" in *Fun* and 1869 edition.

146.7.4. *Fiat mist. sumendum haustus, in a cochleyareum:* "Let the mixture be made to be taken in a teaspoon." The final instruction on a prescription often read *fiat mixtura secundum arte* (let the mixture be made according to the rules of art).

BOB POLTER (p. 148)—*Fun,* n.s., VI (29 February 1868), 260–261.

148.3.4. *sometimes:* "rarely" in *Fun.*

148.7.1. *on Robert's:* "upon his" in *Fun.*

148.11.2. *His heavy . . . :* in second edition of 1898 this line reads "His breath was hot and cautery," with "watery" instead of "wortery" in the fourth line.

149.3.3. *brute:* "beast" in *Fun* and 1869 edition.

149.5.3. *Mr. Tweedie's pretty prints:* William Menzies Tweedie exhibited portraits at the Royal Academy from 1857 until 1874, after which, according to the *Dictionary of National Biography,* he was invariably refused.

149.8.3. *pink:* "red" in *Fun,* 1869 edition, and first 1898 edition.

149.12.2. *have:* "know" in *Fun* and 1869 edition.

THE GHOST, THE GALLANT, THE GAEL, AND THE GOBLIN (p. 150)— *Fun,* n.s., VII (14 March 1868), 6.

150.1.1. *clays:* "clay" in 1898 editions.

150.2.4. *pregnant:* "delicate" in *Fun* and 1869 edition.

150.3.4. *far:* "chalks" in *Fun* and 1869 edition; "by chalks" or "by long chalks" was a common colloquialism meaning "by far."

151.2.7. *yon hardy Hieland man:* perhaps related to Wordsworth's reaper, "Yon solitary Highland Lass!"

151.3.3. *bring:* "carry" in *Fun.*

151.4.2. *Hech thrawfu' . . . :* in *Fun,* Gilbert provides this informative gloss to his dialectal expressions: "*Thrawfu'*—baked potato. *Raltie*—seventeen. *Rorkie* [so spelled in *Fun*]—neuralgia. *Thecht*—underdone. *Croonie*—a Zoetrope. *Clapperhead*—seldom. *Fash*—speculate. *Pawkie*—I forget what pawkie means—perhaps stewed mushrooms."

ELLEN McJONES ABERDEEN (p. 152)—*Fun,* n.s., VII (21 March 1868), 16.

The stanza used here is as Scottish as the subject matter, echoing Sir Walter's "Bonnie Dundee."

152.2.1. *hills of:* "beastly" in *Fun* and 1869 edition; "lovely" in 1877 edition. The late-Victorian musician and composer Francesco Berger, who thought the Bab Ballads "*quite classic* of their kind," was particularly fond of "Ellen McJones Aberdeen," but wondered if "beastly" was not a printer's error and that it should read "breezy" (*Reminiscences, Impressions & Anecdotes* [London: Sampson Low, Marston, n.d.], 157). Gilbert seems to have remained unDeesided.

152.2.2. *Dingwall and Wrath:* Dingwall is above Inverness; Cape Wrath is even further north, on almost the same latitude with John o' Groats. In other words,

McClan was the best piper in all of Scotland, from Edinburgh to the Highlands and back down to Glasgow.

152.3.3. *chiels:* lads.

152.3.4. *pibrochs:* martial airs played on the bagpipe.

152.4.3. *his pipes:* "the pipes" in 1877 edition.

152.5.1. *Sassenach:* a Saxon, an Englishman.

153.2.2. *play him:* "render" in *Fun.*

153.2.4. *In My Cottage:* the traditional (and simple) tune "In My Cottage near a Wood" was known in various arrangements and with varying sets of lyrics in the nineteenth century, a popular version being that by R. A. Moreland.

154.2.2. *snivel:* "blubber" in *Fun* and 1869 edition.

THE SENSATION CAPTAIN (p. 155)—*Fun,* n.s., VII (4 April 1868), 43.

155.1.6. *in:* accidentally omitted in *Fun.*

155.2.6. *situation:* "The old Adelphi was for years the recognised house of melodrama and screaming farce" (*Dickens's Dictionary of London:* London, 1879).

155.9.4. *Inchcape Rock:* a rock and lighthouse a few miles off the coast of Arbroath, Scotland, in the North Sea.

156.3.1. *I'll . .* : this line reads "They shall not hear of me" in *Fun.*

156.6.1. *gallant Captain:* "Parklebury" in *Fun.*

156.7.1. *Indeed . . .* : this line reads "'Indeed,' said Tyler, 'Angy's mine'" in *Fun.*

TRIAL BY JURY (p. 157)—*Fun,* n.s., VII (11 April 1868), 54.

As the subtitle states, this is an operetta, or a sort of burlesque of one, and perhaps should not be included with the "Babs." It is offered here for comparison with the expanded version set to music by Sullivan. Gilbert had revised the work for the composer Carl Rosa, who wished to produce the operetta with his wife, the celebrated Madame Parepa, as Angelina; she died unexpectedly and all plans were canceled. Later, when Richard D'Oyly Carte was in need of a curtain-raiser, Gilbert offered him *Trial by Jury,* which marked the beginning of the Gilbert-Sullivan-Carte triumvirate. While it has been pointed out frequently that the names "Edwin" and "Angelina" go back to Goldsmith, Gilbert was more immediately thinking of a pair of newlyweds, Edwin and Angelina Brown, who had appeared in a long series in *Fun* entitled "Letters from a Young Married Lady."

157.2.4. *ca. sa.:* legal abbreviation of *capias ad satisfaciendum,* a writ of execution commanding an officer to take and hold the person named so that he can appear in court to satisfy a debt or damage charge.

157.2.5. *fi. fa.:* legal abbreviation of *fieri facias,* a writ of execution commanding an officer to make the amount of a judgment from the property of the debtor.

158.7.3. *Camberwell:* Camberwell and Peckham, neighboring suburbs of London on the Surrey side, were, and are, quite ordinary and unpretentious districts.

158.7.5. *otto:* ottar, or attar, the scent extracted from flower petals, especially roses.

159.8.2. *Eaton Square:* an elegant address in Belgravia.

THE REVEREND MICAH SOWLS (p. 160)—*Fun,* n.s., VII (18 April 1868), 65.

The condemnation of the stage from the pulpit, frequent in the early part of the nineteenth century, gradually diminished throughout the Victorian period. The clergyman is not so much abused here as the actor. The tragedians performing at

Drury Lane at this time were Samuel Phelps and Barry Sullivan, but the criticism is probably general. Within a few years, however, such comments could serve as Gilbert's estimate of Henry Irving, whose peculiar gait and unnatural pronunciation were acknowledged even by his admirers. Henry James noted how Irving said "Gaw" for "go" and "Naw" for "no." Gordon Craig commented, "For good, Irving said god—sight was seyt—stood was stod—smote became smot—hand was often hond or hend." Early in their remarkably parallel careers Gilbert and Irving were friends; the latter, stage manager for Gilbert's first burlesque, *Dulcamara* (1866), was introduced by Gilbert at the Arundel Club on the evening of Irving's first major dramatic triumph, in Boucicault's *Hunted Down*. From then on, however, they seem to have had almost nothing to do with one another, and Gilbert's antipathies toward Irving's acting and managing steadily increased.

160.5.1. *The:* accidentally omitted in *Fun.*

161.3.3. *counter plain:* "printed card" in 1898 editions.

161.3.4. *Just . . . :* in the 1898 editions this line reads "Go to a theatre where they play our Bard." By this date Gilbert's despair was over the treatment of Shakespeare by Irving and others.

161.6.1. *was:* "wast" in 1869 edition.

161.7.2. *and talked:* the final "and talked" is omitted (accidentally?) from 1869 and 1898 editions.

161.8.4. *then:* "so" in *Fun.*

161.9.1. *I thought . . . :* in 1898 editions the last two stanzas read:

> "I thought *my* gait ridiculous," said he—
> "*My* elocution faulty as could be;
> I thought *I* mumbled on a matchless plan—
> I had not seen a great Tragedian!

> "Forgive me, if you can,
> O great Tragedian!
> I own it with a sigh—
> You're drearier than I!"

In l. 4 "a" is "our" in second edition.

PETER THE WAG (p. 162)—*Fun,* n.s., VII (25 April 1868), 75.

162.2.6. *loved:* in Gilbert's marked copy of the ballads (used to indicate which original illustrations should be in the 1898 edition) he has changed this word to "liked," but it was never so printed.

162.5.1. *this:* "the" in *Fun.*

162.5.1. *the:* "this" in 1869 edition; altered in 1877 edition.

162.6.4. *Poland Street:* "Portland Street" in *Fun* (also two stanzas later). Great Portland Street does not cross Oxford Street into Soho, whereas Poland Street and all the others mentioned in the poem are to be found there.

162.6.5. *youth:* "boy" in 1877 edition.

162.7.3. *cloyed:* "closed" in *Fun.*

163.2.1. *Their eyes . . . :* Gilbert must have recalled these lines when writing the lyrics about the British tar in *Pinafore:* "His nose should pant and his lip should curl,/. . ./His eyes should flash and his breast protrude."

163.2.7. *Il balen:* here is more flashing and striking; in Italian *il baleno* means brilliance, or a flash of lightning. "Il balen" was well known to opera lovers and concert-goers in Gilbert's day as an aria (translated "Bright her Smiles" in the edition Arthur Sullivan prepared for Boosey) sung by the Count di Luna in Verdi's *Il Trovatore.*

163.3.3. Τυπτω . . . : still more of the same; these are forms of the Greek verb "to strike."

163.4.7. *at length they:* "they swore they'd" in *Fun* and 1869 edition.

163.5.3. *Richmond Buildings:* a set of buildings forming a cul-de-sac off Dean Street at number 80, originally built by Thomas Richmond in 1732.

163.5.4. *Royalty:* the Royalty Theatre was at 73 and 74 Dean Street. The "yard," called Richmond Mews, is still there, and is still "dark, dank, and drear."

THE STORY OF PRINCE AGIB (p. 164)—*Fun*, n.s., VII (16 May 1868), 107.

In the *Arabian Nights,* the Third Calender's tale is of Agib, who, after a series of spectacular adventures, loses an eye as a result of his insatiable curiosity. As noted in the Introduction, this is one of the few instances of nonsense writing by Gilbert.

164.1.5. *I:* accidentally omitted in *Fun.*

164.3.2. *Theodolite:* surveyor's instrument for measuring horizontal and vertical angles.

164.3.4. *Zoetrope:* see note to "Captain Reece," p. 338.

164.3.5. *Pantechnicon:* furniture van. Originally a building intended for a bazaar but converted into a furniture warehouse in 1830 (burned in 1874); by extension, the word came to be applied to the vans.

164.4.5. *Oüaits:* Waits. See note to "Sixty-three and Sixty-four," p. 314.

164.6.4. *had:* omitted in 1869 edition; restored in 1877 edition.

165.5.5. *I am Aleck—this is Beth:* William Bailey, in the *Gilbert and Sullivan Journal,* VI (June 1946), 10, suggests that Gilbert intended the first letters of the Hebrew alphabet, "Aleph" and "Beth," here.

166.1.2. *a:* "an" in 1898 editions.

GENTLE ALICE BROWN (p. 166)—*Fun*, n.s., VII (23 May 1868), 111.

This poem was the last in date of composition to be included in the first series of Bab Ballads and was placed last in the volume.

167.8.3. *was now:* "now was" in 1869 edition; altered in 1877 edition.

168.2.3. *life-preserver:* in the United States, a blackjack. Samuel distributes such a weapon to one of the Pirates of Penzance.

PASHA BAILEY BEN (p. 169)—*Fun*, n.s., VII (6 June 1868), 133.

This proud pasha presumably takes his name from two London landmarks, the Old Bailey and Big Ben. The poem is the earliest of those collected for the volume of *More "Bab" Ballads.*

169.6.2. *dog:* "card" in *Fun.*

170.4.3. *Eh:* "Ah" in *Fun* and 1873 edition.

170.8. heading. This and the next four stanzas were first given headings in the 1898 editions.

170.9.4. *Catawampous seeds:* an invention of Gilbert's. "Catawampous," American slang meaning "eager" or "fierce," was popularized in England by Dickens in *Martin Chuzzlewit.*

171.4.1. *Come* . . . : this stanza added in 1873 edition, in which "Lieutenant-Colonel Flare" is the next poem. In *Fun* the poem concludes: "(*To be Continued—Author.*)—(*No!—Editor.*)."

BLABWORTH-CUM-TALKINGTON (p. 172)—*Fun*, n.s., VII (20 June 1868), 153.

This poem is Gilbert's strongest attack upon the clergy. One might compare Lord Macaulay's "The Country Clergyman's Trip to Cambridge," which begins: "As I sat down to breakfast in state,/At my living of Tithing-cum-Boring," and ends with a stanza including these lines:

> Till at last Dr. Humdrum began;
> > From that time I remember no more.
> At Ware he commenced his prelection,
> > In the dullest of clerical drones:
> And when next I regained recollection
> > We were rumbling o'er Trumpington stones.

172.1.4. *Richmond Hill:* a fashionable district in the west of London.

172.1.5. *Epping:* a market town seventeen miles north of London; Epping Forest was a popular recreation and hunting area for Londoners.

172.2.7. *heads:* topics or chief points in a discourse or sermon.

THE SAILOR BOY TO HIS LASS (p. 174)—*Fun*, n.s., VII (27 June 1868), 163.

174.1.3. *starts:* "sails" in 1898 editions, spoiling the internal rhyme.

174.2.2. *que:* "qui" in *Fun* and 1873 and 1877 editions. *Coûte que coûte* (literally, cost what it cost) means "come what may."

174.6.4. *thrice:* "twice" in Routledge's Pocket Library edition (1887, etc.).

174.7.1. *knew:* "know" in *Fun* and 1873 edition; altered in 1877 edition.

174.7.1. *thought:* "hoped" in *Fun* and 1873 edition.

174.7.2. *wished:* "thought" in 1877 edition.

SIR CONRAD AND THE RUSTY ONE (p. 176)—*Fun*, n.s., VII (4 July 1868), 174.

176.1.3. *Talbotype:* he takes his name from the calotype photographic print, a process invented by W. H. Fox Talbot (now superseded).

176.9.3. *I would* . . . : compare Robin Oakapple's words when asked to deny the charge that he is the wicked baronet of Ruddigore: "I would, if conscientiously I could,/But I cannot!"

176.10.4. *King Harry and Aunt Jane:* possibly just a trifle less stirring than the battle cry of Shakespeare's Henry V: "God for Harry, England, and Saint George!"

176.11.3. *glaive:* sword.

176.11.4. *cleave thee to the chine:* in *Yeomen of the Guard*, Wilfred Shadbolt threatens Leonard Meryll with this phrase.

177.3.1. *malapert:* this archaism, as well as "braggadocio" in the last line of the stanza, suggests that Sir Conrad has been reading his *Faerie Queene*.

177.12.4. *Lord Mayor's Show:* the annual pageant on 9 November, inauguration date of the Lord Mayor of London, when he progresses from the City to Westminster to be presented to the monarch.

THE CUNNING WOMAN (p. 178)—*Fun*, n.s., VII (25 July 1868), 205.

Gilbert chose to retain only the last of the three illustrations to this poem when he republished it in 1873. The pastoral setting into which a Lord is introduced is similar to the situation in the first act of *Iolanthe*. The love philter device is akin to that in *The Sorcerer*, or even more like that in Donizetti's *L'elisir d'amore*, in which the quack Doctor Dulcamara offers a very effective Bordeaux as a love potion. Beginning with this poem, Gilbert's ballads frequently occupy the first or second page of the issues of *Fun* in which they were published.

178.1.1. *On:* "In" in *Fun* and 1873 edition.

178.7.4. *humble:* "honoured" in *Fun* and 1873 edition; the same change is made two stanzas later.

178.10.1. *mates:* "pals" in *Fun* and 1873 edition.

178.12.3. *Lord de Jacob Pillaloo:* perhaps his being the Lord of Jacob's Pillow explains his rock-hard indifference to Jane.

178.13.3. *women, it is:* "womankind, it's" in *Fun* and 1873 edition.

178.13.4. *one:* "none" in *Fun* and 1873 edition.

178.14.3. *faithful:* "painful" in *Fun* and 1873 edition.

179.1.3. *The Peer will:* "He's sure to" in *Fun* and 1873 edition.

179.3.3. *secrecy:* "secret for" in *Fun* and 1873 edition.

179.6.3. *rudely:* "coarsely" in *Fun*, 1873 edition, and first 1898 edition.

179.11.3. *countrymen:* "countryman" in *Fun*.

THE MODEST COUPLE (p. 180)—*Fun*, n.s., VII (8 August 1868), 225.

180.1.1. *When man and maiden meet:* there is some similarity here to the dilemma of the "poor little man" Robin and the "poor little maid" Rose, too timid to express their love for one another, in *Ruddigore*.

180.1.4. *For:* "And" in *Fun* and 1873 edition.

180.3.1. *Some . . . :* this stanza eliminated in 1898 editions.

180.5.2. *days:* "hours" in *Fun*; there are some almost equally early romances and betrothals in *Patience* (Patience and Grosvenor), *Princess Ida* (Ida and Hilarion), and *The Gondoliers* (Casilda and the Prince of Barataria).

181.1.4. *frame of mind:* Gilbert turns this phrase into a wretched pun in *H.M.S. Pinafore* when Captain Corcoran suggests to Josephine that the photograph of Sir Joseph Porter "may help to bring you to a more reasonable frame of mind."

181.3.4. *papa's:* "pa's" in *Fun* and 1873 edition.

182.1.1. *into one turn-out:* "in one chariot" in *Fun* and 1873 edition.

182.1.4. *Drove away in gallant style:* "Deposited himself" in *Fun* and 1873 edition.

THE "BANDOLINE" PLAYER (p. 183)—*Fun*, n.s., VII (22 August 1868), 246.

183.4.4. *dainty bandoline:* the *Pall Mall* critics may have had in mind some cross between a bandore (ancient lute) and a mandolin, as even the illustration would support; but "bandoline" was a gummy hairdressing which, from the illustrations, this musician seems sorely to lack.

183.12.4. *Joachim's:* Joseph Joachim (1831–1907), a virtuoso Hungarian violinist famous for his cadenzas to the Beethoven and Brahms violin concertos.

183.14.1. *Piccinni:* Niccolo Piccinni (1728–1800), an Italian opera composer who vied, unsuccessfully, with Gluck.

183.14.4. *Dot-touch-and-go:* apparently Gilbert's compound of "dot and go" (referring originally to the step of a cripple or wooden-legged man, hence "haltingly" or "limpingly") and "touch and go."

184.4.2. *Weston-super-Mare:* a popular seaside resort on the Bristol Channel.

SIR BARNABY BAMPTON BOO (p. 185)—*Fun,* n.s., VII (29 August 1868), 255.

A jester by the name of Barnaby is said to have given his name to a lively dance. In time, the expression "to Barnaby dance" came to describe any quick and uneven movement.

185.4.3. *as:* added in 1898 editions.

185.5.4. *Carrotty:* "Volatile" throughout the poem in 1898 editions.

186.1.1. *There . . . :* this stanza eliminated in 1898 editions when Gilbert changed the illustrations from the high grotesque to the low insipid. In *Fun,* where the stanza came at the bottom of the first column and the cut of the Misses de Plow at the top of the second, a pointing hand is printed at the end of the first line of the stanza.

186.3.4. *Tupper:* see note to "Ferdinando and Elvira," p. 323.

186.5.4. *no:* accidentally "do" in 1873 edition.

186.5.7. *My . . . :* compare the words in the Lord Chancellor's "Nightmare Song" in *Iolanthe:* "the night has been long—ditto ditto my song—."

BOULOGNE (p. 187)—*Fun,* n.s., VIII (12 September 1868), 7.

If not much as verse, this is at least a very detailed description of the holiday city just across the Channel from home.

187.1.6. *from:* "to" in *Fun.*

187.1.7. *South-Eastern mail:* the South-Eastern Railway Company ran a fast and frequent steamer service between Folkestone and Boulogne.

189.1.2. *Masaniello:* a chorus of fishermen open Act II of Auber's *La Muette de Portici,* which, when first performed in London in 1829, was titled *Masaniello; or, The Dumb Girl of Portici.* It is based on a historical figure, a seventeenth-century Neopolitan fisherman who led a brief insurrection against the government.

189.2.1. *Etablissement balls:* the Etablissement de Bains provided, in addition to sea and pool bathing, concerts, dances, and a gambling casino.

189.2.2. *vandyked petticoats:* a vandyke is a cut edge to a garment, like a zigzag or a chevron.

BRAVE ALUM BEY (p. 190)—*Fun,* n.s., VIII (19 September 1868), 16.

Like his fellow Turk Pasha Bailey Ben, the brave Alum Bey has an English name; Alum Bay is at the westernmost tip of the Isle of Wight.

190.2.2. *zenana:* an East Indian harem.

190.2.2. *bul-bul:* the Persian nightingale.

190.2.4. *Backsheesh:* gratuity or alms-giving.

190.2.4. *Rahat Lakoum:* the confection "Turkish delight."

190.3.2. *kismet:* fate, in Turkish.

190.3.2. *tchibouk:* a type of Turkish tobacco pipe (usually spelled "chibouk"); the Bey is smoking one in the middle illustration.

190.3.4. *ka-bob:* Gilbert neatly finishes off his whimsical series of Eastern terms by putting the genuine menu item not in the kettle but in the eye.

190.4.4. *Seringapatam:* town in southern Mysore, India.

191.4.1. *furnace of:* "fire of red" in *Fun*.

191.6.2. *garment:* "raiment" in *Fun*.

191.8.1. *it knows how:* "a beggar" in *Fun* and 1873 edition.

191.9.1. *seized on:* "collared" in *Fun* and 1873 edition.

191.9.2. *Pacha:* Pasha; hence just more Turkish nonsense.

192.1.2. *Get it over, my tulips:* "You'd best get it over" in *Fun* and 1873 edition.

192.1.3. *lay:* "get" in *Fun* and 1873 edition.

192.1.4. *cling to:* "collar" in *Fun* and 1873 edition.

192.4.3. *further:* "farther" in second 1898 edition.

192.5.2. *something:* "summut" in *Fun;* "summat" in 1873 edition.

192.5.4. *drawing:* "initial" in *Fun,* since the illustration came first there rather than last.

GREGORY PARABLE, LL.D. (p. 193)—*Fun,* n.s., VIII (3 October 1868), 35.

In *Fun* the title is "Doctor Parable, LL.D."

193.3.4. *Eton Gram:* even at Eton at this time the old *Eton Latin Grammar* was being replaced by the *Public Schools Latin Primer,* but it was not long before a new Eton grammar asserted itself. Gregory undoubtedly had the old one.

193.3.14. *Henry:* James Henry (1798–1876), a great Virgilian scholar who wrote several volumes of notes to the *Aeneid.*

194.1.3. *Balbus:* "The Romans also built towns wherever they were wanted, and, in addition, a wall between England and Scotland to keep out the savage Picts and Scots. This wall was the work of the memorable Roman Emperor Balbus and was thus called Hadrian's Wall" (Walter Carruthers Seller and Robert Julian Yeatman, *1066 and All That* [London: Methuen, 1930], 4).

194.3.11. *musa musae:* beginning of the declension of the word for "muse," a first-declension noun.

194.3.17. *Amas:* you (singular) love; Ovid, of course, wrote the *Ars Amatoria.*

195.1.7. *for:* "to" in *Fun*.

195.1.9. *Boucicault or Baring:* Dion Boucicault came of humble, even dubious, origins to make a fortune as a writer of melodramas in America and England. The Barings were a famous banking family: the merchant founder of the firm, Francis Baring, was knighted; one of his sons was created Lord Ashburton and a grandson became the first Lord Northbrook.

195.1.10. *very:* "jolly" in *Fun* and 1873 edition.

195.1.12. *My child . . . :* in *Fun* and 1873 edition the last three lines of this stanza read:

> Come, Mary, we will go and try
> If he would like to marry thee,
> If not, thy bride the maid shall be.

195.4.2. *took a parchment:* compare the act of Otto in "The Baron Klopfzetterheim" and see note (on Balfe's *Bohemian Girl*), p. 315.

195.4.8. *Duke of Gretna Green:* Gretna Green, just over the border into Scotland, has been famous since 1754 as a place where eloping couples could be married by the village blacksmith. The first act of Gilbert's comedy *Engaged* is set in the garden of a cottage strategically located on the border near Gretna Green.

LIEUTENANT-COLONEL FLARE (p. 196)—*Fun*, n.s., VIII (10 October 1868), 46.

196.1.1. *The earth* . . . : note the similarity in meter, language, and sentiment of this stanza to "The British Grenadiers."

196.3.6. *stifling:* "laying" in *Fun* and 1873 edition.

196.7.4. *He'd* . . . : in *Fun* and 1873 edition this line reads "They'd always change for his."

197.2.6. *teary dew:* in *Fun* this poetic sentiment receives the footnote comment, "Very pretty."

THE HERMIT (p. 198)—*Fun*, n.s., VIII (17 October 1868), 62.

198.9.1. *Chatham:* the Royal Dockyards at Chatham were built and maintained, beginning in 1856, in part by convict labor. The same was true at Devonport from 1866. The huge breakwaters at the Portland naval station were built by prisoners from 1849 to 1872.

199.2.1. *Then:* accidentally "Men" in *Fun*.

ANNIE PROTHEROE (p. 200)—*Fun*, n.s., VIII (24 October 1868), 65.

The charming young couple in this ballad are related to Phoebe Meryll and Wilfred Shadbolt in *Yeomen of the Guard*. In both instances the sweethearts of what might be termed penal officers are in love with gentlemen about to be executed but reprieved at the last moment.

200.3.2. *Cal-craft:* William Calcraft was executioner for London from 1829 to 1874. For an additional fee he offered his services in the provinces. After one multiple execution the crowd cheered, "Calcraft, Calcraft, he's the man!" The last public execution in London occurred only a few months before this poem appeared.

201.1.2. *collared head:* "the meat of the head and other parts of a pig, ox, etc., boiled, cut into small pieces and pressed into the shape of a roll, often with the skin laid round" (*Oxford English Dictionary*); our "headcheese."

201.1.3. *This collared* . . . : in *Fun* and 1873 edition the last lines of this stanza read: "This reminds me I must settle on the next ensuing day/The hash of that unmitigated villain PETER GRAY."

201.1.4. *Peter Gray:* also the name of the unfortunate young man in the American folksong who, when rejected by his sweetheart, goes west and is scalped by Indians.

201.2.4. *gentle Annie:* both "Gentle Annie," a song by Stephen Foster, and "Peter Gray" were sung by minstrel groups in London in the sixties.

202.2.3. *If you* . . . : in *Fun* and 1873 edition this line reads "If you appear with that, you may depend you'll rue the day."

202.5.1. *stock:* a broad, stiffened band worn as a cravat.

203.2.2. *having:* "as I'd" in *Fun* and 1873 edition.

203.3.1. *could not:* "couldn't" in *Fun*.

203.3.4. *you monster:* "old fellow" in *Fun* and 1873 edition; "young Gilbert" in 1877 edition.

THE CAPTAIN AND THE MERMAIDS (p. 204)—*Fun*, n.s., VIII (7 November 1868), 85.

204.3.4. *his:* "those" in *Fun* and 1873, 1877, and first 1898 editions.

204.3.6. *Timbs:* John Timbs (1801–1875), a prolific writer of books on matters curious and antiquarian.

204.5.5. *kerseymere:* a woolen cloth for men's wear (usually "cassimere").

204.6.3. *And . . . :* in 1877 edition this line reads "And, when the day was dry."

204.6.5. *there every day:* "from morn till night" in 1877 edition.

204.7.1. *sneered pooh-pooh:* "laughed a few" in *Fun* and 1873 edition; "laughed, 'Pooh! pooh!'" in 1877 edition.

204.7.6. *smalls:* close-fitting knee breeches.

205.2.3. *Cleggs:* "him" in *Fun* and 1873 edition.

205.10.4. *You're only half a captain:* similar jokes are made at Strephon's expense in *Iolanthe,* who is "a fairy down to the waist—but his legs are mortal."

AN UNFORTUNATE LIKENESS (p. 206)—*Fun,* n.s., VIII (14 November 1868), 96.

206.2.1. *ben.:* benefit.

206.5.2. *with all my skill:* "it's evident" in *Fun* and 1873 edition.

206.n.2. *she shall:* "shall she" in *Fun* and 1873 edition.

206.n.6. *Act II:* "Act IV," mistakenly, in *Fun* and all editions.

207.10.1. *cellar-flaps:* see note to "John and Freddy," p. 329.

208.3.2. *a:* accidentally omitted in 1898 editions.

A BOULOGNE TABLE D'HOTE (p. 208)—*Tom Hood's Comic Annual for 1868* (London: Fun office, 1868), 78.

This and the next two poems were published under the collective title "A Batch of Ballads." The date of publication of the annual, actually *for* 1869, was probably in the latter part of November. The air to which the ballad is set, correctly entitled "I Vowed that I Never Would Leave Her," was composed and sung by Arthur Lloyd.

THE RAILWAY GUARD'S SONG (p. 210)—*Tom Hood's Comic Annual for 1868,* 79.

The air "Crescendo Galop" has not been traced.

"THE UNDECIDED MAN" (p. 211)—*Tom Hood's Comic Annual for 1868,* 79.

The air to which the ballad is set, more fully titled "She Lodges at a Sugar Shop," was composed by G. W. Hunt and sung by Alfred Vance. This air and "I Vowed that I Never Would Leave Her" had been used by Gilbert in his first extravaganza, *Dulcamara,* in 1866.

PREMONITORY SYMPTOMS (p. 212)—*Fun,* n.s., VIII (28 November 1868), 117.

212.5.7. *never will cross again:* the same sentiment, presumably for the same reason, is expressed by the Duke of Plaza-Toro and suite in *The Gondoliers:*

> If ever, ever, ever
> They get back to Spain,
> They will never, never, never
> Cross the sea again!

LOST MR. BLAKE (p. 212)—*Fun,* n.s., VIII (28 November 1868), 121.

212.1.3. *on Sunday:* "on a Sunday" in 1877 edition.

212.2.1. *particular:* "special" in *Fun* and 1873 edition; altered in 1877 edition.

212.2.2. *at the church:* "at church" in 1877 edition.

212.2.4. *nasty:* added in 1898 editions.

213.1.2. *the width:* "the proper width" in *Fun* and 1873 edition.

213.2.4. *ecclesiastical:* "exaggerated" in *Fun* and 1873 edition.

213.4.1. *Mrs. Grundy:* the embodiment of prudish respectability—from the character who never appears but is frequently referred to in Thomas Morton's comedy *Speed the Plow.*

213.4.2. *Koh-i-noor:* the Kohinoor diamond, over a hundred carats in weight, became a British crown jewel in 1849.

214.1.1. *say she:* "say that, 'she [the rest of the line a quotation]'" in 1877 edition.

214.4.4. *the dinner:* "the parlour dinner" in *Fun* and 1873 and 1877 editions.

215.1.1. *farther:* "further" in *Fun* and 1873 edition.

215.1.1. *on Sundays:* added in 1898 editions.

215.1.4. *into:* "in" in *Fun* and 1873 edition.

215.3.3. *their evenings:* in *Fun* (where the drawing placed last in this edition was first) a parenthesis was added: "as shown in the initial."

LITTLE OLIVER (p. 216)—*Fun,* n.s., VIII (5 December 1868), 132.

216.2.3. *Minnie-haha:* "From the waterfall he named her,/Minnehaha, Laughing Water."

216.7.3. *Knee-suitor:* Pliny, in his *Natural History,* tells of Apelles' advice to his shoemaker, *Ne supra crepidam sutor judicaret,* which is usually translated, "Let the cobbler stick to his last." Oliver was perhaps a better punster than Latin scholar.

216.9.4. *Niedermeyer's opera:* a reference to the Swiss composer Louis Niedermeyer's *Marie Stuart,* first performed on 6 December 1844. The name is spelled "Neidermeyer" in *Fun* and all editions of the "Babs."

216.10.3. *Who ardently:* "And that the dame" in *Fun* and 1873 edition.

217.2.2. *Esmeralda's kid:* in Hugo's *Notre-Dame de Paris,* the gypsy dancing-girl Esmeralda has a pet goat, Djali, who dances and performs tricks. H. J. Byron wrote an extravaganza in 1862 entitled *Esmeralda; or, The "Sensation" Goat.*

217.5.3. *The upper:* "At length the" in *Fun* and 1873 edition.

217.10.1. *in tone consoling:* "his hands still wringing" in *Fun* and 1873 edition.

217.10.3. *The song . . . :* in *Fun* and 1873 edition this line reads "The ballad that you heard her singing."

217.14.2. *Sensation:* melodrama.

WHAT IS A BURLESQUE? (p. 218)—*Belgravia Annual,* ed. M. E. Braddon (London, 1868), 106–107.

Perhaps all that can be said for these lines is that they provide a fair description of Victorian theatrical burlesques. As drama critic for *Fun* and *The Illustrated Times* Gilbert was forced to witness dozens of them.

THE PHANTOM HEAD (p. 220)—*Fun,* n.s., VIII (19 December 1868), 151.

221.4.4. *Second James:* these three must have been among those sentenced to death at the Bloody Assizes (1685) for supporting the Duke of Monmouth in his attempt to overthrow James.

221.5.2. *Those:* "That" in *Fun;* an error.

THE POLITEST OF NATIONS! (p. 222)—*Fun,* n.s., VIII (2 January 1869), 173.

Gilbert offers a standard Victorian assessment of the French in this trivial poem.

222.2.8. *by chalks:* by far.

WOMAN'S GRATITUDE (p. 223)—*Fun,* n.s., VIII (9 January 1869), 176–177.

The situation here is similar to that in Gilbert's serious drama *Broken Hearts,* in which the misshapen dwarf Mousta loves in vain and is reminded rudely of his unlovable appearance by the handsome Prince Florian. In this poem and that play Gilbert is most guilty of the charge of unfeeling inhumanity.

224.2.7. *The cat . . . :* i.e., "A cat may look at a king."

224.6.8. *springald:* a youth or stripling; common in Tudor times, the word was revived by Scott and Byron.

THE BABY'S VENGEANCE (p. 225)—*Fun,* n.s., VIII (16 January 1869), 188.

The changeling motif and the willingness of the two parties to rectify the situation, also found in "General John," was used again by Gilbert in *H.M.S. Pinafore* and *The Gondoliers.* There is also a prefiguring here of the concept of the Statutory Duel of *The Grand Duke,* in which rivals draw cards and

> The winner must adopt
> The loser's poor relations—
> Discharge his debts,
> Pay all his bets,
> And take his obligations.

225.1.2. *Bromptonville:* Brompton?

225.1.4. *Polygon, Somers Town:* then, as now, a blighted area just above the Euston train station.

225.2.3. *herited:* "inherited" in 1877 edition.

226.2.2. *dustman:* one who removes ashes and other refuse; in America, the garbage man. Frederick's occupation, and the foster-mother's mangling, suggest figures in Dickens' *Our Mutual Friend.*

226.4. heading. This heading appears in the 1877 edition to introduce Paley's confession.

226.4.3. *wed ten years or so:* "whom you ought to know" in *Fun* and 1873 edition.

226.4.4. *Drum Lane, Ealing:* now the Ealing Road, this was the lower portion of Ealing Lane in Old Brentford, just north of the Thames and too close to the wharves and gasworks to be a good address. Some of the low row houses, dating from 1831, still remain.

226.5.1. *her:* "their" in 1877 edition.

227.1.1. *One . . . :* in *Fun* and 1873 edition this stanza begins:

> One day—it was quite early in the week—
> I *in my cradle having placed the bantling—*

> Crept into his! He had not learnt to speak,
> But I could see his face with anger mantling.

The "bantling" changed to "brat" reminds us of Don Alhambra's use of "bratling" to describe a parallel case in *The Gondoliers*.

227.2.2. *There . . .* : this line reads "No wickedness but I was game to try for it" in *Fun* and 1873 edition.

227.4.4. *shake-down:* a make-shift bed, usually of straw shaken down on the ground or floor.

227.5.5. *for:* "far" in *Fun* and 1873 edition.

228.2.3. *jean:* formerly pronounced "jane."

THE TWO OGRES (p. 229)—*Fun*, n.s., VIII (23 January 1869), 204.

This is the first of the poems to be titled "The Bab Ballads" in *Fun*. The first collected edition of "Babs" was out, and it was probably thought that the use of the title for each new poem would help the sales of both magazine and book.

229.2.1. *Wickham Wold:* the rolling country north of Portsmouth, in Hampshire.

229.2.2. *Each . . .* : in *Fun* and 1873 edition this line reads "One grown up—one a lad."

229.2.4. *was as:* "one was" in *Fun* and 1873 edition.

229.3.3. *elder:* "younger" in *Fun* and 1873 edition.

229.4.3. *to:* accidentally "too" in 1898 editions.

229.5.2. *ate:* pronounced to rhyme with "net."

229.11.4. *zoetropes:* see note to "Captain Reece," p. 338.

229.12.1. *when he was quite a youth:* "before he grew so big" in *Fun* and 1873 edition.

229.12.3. *so bad, to tell the truth:* "of course, a reckless pig" in *Fun* and 1873 edition.

229.14.1. *Expound:* "You hound" in *Fun* and 1873 edition.

230.4.1. *his Mentors:* James' logic, and his mentors' difficulties in discovering the fallacy, is like Robin Oakapple's attempts to defraud his ancestors in *Ruddigore* and Sir Roderic's annoyed perplexity: "These arguments sound very well, but I can't help thinking that, if they were reduced to syllogistic form, they wouldn't hold water."

230.6.1. *and penal woes:* "unworthy son" in *Fun* and 1873 edition.

230.6.3. *those:* "one" in *Fun* and 1873 edition.

230.6.4. *dare:* "dares" in *Fun* and 1873 edition.

230.7.3. *Drury Lane:* where good boys would be enjoying the best pantomime in London, especially at this time, under F. B. Chatterton's management.

230.9.4. *Lemprière:* John Lemprière's *Bibliotheca Classica, or Classical Dictionary,* was first published in 1788. E. H. Barker offered an edition "abridged for public and private schools of both sexes" in 1833.

230.10.1. *But . . .* : in *Fun* and 1873 edition this stanza reads:

> But as for APPLEBODY BLAND,
>   Who only eats the bad,
> A fitting recompense we've planned
>   For that deserving lad.

230.11.1. *wicked youths:* "naughty boys" in *Fun* and 1873 edition.

230.11.3. *Hackney Road Reformatory School:* no institution with this name has been traced. By 1869, the Reformatory and Refuge Union claimed that there were two hundred ten reformatories, refuges, and industrial schools in the country giving shelter to twenty thousand youths (see *Conference of Managers of Reformatory and Industrial Institutions* [London, 1869], ix).

MISTER WILLIAM (p. 231)—*Fun,* n.s., VIII (6 February 1869), 217. No. 60.

This was the first of the "Babs" to be given a number in *Fun*—"No. 60" (see Introduction, p. 13). When published in *More "Bab" Ballads* it was placed first. When both sets of collected poems were joined in the 1898 edition, interspersed with Savoy Opera lyrics, the order was left exactly as it had been in the separate volumes with the exception of this poem, placed later. The explanation is found in a letter from Gilbert to Routledge: "I find that in the enclosed proofs three Bab Ballads, written in very similar metre, occur together (with a Savoyard interposed)—viz 'Gentle Alice Brown' 'Mister William' & 'The Bumboat Woman's Story.' Would it not be well to take the middle one of these (Mister William) & transfer it elsewhere, substituting for it a Bab Ballad of totally different metre? Its [sic] not important, but might be worth considering" (letter, dated 14 November 1897, in the Pierpont Morgan Library).

231.3.4. *deal in:* "plan" in *Fun* and 1873 edition.

231.5.3. *Is free . . . :* in *Fun* and 1873 edition this line reads "May then for half an hour perpetrate a deed of shame."

233.4.2. *the disgusting:* "uncongenial" in *Fun* and 1873 edition.

233.4.3. *For when:* "When quite" in *Fun* and 1873 edition.

233.5.1. *garroter:* there was a rash of garrotings, or strangulations, in the London streets in the sixties.

233.8.1. *ticket:* a ticket-of-leave, as seen in the illustration; this is an "order of license" giving a convict his liberty under certain restrictions before his sentence has expired (comparable to parole in the United States).

THE MARTINET (p. 234)—*Fun,* n.s., VIII (13 February 1869), 228. No. 61.

234.4.2. *half-pay:* Gilbert would seem to be fusing, or confusing, the story of Captain Reece with that of Captain Cleggs ("The Captain and the Mermaids"), who is put on half-pay for being but half-man.

234.11.1. *Then William Lee:* compare stanza eleven of "Captain Reece," p. 143.

235.3.2. *did not:* "didn't" in *Fun* and 1873 edition.

235.5.4. *Shame:* the romantic crew of *H.M.S. Pinafore* also cries "Shame!" when Dick Deadeye realistically points out comparable distinctions of rank.

235.12.3. *straightway:* "William" in *Fun* and 1873 edition.

THE KING OF CANOODLE-DUM (p. 236)—*Fun,* n.s., VIII (20 February 1869), 238–239. No. 62.

"Canoodle," originally American slang for "fondle," was anglicized by Gilbert's colleague George Augustus Sala in 1864. By the date of this poem the word had come to mean "coax" as well. Canoodle-Dum is the see of the colonial bishop in Gilbert's story "A Christian Frame of Mind," *Fun,* 8 January 1870. The concept of a tropical isle choosing to model itself on English lines is elaborated upon in *Utopia Limited,* where the whimsy of a Frederick Gowler is replaced by a quasi-serious satire of English institutions.

236.2.2. *Hum! Golly de do to-day:* typical refrain to a song in minstrel dialect.

236.2.3. *Buckra:* a Negro's term, often contemptuous, for a white man (from the Efik word *mbākara*).

236.3.7. *William the Fourth:* Frederick's choice is a good one for a mariner to make, for William, who ruled in his old age from 1830 to 1837, was known as the Sailor King.

236.5.4. *Grinnidge's Naval Fane:* Greenwich's Royal Naval College and Museum of Naval Architecture.

236.5.8. *"Angel" at Islington:* this famous inn had been the first stop on the old North Road from London. It was an omnibus terminus in Gilbert's day.

236.6.2. *At Canoodle-Dum to:* "To stop with him—yes" in *Fun* and 1873 edition; "In his capital to" in 1877 edition.

237.3.7. *jacky:* the rhyming of this word with "tobaccy" occurs also in *H.M.S. Pinafore:* "I've snuff and tobaccy, and excellent jacky."

237.4.3. *darning their eyes:* sailors were as well known as was Sam Hall for their "damn your eyes's."

237.4.4. *that:* omitted in 1877 edition.

237.4.7. *wore—stitches:* "wore breeches" in 1877 edition; "were breeches" in Routledge's Pocket Library edition (1887, etc.). In 1873 edition "stitches" is in very small print.

237.6.5. *who loves a:* "a walking" in *Fun* and 1873 edition; altered in 1877. "Bathos" receives the comment "Fine" at the bottom of the page in *Fun*.

237.6.7. *C.B.:* Companion of the Bath. Sir Blennerhasset Portico ("The Mystic Selvagee"), Sir Joseph Porter (*H.M.S. Pinafore*), and Captain Corcoran (*Utopia Limited*) are all even higher in the Order of the Bath: Knight Commander, or K.C.B.

237.7.1. *officer:* "rebel, he" in *Fun* and 1873 edition.

237.7.8. *That Admiral slowly:* "These horrible pirates" in *Fun* and 1873 edition.

237.8.6. *They:* "The," by mistake, in 1873 edition.

237.8.6. *the:* "his" in *Fun* and 1873 edition.

FIRST LOVE (p. 238)—*Fun,* n.s., VIII (27 February 1869), 248. No. 63.

238.1.4. *At:* accidentally omitted in *Fun*.

238.1.4. *hundred:* "thousand" in *Fun* and 1873 edition; here Gilbert's moderating seems justified.

238.9.2. *Godfrey's Grenadiers:* Daniel Godfrey, of a family of military bandmasters, held such a post with the Grenadier Guards from 1856 to 1896. He wrote and adapted many songs and dances for military band.

238.9.3. *Coote:* Charles Coote formed a quadrille band in 1848 which was popular in aristocratic circles. He, too, composed and arranged many dance pieces, mostly from opera airs.

238.9.3. *Tinney:* F. G. Tinney was pianist to the Duchess of Bedford and composer of dozens of waltzes, quadrilles, and galops which he conducted "at Her Majesty's State Balls, and the Nobility's Soirées Dansantes." For several years "Coote and Tinney" were partners in a music publishing firm.

238.13.2. *M.B. waistcoat:* a long coat or cassock waistcoat worn by some clergymen, first recorded in 1853. The abbreviation stands for "mark of the beast," a reference to the supposed Popery implied by such apparel.

239.4.1. *Bayard:* the heroic French knight, Chevalier de Bayard (1475–1524), known as "le chevalier sans peur et sans reproche."

239.9.4. *sluggard:* old Aaron is quoting scripture to Nell: "Go to the ant, thou sluggard; consider her ways and be wise" (Proverbs 6:6).

239.10.3. *pugnacious:* "disgraceful" in *Fun* and 1873 edition.

THE HAUGHTY ACTOR (p. 240)—*Fun*, n.s., IX (27 March 1869), 31. No. 64.

241.1.6. *was:* "but" in *Fun.*

241.4.4. *Utility:* in a theatrical company, the utility actor was called upon to play a variety of small parts. "First amputation" would correspond to "First Gentleman" or leading man, a starring "line of business."

242.2.5. *placed upon the shelf:* Gilbert used this expression again in another courtroom situation, in *Trial by Jury* when the Judge decides: "Put your briefs upon the shelf,/I will marry her myself!" The rhyming of "pecker" with "Exchequer" also occurs in that opera.

242.3.4. *Nisi Prius:* trial of a civil action (literally, "unless sooner").

242.4.4. *In Banco or in Error:* the former, meaning "on the bench," is applied to sittings of the Superior Court of Common Law (as distinguished for sittings of Judges at Nisi Prius or on circuit); the latter refers to a court of appeal from a previous decision.

THE TWO MAJORS (p. 243)—*Fun*, n.s., IX (3 April 1869), 41. No. 65.

The situation in this poem, in which two cowardly rivals for the hand of a simple maid decide not to fight for her after all, has its counterparts in *Iolanthe* and, even more closely, *Utopia Limited.*

243.3.4. *Makredi Prepare:* a pun on the words addressed to a weaponed soldier.

243.4.2. *their:* "them" in second 1898 edition.

243.5.1. *For . . . :* this stanza eliminated from 1898 editions.

244.2.4. *Vivandière:* see note to "Lorenzo de Lardy," p. 330.

244.3.1. *we know:* "you see" in *Fun* and 1873 edition.

244.4.1. *It . . . :* this stanza eliminated from 1898 editions.

245.1.2. *my:* added in 1898 editions.

245.2.1. *has:* "had" in 1873 edition; altered in 1877 edition.

THE THREE BOHEMIAN ONES (p. 246)—*Fun*, n.s., IX (10 April 1869), 51. No. 66.

This poem was first reprinted by Rowland Grey in "The Author of Pinafore: Sir W. S. Gilbert as I Knew Him," *Century Magazine*, LXXXIV (October 1912), 849–850.

246.8.4. *Zion Villa, Clapham Rise:* Clapham residents had a reputation at this time for evangelical, nonconformist religious beliefs; if there was not a villa, there was at least a Zion chapel there. Sir Jasper probably felt very much at home in "that sanctified ville," as Thomas Ingoldsby called it.

247.3.1. *St. George's . . . :* well-known London hospitals.

247.4.4. *diachylum:* an adhesive plaster.

247.8.1. *Interea:* in the meanwhile.

THE POLICEMAN'S BEARD (p. 248)—*Fun*, n.s., IX (1 May 1869), 75. No. 67.

249.2.4. *inside places:* seats inside a coach or carriage.

249.3.2. *Lieutenant Colonel Henderson:* when Sir Edmund Henderson, lieutenant-colonel in the Royal Engineers, became Chief Commissioner of Metropolitan Police in 1869, he introduced several changes and reforms. His actual order on beards read: "Beards and Moustaches.—The metropolitan police will in future be permitted to wear beards and moustaches." The *Police Service Advertiser* recorded that "The 'order' was received with general satisfaction by the men, many of whom said it would save them a few minutes every morning in the use of the rasor" (3 April 1869, p. 4).

THE BISHOP OF RUM-TI-FOO AGAIN (p. 250)—*Fun*, n.s., IX (8 May 1869), 85. No. 68.

250.1.4. *Last summer twelvemonth:* "The Bishop of Rum-ti-Foo" had actually appeared in *Fun* on 16 November 1867.

250.2.3. *Synod, called Pan-Anglican:* see note to "The Bishop of Rum-ti-Foo," p. 334.

250.4.5. *Payne-cum-Lauri:* see note to "The Bishop of Rum-ti-Foo," p. 335.

250.4.7. *fruits of Progress:* compare the subtitle to *Utopia Limited,* "The Flowers of Progress."

250.6.7. *Royal N.:* Gilbert used this abbreviation for a rhyme again in *H.M.S. Pinafore:*

> We're smart and sober men,
>   And quite devoid of fe-ar,
> In all the Royal N.
>   None are so smart as we are.

251.2.2. *unseemly:* "disgraceful" in *Fun* and 1873 edition.

251.3.8. *Cutch-chi-boo:* in *Fun* and 1873 edition a footnote says this dance is "described by Mungo Park." If that famous Scottish explorer of the Niger does so, it is not by name, though he describes certain dances which "consisted more in wanton gestures than in muscular exertion or graceful attitudes. The ladies vied with each other in displaying the most voluptuous movements imaginable" (*Travels in the Interior of Africa* [New York: Cassell, n.d.] I, 68–69). There is also, of course, the coochy dance, or hootchy-cootchy, described by side-show barkers at fairs and circuses.

A WORM WILL TURN (p. 252)—*Fun*, n.s., IX (15 May 1869), 104. No. 69.

252.8.3. *sloped:* ran off.

252.8.4. *forged:* "died" in *Fun* and 1873 edition.

253.5.1. *And . . . :* this stanza eliminated in 1898 editions.

THE MYSTIC SELVAGEE (p. 254)—*Fun*, n.s., IX (22 May 1869), 112. No. 70.

A selvagee (or "salvagee," as spelled in *Fun* and the 1873 edition) is "a strong and pliant hank, or untwisted skein of rope-yarn marled together, and used as a strap to fasten round a shroud or stay, or slings to which to hook a tackle to hoist in any heavy articles." For this and all the following definitions of nautical terms the reader must hold responsible Admiral W. H. Smyth, compiler of *The Sailor's Word-Book* (London: Blackie & Son, 1867).

254.1.2. *Sir Blennerhasset Portico:* Harmon Blennerhasset, an Irishman, established an elaborate mansion on an island in the Ohio River in 1798.

254.1.4. *K.C.B.:* Knight Commander of the Bath.

254.1.8. *Rodney:* Admiral Rodney, who defeated the French fleet off Dominica in 1782, capturing their flagship and commander, was voted the thanks of the nation and created Baron Rodney of Stoke-Rodney.

254.2.1. *Benbow? Cornwallis? Hood?:* Admiral John Benbow (1653–1702) also encountered the French in the West Indies and died there from a ball which had shattered his leg. Admiral William Cornwallis (1744–1816) was commander-in-chief of the fleet in the West Indies not long after Rodney's retirement. Admiral Samuel Hood (1724–1816) served under Rodney and felt, probably rightly, that if his superior had not stopped the rout of the French when he did, the English might have taken twenty more ships.

254.3.10. *Eheu fugaces:* in bk. 2 of the *Odes,* Horace writes:

> *Eheu! fugaces, Posthume, Posthume,*
> *Labuntur anni; nec pietas moram*
> *Rugis et instanti senectae*
> *Afferet, indomitaeque morti.*

(Alas! Posthumus, Posthumus, the flying years glide by; nor can religion give pause to wrinkles, and approaching age, and invincible death.) The lines were best known to Victorians as treated epigrammatically in the *Ingoldsby Legends:*

> What Horace says is
> Eheu fugaces
> Anni Labuntur, Postume, Postume!
> Years glide away, and are lost to me, lost to me.

254.5.9. *swifting in:* "when the lower rigging becomes slack at sea, single blocks are placed on each shroud about 8 feet above the deck, a hawser rove through them, and the rigging swifted in, to bring a fair strain."

255.1.2. *Peak-halliard blocks:* "the . . . tackles by which the outer end of a gaff is hoisted, as opposed to the *throat-halliards.*"

255.1.6. *maintop-stay:* "the *main-topmast stay* is attached to the hounds of the foremast, or comes on deck."

255.2.2. *deadeyes:* "a sort of round flattish wooden block, or oblate piece of elm, encircled, and fixed to the channels by the chainplate: it is pierced with three holes through the flat part, in order to receive a rope called the laniard, which, corresponding with three holes in another dead-eye on the shroud end, creates a purchase to set up and extend the shrouds and stays, backstays, &c., of the standing and topmast rigging."

255.2.4. *cutter's:* "a small single-masted, sharp-built broad vessel, commonly navigated in the English Channel, furnished with a straight running bowsprit, occasionally run in horizontally on the deck; except for which, and the largeness of the sails, they are rigged much like sloops."

255.2.7. *Breast backstays:* "they extend from the head of an upper-mast, through an outrigger, down to the channels before the standing backstays, for supporting the upper spars from to windward. When to leeward, they are borne abaft the top-rim."

255.5.4. *unshipped:* "Unship. To remove any piece of tackle from its situation in which it is generally used. . . ."

255.5.8. *said:* "says" in *Fun.*

EMILY, JOHN, JAMES, AND I (p. 256)—*Fun*, n.s., IX (29 May 1869), 115. No. 71.

256.1.3. *And:* first added in Routledge's Pocket Library edition (1887, etc.). The same is true at this point in the next stanza.

257.1.3. *Some:* "Young" in *Fun* and 1873 edition.

257.2.3. *pads:* paddies, slang for Irishmen.

257.8.1. *crusher came down:* "constable fell" in 1877 edition.

257.8.3. *Let . . . :* this line first italicized in 1898 editions.

258.2.2. *scenes:* "scene" in *Fun.*

THE GHOST TO HIS LADYE LOVE (p. 259)—*Fun,* n.s., IX (14 August 1869), 233.

This poem is not one of the numbered series of ballads, nor is it a typical "Bab." It bears a resemblance to Sir Roderic's ghost song in *Ruddigore,* which includes the lines: "And then each ghost with his ladye-toast to their churchyard beds takes flight,/With a kiss, perhaps, on her lantern chaps, and a grisly grim 'good-night.'"

PRINCE IL BALEINE (p. 260)—*Fun,* n.s., IX (28 August 1869), 253. No. 72.

If this prince derives his name from the Italian "il baleno" (brilliance), perhaps it is to suggest his splendor; if from the French "la baleine" (whale), perhaps to suggest his size in the estimation of his admirers. See note to "Peter the Wag," p. 341.

260.3.5. *dolce far niente:* sweet idleness. Gilbert liked the rhyming possibilities of this expression and used it in *Iolanthe, The Gondoliers,* and *Utopia Limited.*

261.9.5. *Prince's happy valet:* a punning allusion to the Happy Valley of Samuel Johnson's Prince Rasselas.

THE WAY OF WOOING (p. 262)—*Fun,* n.s., X (11 September 1869), 13. No. 73.

According to Jane Stedman, *Gilbert Before Sullivan* (Chicago: University of Chicago Press, 1967), 244, the 1872 version of Gilbert's *Happy Arcadia* included this poem as a solo number.

262.1.8. *thus:* "this" in 1877 edition.

262.1.12. *As:* "But" in 1873 edition.

263.1.5. *thumb:* "tongue" in Routledge's Pocket Library edition (1887, etc.).

263.1.9. *to:* omitted (accidentally?) from 1898 editions.

THE SCORNFUL COLONEL (p. 264)—*Fun,* n.s., X (25 September 1869), 31. No. 74.

264.2.1. *his lip would curl:* similar behavior is asked of the British tar in *H.M.S. Pinafore:* "his lip should curl."

264.4.3. *By sections, 'Phew'!* compare the command of the Colonel of Dragoons in *Patience:* "By sections of threes—Rapture!"

THE VARIABLE BABY (p. 266)—*Fun,* n.s., X (9 October 1869), 51. No. 75.

The illustration of Jeremiah Stutely in his old age is very like one used by Gilbert the following February in "The Reverend Simon Magus" to portray the ninety-five year old vicar.

266.4.4. *moon of honey:* in his long poem *Miss Kilmansegg and Her Precious Leg* Thomas Hood (the elder) had written:

> But of all the lunar things that change,
> The one that shows most fickle and strange,
> And takes the most eccentric range,
>   Is the moon—so called—of honey!

266.11.3. *Crichton:* see note to "The Baron Klopfzetterheim," p. 315.

266.12.3. *a sell:* a great disappointment.

267.9.2. *gaby:* fool.

THE LADIES OF THE LEA (p. 268)—*Fun*, n.s., X (30 October 1869), 75. No. 76.

The title of this poem is a pluralization of a song by Henry Smart, "The Lady of the Lea," with lyrics by W. H. Bellamy. The new curate James is perhaps the sort Dr. Daly (*The Sorcerer*) was in his youth: "Ah me, I was a fair young curate then!"

269.1.4. *jack-a-dandies:* a slang expression for fops; Gilbert is suggesting that each of James's fingers is a dandy.

270.5.3. *feet:* "hands," erroneously, in *Fun*.

HONGREE AND MAHRY (p. 271)—*Fun*, n.s., X (20 November 1869), 105. No. 77.

Gilbert changed the subtitle of this poem twice. In *Fun* and the 1873 edition it reads "A Transpontine Romance." To make his meaning more explicit, he changed this to "A Recollection of a Surrey Melodrama" in the collection of *Fifty "Bab" Ballads* (1877). The final choice, "A Richardsonian Melodrama," refers to the kind of drama offered by Richardson's Show, the best known of the nineteenth-century booth theaters that played the fairs around London and toured the provinces. This is the same John Richardson whose show is included by the Colonel of Dragoons (*Patience*) in his recipe for a Heavy Dragoon. Another *Fun* regular, Henry S. Leigh, had written a poem lauding these performances, which began "Look always on the Surrey side/For true dramatic art."

271.1.2. *Hongree:* Henri as pronounced by English booth-theater actors. Mahry is, of course, Marie.

271.1.2. *Chassoores:* again a debased English pronunciation, of "chasseurs."

271.1.3. *Mahry Daubigny:* William Gilbert, W. S. G.'s father, wrote a story about French Huguenots which included a Gregory D'Aubigny and a Mrs. Dubosq; perhaps Mahry and Jooles are among their ancestors.

271.2.5. *dog:* "dodge" in *Fun* and 1873 edition.

271.3.3. *actuates:* "animates" in *Fun* and 1873 edition.

271.3.11. *ungrammatical:* compare Phyllis, in *Iolanthe*, whose grammar's as good as her neighbours'.

271.3.13. *No such . . . :* in *Fun* and 1873 edition this line reads "How different to this unreflecting boor."

271.3.14. *Of:* "Was" in *Fun* and 1873 edition.

271.4.3. *that sad war:* the Hundred Years' War. By the Treaty of Troyes (1420),

Henry V was to marry Catherine of Valois, daughter of Charles VI, and become king of France (as well as England) upon her father's death. His scheme was thwarted by Joan of Arc and the Dauphin, crowned Charles VII at Reims in 1429, while Henry's eight-year-old son sat on the English throne with John of Lancaster, duke of Bedford, as regent and leader of the king's troops in France.

272.2.6. *These . . .* : this line omitted in 1877 edition.

272.2.7. *soul:* "man" in *Fun* and 1873 edition.

272.3.9. *a:* "three" in *Fun* and 1873 edition; altered in 1877 edition.

273.1.15. *could:* "would" in 1877 edition.

273.3.4. *killed:* "slew" in *Fun,* 1873 edition, and first 1898 edition.

273.3.6. *married:* "gave fair" in 1877 edition.

ETIQUETTE (p. 274)—*The Graphic,* I (25 December 1869, Christmas Number), 6–7.

This is the only poem from a source other than *Fun* that Gilbert chose to collect (in *Fifty "Bab" Ballads* and again in the 1898 edition). Many of its features were reworked by Gilbert in his German Reed musical piece *Our Island Home.* Swinburne, writing to Rossetti on 1 March 1870, remarks: "By the way what a splendid 'Bab' that was in the Graphic for Christmas Day about the shipwrecked men and their common friend—I thought it one of the best—and it took me about an hour to read out en famille owing to the incessant explosions and collapses of reader and audience in tears and roars of laughter" (*Swinburne Letters,* II, 106).

274.1.1. *Cariboo:* no actual Cariboo or Caribou bears any relation to Gilbert's land of this name.

274.2.3. *Baker, Croop, and Co.:* apparently Gilbert's invention.

274.3.3. *Alexander Selkirk:* the Scottish sailor marooned on Juan Fernandez Island for four years who is said to have given Defoe his idea for *Robinson Crusoe.*

275.2.1. *mus ridiculus:* not a species of turtle or oyster, this is Horace's "trifling mouse" (Ben Jonson's translation). The line from the *Ars poetica* reads: *Parturient montes, nascetur ridiculus mus* (The mountains are in labor, and only bring forth a mouse).

275.3.2. *Charterhouse:* the famous old London school which Thackeray, among others, attended and wrote about; removed in 1872 to Godalming, Surrey.

275.5.1. *sociably:* "pleasantly" in *The Graphic* and 1877 edition.

276.1.4. *both:* "each" in *The Graphic.*

276.2.4. *vessel:* "frigate" in *The Graphic* and 1877 edition.

276.3.2. *So . . .* : compare Bunthorne's line when offering himself in a lottery: "Such an opportunity may not occur again" (*Patience*).

276.3.2. *occur:* "be found" in 1877 edition.

277.1.2. *Portland:* a major convict prison on the Dorset coast.

277.2.2. *an unattractive:* "a gentlemanly" in *The Graphic* and 1877 edition.

277.5.3. *loathes with horror grim:* "hates, in layers thick" in *The Graphic* and 1877 edition.

277.5.4. *disagrees with him:* "always makes him sick" in *The Graphic* and 1877 edition.

THE REVEREND SIMON MAGUS (p. 278)—*Fun,* n.s., X (5 February 1870), 215. No. 78.

The reverend's appropriate name is that of the first-century Samarian magician whose followers believed him to be the Messiah. He offered Peter money for the gift of the Holy Spirit, thereby lending his name for all time to the practice we know as simony.

278.1.1. *advowson:* the right of presentation to a vacant benefice.

278.2.4. *Otium-cum-Digge:* the phrase *otium cum dignitate* (leisure with dignity) is applied to one living in a retirement earned by worth.

278.9.4. *pretty:* "very" in *Fun* and 1873 edition.

279.6.2. *there is:* "is there" in *Fun.*

279.9.4. *Of course:* in *Fun* and 1873 edition these words conclude Simon Magus' speech; in 1877 edition they are spoken by the agent.

MY DREAM (p. 280)—*Fun,* n.s., XI (19 March 1870), 15. No. 79.

A poem by William Sawyer that appeared in *Tom Hood's Comic Annual for 1868* may have given Gilbert the idea for this "Bab," though topsy-turveydom is, of course, a realm in which Gilbert had long dwelt. Some of the stanzas from Sawyer's poem, "Turvey Top," are very like Gilbert's, albeit more satiric:

> 'Twas after a supper of Norfolk brawn
>   That into a doze I chanced to drop,
> And thence awoke in the grey of dawn,
>   In the wonder-land of Turvey Top.
>   • • •
>
> The people there are not tall or short,
>   Heavy or light, or stout or thin,
> And their lives begin when they should leave off,
>   Or leave off where they should begin.
>   • • •
>
> There childhood with nought of childish glee,
>   Looks on the world with thoughtful brow;
> 'Tis only the aged who laugh and crow,
>   And cry "We have done with it now!"
>   • • •
>
> They didn't believe in the wise and good,
>   Said the best were worst, the wisest fools;
> And 'twas only to have their teachers taught
>   That they founded national schools.
>   • • •

Gilbert later used the idea of his ballad for his play *Topsy-turvydom,* an extravaganza which opened at the Criterion Theatre on 23 March 1874.

280.4.2. *binomial theorem:* their skill in this and differential calculus puts these babies in a class with that very model of a modern Major-General in *Pirates.*

280.5.3. *forget:* "forgot," by mistake, in 1873 edition.

281.1.4. *practical experience:* the same sort of logic prompted the Mikado to make Koko, condemned to death for flirting, the Lord High Executioner:

> Who's next to be decapited
> Cannot cut off another's head
>   Until he's cut his own off.

DAMON *v.* PYTHIAS (p. 282)—*Fun,* n.s., XI (26 March 1870), 31. No. 80.

In Roman legend, Damon and Pythias were such devoted friends that when the latter, condemned to die, wished to visit his home one last time, the former consented to serve as hostage in his stead and to submit to the death sentence if his friend did not return.

282.8.4. *fingered:* "tasted" in *Fun* and 1873 edition.

282.10.1. *too:* "two" in *Fun* and 1873 edition.

283.1.1. *Enthusiastically . . . :* this stanza omitted in 1898 editions.

283.5.1. *in robe and fur:* "at Westminster" in *Fun* and 1873 edition; by 1898 the law courts were not in Westminster, but in new quarters in the Strand.

283.8.3. *And thus . . . :* this line reads "And then they paid each other's debt" in *Fun* and 1873 edition.

THE BUMBOAT WOMAN'S STORY (p. 284)—*Fun*, n.s., XI (9 April 1870), 45. No. 81.

This poem is one more source for *H.M.S. Pinafore*, where Poll Pineapple, alias Little Buttercup, plies the same trade. In 1951, Sadler's Wells Theatre Ballet presented *Pineapple Poll*, in which the bumboat woman's story was set to a variety of Sullivan's Savoy music.

284.4.3. *Hot Cross Bun:* the same ship appears in *Our Island Home.*

284.4.4. *thirty:* "seventy" in 1898 editions.

284.5.3. *Seventy:* "Twenty" in 1898 editions; Gilbert was apparently trying to bring these figures more in line with probability—which seems pointless, given the story in which they are used.

285.4.3. *big big D—:* the expression Captain Corcoran never (well, hardly ever) uses in *H.M.S. Pinafore.*

286.1.3. *I can hand, and reef, and steer:* just as Captain Corcoran can, "though related to a peer." The phrase "hand, reef, and steer" is a recurrent one in Charles Dibdin's song "A Drop of the Creature." Dibdin had set the pattern in the eighteenth century for nautical songs about Jack Tars and the Polls they must leave behind, and Gilbert often echoes him. "Bill Bobstay," for instance, a minor character in *Pinafore,* is the subject of one of Dibdin's songs.

286.4.1. *He up . . . :* compare Richard Dauntless' seaman's lingo in *Ruddigore:* "Then our Captain he up and says, says he."

THE FAIRY CURATE (p. 287)—*Fun*, n.s., XII (23 July 1870), 32–33. No. 82.

This "Bab" is a major source for the plot and incidents of *Iolanthe.* Just as "The Rival Curates" become poets in *Patience,* Georgie's profession changes from clerical to political in the opera, in which the Fairy Queen, with a borough or two at her disposal, gets Strephon (a fairy down to his waist) into Parliament.

287.2.6. *moon of honey:* see note to "The Variable Baby," p. 358.

287.4.4. *There's:* "He's" in *Fun* and 1873 edition; altered in 1877 edition.

288.1.10. *But:* "'Twas" in *Fun* and 1873 edition.

288.1.12. *the:* "his" in *Fun* and 1873 edition; altered in 1877 edition.

288.4.10. *spencers:* not High-Church vestments at all, but short coats similar to pea jackets, for outdoor wear.

288.5.1. *quandary:* this wrenching rhyme with "fairy" is repeated in *Iolanthe.*

289.1.10. *Then:* "But" in 1877 edition.

289.2.4. *'Tis my mother:* compare Lord Mountararat in *Iolanthe:*

> This gentleman is seen,
> With a maid of seventeen,
> A-taking of his *dolce far niente;*

And wonders he'd achieve,
For he asks us to believe
She's his mother—and he's nearly five-and-twenty!

Similar results occur when a picture gallery comes to life in *Ages Ago:*

So strange a meeting ne'er was seen,
For sure as I'm alive,
His grandmama is seventeen,
And he is sixty-five.

289.footnote. *Like a bird:* in *Fun* this reads "'Like a bird'—any bird"; in 1877 edition the gloss to the note is "Slang expression."

PHRENOLOGY (p. 290)—*Fun,* n.s., XII (6 August 1870), 45. No. 83.

290.1.4. *garroted:* see note to "Mister William," p. 352.
291.2.4. *Generenerosity:* "Impecuniosity" in *Fun* and 1873 edition.
291.3.3. *ears:* "ear" in 1873 and 1898 editions; altered in 1877 edition.
291.4.4. *Sorte tuâ contentus sis:* may you be content with your lot. Compare Horace in bk. 1 of the *Epistles, Laetus sorte tua vives sapienter.*
291.7.1. *Policeman:* "That Crusher" in *Fun* and 1873 edition.
291.12.1. *Policeman's:* "Pleeceman's" in *Fun* and 1873 edition.
291.12.4. *I:* accidentally omitted in 1873 edition.

THE PERILS OF INVISIBILITY (p. 292)—*Fun,* n.s., XII (20 August 1870), 65. No. 84.

Gilbert may have recalled the Ingoldsby Legend, "The Spectre of Tappington," with its mysteriously disappearing breeches, when writing this ballad.
292.2.3. *said:* accidentally omitted in *Fun.*
292.11.4. *hoist . . . :* in *Hamlet* the line reads "Hoist with his own petar" (III, iv, 208).
293.1.2. *twigged:* understood.
293.4.2. *stock:* a broad, stiffened band worn as a cravat.
293.8.1. *this:* "the" in 1877 edition.
293.8.3. *Already:* "All ready" in *Fun.*
293.9.3. *he:* "he's" in *Fun.*

THE WISE POLICEMAN (p. 294)—*Fun,* n.s., XII (22 October 1870), 156. No. 85.

Among the most frequently mentioned and illustrated incidents in Victorian comic papers is that of the policeman on his beat mildly wooing a maid or cook, chiefly for the sake of a bit of warmth or food in the servants' quarters or kitchen.
295.10.2. *Mr. Knox:* Alexander Andrew Knox was police magistrate at the Marlborough Street Court 1862–1878.

A DROP OF PANTOMIME WATER (p. 296)—*The Graphic,* II (25 December 1870, Christmas Number), 20.

296.1.11. *rosey:* rosé, or wine generally.
296.1.13. *burrage:* usually spelled "borage."
296.1.16. *Professor von Pepper:* John Henry Pepper, an analytical chemist and lecturer, director of the Royal Polytechnic Institute 1852–1872. The board of the

Polytechnic conferred the title of Professor upon him. He became well known for displaying an optical illusion known as Pepper's Ghost, modeled on Dickens' Haunted Man. George Grossmith, who later originated the comic baritone roles in nine of the Savoy Operas, made his professional debut at Professor Pepper's "Institute" on 11 November 1870, performing a sketch written by his father and scored by himself entitled "Human Oddities."

296.1.17. *proxy of hydrogen-oxy:* a scientific instrument that gained public attention in the sixties with the Hydro-Oxygen Microscope, which, when exhibited at Stanley's Rooms in Old Bond Street, was described as "Unrivalled for the Brilliancy of the Light, the Splendour and Variety of New Objects, and its great Magnifying Powers."

296.1.37. *skinful:* a full wineskin.

298.1.17. *cadis:* Muslim judges.

OLD PAUL AND OLD TIM (p. 299)—*Fun*, n.s., XIII (28 January 1871), 35. No. 86.

This poem, Gilbert's last in *Fun*, where it is mistakenly numbered "85," registers his displeasure with Frenchmen avoiding conscription during the Franco-Prussian War.

299.3.4. *nothing to choose:* compare Phyllis' reaction to her two lordly suitors in *Iolanthe:* "You are both Earls, and you are both rich, and you are both plain. . . . There's really nothing to choose between you."

299.4.2. *much too:* "of you" in *Fun* and 1873 edition.

299.4.4. *get:* "go" in *Fun* and 1873 edition.

299.5.4. *war-horse in "Job":* see Job 39:19–25.

299.6.2. *enemy's:* "enemies'" in *Fun*.

299.6.3. *shakos:* stiff military headgear with an upright plume.

300.1.4. *proofs:* "proof" in *Fun*.

301.1.2. *cripple:* "crippled" in *Fun*.

301.1.3. *A crippled old man:* "An elderly one" in *Fun* and 1873 edition.

"EHEU! FUGACES" (p. 302)—*The Dark Blue*, III (April 1872), 142–143.

This poem is similar in subject and sentiment to the much earlier "At a Pantomime." For a comment on the Latin expression (from Horace) used as the title, see note to "The Mystic Selvagee," p. 356.

JESTER JAMES (p. 303)—*Time*, I (April 1879), 54–57.

In this new publication of Edmund Yates's the poem is headed "THE BAB BALLADS, New Series, No. I." "The Policeman's Story" is No. II.

303.1.4. *his quips passed muster:* Jack Point, in *Yeomen of the Guard*, offers to try his jests first on the Lieutenant's chaplain.

304.5.4. *recruit:* recuperate.

305.6.3. *Sally Lunns:* see note to "Pantomimic Presentiments," p. 321.

THE POLICEMAN'S STORY (p. 307)—*Time*, I (May 1879), 166–168.

307.4.4. *Boeotian:* doltish, boorish; the Athenians so regarded the Boeotians.

308.2.4. *your misfortune:* Lord Tolloller, in *Iolanthe*, assures Phyllis that "high rank involves no shame."

308.3.4. *the total's one and six:* obviously the laws of mathematics undergo transformation too, when applied to the fine of a peer.

THE THIEF'S APOLOGY (p. 309)—*Illustrated Sporting and Dramatic News,* XXII (6 December 1884), "Holly Leaves" (Christmas number), 267.

For eight years (1880–1887) Gilbert contributed to the Christmas number of the *Illustrated Sporting and Dramatic News.* Six of his contributions were prose items; two were poems, one of which, "Only Roses," XVI (10 December 1881), 323, reappeared five years later as Mad Margaret's ballad in *Ruddigore* and is excluded from this volume for having declared itself one of the songs of a Savoyard.

309.1.1. *pipes and tabors:* the rhyming of this phrase with "neighbours" occurs also in *Iolanthe.*

309.6.2. *wicked world:* Gilbert published a story entitled "The Wicked World" in *Tom Hood's Comic Annual for 1871,* which he turned into a successful "fairy comedy" in 1873, burlesqued a few months later in the extravaganza *The Happy Land,* and in 1909 rewrote as a comic opera, *Fallen Fairies,* with music by Edward German.

311. This illustration was originally the last one to "The Policeman's Story."

INDEX OF TITLES